Personal Service Companies A Practical Guide

by

ANDERSONS, Chartered Accountants

with contributions from

R. ANDERSON, Barrister

Disclaimer

This work is intended to be a *Guide* to the subject matter covered. Neither the Author nor the Publishers are engaged in rendering direct legal, management or taxation advice. Readers entering into specific transactions are advised to first seek the advice of a competent professional adviser. The Publishers and Author expressly disclaim all and any liability and responsibility to any person, whether a purchaser of this work or otherwise, in respect of anything done or omitted to be done by any such person in reliance, in whole or in part, upon the contents of this work.

Published by
Tolley
2 Addiscombe Road,
Croydon, Surrey CR9 5AF

Printed in Great Britain by
Redwood Books,
Trowbridge, Wiltshire

ISBN 0 75451 102-2

About the Author

This book was written by Andersons, Chartered Accountants. Established in 1981, this firm can trace its origins back to Mr Barstow, one of the founders of the Society of Accountants which later became the Institute of Chartered Accountants. Traditionally, the specialisation of this firm has been assisting businesses in the sector which, since the advent of the EC, is now classified as small and medium-sized enterprises. The firm has a declared specialisation in helping genuine and aspirational Personal Service Companies to achieve their potential.

The Authors acknowledge contributions from R Anderson, Barrister. A specialist in the field of taxation and a regular contributor of articles (most recently in 'Taxation'). Mr Anderson has extensive experience of representation before the General and Special Commissioners and the Courts of Law up to and including the House of Lords (most recently in *Fitzpatrick v CIR*).

ANDERSONS
Chartered Accountants
www.andersonaccounts.co.uk
212 Picadilly
London
W1J 9HG
Tel: 020 7917 9505
Fax: 020 7439 0262
E-mail: coacc.fsnct.co.uk

Authorised to conduct investment business by ICAS

R. ANDERSON
Barrister
Pepy's Chambers
17 Fleet Street
London
EC4Y 1AA
Tel: 020 7936 2710
Fax: 020 7936 2501
E-mail: anderson@cqm.co.uk

Barrister (of Gray's Inn)

Acknowledgements

We reproduce, with their kind permission, extracts from the publications of:

HM Customs & Excise
The Inland Revenue
The Stationery Office
Companies House
The Accounting Standards Board
Transaction Technology (Software) Limited

This book is dedicated to the firm of Barstow & Millar, Chartered Accountants, and to all who worked in the firm.

Contents

Foreword

By
Rt. Hon. the Lord Howe of Aberavon, CH, QC*

To be or not to be? To start up a new business or not? Once upon a time it was probably quite a simple question. But not today. For it's no longer enough to know that you have a product to sell, the premises in which to start, the capital and know-how with which to launch the business.

More important than any of that, you may find, is to discover the right legal dress to wear when you enter the market. The simplest way to be your own boss, you may think, is to be self-employed. But is it? Can't you, for example, limit your liability for disaster by 'becoming' a company? But aren't you now an employee of the company? And doesn't that alter your status in the eye of the law? And of the tax system? The answer may depend on the nature of the contract under which you work. Or of the company that you've become. Is yours a contract of service? Or for the supply of services? Have you perhaps become – a Personal Service Company?

Almost every one of the words I've written so far rings bells in the mind of a lawyer. And they ring even more loudly in the mind of a tax inspector. And so, inevitably, the legal jungle through which this book seeks to guide the reader, grows even denser.

And nowhere does the legal undergrowth grow more quickly than in the tax field. Thirty years ago there were 'only' 2,000 pages of direct tax legislation. Today there are almost 7,000 – 600 of them added by last year's Finance Act. And some of those new pages were aimed at the very gateway, through which you might choose to steer your own new business – targeted directly at the Personal Service Company.

And no wonder. For the rising popularity of the Personal Service Company appears to have been largely 'tax-driven' – or, more accurately, driven by the prospect of (perfectly lawful) tax-avoidance. 'Perfectly lawful' perhaps – but on a scale that threatened to deprive the Treasury of their reasonably expected share of your income. And so the law gets changed – again and again.

This is the kind of end-game puzzle that you could not have been expected to bargain for, when you decided to set up in business. And it's the kind of troublesome puzzle from which this book seeks to protect you. Make the most of it!

* Geoffrey Howe was Chancellor of the Exchequer (1979-83), Foreign Secretary (1983-89) and Deputy Prime Minister (1989-90)

Preface

The Personal Service Company is a creature of our time. It has its origins in the shift to a fast-moving service-based economy. The declared intention of the Government is to bolster that new economy. It appears contradictory, therefore, for the Government not only to continue to apply an administration burden to that sector much of which, particulrly in the field of taxation, can barely be understood but to then add to that burden by introducing legislation aimed specifically at the taxation of Personal Service Companies.

This latest piece of legislation (colloquially known as 'IR35' after the number of the Inland Revenue Tax Bulletin (No. 35) which first heralded the legislation) has been greeted with horror throughout the knowledge-based industry (to such an extent that at the time of writing a Judicial Review of the legislation is being attempted) and it has to be admitted that it does have something of a draconian appearance (only 30/100 on review by the Tax Faculty).

What matters, however, is not so much the appearance of the legislation but its underlying intention and the manner in which it is applied in practice. Some have suggested that the (undeclared) underlying intention is to force a return to employment. The declared intention, however, is to distinguish (with appropriate fiscal sanction) between those Personal Service Companies which are properly-run on a self-employed basis and those Personal Service Companies which are improperly-run on a disguised employment basis.

Whatever the true intention, the legislation implementing IR35 merely takes its place in the increasing administrative burden which is imposed upon all SME's and which it is hoped the Government will alleviate in the future. For the meantime, however, the objective of this book is to exclude the irrelevant and pull together in one place everything that is relevant to the operation of a Personal Service Company today. The unique nature of a Personal Service Company is such that many areas such as secured borrowing, insolvency and the like are largely irrelevant and can be excluded.

What it is sought to do in the first edition of this book is to pull together in one place the principal requirements currently imposed upon a Personal

Service Company. Those requirements will change as the practices of law, management and taxation develop (and are hopefully tempered) and accordingly the authors make a call for assistance in future editions to keep pace with those developments as they affect Personal Service Companies.

The maxim *ignoranti juris neminem excusat* (ignorance of the law is no excuse) has traditionally been rigorously applied by the Revenue Authorities and the Courts of Law. Hand-in-hand with that principle, however, has traditionally been a ready supply of (free and easy to understand) information about the requirements which must be complied with. In researching this book, however, the authors were horrified to discover that equation to now be significantly out-of-balance in that information, ignorance of which is no excuse,.was in many areas not at all readily forthcoming (and even in some instances required to be paid for).

The authors do, however, owe a debt of gratitude owed to the whole editorial team at Tolleys, we would like to record our thanks (in alphabetical order) to the following:

Veronica Baker; John Barbour; Tom Cody; Nigel Goldie; Ian Moffat; Ken Rozier; John Speirs.

ANDERSONS
Chartered Accountants
www.andersonaccounts.co.uk
212 Picadilly
London
W1J 9HG
Tel: 020 7917 9505
Fax: 020 7439 0262
E-mail: coacc.fsnet.co.uk

Authorised to conduct investment business by ICAS

R. ANDERSON
Barrister
Pepy's Chambers
17 Fleet Street
London
EC4Y 1AA
Tel: 020 7936 2710
Fax: 020 7936 2501
E-mail: anderson@cqm.co.uk

Barrister (of Gray's Inn)

The Scheme of the Book

The modern economy, so far as it relates to the knowledge-based sectors, appears to have created a situation where - in much the same way as 'greatness' – some are born to Personal Service Companies while others have Personal Service Companies thrust upon them.

Whatever the starting-point, however, once in possession of a Personal Service Company there can be little doubt that the legal, administrative and taxation burden (the most recent being the infamous 'IR35) is considerable. Indeed, so complex and weighty has the burden become that the demand from all sides for its alleviation has achieved a degree of unaninimity rarely seen in modern times and now demands an answer.

Against that background, the aim of the first edition of this book is a modest one. It seeks to aid that burden in the meantime by stripping away all that is irrelevant or extraneous and concentrating instead on what is relevant so as to gather together in one place all of the matters which are essential to the birth, life, and death of a Personal Service Company.

Armed with such a knowledge, those involved in a Personal Service Company should, in theory – perhaps in very strict theory – be able to regulate the affairs of their company themselves and avoid the consequences of ignorance being no excuse. In practice, however, it is at present more likely to be found that the affairs of a Personal Service Company will run more smoothly with professional assistance. Even better, a Personal Service Company may be able to establish a synergetic effect where the individuals behind the company and the professional advising the company share a common understanding of the objectives which they are trying to achieve.

This book is aimed at helping to achieve that common understanding. It is aimed at the individuals involved in Personal Service Companies but is also aimed at being of use and benefit to those who are required to give professional advice to Personal Service Companies. As life moves on and the real impact of IR 35 and other legislation becomes clearer, it is hoped to keep pace with those developments and to focus ever more closely upon the specific needs and requirements of Personal Service Companies.

For present purposes, however, the intention is to set out the basic legal, administrative and taxation considerations applicable to starting, running, and leaving a Personal Service Company. The approach adopted in the book – presented in Parts – is as follows:

Part A: An introduction to a Self-employment
Part B: Starting a Personal Service Company
Part C: Running a Personal Service Company
Part D: Leaving a Personal Service Company

Part A

Part A consists of an introduction to Self-Employment. It reviews the considerations which effectively apply to everyone considering setting out in business before the decision is reached to become self-employed using the commercial vehicle of a Personal Service Company. It provides, that decision having been reached, an overview of the aspects of law, administration and taxation which will apply to Personal Service Companies. It also considers the preliminary decisions which require to be arrived at before starting up a Personal Service Company.

Part B

Part B deals with starting up a Personal Service Company. It consists of an Introduction and three sections. It deals with the legal, administration and taxation aspects.

Part C

Part C deals with running of a Personal Service Company. It consists of an Introduction and three sections (legal, administration and taxation).

Part D

Part D deals with leaving a Personal Service Company.

Part A

AN INTRODUCTION TO SELF-EMPLOYMENT

Introduction

Today's economy, and the employment framework which it supports, has been described as 'flexible'. What that means, it appears, is a shift away from long-term 'employment' under a single contract with one 'employer' towards short-term 'contracting' under a series of contracts with a number of 'clients'.

For those involved in the knowledge-based sectors of the economy that 'flexibility' can place them in a parlous position. Some companies might insist upon dealing only with contractors and refuse to take on any employees. Other companies might retain the traditional structure of employees but also take on some contractors. Some workers will clearly fall into the category of contractors and some will clearly fall into the category of employees but others will occupy a grey area in between and as an initial short-term contract is renewed and lengthened it is increasingly becoming unclear as to whether a worker is or is not an employee.

Against that background – in much the same way as 'greatness' – it is likely that some workers will be born to be self-employed while other workers will, under modern conditions, have self-employment thrust upon them. However, such a decision is not one to be taken lightly. While employment might have its strictures and controls it does offer security and is accompanied by a bundle of hard-fought-for employment rights. Self-employment, on the other hand, is accompanied by no such rights and can be a long and rocky road although it does offer the possibility of freedom and personal gain. The point is, however, that self-employment is not something that a person should be driven into or fall into by default. The nature of self-employment is such that it should only be adopted by way of an active choice after due consideration. We consider briefly in this section the question of whether or not to be self-employed.

Should a firm and positive decision to become self-employed be made, however, then a further series of decisions require to be made. There are a number of methods - known as commercial vehicles - under which self-employment can be undertaken and these are essentially being a sole trader, a partnership or a limited company. There are advantages and disadvantages to the use of each type of commercial vehicle and it is largely a matter of individual choice according to circumstances. We consider briefly in this section the advantages and disadvantages of each of the commercial vehicles.

There is, however, one factor which is at present bearing down heavily upon such decisions and that is the aspect of taxation and in particular the operation of the PAYE system and the deductability of National Insurance Contributions.

Companies who are entering into a contract with a specialist to perform a task over a short period of time are reluctant to engage that specialist as an 'employee' because not only would that person instantly acquire a bundle of employment rights but the company would also have to go to the trouble of operating a PAYE system in respect of that person's remuneration and company would also have to pay Employer's National Insurance Contributions. Initially, such companies paid such workers gross remuneration as self-employed sole traders or partnerships but the Inland Revenue intervened and insisted upon the operation by companies in such circumstances of the PAYE system and the payment of Employer's National Insurance Contributions. Only by using an Agency (which then had the same problem) or by using the worker through the commercial vehicle of a limited liability company (which was a separate entity) could that problem - at that time - be avoided. Some companies therefore insisted upon the use of companies (to such an extent, and with such savings, apparently, that the Government claimed to have received complaints from other more traditional enterprises that those companies were becoming anti-competitive!) Overall, however, there was pressure from such companies for their short-term workers to operate through the medium of a limited liability company which, when supplying personal services, became known as a Personal Service Company.

Those operating Personal Service Companies also became aware of certain taxation advantages. In particular, extracting funds from their companies by way of dividend rather than remuneration also offered certain tax advantages including the avoidance of National Insurance Contributions. Overall, therefore, there was pressure on short-term workers to take advantage of these taxation opportunities by operating through the medium of a limited liability company which, when supplying personal services, became known as a Personal Service Company.

The combined pressures on companies to engage Personal Service Companies and on workers to operate through Personal Service Companies appears to have led to a proliferation of Personal Service Companies (to such an extent that, according to the Government, some employees left their employment on the Friday only to return to exactly the same job in the guise of a Personal Service Company on the Monday!). The proliferation was such that it was said by the Government to have had an effect upon the public purse, particularly as regards the ingathering of National Insurance Contributions, which was in the order of £300 million per annum.

The Government declared its intention (in the infamous Inland Revenue Tax Bulletin No. 35 - hence the term 'IR35') to take measures to 'counter avoidance in the area of personal service provision' and that legislation (made effective from 6 April 2000) is now in fact in place although, unusually, it is at the time of writing subject to an application for Judicial Review. We consider briefly in this section the likely application of IR35 in relation to the choice of a Personal Service Company as the commercial vehicle for self-employment.

The intention of the legislation in relation to the legislation implementing IR35 appears to be to leave genuine Personal Service Companies (they exist in a number of sectors other than the knowledge-based sectors such as in acting) unaffected but for those Personal Service Companies which are effectively disguised employment, to produce what might be called a 'level playing field' by making all those who provide personal services – whether through the commercial vehicle of a Sole Trader, a Partnership, *or* a Personal Service Company – subject to the same rules particularly with regard to PAYE and National Insurance Contributions.

While that might be, in principle, a laudable aim for the country as a whole, the legislation itself (which was awarded a score of only 30/100 on review by the Tax Faculty) has been described as draconian. It appears that the intention of the Inland Revenue is to approach the matter on a contract-by-contract basis. In something of a radical departure from the way in which taxation matters have traditionally been dealt with in the United Kingdom, the Inland Revenue offer advance clearance of contracts failing which as at 5th April the new tax rules will bite with tax and NIC payable by 19 April.

The application of these new tax rules (presumably with interest and penalties if operated in arrears) is such that while allowance will be given for expenditure which an employee (under the Schedule E rules) would have made, the actual expenditure incurred by the Personal Service Company is disallowed and replaced by an allowance of only 5% thereby creating a substantial loss. Furthermore, it may prove difficult in practice for the Personal Service Company to itself obtain tax relief for the tax and NIC which it has been required to pay under the new rules.

This appears to have produced a situation – and some have suggested, rightly or wrongly, that this is the undeclared intention of the Government – which in practice might very well be that to be self-employed through the commercial vehicle of a Personal Service Company which fails the IR35 Test in relation to a substantial number of its contracts is to have the worst of all worlds and is a positive disincentive to using Personal Service Companies as the commercial vehicle for self-employment. This is clearly an additional factor which now requires to be borne in mind when deciding which commercial vehicle to use for the purposes of self-employment.

The result appears to be that genuine Personal Service Companies are to be allowed to continue as before while those Personal Service Companies which are effectively a disguised form of employment are to be penalised. What seems to be rather unfair, however, is that the test for distinguishing between the two types of Personal Service Company (the existing Employment/Self-employment test) is rather etherial and operated retrospectively could have very significant, if not fatal, consequences for the company concerned. That, however (pending the outcome of the Judicial Review) is what we are given to work with. This book, in the following sections, concentrates upon what is involved in being a genuine Personal Service Company. For the purposes of this section, however, the fact that a descent into such murky waters may be required in the future should be taken on board in relation to the decision whether to become self-employed and, if so, what commercial vehicle to use.

AI1 – Pre-considerations

Introduction [AI1.1]

Those who have acquired knowledge or skills in the new technologies are indeed fortunate. They are likely to be in demand and to command a premium in the marketplace.

For those contemplating the marketing of their knowledge or skills, however, there are a number of pre-considerations which ought to be taken into account.

To be or not to be self-employed [AI1.2]

Knowledge or skill can be utilised in a number of ways. Essentially, a distinction can be drawn between persons using their knowledge or skill in working for someone else (where they are generally known as employees under a contract of service) and persons using their knowledge or skill to work for themselves (where they are generally known as self-employed and, in relation to their clients, are under a contract for service).

Each category is attended with its own advantages and disadvantages.

The distinction [AI1.3]

In years gone by, the distinction between employment and self-employment was relatively clear-cut. The vast majority of people were in employment and those who embarked upon self-employment made a clear and conscious decision to do so. In recent years, however, the picture has changed. Whereas previously, workers would leave school and/or university with the expectation of securing employment with the same employer for a significant number of years, workers today must expect to have not just a number of employers but perhaps a number of different vocations as well.

Given that the current requirement of employers – particularly in the modern technology industries – is for the use of the services of a skilled person in order to complete a specific task over a short period of time, this change has resulted in something of a revolution in the working framework of these industries.

There appears to have been a move away from the formal engagement of employees under long-term contracts of service and a move towards putting out short-term contracts for services. By virtue of that fact, from the point of view of the employer, this not only avoids some of the inconveniences of dealing with the protections which the status of employee affords but also carries a number of tax advantages.

The movement appears to have become more pronounced in recent years but appears, however, to have resulted in the distinction between employment and self-employment having becoming much more blurred. Increasingly, many of those who consider themselves in employment may in fact be self-employed and many of those who consider themselves to be self-employed may in fact be employed.

The distinction is not without significance. Whilst those in 'employment' are subject to the rigours of direction and control, they do enjoy a recognised status protected and hedged by an increasing number of benefits and rights and entitlements such as protection against redundancy, maternity leave, and the like. Those in 'self-employment', on the other hand, whilst having significantly more freedom from control, enjoy none of these benefits and protections. Perhaps the worst position to be in is to be self-employed and without the benefits and protection of employment while still being subject to direction and control.

Given the importance and significance of the distinction between being employed and being self-employed, the position and status adopted should not be something which is slipped into by default but should be the result of a conscious decision.

It is, in all probability, the temperament of the individual concerned, as much as anything else, which should be the determining factor in this decision.

The right temperament? **[AI1.4]**

Some people, from a very early age, have a temperament which causes them to pepper their conversations with their desire to 'start up on their own'. They may or may not succeed (and there should be no shame in trying and failing and trying again) but such people give the impression of having self-confidence, energy, support, a burning desire to succeed, and the strength to drive through gap periods of no work to achieve success and substantial material reward. People with these identifiable characteristics are those whom banks and other funders are prepared to support in their pursuit of self-employment. They have, in short, something which can be variously described but is often known as an 'entrepreneurial spark'.

Other people may prefer a more settled existence. They may draw comfort from familiar surrounding, familiar co-workers, and the familiarity of the tasks which they are asked to perform. Such people, although sometimes able to cope with it very well if they have to, may not like rapid change. People with these identifiable characteristics are those whom funders are not prepared to support in their pursuit of self-employment.

Of course – rather like 'greatness' – self-employment is something which some people choose or are born to and something which others aspire to or have thrust upon them. It may be that redundancy or the fact that employers in the area in which the person wishes to work have indicated that they will only take people on on a self-employed basis, which has led to the *need* to become self-employed.

What ought to be appreciated, however, is that self-employment should not be regarded as just an easy option in comparison to employment. For all but the lucky few, self-employment involves a long and rocky road and to succeed it is essential that the tools of self-employment are there at the outset. If a person has a gut feeling that self-employment is not for them then they should not allow themselves to be coerced into going down that route and they should continue working under a contract of service.

The commercial vehicle for self-employment [AI1.5]

Having, after due reflection, made the conscious decision to become self-employed, it should then be appreciated that there are a number of ways in which this can in fact be done.

In the UK there are essentially three methods (sometimes known as 'commercial vehicles') under which self-employment may be pursued:

- as a sole trader;
- in partnership; or
- as a limited liability company.

For a detailed comparison of these vehicles, see **AI1.7–AI1.29** below.

Similarities [AI1.6]

The distinction between the three commercial vehicles listed above was formerly considerably more marked than it is today. Under modern business conditions, much the same considerations apply to each.

For example:

- the keeping of proper accounting records;
- the rigours of the VAT system (given a sufficiently high level of earnings);
- taxation generally; and
- NIC.

In essence, therefore, the distinctions between the three commercial vehicles are getting narrower, a factor emphasised by IR35.

Sole trader [AI1.7]

'Sole trader' is the term which is used to describe a single self-employed 'individual' carrying on the business alone. No formalities are required at all in order to commence trading. The sole trader can put money in and take money out of the business at will. There is complete freedom of contract.

The record-keeping requirements for tax purposes are, however, now stricter. The sole trader is taxed as an individual. There is no requirement for an audit and no publicity is given to earnings.

The sole trader owns all of the business although when the sole trader departs it is normally only any assets and not a business which is sold on.

The sole trader is liable to bankruptcy for any debts.

Partnership [AI1.8]

'Partnership' is the term used to describe where two or more self-employed 'individuals' carry on business together. The UK recognises two types of partnership – general and limited.

General partnership **[AI1.9]**

If there is no written partnership agreement, the terms of *Partnership Act 1890* will govern their relations. Accordingly, a general partnership could commence trading with little or no formality. However, it is generally considered advisable to have a partnership deed drawn up before trading and the cost of paying solicitors to do this often exceeds the cost of setting up a company.

Payments into and out of the partnership are relatively informal. Partners have wide freedom of contract. The record-keeping requirements for tax purposes are, however, now stricter. Partners are taxed as individuals. There is no requirement for an audit and no requirement to publish accounts.

Business Names Act 1985 requires some disclosure of partners' names. The maximum number of partners (except for certain professional partnerships) is 20.

Subject to any provisions in a partnership deed, most decisions (except the admission of new partners or a change in the nature of the trade being carried on) will be by a majority of the partners.

Disposing of an interest in a partnership can be difficult since leaving brings the partnership to an end and the consent of the other partners would be required for any someone else to purchase the leaving partner's share.

The partners are liable to bankruptcy for any debts.

Limited partnership **[AI1.10]**

A limited partnership is much more likely to require a formal deed before any trading can commence. Matters are normally a little more strictly controlled in a limited partnership although paying funds in or out remains relatively informal. In theory, freedom to contract exists although this may be restricted by any partnership deed. The record-keeping requirements for tax purposes are, however, now stricter.

Partners are taxed as individuals. It is possible to dispose of a share in a limited partnership and a limited partner cannot stand in the way of the introduction of a new partner. There must be at least one general partner who will be generally liable. The liability of the other partners will be limited in contract but not necessarily in negligence. Under the *Limited Partnerships Act 1907*, the limited partner is not allowed to take any part in the management of the firm (and becomes an unlimited general partner in the event of doing so).

It should be noted that in Scotland partnerships are regarded differently in law from the way in which they are regarded in England and Wales and Northern Ireland.

Company [AI1.11]

'Company' is the term used to describe the situation where a legal entity is created which is separate and distinct from the individuals who created it, its shareholders and directors.

Normally a company will have at least two shareholders (members) and two directors (possibly the same people in each case) as well as a company secretary. It is now possible to have a company with a single person as both director and shareholder although another person must act as company secretary is still required. Since 1980, there has been no limit on the maximum number of members.

A company does not legally exist prior to registration and therefore ought not to trade before the necessary formalities of incorporation or transfer have been completed. The administration of a company operates at two levels. The day-to-day decisions are taken by the directors. The activities of the directors are overseen by the shareholders in general meeting.

The assets and liabilities of a company are those of the company alone and paying money into or taking money out of a company can only be achieved in certain defined ways.

A company does not have complete freedom of contract and can only act within its powers (*intra vires*) which are set out in its Articles of Association.

The record-keeping and accounting requirements of a company are stricter. A company is separately taxed. The accounts of a company (in restricted form when the company is small) must be published annually and when turnover reaches a certain stage an audit is compulsory.

It is relatively easy to dispose of shares in a company although the market for a minority share in a private company is not great. Whatever happens to an individual shareholder has no direct effect on the company which lives on. Unless signed away in a contract, the liability of shareholders for the debts of a company is limited to the amount due on their shares.

Taxation [AI1.12]

The taxation rules applicable to sole traders and partnerships and that applicable to companies differ and there are in effect two separate taxation regimes. The same applies to National Insurance. There are also different rules relating to benefits and pensions.

Sole traders and partnerships pay Income Tax on any profits and Capital Gains Tax on any capital gains. There are taxation rules particular to sole traders and partnerships for assessing the sum upon which tax requires to be paid and the time of payment.

Companies pay only Corporation Tax on both profits and any capital gains. There are taxation rules particular to companies for assessing the sum upon which tax requires to be paid and the time of payment.

It is open to the Chancellor of the Exchequer to seek the approval of Parliament for adjustments to these separate taxation regimes which can have the effect of either bringing them closer together or pushing them further apart.

In previous years, there has been a tendency for it to be advantageous, from a taxation point of view, to start business as either a sole trader or a partnership but there also came a point at which it would be advantageous, from a taxation point of view, to continue business as a company. There was a trend, therefore, for businesses to begin as sole traders or partnerships and then later incorporate as a company.

In recent years, however, the policy has been to seek to stimulate commerce by creating the small companies rate for Corporation Tax and bringing that rate down to the rate of taxation paid by individuals. This has had the effect of reducing the advantages and that trend.

It has also been the case, however, that the manipulation of funds within a company and the payment of those funds by way of dividend has had a significant effect upon the amount of tax and National Insurance being collected to which the Inland Revenue has responded with IR35, the likely effect of which is considered in detail at **CM3** and **CT4** below.

Taxation will always be a factor in the decision whether or not to incorporate but it should rarely, if ever, be the sole consideration.

Disadvantages of incorporation [AI1.13]

There are a number of disadvantages of incorporation.

Formalities [AI1.14]

In contrast to the relative informality of being a sole trader or partnership, companies are subject to more structured formalities such as keeping records of members, directors, meetings, shares and the like and making returns of some of these to the Registrar of Companies.

These formalities are enshrined in the *Companies Acts* and there are penalties for non-compliance.

Cost [AI1.15]

In contrast to being a sole trader or partnership which could, in theory, be started up and run at virtually no cost, starting up a company will involve a fee for incorporating the company (currently £20) or buying the company off-the-shelf (currently about £100). It will also be necessary to purchase materials for meeting the various recording requirements of the company (perhaps £100) and there is an annual fee (currently £15) for submitting the annual return.

The more successful a business (even as a sole trader or partnership) the greater the costs associated with running it become and in the case of a company, crossing the turnover threshold (currently £1 million) will introduce the legal requirement for an audit together with its associated fee.

Capital [AI1.16]

In contrast to a sole trader or partnership which can pay money into and take money out of the business with the minimum of formality, the business belongs not to the individuals but to the company and there are strict rules to be followed for paying in and taking out money.

Publicity **[AI1.17]**

How well or how badly a business is performing is something which, in the case of a sole trader or partnership, is known only to the individuals involved, their accountant and the taxman (the latter two being under a professional obligation to keep the information confidential). A company, however, is obliged to file accounts with the Registrar of Companies and although the level of detailed disclosure required from smaller as opposed to larger companies is much reduced, disclosure in general is nevertheless required.

Dissolution **[AI1.18]**

Ceasing to trade is a relatively easy and painless process for sole traders and partnerships. It requires more care, however, to wind-up a company without undue disadvantage.

Advantages of incorporation **[AI1.19]**

There are a number of advantages to being incorporated.

Administration **[AI1.20]**

In a situation where a number of sources of revenue exist, it can often be a difficult task to first of all control those different sources of revenue and then allocate against the appropriate amounts of expenditure to arrive at the sum upon which tax should be charged before going on to consider other important matters such as benefits and pensions. A company provides a stable platform from which this can be done to best advantage.

Pensions **[AI1.21]**

One of the most important considerations for someone supplying personal services on a self-employed basis is their pension provision. Sole traders, partners and employees are all strictly controlled in that respect. Companies are also controlled but company pension schemes, particularly if self-administered, can offer greater flexibility.

This is, however, an area which requires to be carefully monitored and advice taken from someone authorised to give investment advice.

Investment **[AI1.22]**

The nature of a company allows investment to be attracted to the business because investment is separate from management. Thus, in exchange for shares, some individuals may contribute cash whilst others may contribute expertise and effort.

Financing **[AI1.23]**

The nature of a company as a separate entity allows a company to enter into its own separate borrowing arrangements which, in theory, will not affect the individuals behind the company. In practice, however, it can sometimes be difficult to obtain financing in isolation for a small company as banks will often insist upon personal guarantees from the individuals as well.

Perpetual succession **[AI1.24]**

When a sole trader or a partner decides to stop working then while the assets within the business can be sold, goodwill usually disappears with the individual concerned and the business itself dies. That is not necessarily the case in a company because of its legal identity separate from the individuals who, as shareholders or directors, are behind it. If an individual leaves, that company will live on until struck off and while the leaving of an important individual can affect the value of the shares in the company, if sufficient other individuals of 'worth' remain, then the shares of that company will retain a value and can be sold.

Separate legal personality **[AI1.25]**

It can often be an advantage to an individual who pursues a number of activities to put these into a company. That means that the activities will not be confused and that in the unfortunate event of something befalling one of the activities then the other activities will be relatively unaffected. This is only possible because the law regards a company as a separate legal 'person' from the 'individuals' who as shareholders or directors are behind it.

In fact, the legislation in the form of the *Companies Acts* does not spell out this situation in any detail and it was left to the courts to interpret this legal situation. The House of Lords did so in *Salomon v A Salomon & Co Ltd [1897] AC 22.*

The facts of that case were that Aron Salomon was a manufacturer of shoes in London. He wished to expand his business and also give his wife and children a share in it. Aron Salomon therefore incorporated a company which he named A Salomon & Co Ltd in which he, his wife and his five children held shares and to which, in return for cash, shares and debentures in his name, he sold his existing shoe manufacturing business. For reasons outside his control, the trade and the company declined and despite his best efforts (including the mortgage of the debentures) went into liquidation.

One-man companies of this sort were a new concept at the time and after the mortgagee of the debentures raised a claim the liquidator sought to have Aron Salomon made personally liable for the debts of the company. Approaching the matter as a novel abuse of the *Companies Acts*, the judge held that the company was a mere agent which Aron Salomon as principal had to indemnify. This decision was upheld by the Court of Appeal. However, the House of Lords overturned these decisions, holding that shareholders are neither agents nor trustees of the company which is a separate legal entity from them and that the declared intention of the legislation was that subscribers, as members, were not liable in any shape or form except to the extent and in the manner provided in the legislation.

Although frequently attacked and criticised by academics, that principle has remained ever since. The principle was reaffirmed by the Privy Council comparatively recently in *Lee v Lee's Farming Ltd [1961] AC 12*, a case which will be of particular relevance to those considering incorporating a Personal Service Company. The facts of that case were that Mr Lee was the shareholder, director and pilot of a company which used an aircraft for farming purposes in New Zealand. He was killed in an aircrash and the question was whether he was an employee of the company for the purpose of his heirs receiving workmen's compensation under legislation peculiar to that country. The Court of Appeal there held that he was not so entitled as he was not sufficiently separate from the company but that decision was overruled by the Privy Council which applied the case of Salamon holding that the company and Mr Lee were separate legal persons and it was possible for the shareholder/director to have a contract with the company which could be the basis for such a claim.

Clearly, separate legal personality is capable of being abused and, therefore, in a number of carefully defined circumstances the courts have indicated that they have been prepared to look behind the *Salomon* principle – known as 'lifting the corporate veil'. It is difficult to provide a systematic and exhaustive list of the circumstances in which the courts will do this but a number of examples might illustrate the approach

The first of these relates to the willingness of the courts to lift the corporate veil in order to combat fraud. If a company is found to be 'a mere cloak or sham' then the shareholders/directors may find themselves personally liable (*Gilford Motor Company Ltd v Home [1933] Ch 935*). This has recently been reinforced on a statutory basis with the *Insolvency Acts* providing that in the case of fraudulent or wrongful trading or trading under the name of a previously insolvent company shareholders/directors may find themselves personally liable.

Technical breaches of the *Companies Acts* such as allowing the number of members of a public company to fall below the statutory minimum or misdescribing the company on cheques or other commercial papers may also result in those behind companies losing the protection of the separate personality.

The second of these relates to taxation where the courts have shown a willingness to lift the corporate veil to combat tax evasion.

Limited liability **[AI1.26]**

The ultimate advantage of incorporation as a company is, of course, or is said to be, the protection of limited liability. Any liability is that of the company alone and the liability of the individuals behind the company is limited to the amount which they have agreed to contribute in shares. Previous practice was for shares to be only partly paid-up so that in the event of difficulty the company or liquidator would make a call for the shares to be made fully paid up. Modern practice is for a small number of shares to be issued (perhaps 2 shares of £1 each) and for these to be fully paid up.

The principle of limited liability (provided nothing is done contractually to interfere with that principle) is that having paid fully for those shares, no further liability can attach to the individuals behind a company which has failed. Although this is a strict legal principle which will always be upheld by the courts, in practice the principle is often interfered with on a contractual basis.

For example, where a small company approaches a bank for a loan it will often find that in return for the loan the bank will require not only a floating charge over all the assets of the company but also (and the signing of such a document clearly destroys the principle of limited liability) a personal guarantee signed by the shareholder/directors guaranteeing the indebtedness of the company to the bank.

Clearly, this is something of a belt-and-braces approach and with a strong enough bargaining position and the help of professional advisers it can sometimes be possible to persuade the funders to accept the security provided by the company alone and leave the principle of limited liability intact.

Other situations of particular relevance to Personal Service Companies are where the client contracting with the company insists that the contract is guaranteed by the individual behind the company.

Where a company is solvent and no document is signed affecting the principle of limited liability, then the courts will apply this principle. Most people do their level best to make their companies a success and where, despite their best endeavours, the company fails, then the fact that the individual has not lost everything he owns including the house in which his family lives is a factor which encourages entrepreneurs to take the risks which are the lifeblood of the economy.

There have, however, been situations where the unscrupulous have abused the principle of limited liability to the detriment of ordinary creditors and to such an extent that the Government has intervened with legislation in a number of clearly defined circumstances. These relate to wrongful trading and fraudulent trading. Where, however, the individuals behind a company *knowingly* continue to trade in a fraudulent or wrongful way (i.e. in the knowledge that the company is unlikely to be saved) then in those clearly defined circumstances only the *Insolvency Acts* allow the principle of limited liability to breached and personal liability attached to the individuals concerned. However, this applies only to companies in difficulties.

Such situations can be clearly recognised when encountered and with professional help it is possible to steer a course to safety for a company in trouble without the risk of losing limited liability.

Barriers to incorporation [AI1.27]

The main barriers to incorporation are for those below the age of majority and previous involvement in a company that failed.

Age [AI1.28]

There is in theory no age barrier to being involved in a company and the matter is generally regulated by the law of contract applying wherever the contract was entered into. Thus, a minor could set up a company although any contracts made may be avoided within a reasonable period of attaining majority and for that and other reasons minors might find it difficult, though not impossible, to run a company commercially.

Previous behaviour [AI1.29]

If this is the first occasion upon which the individuals have sought to incorporate a company then there are unlikely to be any barriers to their progression. Where, however, they have previously been involved in a company which has failed then there have been a number of barriers recently introduced by the *Company Directors Disqualification Act 1986*.

An overview of what is involved in a Personal Service Company [AI1.30]

Where the decision has been made to become self-employed and should the decision be made to select as the commercial vehicle a Personal Service Company then a number of considerations come into play in relation to what being a Personal Service Company involves.

There seems little point in trying to define the term 'Personal Service Company'. It is neither a legal term nor a term of art. A Personal Service Company can, however, be described as a company which exists to provide personal services. That description can cover a range running from a single member company with a single client to a company which has several members and several clients.

Wherever it falls in the range, however, a Personal Service Company is likely to have several defining characteristics. While technically a trading company, a Personal Service Company is likely to be more stable than many other types of trading companies. Personal Service Companies are unlikely to have to speculate or to carry much in the way of stock or goods. Instead, Personal Service Companies are likely to be concerned with the provision, in consideration for an agreed level of remuneration, of services in relation to which the personal characteristics of those supplying the services are likely to be of importance to the client.

As a result of these characteristics, Personal Service Companies may be able to avoid many of the considerations which other companies have to take into account. Personal Service Companies are unlikely to:

- offer shares to the public;
- become a member of a group of companies;
- borrow heavily; or
- make losses (unless mismanaged).

Despite these advantages, however, it is important to appreciate that for the purposes of law, management and taxation a Personal Service Company is no different from any other company. There may be a number of areas with which a Personal Service Company need not concern itself and there may be a number of exemptions for which a Personal Service Company can apply but at the end of the day a Personal Service Company is subject to the same basic obligations as any other company.

These basic obligations apply throughout the life of a Personal Service Company.

Law **[AI1.31]**

Strictly speaking, the word 'company' has not been legally defined but it has, in the past, been generally understood to mean an association of a number of people for a common purpose. In the past, that was just what being a company did mean and, indeed, so difficult and complex was the process of creating a company that a profession grew up devoted to the promotion and creation of them.

Today, the creation of a company is a relatively simple, inexpensive and easy undertaking. Furthermore, the requirement (for long something of a legal fiction) that a 'number of people' be involved, has formally been done away with (by the introduction of *Companies (Single Member Private*

Limited Companies) Regulations 1992 (*SI 1992/1699*) allowing single member companies). Therefore, in effect a company might now be seen – for present purposes – as a device to personify a business and divorce that business from its members despite the fact that those members are controlling the business. That, in effect, is what many Personal Service Companies are today.

It might have been thought that, in relation to a company such as a Personal Service Company, where, for example the:

- shareholders and directors are the same individual or individuals;
- company does not offer shares to the public;
- company has no borrowings from a bank;
- company has no creditors;
- company has no other employees; or
- company has no body of suppliers,

that a different or at least more relaxed regime might apply to such companies.

That would, however, be a dangerous assumption to make. There is at present no separate code of requirements for single member companies. There is a Company Law Review under way at present which is considering the simplification of company law for 'small' (i.e. private companies with a small level or turnover or assets) companies generally but even that Review does not currently propose a separate code of requirements for single member companies or companies where the shareholders and directors are the same individuals.

Instead, what faces companies (including Personal Service Companies) is a large and complex body of law contained in the *Companies Acts* and associated legislation. Of that legislation, 95% is for the protection of investors and creditors, aimed at public companies whose shares are offered to the public and that notwithstanding the fact that 95% of companies in existence are private.

Certainly, exemptions are from time-to-time available but the overall structure of the present law relating to companies in the UK is such that in many areas exactly the same requirements will apply regardless of whether it is a public company that offers its shares to the public or a private Personal Service Company with a single shareholder/director.

These requirements are reinforced by sanctions in various forms. Therefore, it is important for those who have decided to become self-employed and who are marketing their knowledge or skills through a Personal Service

Company to appreciate that no special code or considerations apply to them. For all essential purposes their Personal Service Company is in exactly the same position as any other company.

Advantages and disadvantages **[AI1.32]**

The legal consequences of incorporation for all companies include the fact that:

- it is a legal entity or person separate and distinct from its member(s);
- its liability (unless given away) is limited;
- it can own and deal with property in its own name;
- it can sue and be sued in its own name;
- it is capable (until its life is brought to an end) of perpetual succession; and
- its shares are transferable.

Those advantages come at a price as there:

- are certain formalities to be observed at the birth of a company;
- is a certain loss of privacy and various disclosures require to be made throughout the company's life; and
- is even formality and expense involved in the final dissolution of a company.

Incorporation, therefore, involves a balance. The advantages, such as limited liability, are balanced by the disadvantages, such as disclosure. The *Companies Acts* are there to see that the balance is properly maintained. A failure to observe the requirements of the *Companies Acts* may not have any immediate consequences but it can, in the long run, result in those involved being disqualified from being directors.

It is important for those contemplating marketing their knowledge or skill through the medium of a Personal Service Company to keep two principles at the forefront of their mind.

Firstly, a failure to appreciate and maintain the distinction between the legal person which is themselves as the shareholder(s) and the legal person which is the company is likely to lead to legal difficulties. Secondly, the legal obligations presently imposed upon a Personal Service Company are, to all intents and purposes, the same as those imposed upon any other company.

Management **[AI1.33]**

The management of a company, as we shall consider in more detail below, is divorced from the ownership of a company.

The shareholders, as the owners of the company through its shares, establish the constitution of the company (the essential documents regulating the affairs of the company) and appoint the directors but then hand over the running of the business to the directors (as a Board). These principles still apply even where there is only one member and one director who is the same individual.

Effectively, therefore, the directors manage the affairs of the company and indeed constitute its management.

This is a responsible and increasingly onerous position that has:

- a number of powers;
- a number of duties; and
- a measure of liability.

The powers of the directors as the management of the company are to be found in a document known as the Articles of Association. This document can take a number of forms but if adopted in the standard format gives the directors extensive powers in the management of the company's affairs.

For example, the directors are likely to have the power to:

- allocate or 'allot' shares;
- run the company's bank account and cheques;
- borrow on behalf of the company where necessary;
- pay dividends; and
- generally to do everything else which is necessary for the running of the company.

The duties of the directors as the management of the company are to be found in a blend of statute law and case law. The *Companies Acts* impose duties upon directors (see further **CL2.37** below).

The common law, as considered at **CL2.28**, has also recognised a number of fiduciary duties which have been imposed upon directors such as the duty:

- to act in the best interests of the company; and
- not to compete with the company.

Directors' liability **[AI1.34]**

So far as the liability of the directors for the management is concerned, it has to be borne in mind that a company, although a legal person, is an artificial person. Although a company can be fined it cannot, as the ultimate sanction, be put in jail. Nor can pressure be brought to bear upon a company to coerce it into altering its behaviour.

For that to be effective, pressure must be brought to bear upon the human agents through whom the company acts, i.e. the directors. Throughout the *Companies Acts* and *Taxation Acts*, therefore, where certain requirements are imposed upon companies, sanctions (in the form of penalties or other measures) have been imposed upon the directors for non-observance.

The list of requirements which even a Personal Service Company has to observe, grows ever-longer. In the enforcement of those requirements the legal maxim *ignorantia juris non excusat* (ignorance of the law is no excuse) is likely to apply. In relation to that vast and complex body of requirements, the aim of this book is to strip out those which do not apply (such as those that apply only to listed companies) and to gather together in one place those requirements, and only those requirements, of which Personal Service Companies need to be aware.

Taxation **[AI1.35]**

Many of the requirements which are today imposed upon companies, and Personal Service Companies, are fiscal in nature.

With minor variations, these fiscal requirements will in fact apply in much the same way to all self-employed businesses whether the commercial vehicle chosen is that of a sole trader, partnership or company.

Value Added Tax **[AI1.36]**

VAT is a tax which is obligatory upon traders – including Personal Service Companies – whenever a defined turnover threshold is reached.

Most Personal Service Companies will exceed that turnover threshold and be involved in the VAT system (indeed, it is probably possible to go so far as to say that if the current turnover threshold is not being exceeded then the disadvantages will have exceeded the advantages of having a Personal Service Company).

This tax is an indirect tax which is imposed upon the ultimate consumer. There will often be a chain of suppliers and purchasers on the way to the ultimate consumer in which a Personal Service Company is likely to find itself.

The obligation of a Personal Service Company in that situation is simply to:

- charge output VAT on its supplies;
- offset allowable input VAT on its purchases; and
- account for any balance to Customs & Excise.

The regime is stringent. Professional assistance will often be required, at least in the first instance.

It will be appreciated that in these circumstances, a Personal Service Company is acting as an unpaid tax collector. A major area of difficulty for traders generally is where they treat VAT moneys as moneys of the trader. It is important to recognise, therefore, that these moneys properly belong not to the company but to the Treasury and should be separately treated and accounted for accordingly.

Registration for VAT purposes carries with it a legal obligation to comply with the requirements of the VAT system and that involves not only the requirements in relation to proper VAT invoices (see **BM3.22** below) but also the requirement to keep proper records for VAT purposes (see **BM3.21** below) in relation to not only supplies made by the business but also supplies received by the business.

PAYE, NIC and benefits **[AI1.37]**

Having introduced a system for the administration of VAT and stripped out that aspect, the next hurdle which the directors of a Personal Service Company are likely to face is the imposition of PAYE, NIC and benefits.

The income of a Personal Service Company is the income of the company and the extraction of any profit from that company is usually something to which the attention of the directors is turned at the end of the year.

During the year, however, those involved in the Personal Service Company will want to draw out sufficient funds to meet their day-to-day living expenses. This will be drawn out in the form of a salary which is paid by the Personal Service Company to its directors or other employees. That salary is deductible against Corporation Tax in the hands of the company and taxed in the hands of the director or member under Schedule E.

However, as a direct tax emoluments from an office or employment chargeable to taxation under Schedule E require to be deducted at source by the company under the system known as Pay-As-You-Earn (PAYE). The Personal Service Company will require to introduce a system which will allow it to do that on a periodical (probably monthly) basis.

Furthermore – and this is often a particular consideration in the case of Personal Service Companies – those involved in the company may enjoy, privately, some of the assets of the company such as accommodation, holiday villas, cars, or even yachts. These are regarded as benefits. The legislation relating to benefits has become increasingly complex over recent years and a wide range of 'benefits' are now taxable in the hands of all employees and even more in the hands of higher-paid employees and directors.

The Personal Service Company will require to introduce a system which will allow it to identify and account for those benefits (some of which may have to be included in emoluments and taxed thereunder). Moreover, the emoluments (including benefits) of employees and employers are, to a greater or lesser extent, subject to National Insurance Contributions (NIC). The Personal Service Company will need to introduce a system which will allow it to account for the appropriate NIC.

As an additional requirement, the legislation implementing IR35 impacts on PAYE and NIC. The contracts of Personal Service Companies may be made subject to the IR35 Test. If that test is failed then what is known as a 'relevant engagement' exists to which special rules apply resulting in a 'deemed' (or presumed) payment of remuneration upon which PAYE and NIC will then be due (whether or not that remuneration is in fact paid out).

PAYE, NIC and benefits are often dealt with and accounted for together. In addition to its periodical obligations, a Personal Service Company as an employer will have obligations at the year-end particularly as regards reporting to the Inland Revenue and employees. The regime is stringent. Professional assistance will often be required, at least in the first instance.

Corporation Tax **[AI1.38]**

Having introduced a system for the administration of VAT and stripped out that aspect, and dealt with and accounted for PAYE, NIC and benefits both periodically and at the year-end, the next hurdle which a Personal Service Company is likely to face is its liability for Corporation Tax.

Whereas individuals pay Income Tax and Capital Gains Tax. Companies only pay Corporation Tax.

Whereas previously it was the responsibility of the Inland Revenue to assess the Corporation Tax due by a company, the position has very recently been changed to one of self-assessment so that companies are now required to make a company Tax Return in which they assess their own liability to Corporation Tax (self-assessment).

The system is, of course, subject to review. The regime is stringent. Professional assistance will often be required, at least in the first instance.

The rise in popularity of Personal Service Companies **[AI1.39]**

The rise of the Personal Service Company appears to have been largely tax-driven.

Some employers appear to have begun the process by declaring some people to be self-employed and refusing to pay the employer's NIC in respect of those people. The National Insurance Agency disagreed and, in a number of test cases, such people were held to be employees for the purposes of that legislation. The employers were required to pay (in arrears and with penalties) the outstanding NIC.

In response, some employers adopted a policy of refusing to engage such people directly and instead engaging such people only through the medium of an agency – thereby passing the problem of NI to the agency. In the normal course of events, under the same principles, the agency will be required to pay employer's NIC in respect of the persons it has on its books. However, that rule does not apply if the entity which the agency has on its books is a limited liability company and this appears to have been a significant factor in the rise in the number of Personal Service Companies.

Nevertheless, there will often be sound reasons for the creation of a Personal Service Company. Where individuals derive income for personal services from a number of sources but wish to simplify the administration of their affairs, it has long been the practice to set up a limited company as a separate entity into which all income can be pooled and then administered in a more organised and settled manner. The principle should not be lost sight of, therefore, that it has long been (and remains) entirely permissible for those pursuing self-employment through the provision of personal services to do so through the medium or commercial vehicle of a Personal Service Company.

'Umbrella' or 'composite' companies [AI1.40]

Driven to be a Personal Service Company but reluctant to devote the time and effort necessary to run a Personal Service Company, some workers in the knowledge industry have moved into what are known as 'umbrella' or 'composite' companies. The contract flow in such situations is likely to run as follows:

client → [possibly with agency inbetween] → umbrella or composite company.

That umbrella or composite company is likely to have a large number of clients. The remuneration from that client will be passed through the umbrella or composite company (who will deduct a fee for their services) and will then be paid out (in the most fiscally advantageous manner possible) to the worker who actually provided the services. It remains to be seen how IR35 will apply to umbrella or composite companies but its main purpose is clearly the channelling of remuneration and there is clearly no opportunity for the worker to develop the company for their benefit.

Caveat: Personal Service Companies and IR35 [AI1.41]

Where the decision to become self-employed has been taken and, after due consideration of what is involved in such an undertaking, the decision is taken to use as the commercial vehicle a Personal Service Company there remains, as a result of recent legislation, a caveat.

Background [AI1.42]

As already noted, a shift in working patterns has led some employers to move from long-term contracts of service to short-term contracts for services and this movement has become pronounced in the modern technology industries partly as a means of avoiding some of the difficulties associated with the status of employment and partly as a result of the tax advantages which this offers.

Indeed, this movement has become so pronounced that – according to the Treasury – it now requires something to be done about it. The movement, it is said, has reached the stage where it has become anti-competitive in that those within the industry adopting traditional methods of employment now claim to find it difficult to compete with those in the industry who are operating without the costs of any employees whatsoever. The movement has also, it is said, become so pronounced that the fiscal balance of the country (particularly in the area of NIC) is becoming affected. Furthermore, that the movement is to a large extent artificial in that those who are directed as employees on the Friday are leaving, only to return on Monday as self-employed but essentially subject to the same level of direction. As a result, legislation to correct the movement was proposed.

The proposal was first announced as part of the 1999 Budget, when the Inland Revenue issued a Press Release entitled, *IR35 – Countering the Avoidance in Personal Services*. That proposal has now been translated into legislation.

The Inland Revenue's approach [AI1.43]

Although yet to be tested in practice (and now subject to an application for judicial review) at the time of writing this book, the Inland Revenue approach appears to apply these new rules on a contract-by-contract basis. Essentially, a test – what we might call the 'IR35 Test' – will be applied to each contract and each contract will be determined as being either a 'relevant engagement' or a 'non-relevant' engagement'.

Where the contract has failed the IR35 Test and been determined to be a relevant engagement then – regardless of the actual expenditure by the Personal Service Company – only certain defined expenses will be allowed to be deducted from the income flowing from the 'relevant engagement'. The balance will be regarded as a 'deemed payment' upon which (irrespective of whether the sums concerned have or have not been paid out) PAYE and NIC will then be payable.

The possible consequences for Personal Service Companies [AI1.44]

Faced with the prospect of an IR35 Test, the consequences for a Personal Service Company could be significant. The position is aggravated by the fact that, under review, audit or Corporation Tax self-assessment, the position might not be examined closely until several years later.

The Inland Revenue has now offered to test contracts in advance and to issue an opinion on whether the contract is a relevant engagement or a non-relevant engagement. The IR35 Test is, however, a complex one and a number of opinions might be possible on the same set of facts.

A substantial Personal Service Company is likely to be able to accommodate and absorb a few of its contracts being determined to be 'relevant engagements'. However, for a small Personal Service Company with only one client and one contract, the consequences of a determination that a particular contract is a relevant engagement is likely to be financially significant.

In practice [AI1.45]

In short, the caveat is that the effect of IR35 in practice (and it applies to partnerships as well) might turn out to be such that after the application of the legislation none of the advantages (but all of the disadvantages) of being a limited company will be present, whilst the individuals behind the Personal Service Company will, financially, be in a worse position than they would have been in had they been a sole trader or an employee.

The prospect of that happening must now be added as another pre-consideration to be taken into account when deciding whether or not to embark upon self-employment as a Personal Service Company.

Summary [AI1.46]

Each individual's set of circumstances is different and the most appropriate solution for each individual is therefore likely to be different. The new limited liability partnership could turn out to be advantageous and there are further changes in the pipeline for company law. In these decisions professional advice will often assist. The difficulties of self-employment should not be underestimated and nor should the potential effects of the legislation implementing IR35. Nevertheless, if you have a genuine desire to become self-employed in the knowledge industry and the commercial vehicle which you have chosen for that task is a genuine Personal Service Company then you should not, by any means, be put off.

Part B

STARTING A PERSONAL SERVICE COMPANY

Introduction

Having made the firm and positive decision to become self-employed and having made the firm and positive decision to use a Personal Service Company for that purpose, attention can turn to starting a Personal Service Company.

Starting a Personal Service Company – in common with starting any other private limited company – is something which, ideally, should not be rushed into but which should be carefully considered and prepared for over a period of time. In theory, as one would expect from a developed commercial country, it ought to be – and is – possible for individual(s) to do this themselves but, in practice, professional advice will often assist the process.

Starting up a company used to be an expensive, complex, cumbersome and technical process (so technical, in fact, that a body of professionals sprang up devoted to the process) the technical name for which is 'promoting'. Today, starting up a company is a simple process and much of the previous body of law which applied to the process of promoting is, while still good law, of little relevance. Nevertheless, there are still circumstances, setting up a Personal Service Company with others and with a specific project in mind, where the law relating to promotion could still be of relevance and we consider that briefly in this section.

The involvement of others (or not, as the case may be) is something which will also have to be considered. It has, since 1992, been possible for an individual to largely incorporate a company alone (something which, although by no means determinative, might be regarded by some as pointing more towards disguised employment than self-employment). It is also possible, of course, to involve others in the company either as substantial shareholders or as minor shareholders. We consider the shareholding structure in this section. To whatever extent others are involved in a company, however, this is a matter which should be approached with care and which should be made the subject of special provision. This is an area where, at present, professional assistance is advisable.

Thereafter, no matter what route is taken to the establishment of a company, it will be necessary to settle upon (and have to hand for the purposes of starting the company) the officers of the company, the name to be used by the company, and the situation of the first Registered Office of the company. We consider each of these factors in this section.

Following upon that, we consider in this section the legal, administrative and taxation considerations applicable to starting a Personal Service Company.

BI1 – Preliminaries

Introduction [BI1.1]

Most Personal Service Companies are likely to be set up in advance of any commercial opportunities arising and in that respect the preliminaries to be established – so as to be able to implement them swiftly once the Company has in fact been set up – will include consideration of:

- formation;
- shareholding structure;
- management structure; and
- name.

Promotion [BI1.2]

The period between making the decision to use the commercial vehicle of a Personal Service Company and actually setting it up is known as 'promoting the company'.

In days gone by, when setting up a company was a difficult and expensive exercise, the promotion of a company was undertaken by professional promoters. So many difficulties arose in that respect that the common law had to evolve a number of remedies to deal with the concept of promotion.

Now that the setting up of a company is a quick, inexpensive and relatively easy exercise, the law relating to promotion (although still in existence) is less relevant. It is still possible to envisage circumstances where the law relating to promotion could be relevant to Personal Service Companies. For example, where a number of individuals come together to form a Personal Service Company to take advantage of a commercial opportunity but when the company is formed it takes the name of one of the promoters only.

With the benefit of foresight and time, a Personal Service Company can be set up by the individual concerned themself. Alternatively, off-the-shelf companies (see **BL3** below) can be purchased very quickly indeed although changing the name of the company to the name you want to use can take a little time. By either route, therefore, the Personal Service Company will, in the ideal situation, already have been established with its chosen name and notepaper when any business opportunity comes along afterwards. In these circumstances there are rarely any difficulties – the company, already validly in existence, enters into any necessary contracts in its own name. Where the difficulties arise is where the business opportunity comes along first and it is desired to preserve and take advantage of that business opportunity while intending to run the business opportunity through the medium of a company which has yet to be set up and come into existence.

The concept of promotion [BI1.3]

For a number of reasons (mostly to do with anti-avoidance) no formal legal definition of the concept of promotion or promoter has been attempted but the concept has nevertheless been judicially described from time-to-time.

One of the better descriptions is that given by Cockburn J in the case of *Twycross v Grant (1877) 2 CPD 469*. He said:

> 'A promoter, I apprehend, is one who undertakes to form a company with reference to a given project and to set it going and who takes the necessary steps to accomplish that purpose. That the defendants were promoters of the company from the beginning can admit of no doubt. They framed the scheme; they not only provisionally framed the company but were, in fact to the end its creators, they found the directors and qualified them, they prepared the prospectus; they paid for printing and advertising and the expenses incidental to bringing the undertaking before the world...'.

That judicial description is indicative of some of the actions that the courts will take into account when they are determining who is or is not a promoter. Since the circumstances can vary infinitely, no stricter definition has been attempted but the courts will look at these factors.

Clearly, the individual who takes steps to set up a Personal Service Company is likely to be viewed as a promoter. That individual is likely to have:

- framed the scheme to provide personal services to the client through the medium of a company;

- submitted the necessary forms to the Registrar of Companies;
- appointed the director(s) (if only himself or herself); and
- paid for the printing of the stationery of the company.

In the unlikely event of any question about it arising, the individual who has set up a Personal Service Company is undoubtedly likely to be regarded by the courts as a promoter. There appears to be no specific authority relating to off-the-shelf companies but as the real power behind the throne there is a likelihood that the individual who buys an off-the-shelf company to become a Personal Service Company will also be regarded by the courts as a promoter.

The significance of being a promoter **[BI1.4]**

The significance of being a promoter derives from the way in which companies were set up historically. It was considerably more difficult then to set up a company than it is now and indeed there were a number of individuals who at that time specialised in the then complex business of setting up, companies.

Difficulties arise where, for example, an expensive and valuable coal deposit or piece of property is discovered. In order to raise the necessary capital to develop the discovery it is decided to set up a company to which many people will contribute small amounts of capital. In the meantime, in order to protect the discovery, one of the individuals whose idea it is to set the company up takes it in his or her own name.

In due course the company is set up but the individual, in reselling the discovery to the newly-formed company, demands a higher price. Those involved in the company are naturally aggrieved and maintain that the discovery was made and secured with the company in mind. In law, however, the individual concerned was not acting as the agent of the company because by not being in existence at that time the company did not have the legal capacity to appoint an agent. Only the courts of equity could prevent such abuses and over the years a large body of common law has grown up aimed at controlling abuses by individuals promoting companies.

Clearly, the aggrieved persons in such situations are the shareholders of the company. The extent to which individual shareholders have a remedy is, in fact, an uncertain area of law but since in the case of Personal Service Companies the shareholder(s) and promoter(s) are likely to be one and the same person they are unlikely to complain about each other even if legally they could. In previous years the remedy has been at the instance of the company itself as a separate entity and while such an action might be legally more possible again, because the company and the individual promoter behind it are essentially the same, proceedings are unlikely. If there is only one individual in the Personal Service Company and that is the individual who promoted the company then a dispute relating to promotion is unlikely ever to occur.

However, it is just possible to envisage some circumstances in which – provided others are involved – a promotion dispute could arise in relation to Personal Service Companies. Suppose that an individual secures from a client an agreement to provide certain services for a very lucrative return. That individual might suggest to

- others that they join together in a company to be formed which will provide those services and secure that return;
- a bank that they extend lending facilities to allow a company to be formed to purchase expensive new equipment to provide those services and secure that return;
- their spouse or partner that they organise their life around a company to be formed to provide those services and secure that return.

Where those other people have relied upon the existence of that contract with the client when taking steps in relation to the company later formed then were the individual concerned not to put all of the work from that client into the company but were to instead divert some of the remuneration from that client to the individual personally then in certain circumstances that individual might be liable as a promoter for breach of his or her fiduciary duties to the company.

While an individual, in the setting up of a Personal Service Company, is likely to be regarded in law as a promoter provided that the individual who promotes the company is the only individual within the company there are unlikely to be any legal consequences flowing from the concept of being a promoter.

The shareholding structure [BI1.5]

The structure or allocation of the shares in the company is essentially a personal decision for those involved. A number of possible scenarios and considerations are detailed below.

The first aspect is whether the Personal Service Company is to be a single member company or a multi-member company.

Single member companies [BI1.6]

Although historically the corporation sole has legally existed for some time and the consequence in law for having less than two members was the removal of limited liability, the concept of having two members has long been something of a legal fiction with individuals taking on as a member someone who was merely a figurehead and without any real beneficial interest in the company. Even that requirement has been removed by the *Companies (Single Member Private Companies) Regulations 1992* (*SI 1992/1699*) and it is now legally possible to have a private company limited by shares which has only one member or shareholder.

However, whilst it is possible to have a company with only a single member, it is not yet possible to have a company which is run by only one person. Although that single member may also be the sole director, there is still a provision that the company secretary may not be the same person as a sole director.

So far as the shareholding structure is concerned, however, this obviously gives 100% control of the company to that single member.

The concept of the single member company is in fact a relatively recent (1992) introduction and not much of a body of law has grown up around it. The concept seems to have been introduced rather reluctantly. Nevertheless, there is no reason why those contemplating setting up a Personal Service Company should not choose to be a single member company.

Although shareholding is not mentioned specifically as one of the tests for employment to be utilised in the IR35 Test, it perhaps bears mentioning that, in practice, a single member Personal Service Company with only one client is perhaps closer to employment whereas a multi-member Personal Service Company with a number of clients is perhaps closer to self-employment.

Multi-member companies [BI1.7]

The involvement of other people in a Personal Service Company which is the brainchild of, and utilises the personal services of, one individual is unobjectionable and can be achieved without losing sight of the objective of the company. It is important, however, to understand what is involved.

In the first place, it should be appreciated that the courts and others will almost always regard a share as an item of property. Thus, no matter what the motive or understanding is for giving shares, for example, to spouses, mentors, management personnel or employees and no matter what compensation might afterwards be adjusted, the share itself will usually be regarded as an item of property belonging to the person in whose name it is.

It should also be noted that the coming together of individual shares can have consequences for the company. The control of a company is almost always a matter of simple arithmetic. Some significant percentage holdings are considered below.

95% shareholding **[BI1.8]**

A 95% shareholding in a company is only a little less than 100%. This is recognised, and the significance of the 95% shareholding is that in certain circumstances the minority 5% have the right to insist that they be bought out thereby leaving the effective controller completely in charge.

75% shareholding **[BI1.9]**

Many shareholders decisions are taken on the basis of a simple majority. Some, however, require the approval of 75% (e.g. special resolutions, see **CL3.11** below). Clearly, holding such a majority allows a particular shareholder to ensure that those decisions are put into effect.

51% shareholding **[BI1.10]**

Having a majority (albeit only 51%) allows those shareholders to ensure that most of the decisions they consider appropriate, are taken.

50% shareholding **[BI1.11]**

A 50% shareholding can clearly result in a deadlock situation and unless specific provision is made for this eventuality, recourse to the courts may be necessary in order for this to be resolved.

Less than 50% shareholding **[BI1.12]**

A number of people might join together to form a company and divide the shares equally between them. Where, for example, three people divide shares as equally as possible, it is necessary to bear in mind that the decision of two of these individuals will always outvote the wishes of the third.

The involvement of others [BI1.13]

In principle, there is no objection (and, in relation to the IR35 Test, perhaps even some advantages) to the 'main' person or persons involved in providing the services in a Personal Service Company distributing some of the shares in that company, provided that professional advice has been taken and a full understanding gained of what is involved. It will often be advisable to make specific provision.

Some of the main points to take into account are discussed at **BI1.14** to **BI1.18** below. See also the minority protection section in **DL1.5**.

Spouses [BI1.14]

The rights of married couples are now well-recognised and well-established. The spouse who remains at home is as likely to be regarded as fully contributing to a business (even where it is in the form of a company) as the spouse who actually goes out and does the work.

This arrangement is likely to be recognised in the event of any divorce by the award of a capital sum from one spouse to the other, either in a settlement or by way of a court order. However, as noted at **BI1.7** above, any shares issued by one spouse to another are likely to be still regarded as an item of property which one spouse buys from the other at an agreed or determined value, in partial or full satisfaction of the capital sum.

Sometimes spouses agree to distribute shares in accordance with their input to the company. At one end of the spectrum a spouse might also play no active role in the company but instead stays at home and provides the support which allows the other spouse to go out and earn by providing personal services through the medium of a company.

At the other end of the spectrum a spouse might attend for each full working day and by keeping the books or providing other services (such as marketing or sales), work just as hard as the other spouse who is in fact providing the personal services. Many other spouses will fall somewhere between these two extremes.

Recognising the above legal reality, however, some spouses often divide all of their property – including the shares in any company – along equal lines. While this might, provided that professional advice has been taken and a full understanding gained of what is involved, be unobjectionable in principle the effect in practice is that a 50/50 shareholding results so that whenever a disagreement arises the company is deadlocked.

In order to provide for such a situation, and to avoid the need to go to court, some companies include 'deadlock' provisions in their Articles of Association but as already indicated, this is a matter on which specialist professional advice should be taken.

> Example
>
> In a Personal Service Company, Spouse A holds 75% of the shares and Spouse B holds 25% of the shares. The spouses decide to divorce and after balancing their matrimonial assets a capital sum of £150,000 is agreed. It is agreed between them that provided Spouse B transfers her 25% shareholding in the company to Spouse A then Spouse A will pay to Spouse B then only a cash balance of £50,000 will be needed to meet the capital sum in full and final settlement.

See also the section on divorce and the Personal Service Company in **DL1.12**.

Partners **[BI1.15]**

As things stand at the moment, 'palimony' (rights of partners who are not legally married) is not recognised in the UK (although it is in some States of the USA).

Accordingly, if an unmarried partner owns shares then they are entitled to the value of those shares. They are not, however, at present entitled to any further matrimonial-type award reflecting the unpaid extent to which they might have supported the other partner in the operation of the company.

Mentors or other associates **[BI1.16]**

It is often a good idea (particularly in relation to the IR35 Test) for a Personal Service Company to involve these.

This might involve a mentor or other associate who is giving real input and assistance to the company. There is no objection, and some possible advantage, to giving such individuals shares in the company provided that professional advice is taken and the principles in **BI1.7–BI1.15** fully understood.

Employees **[BI1.17]**

The person or persons providing the main services in a Personal Service Company are often fully occupied with their expertise. They often do not have the time to see to the administration of the company and rely upon others as directors or employees to look after such areas.

In order to tie such individuals more closely to the company it is now often the practice to issue them with a number of shares. The same applies to valued or key employees providing assistance in the area of expertise.

The employee share schemes recently announced by the Chancellor are, in the main, for developing companies and are beyond the scope of this book.

Others **[BI1.18]**

Some individuals like to involve family members or other relatives in their companies and provided that professional advice is taken, there is no reason why they should not be. There may even be some possible advantage to giving such persons shares in the company although family disputes can be more bitter than others and the principles in **BI1.7–BI1.15** above should be borne in mind.

Settling on the officers of the company [BI1.19]

The officers of a company (it is recognised as a formal 'office' rather than an 'employment', although little turns on the distinction in practice) consist of the company secretary and the director(s).

Company secretary **[BI1.20]**

Every company must have a secretary and a single member company which has the same individual as the sole shareholder/director cannot at present also hold the office of company secretary.

Some firms offer a company secretarial service as a business. Some professional advisers (such as accountants and solicitors) will also offer their clients such a service. Alternatively, a spouse, partner, relative, associate or friend may be willing to serve as the company secretary.

The office of company secretary involves an understanding of the powers and duties involved (see **CL1** below), although these are more limited than those of a director. The company secretary, unlike directors is not usually exposed to much in the way of potential liability (although they can be).

Details of the secretary will be needed in setting up the company and the secretary will have an important role to play from the first board meeting.

The director(s) **[BI1.21]**

Every company must now have at least one director (although a company can have as many directors as it likes). In a single member company the sole member can also be the sole director. Directors' duties are increasingly onerous and carry the risk (even if minimal) of exposure to potential liability and, in extreme cases, to disqualification from acting as a director for a number of years (*Company Directors Disqualification Act 1986*).

Several heads are usually better than one and, as noted at **BI1.13** ***et seq.*** above, it may be advantageous to involve others in the Personal Service Company.

Details of the director(s) will be needed in setting up the company and the director(s) will have a vital role to play from the first board meeting.

Types of directors are considered in detail at **CL2.2** below.

Points to consider before becoming a director **[BI1.22]**

In the event of being invited to be a director of a company then there are a number of considerations it might be as well to bear in mind.

In the first place, although the company might appear as a small, informal gathering in which everyone knows each other and gets on well, in the eyes of the law it is a company the same as any other and most of the responsibilities for the behaviour of that company rest upon the shoulders of its directors.

It is important, therefore, before assuming the office of director, to have an understanding of what the position involves (see **CL2** below).

A measure of independence, at least in approach, is called for. Sufficient information must be obtained from the company to arrive at a balanced decision. Sufficient time must be devoted to the office to discharge it properly.

The administration of a Personal Service Company is, from the point of view of administration, no more difficult than any other company. Indeed, it ought to be easier in that because the income of a Personal Service Company can generally be anticipated in advance, there is less need to speculate and therefore it should be easier to avoid many of the pitfalls which trap other types of company.

Settling on the name [BI1.23]

The name under which a business operates has become increasingly important in recent years and in many instances has become an item of value. From the point of view of a Personal Service Company the name or names settled upon under which to run the business may or may not matter.

Where the Personal Service Company is simply a conduit for earnings which will die with the individual whose person services are generating the earnings for the company, then the name settled upon is unlikely to be of much significance.

Where, however, it is hoped that the Personal Service Company will make a name for itself and will go on to have an independent existence with others joining and the whole turning into an asset which can possibly be sold on later, then the name settled upon is likely to be very significant indeed.

Under modern conditions, names can be relevant in four main respects:

- domain names;
- trade mark names;
- trading names; and
- company names.

In theory (although difficult to achieve in practice) it is possible to have the same name running through all four concepts. Thus, 'Spencer Limited' may trade as 'Spencer', use 'Spencer™' or 'Spencer®' as its trade mark and have www.spencer.co.uk as its domain.

The difficulty in practice stems from the current fad for reserving interesting names in the hope of selling that name on later for a profit to someone who wants it.

Should the selection of a name be a matter of importance, a search is carried out through the indices (ideally in the suggested order of domain names; trade mark names; trading names; and company names) and the appropriate names registered.

Domain names [BI1.24]

Domain names are used to identify sites on the internet.

The internet is what is known as 'loosely regulated'. It is an international concept which is largely self-regulating but nevertheless there is a measure of protection to be obtained in relation to names. Various sites on the internet offer the service of registering domain names which includes the service of searching to see whether the proposed domain name is already being used.

Domain names have a suffix intended to designate the type of organisation involved, often the internet service provider involved, and sometimes the country involved.

A few examples of designations (the categories of which are expanding at the moment) are given below:

- .ac
- .co
- .com
- .org
- .net

For example, a business might have a domain name and address of: www.spencer@isp.co.uk.

Acquisition and protection **[BI1.25]**

The rapid and recent growth of the internet means that its regulation generally and particularly in relation to domain names, is not yet fully developed.

So far as domain names are concerned, a practice on the part of a few individuals has grown up of registering as domain names those names which they feel might later have a use and/or a value. This practice is known as 'cybersquatting' and there is very little that can be done about it. It is really a case of the first to think up and register a unique name owns that name.

Essentially, cybersquatting exists in two forms:

- registering a domain name which it is thought might have a use in the future and might be sold at auction; or
- registering the name of an existing company as a domain name and effectively holding the user of that name to ransom.

There is at present no official international regulation of the internet. There is an unofficial form of international regulation in the form of the Internet Corporation for Assigned Names and Numbers (ICANN) a non-profit organisation based in the USA. That organisation has delegated such powers as it has to another organisation called the World Intellectual Property Organisation (WIPO) which operates a dispute resolution system (a form of arbitration) for domain names disputes.

The second form of 'cybersquatting' referred to above, however, the registration of existing trade names as domain names, is a different matter. In the USA, legislation in the form of the Anticybersquatting Consumer Protection Act and the Trademark Cyberpiracy Prevention Act has been introduced specifically to deal with the problem.

In the UK, the common law has been called into effect. For example, a cybersquatter registered Marks and Spencer as a domain name and then offered to sell it back to them for a large sum. However, because Marks and Spencer was not only the name of the company and the trading name of the company but also its registered trade mark, the company was able to persuade the court on the grounds of trade mark infringement and passing off (see **BI1.36** below) to order the cybersquatter to hand the domain name over to them.

Trade mark names [BI1.26]

Added protection for a name can be obtained by registering the name as a trade mark. Under the *Trade Marks Act 1994, section 1*, a trade mark is:

> '...any sign capable of being represented graphically...'.

Businesses often use a symbol as a logo but they might equally well use a name both of which are, of course, capable of being represented graphically. It was previously more difficult to have names registered than to have logos registered but the requirements in this respect have been relaxed considerably.

Trade marks are essentially a means of identification. The idea is that as soon as the trade mark is seen then it is associated in the minds of the public with the supplier and the quality of the supplier. For that reason, a trade mark must be distinctive. In the case of a trade mark for services in particular it must be distinctive and not descriptive so that it is different from any words that others providing services may wish to use in the normal course of business in providing those services. Trade marks are something of a specialist area and a number of professional agencies provide advice in this respect. Hearing Officers are also available for consultation within the Trade Mark Registry.

Acquisition of a trade mark name [BI1.27]

Trade marks are now dealt with under trade mark legislation. There is an official body which deals with trade marks known as the Trade Mark Registry. For administrative convenience, this is situated within the offices of the Patent Office at Newport Gwent from where it covers the whole of the UK.

To obtain a registered trade mark in the UK an application must be made to the Trade Mark Registry. The application will be scrutinised to ensure that it does not conflict with existing or application-pending trade marks and to see whether it meets the necessary criteria. These include the trade mark being capable of being represented graphically and distinguishing the services of one business from another. Applications are entered in the Trade Marks Journal and third parties have three months from advertisement to lodge any objection. Thereafter, registration will be considered and if there are no objections is normally completed in about six months.

An international classification of 42 classes of goods and services has been drawn up and any trade mark registered is registered against one or more of those classes of goods or services. It is possible for a single application to cover more than one class but any protection will only apply in respect of the classes under which registration has been made.

While registration is pending the trade mark name can be identified with ™ and when registered the trade mark name can be identified by ®. Once made, registration lasts for ten years and needs to be renewed for another ten years thereafter.

It is possible, although expensive, to extend trade mark protection throughout the common market (the Community Trade Mark CTM) and also internationally (for example, under the Madrid Protocol System or in the USA).

The Registry of Trade Marks, which requires to be searched, has recently gone on-line (www.patent.gov.uk). On payment of a fee, anyone is entitled to search the index of trade marks. The indices are alphabetical and include, of course, the trade mark itself. The index includes pending applications.

Protecting the trade mark name **[BI1.28]**

It is theoretically possible to have and use a trade mark without formally registering that trade mark. In those circumstances, some protection might be obtained at common law if someone came along later and used the same trade mark in circumstances which the court regarded as 'passing off' (see further **BI1.36** below). The advantage of the registration of a trade mark lies in the additional protection which that affords. It should be noted, however, that protection is afforded only in respect of the official class or classes of goods and services against which the trade mark has been registered.

Once registered, there is an automatic right of action against an infringer using the same trade mark and in the case of similar trade marks against those in the same category where the public are likely to be confused.

Trading names **[BI1.29]**

There is no obligation on a company to trade under the name chosen for the company. It could choose to trade under a different 'trading name'.

There used to be an extensive and effective procedure for the registration of trading or business names so that the public could ascertain the real identity of the persons behind the trading name they are dealing with. *Business Names Act 1985* regulates what must be told to others about the ownership of the business and also allows the Secretary of State to exercise some control, in line with that applied to company names, over which names may be used.

A 'business name' is the name which, unless it is the same as their own name, is used by any sole trader, partnership, or company for the purposes of carrying on business.

Example

Own name	**Trading name**
John Smith	Brixton Joiners
Partners: Albert Brown James Green Peter White	MacPherson & Company, Surveyors (Note – it would not be a trading name if all the partners traded under their own names e.g. Brown, Green, White & Co.)
PSC Limited	Mastersoft

Where name being used is not that of the individual(s) behind the company then the *Business Names Act 1985* applies.

Acquiring a trading name **[BI1.30]**

There is no longer any formal requirement to register a trading name with any Government Department. Instead, a trading name is simply chosen and applied. Most of the business names legislation now relates to disclosure (on which see **BI1.29** above) aimed at ensuring that those dealing with an entity using a trading or business name are able to identify the person behind that trading or business name.

Certain names are excluded from use as trading or business names without special permission. They are common to the names which cannot be used as company names (see **BI1.34** below)

Protecting a trading name **[BI1.31]**

There is no formal system for the protection of trading names. However, the first to establish such a name will obtain a measure of protection under the general law (see passing off at **BI1.36** below).

Company name **[BI1.32]**

Regardless of whatever else a business does or does not intend to do by way of names, if that business decides to trade using the commercial vehicle of a company then it must have a company name.

In practice, conflicts are more likely in regard to domain names (see **AI3.24** above) than company names which is why it has been suggested that registration is approached in this order.

Checking existing company names **[BI1.33]**

Prior to making any application or decision, it is possible to run a check on the names in use by existing companies by consulting the register of company names which the Registrar of Companies is required to keep (*CA 1985, s714*).

Acquiring a company name **[BI1.34]**

On receipt of an application to either name or change the name of a company, the Registrar of Companies will consider whether the name chosen:

- if that of a private limited company carries 'Limited', 'Ltd' or the Welsh equivalent at the end of its name (*CA 1985, s26*) as this warns the public of the company's status;
- is not the same or similar to one appearing in the index of names kept by the Registrar of Companies;
- does not fall into the category of 'sensitive' words which cannot be used without permission;
- does not imply a connection with a government or local authority;
- does not constitute a criminal offence; and
- is not offensive.

Protecting the company name [BI1.35]

Entry of the company's name on the Registrar's index of company names means that others will be prevented from using that name for their company.

This is a protection which sole traders and partnerships do not have. The name they choose can be copied by others as long as they are not guilty of 'passing off' (see **BI1.36** below) or they are not in breach of a trade mark (see **BI1.26** above).

If a company becomes aware that another is using a name that is either the same or similar to its own, there are a number of steps which it can take – for example, in the first instance the matter should be drawn to the attention of Companies House and, where applicable, an action of passing-off can be considered.

Passing off [BI1.36]

The image of a Personal Service Company (as distinct from the individuals behind it) is of importance if it is intended to grow that image with a view to turning it into an asset and possibly selling it on later. If this is the case, then the company name will need to be adequately protected.

This concept of providing the business, as an aid to marketing, with a clear identity which the public can recognise and rely upon is now known as 'branding' and because brands, although intangible, can be protected and assigned they have an independent value. The creation and protection of such rights is one aspect of a field (which includes patents, copyright, design rights and others) known as 'intellectual property'.

Where sufficient time and effort has been put into a business enterprise to the extent that it has a recognised reputation and a measure of goodwill then at common law the courts will protect that enterprise against another enterprise which deliberately sets out to confuse the public and to capitalise upon that reputation and goodwill by using a name which has the effect of 'passing off' the identity of the new enterprise as being that of the original enterprise.

The test for passing off is, however, a tight and restrictive one and it can be a difficult and expensive exercise to pursue or defend such an action through the courts. Professional advice will usually be required in this respect.

Settling on the Registered Office [BI1.37]

The Registered Office is where most of the documentation which a company is required by law to hold is kept, or at least where the location of the documentation, if kept elsewhere, can be ascertained. The Registered Office is also the place where formal notices, writs, summons and the like can be served on a company.

The primary obligation is obviously for the Company to keep Companies House fully advised as to the current location of their Registered Office.

The requirement is that the Registered Office be maintained within the country where the company is incorporated. Thus, if a company wishes to locate its Registered Office (as opposed to a branch office) in another country then at present the only option is to re-incorporate in that country.

Beyond that, there are few restriction upon where the Registered Office must be. Some companies choose to use the offices of their accountants or solicitors to avoid having to change its location as the company moves and develops.

Details of the Registered Office will be required when setting up the company.

Law

For those who have decided to set up a Personal Service Company, there are, three main ways of doing so:

- joining an 'umbrella' Personal Service Company;
- incorporating your own Personal Service Company; or
- purchasing a Personal Service Company 'off-the-shelf'.

BL1 – Joining an 'Umbrella' Personal Service Company

Introduction [BL1.1]

Pressure on the one hand from clients to become a Personal Service Company and pressure on the other hand from the not inconsiderable administrative burden imposed upon Personal Service Companies (perhaps itself an indictment of the system operated within the UK) has resulted in the further development of what are known as 'umbrella' companies. As a result there is often a temptation open to those providing personal services, rather than forming a company to simply join an umbrella company.

In essence, an umbrella company is a single company which acts as an 'umbrella' in providing administrative services (often via the internet) for a number of contractors in the new technology industries.

The basic functions of the umbrella company are to:

- gather in the earnings of the consultant from the client or agency;
- perform the various administrative and taxation requirements in relation to those earnings; and
- then remit the net balance to the consultant.

The consultant will want to ensure that:

- the demand of the client or agency to deal with a Personal Service Company is met;
- the administrative burden is taken off the shoulders of the consultant; and
- the consultant receives his or her net earnings each month.

The umbrella company earns a fee from each consultant.

Features [BL1.2]

The cardinal feature of the above arrangement is that the umbrella company is the company. The consultant does not have a company under this arrangement. A number of features appear to flow from this.

Firstly, if an individual decides to set up a Personal Service Company, then it is as well to take full advantage of such opportunities as are offered by such companies and to really make it work and grow for the individual concerned.

Under an umbrella company arrangement, there is no opportunity for that individual development. The administrative burden might well have been lifted but in effect, however, the consultant is a glorified 'employee' (one stage removed) without any of the benefits and protections which are normally afforded to employees.

Secondly, as will become apparent in this book, developing a Personal Service Company individually is undoubtedly difficult without some professional assistance. A number of professions such as accountants and solicitors are available to provide that professional assistance. Those professions are tightly regulated and carry compulsory indemnity insurance. In the event of any difficulties (such as incorrect or incomplete payment of PAYE, NIC, or benefits), there are avenues of complaint and insurance available. The same cannot be said for many umbrella company organisations. Having said that, there have not in practice been a great number of published difficulties with umbrella organisations many of which are run by perfectly reputable individuals.

Thirdly, under the legislation implementing IR35, the contracts entered into by consultants are likely to come under increasing individual scrutiny from the Inland Revenue. The medium through which that contract is administered is not specifically a factor in the IR35 Test. It perhaps bears mentioning, however, where a consultant has only one contract administered through an umbrella company it is more likely to resemble employment than a consultant who operates several contracts through his or her own Personal Service Company.

Implications of IR35 for umbrella companies [BL1.3]

The ambit of the legislation implementing IR35 has yet to be determined and much will depend on the way in which it is administered.

It is probably fair to say, however, that:

- contracts will come under increasing scrutiny;

- PAYE and NIC will feature larger as a consideration; and
- the financial viability of the Personal Service Company with only one 'relevant engagement' may become questionable.

Umbrella company organisations will also have to address these issues and may, or may not, find their place in any new picture which emerges.

Choosing to use an umbrella company is to throw away the opportunity to fully develop and benefit from an individual Personal Service Company. On balance, umbrella organisations have all the disadvantages and only a few of the advantages of being self-employed through the commercial vehicle of a company.

BL2 – Incorporating your own Personal Service Company

Introduction [BL2.1]

While once a complex and expensive procedure which was so difficult that it allowed for the creation of a class of professional promoters (see **BI1.2** above), the incorporation of any company including a Personal Service Company is now a relatively easy, inexpensive and simple process.

A company is 'born' or incorporated by registration at Companies House and the formalities involve the promoter (the person setting up the company) sending to Companies House:

- the fee for incorporation (currently, £20);
- the Memorandum of Association;
- the Articles of Association;
- Companies Form 10; and
- Companies Form 12.

The Memorandum of Association [BL2.2]

The Memorandum of Association is perhaps the most important of a company's documents. It is of considerable legal significance and essentially regulates the relationship between the company and the outside world.

Under *Companies Act 1985, section 1(3A)* an individual:

> '...may, for a lawful purpose, by subscribing his name to a memorandum of association and otherwise complying with the requirements of this Act in respect of registration, form an incorporated company being a private company limited by shares or by guarantee.'

Further legal significance can be gleaned from the fact that *Companies Act 1985, section 14* provides that when registered the Memorandum of Association binds the company and its members as if they had each entered a contract with the others agreeing to be bound by the terms of the Memorandum.

Under *Companies Act 1985, section 3*, the Memorandum of Association should conform to the statutory style laid down from time to time by the Secretary of State – currently *Companies (Tables A to F) Regulations 1985* (*SI 1985/805*) as amended by *SI 1985/1052*. A private company limited by shares will use *Table B*.

The Memorandum of Association details the:

- name of the company;
- Registered Office of the company;
- objects of the company;
- liability of the company;
- share capital of the company; and
- subscription to form the company.

Company name [BL2.3]

Companies Act 1985 prohibits companies from trading under a misleading name. Under *CA 1985, s33*:

> '(1) A person who is not a public company is guilty of an offence if he carries on any trade, profession or business under a name which includes, as its last part, the words "public limited company" or their equivalent in Welsh ("cwmni cyfyngedig cyhoeddus").
>
> (2) [Applicable only to public limited companies.]
>
> (3) A person guilty of an offence under subsection (1)...and, if that person is a company, any officer of the company who is in default, is liable to a fine and, for continued contravention, to a daily default fine.'

Company names were considered in detail in **BI1.32 *et seq.*** above.

Registered Office [BL2.4]

The situation of the Registered Office of a company is a vital consideration for the company around which much of the legal personality of the company revolves.

There is no requirement to have the company's Registered Office at the place where it carries on its business (although many companies do) and many companies use the offices of their lawyers or accountants for this purpose. However, the situation of a company's Registered Office is of legal significance.

The situation of the Registered Office will in the first place determine where the company can be incorporated:

- the Registrar of Companies in Scotland will only register in Scotland a company which has its Registered Office in Scotland; and
- the Registrar of Companies in England and Wales will only register in England and Wales a company which has its Registered Office in England and Wales.

Once established within the boundaries of a country, the Registered Office cannot, at present, be moved outside that country. Therefore, if it wanted to re-base in another country (as opposed to simply doing business in another country) then at present it would be necessary to re-incorporate in that other country. Note, however, that this is likely to change in the near future, at least as regards countries within the EC.

Secondly, the situation of the Registered Office (along with the place where the central management and control of the company is situated) will play a large part in determining where the company has what is known as its domicile. That will determine, amongst other things, what law will apply to the company and where the company is to be taxed.

Publication **[BL2.5]**

The office or place where the company has its Registered Office must have the name of the company affixed outside it (in a manner which is both conspicuous and legible – *CA 1985, s348*) and all business letters and order forms of the company must show (in legible lettering) the address of the Registered Office of the company (*CA 1985, s351*) and if more than one address is shown, clearly designating which address is that of the Registered Office.

This clearly directs the public and all interested parties to the Registered Office where many of the company documents which they are entitled to consult are kept.

Delivery of documents **[BL2.6]**

The recorded Registered Office is where (unless another place such as an accountant's office is expressly agreed as well) the Revenue Authorities will send tax papers, some of which may carry time-limits.

The recorded Registered Office is also the place where the leaving of any legal documentation will amount to proper intimation and service upon the company (with possible consequences of legal significance if no response is made by the company within any time limit specified).

Clearly, therefore, the choice for the Registered Office of the company of an address from which a prompt response can, if necessary, be made is crucial. Those involved in Personal Service Companies would be well advised to use either their home address or working office address unless it is likely that they will be absent from there for substantive periods, in which case they should arrange to use the address of a professional adviser as that of their Registered Office.

Legal consequences **[BL2.7]**

It is unsurprising that the law relating to Registered Offices is quite strict given the importance of it. In the first place, *Companies Act 1985, section 287* (inserted by *CA 1989, s136*) provides that every company must have a Registered Office.

- The first Registered Office of a company must be intimated to the Registrar of Companies upon incorporation using Form 10 (see **BL2.17** below).
- The situation of the Registered Office of a company can be easily changed (within the country of incorporation) although some care should be observed in the timing of any change (see the 14-day hold-over referred to at *CA 1985, s287(4)*).
- Any change in the Registered Office of the company must be intimated to Companies House using Form 287 (see **Appendix 1**) although the change only becomes effective in law when Form 287 is in fact registered and during a period of 14 days following such registrations documents will continue to be legally served if served on the former Registered Office.
- A failure to keep the records of the Registered Office of the company up-to-date can have significant legal consequences. Apart from being an offence, it forms one of the grounds upon which – were the

company to fail – the disqualification of the directors might be applied for by the DTI.

- From the point of view of IR35, if the Inland Revenue were investigating whether or not a Personal Service Company fell within the legislation then they would expect to receive company notepaper with the Registered Office details properly marked on it. It is not beyond the bounds of possibility that they might pass by the Registered Office to check whether or not the company publicly displayed having its Registered Office there.

The objects of the company [BL2.8]

The essential legal principle is that as an artificial entity a company can only do what it has the power to do and the power given to a company to do things is to be found in the objects clause of the Memorandum of Association. If the company acts outside the powers it is given, it is said to be acting *ultra vires*.

In order to help minimise the possibility of this, the Memorandum of Association might State:

> 'The objects set forth in any paragraph of this clause shall not be restrictively construed but the widest interpretation shall be given thereto and they shall not, except where the context expressly so requires, be in any way limited to or restricted by reference to or influence from any other object or objects set forth in such paragraph or from the terms of any other paragraph or by the name of the company. None of such paragraphs or the object or objects therein specified or the powers thereby conferred shall be deemed subsidiary or ancillary to the objects or powers mentioned in any other paragraph but the company shall have full power to exercise all or any of the powers or to achieve or to endeavour to achieve all or any of the objects conferred by and provided in any one or more of the said paragraphs.'

In addition, the drafters would specify that the main object clause is:

> 'without prejudice to the other objects of the company'.

and follow that with a clause:

> 'to carry on any other business which can be advantageously or conveniently carried on by the company and which is

> calculated directly or indirectly to benefit the company or to enhance the value or render profitable any of the company's property or rights'.

Companies Act 1985, section 35B now imposes upon directors a specific duty to respect any limitation on their powers flowing from the Memorandum of Association. A member of a company is specifically given the power to bring proceedings to restrain an act by the directors which is outside the powers given to the company by its object clause.

Companies Act 1985 also introduces the power for the majority of the shareholders, by a special resolution in general meeting, to ratify (and thereby make valid) the actions of directors which are ultra vires. However, it is also provided that if directors or others are to be thereby relieved from any liability resulting from their ultra vires actions, then that requires a further specific special resolution.

This, of course, is only of real practical application where there is a plurality of directors and shareholders and will be of very limited practical effect where those who are acting as the directors of the company are also the shareholders (save in exceptional circumstances such as a husband and wife team falling out). It would have no application whatsoever to single member companies.

Examples **[BL2.9]**

In fact, those responsible for drafting and forming companies have a fondness for drafting a main objects clause which closely and specifically matches the purpose for which the company is to be formed and in the case of a Personal Service Company such a clause might run along the lines of:

> 'To carry on business as consultants or advisers on all matters relating to the provision of personal services and [your specialisation] to any trade, business or profession including, without prejudice to the foregoing generality, the provision of services, goods, personnel or any other means of organising, extending, developing, financing, marketing or improving any trade, business or profession and to carry on business as a personal service company.'

The difficulty about such an approach is that the term 'Personal Service Company' has only limited acceptance as a definition and the statement of a main objects clause in that manner could conceivably give rise to a dispute within the company over what remains of the ultra vires doctrine.

The legislature has, however, introduced into *Companies Act 1985, section 3A* an objects clause (likely to be considered to cover the objects of a Personal Service Company) which is intended to be of general application:

> 'To carry on for profit, directly or indirectly, whether by itself or through subsidiary, associated or allied companies or firms in the United Kingdom or elsewhere in all or any of its branches the business of a general commercial company.'

So far as Personal Service Companies are concerned, there are no reported cases pointing to any difficulties in the use of *Table B* in relation to Personal Service Companies so that those considering incorporating such a company should at present feel entitled to rely on *Table B* with the *CA 1985, s3A* main objects clause.

Company liability **[BL2.10]**

Under *Table B*, the liability of the members is limited to their shares. It serves as a warning of that fact to those members of the public contemplating dealing with the company. As will be seen at **BM2.3** below, shares can be authorised and issued and fully or partly paid but once issued and paid in full then that is the limit of the liability of the members.

This limited liability attaches in principle to shareholders who are also officers of the company (e.g. a director or company secretary) or employed in some other capacity. Note that the extent to which directors can be found personally liable is an area that seems to be growing. *Companies Act 1985, section 307*, permits a company whose liability is limited to alter its Memorandum of Association so as to make the liability of the directors (as opposed to the shareholders) unlimited, although there are few recorded instances of the use of this section.

Share capital **[BL2.11]**

The share capital clause states:

- what the capital is;

- how it is divided up; and
- its number and value as it is available for issue to the members of the company.

Share capital might be in the form of preference shares, ordinary shares, or both or otherwise. In either case this clause should declare that the:

> 'company's share capital is £ [a specified sum]'.

This clause should also specify the manner in which that share capital is divided up e.g:

> 'divided into [specified number] of [specified class such as "ordinary"] shares of [specified amount] each.'

This states the share capital initially available to the members. It is known as the 'authorised' or 'nominal' capital but it does not all have to be issued at once and is distinguished from the 'allotted issued' capital.

Thus, a company might have an authorised share capital of £1,000 divided into [an 'authorised' or 'nominal' capital] of 1,000 Ordinary Shares of £1 each of which the company might at the outset 'allot' or 'issue' only 100 shares of £1 each keeping back the balance for possible issue later.

Even when shares are allotted or issued, there is no requirement to pay their full value at that time. For example, those 100 shares of £1 each could be issued partly paid to the extent of 50p each. That would mean that the company (or a liquidator) could later call on the member to contribute to the full extent of their liability by paying the other 50p to make the shares fully paid up.

A tradition has arisen of giving small private limited companies an authorised or nominal share capital of £100 and issuing only a handful (often two) of these shares theoretically fully paid although the actual pounds are rarely handed over in practice.

Note that a company can, subject to the provisions of *Companies Act 1985*:

- increase or reduce the capital;
- purchase its own shares;
- consolidate, sub-divide, or otherwise deal with the shares forming the capital; or
- convert paid-up ordinary shares into stock and re-convert that stock into paid-up preference shares, redeemable or irredeemable.

So far as Personal Service Companies are concerned, any decision as regards its share capital will depend upon the likely future ownership of the company. If it is anticipated that others are likely to join the company later, then it may be convenient to specify a large authorised or nominal capital which can be issued later. If that is not the case, then the authorised or nominal capital might be set at the traditional £100.

The subscription to form the company [BL2.12]

The final clause of *Table B* reads:

> 'We, the subscribers to this memorandum of association, wish to be formed into a company pursuant to this memorandum; and we agree to take the number of shares shown opposite our respective names.'

Originally and historically attached with great significance and solemnity, this declaration of association now amounts to a statement that those promoting the company wish to form or incorporate the company by becoming its first members.

In fact, following *Companies (Single Member Private Limited Companies)Regulations 1992* (*SI 1992/1699*) it is possible for a private limited company to be incorporated with only a single subscriber (see **BI1.6** above).

Each subscriber should insert (in their own hand) their names and addresses, the number of shares they wish to subscribe for, add the total number of shares subscribed for, and then date and sign the Memorandum in front of a single witness who must attest the signature.

The Articles of Association [BL2.13]

Before the Registrar of Companies will allow a company to be incorporated, that company needs to have Articles of Association. These regulate relationships within the company as well as such matters as the relationship of the shareholders with:

- each other;
- the directors; and
- the internal organisation of the company generally.

The legislature provides a statutory style for a set of Articles of Association as laid down from time to time by the Secretary of State. These are currently *Companies (Tables A to F) Regulations 1985 (SI 1985/805)* as amended by (*SI 1985/1052*) in which *1985 Table A* contains model Articles of Association.

A company that adopts *1985 Table A* without modification need not deliver Articles of Association to the Registrar of Companies. The Registrar will endorse the Memorandum of Association 'registered without Articles of Association' and thenceforth the statutory *1985 Table A* will apply to the company (*CA 1985, s8(2)*). Alternatively, under *Companies Act 1985, section 7* a private company limited by shares may register its own complete set of Articles of Association or modified *1985 Table A* Articles.

The precise form which the Articles of Association for a particular company should take depends largely upon the nature of the company itself. *1985 Table A* consists of some 118 clauses intended to apply to both public and private companies. It is, therefore, considerably more detailed than that required as a set of Articles for a small private company. Furthermore, *1985 Table A* is usually modified in the case of a private limited company. Articles of Association can also later be altered.

The major considerations for the modification of *1985 Table A* can be considered from the point of view of the potential shareholding.

100% control [BL2.14]

If one shareholder holds all the shares in a company, *1985 Table A* will be far more than is strictly needed. However, if it is not anticipated that there will be any other shareholders to cause any potential conflict then for speed and simplicity it would be possible to use *1985 Table A* and amend the Memorandum to that effect, provided it is always borne in mind that if it is later decided to let others become shareholders in the company then it may be wise to use the 100% control to amend the Articles of Association in advance to cater for that new eventuality.

Majority control [BL2.15]

The Articles are intended to regulate a situation where there is a majority shareholder (whether the company is public or private). While *1985 Table A* as it stands may be satisfactory for public companies, it is usual for those behind private companies to want to regulate the manner in which shares may be transferred and to ensure that any unwelcome third parties do not become shareholders in the company. If, therefore, it is intended that the company will have a number of shareholders then professional advice ought to be taken on the modification of *1985 Table A* to create Articles tailored to the particular needs of that company.

If, however, one party holds the vast majority of the shares and only a small token minority of shares are held by another party then for speed and simplicity it would be possible to use *1985 Table A* and to have the Memorandum noted to that effect. It should always be borne in mind, however, that if it is later decided to let others become shareholders, then it may be wise to use that majority control to amend the Articles in advance to cater for that new eventuality.

50% control [BL2.16]

Where shares are held in equal amounts (a common situation where spouses or partners are involved, see **BI1.14** above) there is the possibility that any difference of views will result in deadlock. The Articles of Association of a 50/50 company are usually modified to cater for this possibility.

Form 10 [BL2.17]

Form 10 (*First directors and secretary and intended situation of Registered Office*) contains the essential company information as required by *Companies Act 1985, section 10*. It records on incorporation the all-important Registered Office of the company together with the first directors and the company secretary.

Form 10, is reproduced in **Appendix 1**.

Form 12 [BL2.18]

Form 12 (*Declaration on application for registration*) has considerable legal significance. The legislature was anxious to ensure that the proper procedures were followed before allowing the incorporation of companies with limited liability and delegated the duty to ensure that to the Registrar of Companies who in turn is entitled to rely upon a declaration by those incorporating the company that the proper procedures have been complied with.

Form 12 is that declaration and it has statutory effect by virtue of the *Companies Act 1985, section 12.*

Form 12 is reproduced at **Appendix 1**.

BL3 – Purchasing a Company 'Off-the-shelf'

Introduction [BL3.1]

Company formation agencies (now including Companies House itself) exist from whom it is possible to purchase a company which has already been incorporated and which is lying on the shelf ready for use (hence the description 'off-the-shelf' companies). Company formation agents can easily be located through local telephone books or newspapers. They will have a number of company styles on their database from which they can find something suitable for a particular company's needs.

To ascertain which is most suitable, the agency is likely to ask:

- How many shareholders do you anticipate the company having?
- How many directors do you anticipate the company having?
- What is the main purpose of the company?

The formation agents will probably be able to offer both single member and traditional companies. However, it is unlikely that you will be able to purchase a Personal Service Company as such off-the-shelf but you will probably be able to purchase a traditional company which will do the job, at least as far as incorporation.

Off-the-shelf companies will already have a Memorandum, Articles as well as directors and a company secretary. These will resign in your favour.

The nature of the transaction [BL3.2]

In exchange for the fee, you are likely to receive:

- Memorandum of Association;
- Articles of Association;
- signed Stock Transfer Forms for all the shares issued;
- signed resignation of the directors; and
- signed resignation of the secretary.

Post-transaction requirements [BL3.3]

The following steps may need to be taken upon receipt of the company documentation in an off-the-shelf transaction.

✓ Check the Memorandum of Association and the Articles of Association to see that their terms are adequate for the purposes of the company.
✓ Consider the need for changing the name of the company.
✓ Register the transfer of shares.

These areas are covered in more detail in **Chapter CL4**.

Management

A company is 'born' or 'incorporated' by registration – that is by entry by Companies House on the Register of Companies. The evidence of that is the Certificate of Incorporation.

Armed, therefore, with a Certificate of Incorporation either from the process of incorporation itself (see **Chapter BL2** above) or from purchasing a company 'off-the-shelf' (see **Chapter BL3** above), the company which is now in existence should proceed to the execution of the essential management tasks.

BM1 – First Board Meeting

Introduction [BM1.1]

A company legally exists from the point of registration but the company can do little in practice until the first Board Meeting has been held and a number of practical matters agreed. There is in fact no statutory requirement covering the holding of a first Board Meeting but it is advisable to have such a meeting as soon as possible.

The underlying responsibility for arranging the first Board Meeting, which will either appoint or confirm the appointment of the directors and company secretary, rests with the promoters of the company. In the case of self-incorporation, the first directors and secretary will have been intimated on Form 10 and as their first task they can pick up the arrangement of the first Board Meeting. In the case of a company purchased off-the-shelf, the existing directors and company secretary will have resigned with their replacements to be appointed at the first Board Meeting and so responsibility for the arrangement of the meeting will devolve to the promoters.

Notice [BM1.2]

Reasonable notice of the first Board Meeting will need to be given to all of those involved in the company. However, in small companies where the shareholders and directors are the same individuals, this is rarely a problem in practice.

Agenda [BM1.3]

There is no set procedure for the first Board Meeting and nor is there any formal requirement for an agenda. The promoters should keep a record of the intimation sent out and to whom.

An example of a suggested agenda is given below.

[Name]
[Address]

Dear [ ]

Notice of first Board Meeting

A copy of the Memorandum of Association and Articles of Association of the company [company name] are enclosed and you are invited to attend the first Board Meeting of [company name] to be held at [place] on [date] at [time] for the purpose of considering the following business:

1. To receive a report on the incorporation of the company.
2. To appoint a Chairman.
3. To appoint the directors of the company.
4. To appoint the company secretary.
5. To allot shares as required and record the allotment.
6. To issue share certificates.
7. To adopt the seal of the company (if any).
8. To establish the Registered Office of the company.
9. To establish the bank accounts of the company.
10. To authorise reimbursement of pre-incorporation expenditure.
11. To consider any pre-trading expenditure by the company.
12. To consider the registration of the company for taxation purposes.
13. To establish the Accounting Reference Date of the company.
14. To appoint the auditors of the company (if any).
15. To receive notification of interests by directors.
16. To consider the method of contracting of the company

To receive a report on the incorporation of the company **[BM1.4]**

The meeting may first receive a report on the incorporation of the company, either self-incorporated or bought off-the-shelf. The meeting will want to satisfy at the outset that a company validly exists and that it has been incorporated as envisaged by the promoters. This will be reflected in the constitution of the company, the Memorandum and Articles.

The Memorandum and Articles of Association will also establish who is entitled to be present at the meeting, any quorum necessary, and all the requirements which have to be met to constitute the meeting validly.

To appoint a Chairman [BM1.5]

It will generally be appropriate to appoint a Chairman (for this meeting) to control and direct the meeting.

To appoint the directors of the company [BM1.6]

The first director(s) will have been appointed by Form 10 when the company was incorporated (see **BL2.17** above). In the case of an 'off-the-shelf' company, the agency's founding directors will have resigned and it is the new director(s) who will need to be appointed at this time.

Under *Companies Act 1985, sections 288* and *289*, within 14 days of appointment, resignation, death, removal or change of a director, the company must notify the Registrar of Companies using Form 288 (reproduced in **Appendix 1**).

The company is under a legal obligation (*CA 1985, s288(1)*) to maintain a Register of directors that should be kept at the Registered Office. The purpose of this Register is to allow anyone to ascertain at any point in time exactly who have the legal responsibility that the position of director entails.

As a minimum, the Register must detail a director's:

- name and any former name (both christian name and surname);
- usual residential address;
- nationality;
- business occupation (if any);
- particulars of other directorships held (unless ceased more than five years previously); and
- date of birth.

Directors are normally individuals. It is possible, however, for a company (or in Scotland a partnership or firm, which has a separate legal identity) to be the director of another company in which case what must be recorded is the name and registered office of the company or the name and principal office of the firm.

Contract of employment **[BM1.7]**

The *Companies Acts* impose various legal obligations on directors regardless of whether have a written contract with the company.

In a Personal Service Company, the same individual is likely to be both a shareholder and a director and can therefore prevent their own dismissal as director. This has led the Employment Appeal Tribunal to hold that such persons fall outside the definition of 'employee'.

This does not mean, however, that a shareholder and a person holding the office of director (where these are the same person) cannot enter into a contract of employment with the company and become employees. Service contracts between companies and directors are common but are really only needed where the directors are not shareholders (unlikely in the case of Personal Service Companies, at least at start up). It is possible that as the company grows and develops, others may be brought in as directors and real consideration given to having directors' service contracts drawn up.

To appoint the company secretary **[BM1.8]**

The first secretary of the company will have been appointed by Form 10 (see **BL2.17** above) when the company was incorporated. If the company was purchased off-the-shelf, the agency's founding company secretary will have resigned and one will need to be appointed at this time.

The company secretary will be appointed by the shareholders. Where a company is being purchased off-the-shelf, a secretary will already have been appointed. Following the sale, the secretary will resign and another will need to be appointed.

Registration **[BM1.9]**

Under *Companies Act 1985, ss 288* and *290*, within 14 days of appointment, resignation, death, removal or change of a secretary, the company must notify the Registrar of Companies using Form 288.

It is a legal requirement (*CA 1985, s288(1)*) that the company maintains a Register of company secretaries that it keeps at its Registered Office. The purpose of this Register is to allow anyone to ascertain at any point in time exactly who is responsible for performing the function of secretary and responsible for the legal duties that position entails.

As a minimum, the company secretaries register must detail:

- name and any former name (both christian name and surname); and
- usual residential address.

Company Secretaries are normally individuals. It is more frequent, however, for the services of another company to be contracted to fulfil this position, in which case what must be recorded is the name and registered office of the company or the name and principal office of the firm.

Contract of employment **[BM1.10]**

The *Companies Acts* impose various legal obligations on company secretaries even if there is no written contract with the company. In the case of a Personal Service Company, the same individual may be both a shareholder, director and secretary (although a sole director cannot also be the company secretary and is thus protected from dismissal and probably will not fall within the definition of employee.

That does not mean, however, that a person holding all of these offices cannot enter into a contract of employment. Service contracts between companies and company secretaries are common but are really only needed where the latter stands at arm's length from the shareholders (unlikely in a Personal Service Company, at least when it first starts up). It is possible that as the company grows and develops others may be brought in as directors and then real consideration would need to be given to having secretaries' service contracts drawn up.

Where an agency is employed to provide the services of secretary, they are likely to have a standard form of contract specifying the services the company will receive for the fee.

To allot shares as required **[BM1.11]**

The authorised share capital of the company will be apparent from the Memorandum of Association. Whether or not the directors have the power to issue the share capital which has been authorised will be apparent from the Articles of Association. The shares subscribed for will be detailed on the Memorandum and these are deemed to have been allotted immediately upon incorporation.

An off-the-shelf company's founding members will have provided Stock Transfer Forms and those shares can be allotted at this meeting. If it is considered desirable to issue any additional shares, then this may be a convenient point at which to do so.

To issue share certificates [BM1.12]

As the Register of Members is made up, it may be convenient to authorise the secretary to issue the share certificates and to establish what the requirements of the company are in that respect.

To adopt the seal of the company (if any) [BM1.13]

The meeting may wish to establish the company's policy on seals. It is no longer strictly necessary for a company to have a seal, however, it can be useful for entering into formal contracts, particularly those overseas.

To establish the Registered Office of the company [BM1.14]

The first Registered Office of the company will have been appointed by Form 10 (see **BL2.17** above) when the company was incorporated. The Registered Office of an off-the-shelf company will need to be altered. The Secretary will do so using Form 287.

To establish the bank account of the company [BM1.15]

The company's bank account is operated by the Board, a number of whom are designated as the authorised signatories (usually two for security).

The minutes of the first Board Meeting should record what bank accounts are to be opened in the name of the company, and who the designated signatories are to be.

Most banks have their own procedures for opening bank accounts which quite often include having sight of a certified extract of the minutes of the Board Meeting relating to the bank account. Copies of the Certificate of Incorporation, Memorandum of Association and Articles of Association will often also be required.

To authorise reimbursement of pre-incorporation expenditure [BM1.16]

It quite often happens that a business opportunity arises at or about the time of incorporation (it may often be the stimulus for the incorporation itself). However, as a result, the promoters of the company sometimes require to make expenditure themselves to preserve that business opportunity for the company when it is later formed.

Legally a company cannot enter into contracts before it has come into existence and therefore the strict legal position (somewhat modified by the common law) is that the company cannot sue for the opportunity which had been anticipated for it prior to incorporation, nor can a promoter sue for reimbursement of expenditure incurred on behalf of the company prior to incorporation.

There have been difficulties in this area in the past. In practice, of course – particularly in small companies – no difficulty arises and the opportunity is simply handed to the company and the promoter is simply reimbursed for any pre-incorporation expenditure. However, in light of the strict legal position it is best if this is formally recorded in the minutes of the first Board Meeting once the company is incorporated.

To consider any pre-trading expenditure [BM1.17]

There is an important distinction between a company being incorporated and a company commencing trading. The distinction can have important tax consequences and it will normally be appropriate for the Board to consider at this stage the reimbursement of the company of any pre-trading expenditure.

To consider the registration of the company for taxation purposes [BM1.18]

Arising out of a consideration of its likely tax position, the Board is likely to arrive at a number of decisions about registration for tax purposes and to instruct the appropriate registrations accordingly.

To establish the Accounting Reference Date [BM1.19]

The Accounting Reference Date is a matter of importance for most companies. A company is obliged by law to produce accounts. The time limit for the production of those accounts is determined by reference to the Accounting Reference Date which can be determined by choice or automatically.

The company has the option, up to the end of a period of nine months after the date of incorporation, to intimate to Companies House the date which the company wishes to adopt as its Accounting Reference Date. This can be of importance to some companies whose trading pattern is, or is likely to be, such that drawing up the accounts to a specific date is going to make more logical and accounting sense.

However, if that option is not adopted by the company within that time-limit, then an Accounting Reference Date will be automatically allocated using the anniversary of the date on incorporation. Thus, if a company were incorporated on 1 July, its Accounting Reference Date would be 31 July and on 31 July the following Year the first financial year of the company will have ended with the obligation in law to, for example, deliver accounts to Companies House within 10 months of that date.

To appoint the auditors of the company (if any) [BM1.20]

Most small companies with a limited turnover (currently less than £1 million) are no longer legally obliged to appoint auditors, although there are often still good reasons for doing so.

If auditors are to be appointed they normally like to be involved in the affairs of the company at an early stage in order to guide the company in the creation of suitable systems.

To receive notification of interests by directors [BM1.21]

It often happens – particularly in small companies – that those who are directors may also have an interest in the shares of the company.

There is nothing objectionable about that in principle but the law requires, under *Companies Act 1985, section 325*, that all companies (irrespective of their size) maintain a Register of the interests of the directors in the shares of the company. Note that where the company has issued debentures (very rare in small companies but essentially loans in the form of Stocks which are usually redeemable) this requirement applies.

The interests of a director are widely defined in *Companies Act 1985, Schedule 13* and include, for example, options on shares and the interests of the director's family.

Under *Companies Act 1985, section 324*, the director must intimate in writing within five days of the matter coming to his or her attention, their interest in the company.

Upon notification, the company is required to enter that interest in the Register of Interests which it maintains.

To consider the method of contracting for the company [BM1.22]

We consider later (see **Chapter CM2** below) the manner in which a company can enter into contracts which may be attended by a greater or lesser amount of formality (with or without the use of a company seal).

Some companies prefer to enter into contracts on behalf of the company with a degree of formality and in that respect some companies maintain a Register of all documents (including contracts) it executes.

In the case of Personal Service Companies, the legislation implementing IR35 is, however, likely to make their contracts of more than usual importance. It might well be to the advantage of Personal Service Companies, in relation to all their contracts, to:

- enter into them with a degree of formality;
- preserve them carefully; and
- keep a Register of them which could be produced in the event of any IR35 Test being applied.

BM2 – Initial Issue or Allotment of Shares

Introduction [BM2.1]

As noted at **BL2.11** above, when a company is incorporated the Memorandum of Association specifies what the authorised share capital of the company is to be (although this can be altered later – see **Chapter CL4** below).

The amount of share capital which a company is authorised to have is not necessarily (although it can be) the amount of share capital which the company has actually issued. A company could issue all of its authorised share capital to the subscribers upon incorporation or alternatively only issue a few, but may decide to issue more later.

The decision to issue more shares can be made at any time but it is a decision which is often made at the first Board Meeting.

So far as the initial issue or allotment of shares is concerned, however, the task of issuing these shares will fall to the person appointed (probably at that same first Board Meeting) as the company secretary and the purpose of this section is to consider what is required in that respect.

Authorised share capital [BM2.2]

The company secretary should first check the Memorandum of Association where the authorised (or 'nominal') share capital of the company will be specified. The secretary is not permitted to issue more shares than the authorised total. (If it is desired to do this then the Memorandum of Association will require to be altered to alter the authorised Share Capital on which see **Chapter CL4** below).

Fully paid and partly paid shares [BM2.3]

The usual practice today is for all shares (of whatever type) to be issued fully paid. Consideration, possibly in the form of assets but usually in the form of cash or a cheque is physically paid over in exchange for the shares which are represented by the Share Certificate. Where the money has not actually been handed over then that is the amount (and under the concept of limited liability, the only amount) which the liquidator could seek from the shareholders.

In days gone by, it was the fashion for shares to be partly paid by having a deposit or proportion of the price of the share paid at the outset leaving the rest of the price to be called in, if necessary, by the company later. The *Companies Acts* and the Articles of Association still reflect that possibility but it is more rarely seen in practice today.

Classes of shares [BM2.4]

Various classes of shares have emerged over the years. It is not advisable to attempt to use such variations except where absolutely necessary and professional advice should be taken wherever they are encountered. They include the following.

Preference shares [BM2.5]

These are shares which are given an entitlement to a fixed dividend in priority to other shares.

The preference is usually stated as a percentage of the nominal value of the preference shares e.g. 10% £1 preference shares, and until those preference shares have received their 10% dividend in full no other class of shares is entitled to a dividend.

The precise terms applicable to preference shares in all eventualities is usually detailed in the Memorandum or Articles of Association. For example:

- they sometimes have preferential votes;
- they may or may not be declared to be cumulative in the sense that if the dividend is not paid in one year then no other share is entitled to participate until the arrears carried forward as well as the dividend for the current year have been paid to the holders of the preference shares; and
- they are also often have special rights to any surplus in the event of a winding-up.

Ordinary shares **[BM2.6]**

In the normal course of events, only one class of shares will be issued and all such shares will have equal rights. These are called ordinary shares.

Such shareholders (also known as 'members') will have one vote for each share. Votes will be cast for matters such as the appointment of directors, dividends, and the like and a simple majority will carry the vote except in those circumstances where the law specifies a greater majority.

It is possible now (since the *Companies (Single Member Private Limited Companies) Regulations 1992* (*SI 1992/1699*)) for a company to have a single member. This certainly precludes arguments.

It is more common, however, at least at present, for companies to have more than one member. It is common, for example, for spouses or partners both to be members and for the company to issue two shares with each spouse or partner holding one share. As earlier noted, this produces a deadlock situation which may not cause difficulties where the spouses or partners are in full agreement but can cause difficulties where the spouses or partners fall out.

Ordinary shares normally rank equally and carry the ordinary rights of shareholders. For example:

- the right to vote (equally);
- the right (equally) to any dividend declared; and
- the right to participate (equally) in any surplus on a winding-up.

It sometimes happens, however, that different classes of ordinary shares (e.g. 'A 'or 'B' Shares) are issued which have slightly different rights attaching to them.

Deferred shares **[BM2.7]**

Deferred Shares are, in a sense, the reverse of preference shares. For example:

- they may have different voting rights;
- they may not be entitled to a dividend until a stipulated amount has been paid to the ordinary shareholders; and
- they may have restricted rights to any surplus on a winding-up.

It used to be common for shares issued to the founders of the company to be in such a class but founders shares are more rarely encountered today.

Redeemable shares **[BM2.8]**

Redeemable shares are shares which may be redeemed by the company on specified terms. *Companies Act 1948, section 58* authorised the issue as redeemable of shares which were preference shares. That was amended by the *Companies Act 1981* to include non-preference shares and the present legislation is to be found in *sections 159–161* of the *Companies Act 1985.*

Further legislation is anticipated laying down further conditions for the issue of redeemable shares. At present, the Memorandum or Articles of Association will specify the circumstances of redemption and the calculation of the redemption price.

Convertible shares **[BM2.9]**

It has, in the past, been quite common for the security given by a company to those who have lent money to the company to specify that the loan can be converted into shares. It the same way, it is sometimes found that provision is made for one class of shares to be convertable, on predetermined conditions, into another class of shares.

Purchased shares **[BM2.10]**

The *Companies Act 1981* introduced the concept of a company purchasing its own shares and the present legislation is to be found in *Chapter VII* of *Part V* of the *Companies Act 1985.* This is a sophisticated concept which carries a number of tax consequences and upon which specialist professional advice is required.

Class rights **[BM2.11]**

The rights attaching to a particular class of shares – for example, rights relating to voting, dividend, and any surplus – are normally fully specified in the Memorandum or Articles of Association os some associated document.

Different classes may be given different rights. For example:

- preference shares may be given no votes;
- Class 'A' ordinary shares may be one vote per share while Class 'B' ordinary shares may be given ten votes per share; or
- other rights might relate to the appointment of directors.

Clearly, the adjustment of class rights (often a requirement of funders especially venture capitalists) can be of considerable significance in relation to the way in which such companies are run.

Authority to issue the authorised share capital [BM2.12]

The directors of a company do not automatically have the power to issue the authorised share capital of a company. Indeed, *Companies Act 1985, section 80* specifically provides that the directors of a company may not issue relevant securities (which includes shares) unless authorised to do so. Accordingly, the power to issue shares is a power which must be specifically given to the directors. That power can be given in two ways, either through the Articles of Association or by an ordinary resolution of the company passed at a general meeting.

1985 Table A does not give this power to the directors and, therefore, would need to be modified. The original terms of *Companies Act 1985, section 80* controlled this authority by providing that such authority given in the Articles must state the maximum period of the authority which must not exceed five years.

Companies Act 1989, section 115 introduced *section 80A* into *Companies Act 1985* and this provides that a private company may by elective resolution elect that the provisions of that section shall apply to it. Once that has been done the company can give the directors the power for an unlimited period to issue shares. Clearly, at the first Board Meeting such an elective resolution is unlikely (unless it was placed on the Agenda) to have been passed but the Articles of Association drawn up or purchased off-the-shelf may give the directors the power to issue shares for a stated period not exceeding five years.

The requirements for membership [BM2.13]

The relationship between a shareholder and the company in which they hold shares is essentially one of contract (albeit a contract heavily influenced by terms implied by statute such as the *Companies Acts*). Technically, therefore (although this is often not observed in practice in the case of small private companies), the contract should be arrived at in the usual manner of offer and acceptance (with, in the case of England & Wales, consideration). A person wishing to become a member of a company should therefore technically make an 'offer' in the form of a formal written application to the company seeking the allotment of a specified number of shares for a specified consideration.

If that offer is accepted by the company and the company secretary has checked that an allotment of the shares is valid, then the company should technically conclude the contract by the issue an unqualified acceptance indicating that a specified number of shares for a specified consideration have been allotted and enclosing an up-to-date copy of the Memorandum of Association and Articles of Association and perhaps also making reference to the existence of the *Companies Acts* as all governing the contractual relationship between the parties which has been entered into.

Although a contract may have been concluded between the parties at this stage (giving them certain personal rights) an allottee does not in law become a member of a company until they have been entered in the statutory Register of Members (*National Westminster Bank and Another v Inland Revenue (HL) The Times, 24 June 1994*).

The consideration for membership [BM2.14]

At the discretion of, ultimately, the controlling shareholders of the company and, administratively, the directors of the company if they have been given that power, a person may be admitted to membership for the company and given shares to reflect that membership in exchange for a consideration which is:

- wholly cash (fully paid or partly paid);
- which is wholly non-cash; or
- which is partly cash and partly non-cash.

Although often, or indeed usually, allotted for cash it sometimes happens that shares are allotted for a consideration which is wholly or partly non-cash such as, for example, for assets, goods, services, property, goodwill, know-how, shares in another company or the like. This introduces a complication in that the non-cash element of a consideration will require to be valued before the shares are allotted and a Return made to Companies House.

The authority for the company secretary to allot shares on these terms and to gather in that consideration before performing the administrative task of actually recording the transaction in the Register of Members and, issuing a Share Certificate is to be found in the minutes of the Board Meeting (in this instance probably the first Board Meeting).

Procedure [BM2.15]

Legislation requires certain registers to be kept by a company (see further **Chapter BM3** below). A register of the shares issued or allotted by the company is not one of those statutory registers but companies may nevertheless find it convenient to keep and maintain such a Register of Allotments which can then be cross-referenced to the other statutory registers which do have to be kept.

Once they have the necessary authority and once the above contract has been concluded, the duties of the company secretary include the following.

Making an entry in the Register of Allotments [BM2.16]

Before proceeding with the procedure for the administrative allotment and issue of the shares the company secretary should carefully check the authority to do that which, again, is to be found in the minutes of the Board Meeting (in this instance probably the first Board Meeting) and as such the company secretary should carefully record and preserve those minutes. With that authority, the company secretary can proceed with the allotment for which a Register of Allotments may be used. This Register is optional but it does offer the company secretary a means of keeping clear track of the shares which have been issued by the company.

Technically, the date of the allotment of shares will be the date from which it appears the shares have been allotted. Unless the minutes provide otherwise, therefore, the date of allotment will be the date of the Board Meeting and that is the date which the company secretary should enter in the Register of Allotments and later in the return to Companies House.

Making the Return to Companies House [BM2.17]

Within one month of the first date of allotment of shares a Return of

Allotment of Shares must be made to Companies House on Form 88(2) which is reproduced in **Appendix 1**. There is no fee payable to Companies House with Form 88(2).

Technically, the date of the allotment of shares will be the date from which it appears the shares have been allotted. Unless the Minutes provide otherwise, therefore, the date of allotment will be the date of the Board Meeting and that is the date which the company secretary should enter in the Register of Allotments (if any) That is also the date from which the one month time limit for the return of Form 88(2) to Companies House should be calculated.

Note that although often, or indeed usually, allotted for cash it sometimes happens that shares are allotted for a consideration which is wholly or partly non-cash such as, for example for:

- assets;
- goods;
- services;
- property;
- goodwill;
- know-how; and
- shares in another company.

This introduces a complication in that the non-cash element of a consideration will require to be valued before the shares are allotted and a Return on Form 88(2) made to Companies House.

Where shares are issued wholly or partly for a non-cash consideration then two consequences follow. Firstly, that non-cash consideration must be valued before the Return on Form 88(2) is made to Companies House and, secondly, the acquisition of shares for a non-cash consideration amounts to a transfer of property which may amount to a chargeable transaction under the *Stamp Act* (which itself will involve a valuation of the transfer).

There are essentially two possible situations here. Either the non-cash consideration is the subject of a written contract or it is not.

Where the non-cash consideration is the subject of a written contract, it is possible to take the written contract to the local Stamp Office (ascertainable from the local telephone directory) and there have it valued and stamped by the Inland Revenue (who will physically attach a stamp to the document as receipt for payment of the stamp duty). A certified copy of that written contract, provided that it is stamped will then be acceptable by the Registrar of Companies as satisfying that part of Form

88(2) where the non-cash consideration for which shares have been allotted must be shown.

Alternatively (although the Registrar will not accept this as an alternative where a written contract exists) where there is no written contract then Form 88(3) may be used. Again, it is possible to take the Form 88(3) to the local Stamp Office (ascertainable from the local telephone directory) and there have it valued and stamped by the Inland Revenue (who will physically attach a stamp to the Form as receipt for payment of the stamp duty). That Form 88(3), provided that it is stamped will then acceptable by the Registrar of Companies as satisfying that part of Form 88(2) where the non-cash consideration for which shares have been allotted must be shown.

Making an entry in the Register of Members [BM2.18]

This Register is statutory and obligatory and is intended to offer interested parties (both within and outside the company) a means, by inspection, of determining at any moment in time exactly who the members of the company are. Clearly, therefore, it is important that the Company Secretary performs his or her statutory duty in maintaining the Register of Members and keeping it always up-to-date.

The minimum information which must, by statute (*CA 1985, s352*) be included is:

- identity:
  - the names and addresses of the members;
  - the date upon which each person was registered as a member; and
  - the date upon which any member ceases to be a member,

- shareholding:
  - the number of shares held by each member (stating the class of share if more than one class);
  - the amount paid up in respect of each share.

It will be appreciated that if this Register is properly maintained then the total number of shares issued by the company will always be reflected in total in the Register of Members from which an interested party will be able to ascertain the names and addresses of the members, the date upon which they became members, and the number of shares they hold. It is the entry on this Register which makes a person a member of a company for voting purposes (not some other oral or written agreement although they might later be enforced) and accordingly if being a member matters then this Register should be checked to ensure that the appropriate entry has been correctly made.

The *Companies Act 1985, section 359* empowers a court to order rectification of the Register of Members where there has been default, unnecessary delay, or the name of any person is, without sufficient cause, entered in or omitted from the Register of Members. Amongst other things, this register will disclose the identity of the person holding the majority of the shares at any point in time and therefore effectively ultimately controlling the activities of the company. Many companies establish the membership of the company at the time when the company is being set up. If the company was self-incorporated then the two persons who subscribed to the Memorandum of Association are, in terms of *Companies Act 1985, section 22*, deemed to have thereby agreed to become members of the company and it is simply a question of entering their names and addresses, date of registration as a member and the number of shares held.

If the company has been purchased 'off-the-shelf' then two employees of the company formation agency will have signed the Memorandum of Association. Their details, if not already entered, should be entered in the Register of Members together with the date upon which they ceased to become members (they ought to have provided you with a signed and dated letter of resignation as members of the company) followed by the names and addresses, date of registration as a member and the number of shares held by those who are taking their place as members.

The number of shares which a company is authorised to have and the number of shares which a company allocates are entirely a matter for the company. Many private companies are formed in a traditional manner with a share capital of £100 divided into 100 shares of £1 each. The company then allots two shares of £1 each to the two individuals who are behind the company and who are also its Directors and Secretary. In strict theory, both of those pounds ought to be paid into the company and reflected in the accounts of the company. It should be appreciated that this is a significant allocation and that it results in two persons each holding an equal shareholding of 50% in the company. This can result in difficulties if differences arise since no-one has overall control and resort often has to be made to the courts.

Where the two individuals are husband and wife the allocation is even more significant in that each spouse, in addition to any matrimonial claims, will be regarded in the eyes of the law as each owning half of a business asset in their own right which, as a separate factor, would require to be factored into any settlement on divorce. Care should be taken at the outset to ensure, so far as possible, that the company is capable of being controlled and reflects the true input of its members.

In the above situation, there is only one class of shares and (if the two pounds have been handed over) they are fully paid up. If those two pounds have not been handed over then (if none of the other circumstances relating to personal liability being present) under the principle of limited liability payment of those two pounds to make the shares fully paid up are all that the Liquidator can call for from the members in the event of the company failing.

It is theoretically possible – although rarely encountered in practice – to issue shares of, say, £10 of which the members are asked to pay only £1 at the time when the shares are allotted. (A Liquidator could, of course, later call for the members to pay the other £9.) In these circumstances, for obvious reasons, the law (*CA 1985, s352*) requires a record of the amount paid and unpaid on those shares.

It is also theoretically possible – and this is a tactic more often encountered in practice being a favourite of venture capitalists – to have different classes of shares. The difference might be between preference shares and ordinary shares or between Class A ordinary shares (carrying special voting rights on certain specified matters) and Class B ordinary shares (with no such rights) or various other permutations are possible. Again, in these circumstances, for obvious reasons, the law (*CA 1985, s352*) requires a record of the classes of shares if there is more than one class of share.

When the number of members exceeds 50 then the Register of Members must, if not itself in the form of an index, contain a separate index of members.

Once the appropriate entries have been made they are currently required (although this is likely to change in the future) to be retained for a period of 20 years following the date upon which an individual ceases to be a member of the company.

The Register of Members must always remain within the country of incorporation. Thus, where a company is incorporated in England and Wales the Register of Members must always remain within the territory of England and Wales and where a company is incorporated in Scotland the Register of Members must always remain within the territory of Scotland.

Traditionally, the Register of Members is kept at the Registered Office of the company but that need not necessarily be so. In incorporating the company it will be inferred that the Register of Members is at the Registered Office of the company. Any change in the place where the Register of

Members is kept should immediately be intimated to Companies House on Form 353a which deals with 'Notice of place for inspection of a Register of Members which is kept in a non-legible (i.e. computer) form, or any changes in that place'. As a running check, the Annual Return (Form 363a) (see **Appendix 1**) contains a section (RM) which enquires where the Register of Members is kept and a section within which the address where it is kept may be inserted.

Making an entry in the Register of Directors' Interests (if applicable) [BM2.19]

If the person to whom the shares are being allotted happens to be a director of the company then there is a further entry which the company secretary must make in another register called the Register of Directors' Interests. The definition of 'interest' is wide and includes the family of the director.

The primary obligation is on the director to notify the interest to the company which the company must record in the register. In addition, the company from its own awareness of its affairs must record in the Register details of shares or rights to subscribe for shares issued by the company to its directors.

This Register is statutory and obligatory and is intended to offer interested parties (both within and outwith the company) a means, by inspection, of determining at any moment in time exactly what interests the directors have in the shares of the company.

Obtaining the consideration for the shares [BM2.20]

While it may or may not be the administrative responsibility of the company secretary to gather in the consideration (cash or non-cash) for the shares, it is the legal responsibility of the directors to ensure that the consideration has been received and properly reflected in the company books.

Issuing the Share Certificate [BM2.21]

The company secretary ought to check that the consideration has been received in full before issuing the Share Certificate. However, *CA 1985* requires a company to issue the Share Certificate within two months of registration of the allotment in the Register of Members.

This area was a particular problem in days gone by when shares were often issued partly-paid and the *1985 Table A* style has extensive provisions dealing with lien (the right to hold onto the share certificate until the share has been made fully paid-up) calling for the balance due, and providing for the forfeiture of the shares where the call has not been answered and payment has not been made. The Articles of private companies may or may not include those Articles. In most cases, however, shares are issued fully-paid and wholly for cash and a cheque is usually forthcoming. In these circumstances, the Share Certificate may safely be issued.

The form which a Share Certificate takes is usually, in terms of the Articles, a matter for the discretion of the directors. It no longer requires to have the seal of the company applied to it (although it can be) and modern Share Certificates can be, and often are, simply printed.

In legal terms, the statutory Register of Members is the important document and it is possible to apply to the courts to have that Register properly reflect the position in law. The Share Certificate then has the legal significance of being *prima facie* evidence of the legal title of that member to the shares in his or her name in the Register of Members.

Share Certificates are normally required to be produced to the company when the share is being transferred. Share Certificates can sometimes be lost. This can be a serious matter in larger companies which sometimes requires the granting of indemnities by the applicant before a replacement Share Certificate is issued. This is less of a problem in small private companies where the shareholders and their shareholdings are all known to each other but nevertheless the replacement of Share Certificates is an area in which the Secretary of the Company should exercise some care.

BM3 – Company Records

Introduction [BM3.1]

One of the most important aspects of the affairs of a company is undoubtedly its documentation. A company which has an efficient method of administering its documentation will find its life easier and the time of its employees free to do other things for the benefit of the company. A company whose documentary administration is in disarray is likely, as insolvency practitioners and Inspectors of the Inland Revenue will testify, to fail and is in fact an indicator of failure. Furthermore, while previously somewhat informal in nature, the requirements for keeping records on the part of companies has been considerably tightened up in recent years and has been given more force. It also goes without saying that a failure to produce any relevant documentation is unlikely to aid the passing of the IR35 Test.

For all of the above reasons, a proper system for maintaining the documentation of the company is important. Furthermore, in order to avoid duplication in maintaining the same records for different purposes it is usually possible to establish an integrated system (now computerised) which will make this task easier. Professional advice is usually of assistance in that respect.

Experience has shown that some time devoted at the outset, during the start-up stage of a business, to establish the best method for that company to maintain its documentation is likely to be time well spent. Accordingly, it is proposed to bring together and consider in this section all that is required in that respect which can be considered under the following headings:

- company information;
    - company books;
    - company publications;
- accounting information;
    - for VAT purposes;
    - for PAYE, NIC and benefits purposes;
    - for Corporation Tax purposes; and
    - for Companies Acts purposes.

The company books [BM3.2]

Every company, in order to administer itself satisfactorily, requires to maintain records of its activities which are often referred to as its 'books'. The manner in which a company does this is (with the exception of the basic statutory record-keeping requirements) largely a matter for the company itself. From leading stationers it is possible to purchase pre-prepared documentation for this purpose or a company can make up its own 'bespoke' documentation.

It perhaps bears mentioning in passing, that the true nature of a company can often be ascertained from its books and that for Personal Service Companies the IR35 Test might have made this a matter of increasing importance. Thus a company which, on headed notepaper, sends in to the Inland Revenue a neatly-kept set of books is perhaps more likely to be regarded as a self-employed entity that the entity which drops them a line on a piece of torn-off paper regretting that no books have been kept.

The Revenue authorities, of course, have their own powers of discovery. However, some of these Registers are required, by statute, to be open to inspection by members of the company without charge and by members of the public on payment of the appropriate charge. Unlikely though that may be in practice, as already noted, a failure to properly maintain these statutory Registers – apart from being an offence – might upon later discovery and reporting result in the individuals involved being disqualified for a number of years from being directors of any company.

- optional books:
  - Register of Allotments;
  - Register of Transfers;
  - Register of Board Meetings; and
  - Register of Contracts;
- statutory books:
  - Register of Members;
  - Register of Directors;
  - Register of Company Secretaries;
  - Register of Directors' Interests; and
  - Register of Charges.

Disclosure [BM3.3]

The advantages (such as they are) of a limited liability company come at a price, the most notable of which is disclosure which is required in various forms. For present purposes, the disclosure requirements relate to the way in which the company approaches going about its business.

This can be considered from the point of view of premises and publications.

Premises **[BM3.4]**

In regard to premises there are no requirements in relation to domain names and trade mark names.

Trading name **[BM3.5]**

The *Business Names Act 1985* requires that where a business or trading name is used by a company then the corporate name must appear at the places where the business is carried on and customers or suppliers are dealt with.

Company name **[BM3.6]**

Companies Act 1985, section 348(1) provides:

> 'Every company shall paint or affix, and keep painted or affixed, its name on the outside of every office or place in which its business is carried on, in a conspicuous position and in letters easily legible.'

So far as it applies to places of business, this requirement is part of the price to be paid for limited liability. By virtue of the fact that companies are required (*CA 1985, ss25* and *26*) to have the word 'limited' (or its equivalent) at the end of their name, this information serves to warn people going to that place to do business that the liability of the entity they are about to do business with is limited.

So far as it applies also to the Registered Office of the company, this requirement is clearly cross-referenced to the requirements that a current record of the Registered Office of the company be maintained at Companies House and on the business letters and order forms of the company so that having obtained the address from that source, an interested party should be able to easily find the company when they go to that address.

So important are these requirements considered that their breach is made the subject of penalties. Under *Companies Act 1985, section 34*:

> 'If a person trades or carries on business under a name or title of which "limited" or "cyfyngedig", or any contraction or imitation of either of those words, is the last word, that person, unless duly incorporated with limited liability, is liable to a fine and, for continued contravention, to a daily default fine.'

Company publications [BM3.7]

Domain names [BM3.8]

Domain names are essentially a form of self-advertisement. There is no requirement to disclose the domain name and nothing is lost by not disclosing the domain name (except, perhaps, that prolonged non-use could result in the name being given to someone else).

Trade mark names [BM3.9]

The opportunity is given to use a symbol (™ or ®) which shows that a trade mark name has been registered or applied for.

There is, however, no requirement as such to use those symbols. Trade mark names operate independently through registration and are not lost through non-use of the symbol (although clearly it is prudent to use them).

Trading names [BM3.10]

Trading names are regulated by the *Business Names Act 1985*. The Act requires that where a business or trading name is being used by a company then the corporate name must appear on:

- business letters;
- written orders for the supply of goods and services;
- invoices and receipts; and
- written demands for the payment of business debts.

Company names **[BM3.11]**

Companies Act 1985, section 349(1) provides:

> 'Every company shall have its name mentioned in legible characters–
> (a) in all business letters of the company,
> (b) in all its notices and official publications,
> (c) in all bills of exchange, promissory notes, endorsements, cheques and orders for money or goods purporting to be signed by or on behalf of the company, and
> (d) in all its bills of parcels, invoices, receipts and letters of credit.'

Again, this requirement is part of the price to be paid for limited liability and by virtue of the fact that companies are required (*CA 1985, ss 25* and *26*) to have the word 'limited' (or equivalent) at the end of its Name, this information serves to warn people in receipt of that correspondence that the liability of the entity they are about to do business with is limited.

The ambit of the legislation should be noted, applying as it does not just to business letters and commercial paper (as might be expected) but to all notices and official publications.

Again, so important are these requirements considered that their breach is made the subject of penalties. The point to note about these penalties is that they not only impose fines on the company and its officers but also attach liability to persons (which would include agents such as lawyers and accountants) acting on behalf of the company.

Under *Companies Act 1985, section 351*:

> '(1) Every company shall have the following particulars mentioned in legible characters in all business letters and order forms of the company, that is to say–
> (a) the company's place of registration and the number with which it is registered,
> (b) the address of its registered office…'

This requirement, again part of the price of limited liability, is clearly designed to ensure that those in receipt of business letters and order forms of the company can ascertain at which Companies House the company was registered and make their way there to obtain the details (including the financial details in the form of the accounts lodged by the company) of the company and thereafter make their way to the Registered Office of the company to consult, if so desired, the details where the company is required by law to maintain there. Again, so important is this requirement considered there are penalties for non-observance.

Directors' names on company correspondence etc. [BM3.12]

Companies Act 1985, section 305 provides:

> '(1) A company to which this section applies shall not state, in any form, the name of any of its directors (otherwise than in the text or as a signatory) on any business letter on which the company's name appears unless it states on the letter in legible characters the name of every director of the company.
>
> (2) This section applies to–
>
> (a) every company registered under this Act or under the former Companies Acts (except a company registered before 23rd November 1916); and
>
> (b) every company incorporated outside Great Britain which has an established place of business within Great Britain, unless it had established such a place of business before that date.
>
> (3) ...
>
> (4) For the purpose of the obligation under subsection (1) to state the name of every director of the company, a person's "name" means–
>
> (a) in the case of an individual, his Christian name (or other forename) and surname; and
>
> (b) in the case of a corporation or Scottish firm, its corporate or firm name.
>
> (5) The initial or a recognised abbreviation of a person's Christian name or other forename may be stated instead of the full Christian name or other forename.
>
> (6) In the case of a peer, or an individual usually known by a title, the title may be stated instead of his Christian name (or other forename) and surname or in addition to either or both of them.
>
> (7) In this section "director" includes a shadow director and the reference in subsection (3) to an "officer" shall be construed accordingly.'

Company invoices [BM3.13]

Where the company is registered for the purposes of VAT, the *Value Added Tax Act 1994* requires that the VAT Registration Number of the company appears.

Companies Act 1985, section 349(1)(d) requires that on its invoices the company has its name mentioned in legible characters.

There is clearly no objection to the incorporation of the address, contact details, website address and/or trading name (if any) and any other marketing information though desirable in the invoices of the Company but the important legal requirement relates to the formal name of the company (the legibility of which should not be obscured by any of the above).

Company business letters [BM3.14]

So far as the business letters of a company are concerned, the interlocking requirements of the *Business Names Act 1985* (which applies to business entities generally) and the *Companies Act 1985* (which applies to companies in particular) provide that business letters must disclose the:

- the company's place of registration and the number with which it is registered; and
- the address of the Registered Office.

There is also a provision in the *Companies Acts* relating to directors' names on company correspondence. A director can sign a business letter of the company and a director can refer to himself or herself in the text of a business letter of the company without consequences but where the business letters of a company puts forward the name of one of its directors (in effect, in what appears to be an official capacity) then *Companies Act 1985, section 305* requires the name of every director of the company (including shadow directors) to be put forward on the business letter. If it is decided to put the names of all the directors (including shadow directors) on the business notepaper then provision is made for the way in which that is to be done. As earlier indicted, some companies (especially listed public companies) attach importance to have a person with a title as a director and in those that title may be used instead of or in addition to either or both of their christian names or surnames. There is also provision to use the name of a corporation or Scottish firm where they are directors. Otherwise, the christian name (or other forename) and surname of an individual e.g David Smith although this may also be relaxed to Dave Smith (if that is how he is known) or D. Smith.

As a matter of practice, it is suggested that – unless there is any particular reason for doing so – companies do not incorporate the names of the directors on their printed business stationery because any change in director would require a new run of printing with a failure to do so carrying the (perhaps remote) possibility of a fine.

The legal requirement to publish the VAT Registration Number applies only to invoices and not to other business correspondence but it is often added to that correspondence and there is no objection to that practice.

Again, there is clearly no objection to the incorporation of the address, contact details, website address and/or trading name (if any) and any other marketing information thought desirable on the business letters of the company but the important legal requirement relates to the company's place of registration, registered number, and Registered Office (the legibility of which should not be obscured by any of the above).

Again, this is part of the price to be paid for limited liability so that persons contemplating dealing with the company can ascertain at which Companies House the company was registered and make their way there to obtain the details (including the financial details in the form of the accounts lodged by the company) of the company and thereafter make their way to the Registered Office of the company to consult, if so desired, the details where the company is required by law to maintain there. Again, so important is this requirement considered there are penalties for non-observance.

As a matter of practice, it is suggested that the situation of the Registered Office be selected with some care with a view to its permanence (perhaps using the offices of an agent such as an accountant or solicitor) because any change in the situation of the Registered Office would require a new run of printing with a failure to do so carrying the (perhaps remote) possibility of a fine.

Company order forms [BM3.15]

The requirements relating to business letters for the same reasons apply equally (except for the provision relating to the names of directors) to the company order forms.

Notices and other official publications of the company [BM3.16]

It should be noted that the obligation to mention the company name in legible characters (*CA 1985, s459*) applies not only to the invoices, business letters, order forms etc. which the company might print up at the outset for constant use but applies equally to any other notices or official publications which the company may later issue and that the same requirement (with possible penalties) apply there also.

Company bank details [BM3.17]

Banks have their own requirements for company bank accounts which normally results in compliance in any event. It should be noted, however, that the obligation to mention the company name in legible characters (*CA 1985, s459(1)(c)*) applies specifically to cheques and that the same requirement (with possible penalties) apply there also.

Commercial paper [BM3.18]

The above requirements cover the needs of most companies trading within the UK. Where, however, a company either grows in size or starts to trade abroad the need for what is known as 'commercial paper' may arise –this is essentially paper documents not used in the normal course of business but used for the easy transmission of funds and includes such items as:

- bills of exchange;
- promissory notes;
- endorsements;
- parcels;
- letters of credit etc.

Involvement in these areas will normally require professional advice and that advice will normally point to the requirements involved but companies should note that the Companies Acts impose (with penalties) disclosure requirements in respect of such commercial paper which the companies will have to observe in they get involved in those areas.

IR35 point [BM3.19]

Strictly speaking, company correspondence has no direct relevance to an IR35 enquiry, but clearly a company which has copies of proper correspondence issued to a number of clients has a better prospect of establishing that it has contracts for services than a company whose transactions, in breach of the legislation, are on plain paper or the back of an envelope and which is much more likely to be regarded as having merely a contract of service.

Accounting information [BM3.20]

It is clearly desirable, for a number of reasons, that a company should keep records. These records might be used to determine whether or not the company has been paid or whether or not the company has paid a supplier. The records might also be used to make up the accounts of the company and might also be used to determine the tax due by the company.

In years gone by, the keeping of records by a company was informal. To a certain extent, the keeping of records is still informal in that the precise method by which any objectives are to be achieved in the above respects are nowhere prescribed. Nevertheless, in every sphere of taxation the official requirements for basic record-keeping have slowly been tightened and companies are no exception in that respect.

The keeping of records is not, traditionally, the favourite activity of the entrepreneur. Nevertheless, despite the official requirements in relation to record-keeping the prudent (and therefore usually successful) entrepreneur will want to have a good accounting system not least because by the production of management accounts such a system will help the company avoid pitfalls and run successfully.

Having said that, the entrepreneur will not wish to spend any more time on the area of accounting and taxation than necessary. One of the problems which has bedevilled this area in the past is, having gather the basic records, needing to input that basic information several times for different purposes. This has in the past necessitated a large and specialised accounting workforce or the requirement to employ expensive professional time.

The advent of computers has, however, improved the situation here markedly. A number of organisations have now developed a number of standard accounting systems, some of them specifically for companies, which will meet the accounting requirements of small companies. Some of these systems will cope with and distinguish VAT and PAYE, NIC and benefits as well as the basic accounting information of the company.

Some of these systems are in the early stages of development and further developments are likely in the future. It is also possible to create or modify a standard system so as to produce a 'bespoke' accounting system. Not all systems are fully integrated but, for example, Transaction Technology (Software) Limited (www.ttsoftware.co.uk) produce for companies a system called IRIS which allows for not only the recording of basic records but also the automatic reproduction of that information for both accounting and taxation purposes.

We have probably not yet reached the stage in the UK where an unqualified company could feel comfortable about meeting all its accounting and taxation requirements itself although in theory that should be possible. Professional advice, at least to some extent, will always be advisable at present. However, the particular arrangement or combination of arrangements which a company arrives at is still essentially unregulated and a matter for that company.

Record keeping for VAT purposes **[BM3.21]**

Because a VAT-registered business effectively operates as the collector of VAT and is, moreover, operating a system of balancing input VAT against output VAT in order to arrive at the collection of that tax, it is understandable that strict requirements, supported by penalties, exist in relation to the records which businesses must keep for the purposes of Value Added Tax. These requirements are contained in the *Value Added Tax Regulations 1995* (*SI 1995/2518*). There is also a VAT Notice (700/21/95) entitled *Keeping Records and Accounts* which explains the requirements.

The requirements are slightly complicated by the fact the at present the UK operates a VAT system which distinguishes between supplies which are 'taxable' and supplies which are 'exempt'. In addition, VAT is applied in the UK at different rates namely:

- standard (17.5%);
- reduced (5%); and
- zero (0%).

Customs & Excise require all of the above to be recorded where applicable, although most businesses will be mainly concerned with taxable supplies at the standard rate.

Records must kept of all supplies which are both *made* (output) and *received* (input) in the course of the business. Both of these requirements revolve around the concept of the 'VAT invoice'.

In addition, a summary of the totals of the output vat and input vat for each tax period must be kept in a VAT account. This VAT account forms the basis for the VAT Return.

VAT invoices **[BM3.22]**

The VAT invoice is central to the VAT system. It is an offence to purport to issue a VAT invoice while not registered for VAT purposes and penalties may be imposed on a business which is registered for the purposes of VAT and does not issue VAT invoices in the correct manner (see **BM3.23** below).

The reason that the VAT invoice is so important and its requirements so particular is to be found in the important role which that invoice pays in the VAT chain of transactions until the ultimate consumer is reached. The same VAT invoice which is used to record the output VAT of one business is used to record the input vat of the business which purchased the supplies.

In order that the VAT system can operate properly and so that, if necessary for the purposes of enforcement, Customs & Excise can follow that chain of transactions, it is important that the information considered essential is properly recorded in those invoices and therefore requirements are imposed to that effect.

Ultimate consumers are often not registered for VAT purposes and if, for that or any other reason, a customer of the company not to be registered for VAT purposes then there is no requirement on the part of the company to issue that customer with a VAT invoice unless the customer asks for one.

Where, however, a customer of the company is part of the VAT chain and is registered for VAT purposes then the company is obliged to give that customer a VAT invoice. There are exceptions to this rule (e.g. self-billing arrangement; the construction industry; gifts of goods; second-hand schemes and margin schemes) but in general the bulk of the company's transactions are likely to be with VAT registered customers and the company will be obliged to issue those customers with a VAT invoice containing certain defined information.

Information required on a VAT invoice [BM3.23]

A VAT invoice requires to disclose the following information:

- an identifying number;
- the name, address and VAT Registration Number of the company;
- the time of supply;
- the date of issue (if different from the time of supply);
- the name and address of the customer; and
- the type of supply.

As regards the type of supply the following must be separately identified:

- sale;
- hire-purchase, conditional sale, credit sale or similar transaction;
- loan;
- exchange;
- hire, lease or rental;
- process (making goods from someone else's materials);
- sale on commission;
- sale on return or similar terms;
- a description which identifies the goods or services supplied, including the:
  - extent of the services or the quantity of the goods;
  - charge made, excluding VAT;
  - rate of VAT;
  - total charge made, excluding VAT;
  - rate of any cash discount offered;
  - each rate of VAT charged;
  - the amount of VAT charged (shown in sterling and for each rate);
  - the total amount of VAT charged (shown in sterling).

Recording output [BM3.24]

A VAT-registered business is required to keep a record of all the supplies which it *makes* as part of its business. A separate record requires to be kept of all exempt supplies made and any supplies made at the standard, reduced or zero rate must also be recorded.

The records must be kept readily available should officers of Customs & Excise ask to see them. They must be complete and up-to-date and they must be easy to find using either a name or a number.

There is no set manner in which these records must be kept for VAT purposes and most standard accounting systems will meet the requirements. However, if the system used does not satisfy the requirements then Customs & Excise have the power to direct the business to make any necessary changes.

Unless making retail supplies and part of a retail scheme, VAT-registered businesses must keep a copy of all VAT invoices issued. Provided, however, that copies are kept of all VAT invoices issued then as a concession (although a limited one in that this is what most accounting systems will show) the requirement extends only to keeping a summary of the invoices showing separate totals for:

- VAT on the sales;
- VAT-exclusive value of what has been sold;
- any exempt sales;
- VAT due on certain postal imports and imported services; and
- credits allowed to customers.

If the value of the taxable supplies (excluding VAT) does not exceed a certain level (currently £350,000) then instead of accounting for output vat on the basis of invoices issued, the business can adopt the Cash Accounting Scheme and instead account for output VAT on the basis of payments actually received.

In order to operate the Cash Accounting Scheme the records of the business must clearly cross-reference:

- payments received to the corresponding sales invoice;
- payments received to the normal commercial evidence (e.g. bank statement, paying-in slip).

Recording input **[BM3.25]**

The requirement is that a VAT-registered business keep a record of all the supplies which it *receives* as part of its business. That includes any supplies received at the standard, reduced or zero rate.

The records must be kept readily available should officers of Customs &

Excise ask to see them. They must be complete and up-to-date and they must be easy to find using either a name or a number.

There is no set manner in which these records must be kept for VAT purposes and most standard accounting systems will meet the requirements. However, if the system used does not satisfy the requirements then Customs & Excise have the power to direct the business to make any necessary changes.

As evidence of the VAT paid which it is sought to offset as input vat, VAT-registered businesses should keep all VAT Invoices upon which they have made payment in the same order as they received them. Provided that that is done as a concession (although a limited one in that this is what most accounting systems will show) the requirement extends only to keeping a summary of the invoices received (ideally cross-referenced by number to the invoices themselves) showing separate totals for:

- VAT charged on the purchases;
- VAT-exclusive value of what has been purchased;
- VAT paid on imports; and
- credits received from suppliers.

If the value of the taxable supplies (excluding VAT) does not exceed a certain level (currently £350,000) then instead of accounting for input vat on the basis of invoices received, the business can adopt the Cash Accounting Scheme as a whole and, in the same way as output VAT, account for input VAT on the basis of payments actually made.

In order to operate the Cash Accounting Scheme the records of the business must clearly cross-reference:

- payments made to the corresponding purchase invoice;
- payments made to the normal commercial evidence (e.g. bank statement, cheque stub).

Accounting for VAT **[BM3.26]**

As earlier noted, provided that the minimum record-keeping requirements are met, there is no set accounting method by which records for VAT purposes must be kept. Most businesses will keep VAT records as part of an integrated accounting system. This can be manual or it can be computerised.

If accounting records are kept on a computer then they must be readily convertible into a satisfactory legible form and be available to Customs & Excise on request who are entitled to have access to your computer to check its operation and the information stored and are entitled to ask for help from anyone concerned in the operation of the computer or its software.

Where the business intends to use a computer as part of its accounting system then Customs & Excise should be informed. Some details of the computer system must be provided when registering (Box 8 of Application for Registration Form VAT 1 asks whether a computer is used for accounting and, if so, that a separate letter be enclosed detailing the type of computer and software used). In addition, the local VAT Business Advice Centre should be notified of the computer system in use.

If a computer bureau is being used then the business is responsible for arranging for the bureau to make the records of the business available to Customs & Excise and this will normally be at the principal office of the business. Customs & Excise have the power to refuse or withdraw approval for the use of computer media in any individual case if their requirements are not met.

Audit and VAT **[BM3.27]**

The audit of a small business is now unlikely to be compulsory. Should an audit take place, however, then that audit is likely to include the VAT system and the VAT records. Customs & Excise may rely upon such an audit or, in the absence of such an audit, may take a closer interest in the records of the business.

Retaining VAT records **[BM3.28]**

The requirement for VAT is that 'business records' be retained for six years. This can cause storage problems in some cases and in those circumstances an agreement may be reached with the local VAT Office permitting the records to be retained for a shorter period.

Alternatively, records may be transferred to microfilm or microfiche provided that copies can easily be produced and that there are adequate facilities for allowing an officer of Customs & Excise to view them when required. A number of specialised agencies now offer microfilm or microfiche services and storage. Clearance from the local VAT Business

Advice Centre should be obtained before any records are transferred to microfilm or microfiche and the business may be required for a limited period of time to operate the old and the new systems side by side.

Customs & Excise have the power to refuse or withdraw approval for the use of microfilm or microfiche.

'Business records' is very widely defined and includes:

- Annual Accounts;
- Balance Sheet;
- Profit and Loss Account;
- Bank Statement and paying-in slips;
- Cash books;
- Books of Account;
- Credit Notes (issued or received);
- Debit Notes (issued or received);
- Documentation covering the dispatch/acquisition of goods to/from EC Member States;
- any VAT Certificates for special treatment;
- import and export documents;
- orders (issued or received);
- Delivery Notes (issued or received);
- Purchase Books;
- Sales Books;
- purchase invoices;
- copy sales invoices;
- any record of daily takings;
- relevant business correspondence;
- the VAT account.

IR35 point **[BM3.29]**

The number of clients which a Personal Service Company has is likely to be a significant factor in determining the application of the IR35 legislation. Evidence as to the number of clients for whom the Personal Service Company has provided services over the period in question will come from the records of sales including VAT thereon.

As noted elsewhere, a Personal Service Company should go out of its way to do as much business for as many clients as possible. In doing that, the Personal Service Company should take care (whether it is asked for and compulsory or not) to issue a VAT invoice in each and every case because in addition to being a legal requirement to do so, that will in fact be the best evidence of the business actually done.

Record keeping for PAYE, NIC and benefits [BM3.30]

The obligations on a company with employees is clearly considerable as is the associated requirements for record-keeping. The following should be used as a checklist for the necessary procedures.

- ✓ Identify the employees.
- ✓ Distinguish lower-paid employees and:
  - identify their basic remuneration;
  - expenses and benefits;
  - operate the PAYE, NIC and benefits system in respect of them;
  - pay them;
  - account to the Inland Revenue;
  - report to those employees;
  - report to the Inland Revenue.
- ✓ Distinguish higher-paid employees and:
  - identify the basic remuneration of those employees;
  - identify the expenses and benefits of those employees;
  - operate the PAYE, NIC and benefits system for those employees;
  - pay the employee;
  - account to the Inland Revenue;
  - report to the employee;
  - report to the Inland Revenue;
- ✓ Distinguish directors:
  - identify the basic remuneration of those employees;
  - identify the expenses and benefits of those employees;
  - operate the PAYE, NIC and benefits system for those employees;
  - pay the employee;
  - account to the Inland Revenue;
  - report to the employee; and
  - report to the Inland Revenue.

The essential legal record-keeping requirement for PAYE and NIC purposes is largely based upon the periodical and year-end working deduction sheets copies of which must be kept.

The essential legal record-keeping requirement for benefits purposes is to keep:

> '...all amounts received and expended and the matters concerning which the receipts and expenditures take place.'

In practice, of course, a compliance visit will result in the inspectors expecting to see proper records being kept.

Record keeping for Corporation Tax purposes [BM3.31]

The Inland Revenue have not, so far, produced a booklet containing record-keeping requirements aimed specifically at companies. Instead, the Inland Revenue have approached the matter of record-keeping across the board and produced two booklets which apply generally to all those self-employed whether as sole traders, partnerships or companies.

The booklets, available from the Inland Revenue, are SA/BK3 *A Guide to keeping records for the self-employed* and SA/BK4 *A General Guide to Keeping Records*. In summary, these booklets require all bank and building society statements, particulars of money paid into and drawn out of the business, details of payments in respect of wages and self-contractors, stock records and indeed covers virtually every record which a business generates to be kept.

The Inland Revenue in fact has its own set of requirements for record keeping. The approach of the Inland Revenue is to focus upon the obligation of the taxpayer to make a correct and complete return and, therefore, these record-keeping requirements are believed to be regarded not as prescriptive in the sense that they must be followed to the letter but as advisory in that they set out what is considered necessary in the way of records to support a correct and complete return. The provisions are contained in the *Finance Act 1998, Sch 18*.

A company which may be required to deliver a company tax return for any period must keep such records as may be needed to enable it to deliver a correct and complete return for the period.

The records required to be kept and preserved include records of:

- all receipts and expenses in the course of the company's activities, and the matters in respect of which the receipts and expenses arise; and
- in the case of a trade involving dealing in goods, all sales and purchases made in the course of the trade.

This duty includes a duty to preserve all supporting documents which includes accounts, books, deeds, contracts, vouchers and receipts.

With certain stated exceptions, the duty to preserve records may be satisfied by the preservation of the information contained in them. The exceptions (where original records in writing must be kept) are:

- the amount of any qualifying distribution and tax credit (issued under *ICTA 1988, s234(1)*);
- the gross amount, tax deducted and actual amount paid (issued under *ICTA 1988, s352(1)*);
- sub-contractor certificates (issued under *ICTA 1998, ss566(1)* and *599*); and
- tax paid under the law of a territory outside the UK or would have been but for a double taxation agreement (under *ICTA 1988, s788(5)*).

The records must be preserved for six years from the end of the period for which the company may be required to deliver a company tax return.

If the company is required to deliver a company tax return by notice given before the end of that six year period (or after the end of that six year period and the company happens to have the records in its possession at that time) then the records must be preserved until any later date on which:

- any enquiry into the return is completed; or
- if there is no enquiry, the Inland Revenue no longer have power to enquire into the return.

Recording income **[BM3.32]**

In general, these provisions require records and supporting documentation to be kept of all amounts received and the matters in respect of which the receipts took place. Where goods are involved, records must also be kept of all sales of services or goods.

Recording expenditure **[BM3.33]**

In general, these provisions require records and supporting documentation to be kept of all amounts expended and the matters in respect of which the expenditure took place. Where goods are involved, records must also be kept of all purchases of services or goods.

Record keeping for Companies Act purposes [BM3.34]

A Personal Service Company is governed by *section 221* of the *CA 1985* which sets out the legal obligations of companies to keep accounting records:

> '(1) Every company shall keep accounting records which are sufficient to show and explain the company's transactions and are such as to–
> (a) disclose with reasonable accuracy, at any time, the financial position of the company at that time, and
> (b) enable the directors to ensure that any balance sheet and profit and loss account prepared under this Part complies with the requirements of this Act.
>
> (2) The accounting records shall in particular contain–
> (a) entries from day to day of all sums of money received and expended by the company, and the matters in respect of which the receipt and expenditure takes place, and
> (b) a record of the assets and liabilities of the company.
>
> (3) If the company's business involves dealing in goods, the accounting records shall contain–
> (a) statements of stock held by the company at the end of each financial year of the company,
> (b) all statements of stocktakings from which any such statement of stock as is mentioned in paragraph (a) has been or is to be prepared, and
> (c) except in the case of goods sold by way of ordinary retail trade, statements of all goods sold and purchased, showing the goods and the buyers and sellers in sufficient detail to enable all these to be identified.'

Taxation

Taxation is likely to be a major consideration for most Personal Service Companies when the company starts trading. However, it should be noted that trading does not necessarily commence at incorporation and the test for determining whether trading has begun is considered below.

Many companies wait until they have commenced trading before they concern themselves with taxation. However, there are a number of voluntary steps which a company may take after incorporation but before commencing trading in relation to:

- Value Added Tax (VAT);
- PAYE, NIC and benefits; and
- Corporation Tax.

BT1 – VAT

Introduction [BT1.1]

It is a simple fact of commercial life that at the very outset of the business heavy expenditure may have to be made (often involving capital expenditure and VAT). Thereafter, trading will begin, sales will come in, and turnover will hopefully increase over the early years of the business. While every business lives in hope, some businesses will have a better idea than others what their turnover in the early years is likely to be.

If it is thought that in the early years of a new company, turnover is unlikely to exceed the current threshold (£52,000) in operation for VAT registration then that business may choose not to register for VAT at incorporation. In this situation, the company will effectively be a consumer and will have to bear the burden of the VAT on the heavy expenditure made at the outset of the venture.

If, however, it is expected that the VAT threshold will be exceeded, the company should register for VAT at the outset. Special rules exist where an existing business is taken over.

Otherwise, there are essentially two ways in which this can be done, either by:

- claiming pre-registration expenditure; or
- voluntary registration.

Pre-registration expenditure [BT1.2]

VAT paid on supplies made to the business before the business registers for VAT purposes may be recovered as input VAT provided that acceptable evidence of the expenditure exists (essentially a VAT invoice) and certain conditions are met which differ for goods and services and as between unincorporated and incorporated businesses.

Unincorporated businesses [BT1.3]

Goods [BT1.4]

In addition to having a supplier's VAT invoice, the following conditions must be met:

- the goods were supplied to the business now registered for VAT purposes;
- the goods were supplied not more than three years before the business was registered;
- the goods were obtained for the business now covered by the VAT registration;
- the goods are still held or are incorporated in other goods still held; and
- a stock account of the goods is compiled showing quantities and dates supplied (and dates of any incorporation or disposal of the goods).

Services [BT1.5]

In addition to having a supplier's VAT invoice, the following conditions must be met:

- the services were supplied to the business now registered for VAT purposes;
- the services were received for the purposes of the business now covered by the VAT registration and related to its taxable activities (allocated in partly taxable activity and partly not);
- the services were supplied not more than six months before the business was registered;
- the services were not related to goods disposed of (e.g. repairs to a machine sold before registration); and
- a stock account of the services is compiled showing the services and the dates received (and the dates of any incorporation of the services into goods disposed of).

Incorporated businesses [BT1.6]

Clearly, different considerations apply to incorporated businesses in that the individual having the goods or services supplied will in law be a different person from the business once it is incorporated.

In addition to having a supplier's VAT invoice, the following conditions must be met:

- the rules relating to goods and services of an unincorporated business (see **BT1.4** and **BT1.5** above) apply;
- the goods and services were imported or obtained by a person who became a member, officer (i.e. director or secretary), or employee of the business on incorporation;
- the person was reimbursed for the full cost;
- the person was not a taxable person at the time of the importation or supply.

Voluntary registration [BT1.7]

Clearly, the VAT rules for expenditure made pre-registration (either voluntarily or compulsory) are reasonably generous in that services provided up to six months before registration and goods supplied up to three years before registration may, if the conditions are met, be treated as input VAT although the benefit of those supplies must still be there and anything sold or consumed (e.g. petrol, electricity or gas) cannot be recovered.

However, it is possible for a business to apply for what is known as voluntary registration before the turnover of that business reaches the VAT threshold at which point VAT registration will by compulsory. (For the procedure for registration see **BT1.8** below).

It will be necessary for the business so applying to prove to Customs & Excise that what it does is, for VAT purposes, a business and that it is going to make taxable supplies in the future as part of that business.

Proof of this may take the form of:

- details of the arrangements made by the business;
- copies of any contracts in the pipeline;
- any relevant planning permission;
- details of what has been purchased for the business;
- details of any patents applied for; and
- details of any options obtained.

Once registered the company will be able to reclaim input VAT on any goods and services supplied for the purposes of the business.

Note that a business is obliged to account for VAT after the date upon which registration was granted and became effective. A failure to recover the VAT from customers could mean the business having to account to Customs & Excise for that VAT even though they have not recovered that VAT from their customers. Ignoring registration can also lead to penalties being imposed.

Voluntary registration has a number of advantages. Firstly, the company will be relieved of the need to avoid penalties by checking carefully for the exact date upon which the turnover threshold is crossed and VAT registration becomes compulsory. Secondly, in practice, the absence of a VAT registration may (rightly or wrongly) suggest to clients contemplating doing business with the company, that it is either new or has a low turnover below the current threshold.

Example 1

Two individuals decide to set up a Personal Service Company.

In January, out of redundancy money made available to them, the two individuals in their own name purchase a substantial amount of equipment, goods and services which they feel they will need. No VAT invoices are obtained from the suppliers.

In May, the company is both incorporated and commences trading but does not register for VAT purposes.

In May the following year, it is drawn to the company's attention that it has exceeded the VAT turnover threshold without registration and a penalty is imposed.

At the end of September, the company completes its first VAT return in which the company output vat the remuneration received to date.

The company's attempt to offset as input VAT the VAT element of the expenditure made on setting up the company is disallowed in relation to the passage of time so far as services are concerned (six months) and due to the absence of satisfactory evidence (no VAT invoices).

Effectively, the individuals have acted as consumers for the purposes of VAT and have had to bear the burden of that VAT personally even though the supplies on which the expenditure was made were for the purposes of a business later charging VAT using those supplies.

Example 2

Two individuals set up a Personal Service Company.

In January, the individuals incorporate PSC Limited. They arrange bank facilities for the company and all purchases of goods and services needed for the future business of the company are taken in the company's name and a supplier's VAT invoice addressed to the company is obtained in each case.

In May, preparations are complete and PSC Limited is ready to commence trading. PSC Limited applies for voluntary VAT registration. The application is granted and registration is achieved. PSC Limited then buys a substantial quantity of the equipment which the company needs for trading purposes at a considerable cost and with a considerable amount of VAT added to the price.

At the end of September, PSC Limited completes its first VAT return in which PSC Limited enters as output vat the remuneration received to date (likely to be below the turnover threshold level) and as input vat enters the VAT expended on the heavy equipment expenditure and the VAT expended on goods and services after incorporation but before trading. The difference will be paid to or by Customs & Excise (and in practice will often in this first return involve a repayment of VAT to the company).

Registration procedure [BT1.8]

The position in relation to VAT can be considered firstly from a territorial and then national point of view.

Territorially, the EC is intended to act as a customs union and the broad intention is that supplies brought into the union from outside the union should suffer VAT but that trading within the union should be tax-free. Importing goods from outside the EC will therefore result in the imposition of VAT (as well as any customs duties). With the advent of the Single Market special rules (also reflected in the VAT Return) have, since 1 January 1993 operated in relation to businesses trading within the EC.

Although VAT is a community tax which is eventually intended to operate throughout the EC in a standard manner, that is not the position at the moment and each Member State is presently allowed to operate VAT in a slightly individualistic manner. The UK presently operates a VAT system which distinguishes between supplies which are 'taxable' and supplies which are 'exempt' (see **BT1.11** below).

Importation from outside the EC **[BT1.9]**

A business devoted to importing or exporting services or goods from outside the EC falls into a specialist area involving special VAT rules. It is unlikely that registration for VAT purposes would be permitted to recover that import VAT as input unless the business happened to be registered for VAT for other purposes. It is beyond the scope of this book and businesses devoted to that area should take professional advice or advice from Customs and Excise.

Individual imports and exports are dealt with as part of the normal VAT system. Goods, and some services, which are imported from outside the EC require (in addition to any customs duty payable) to have VAT added to them upon importation into the UK or the Isle of Man and that can normally be reclaimed as input VAT.

Importation from inside the EC **[BT1.10]**

Goods which are brought into the UK (known as 'acquisitions' to distinguish them for 'imports') from another Member State within the EC are now (from 1 January 1993) subject to new rules as a result of the Single Market.

The overall intention of the Single Market is that two VAT registered businesses doing business within the EC should be able to pass goods to each other at (looked at from the UK perspective) the zero rate of VAT leaving the standard rate of VAT to be imposed as the goods are passed to the consumer. However, to avoid distortions in the market, special intra-EC rules have had to be imposed in two situations.

So far as what are known as 'acquisitions' are concerned, the new rules now provide that if the acquisitions by a non-VAT registered business exceed a certain threshold (currently £52,000) then that business is required to register for VAT purposes in the UK. So far as 'distance selling' is concerned (where a business in the UK arranges for goods from another Member State of the EC to be sold somewhere else outside the UK) if the volume of distance selling exceeds a certain threshold (each Member

State may set their own threshold and in the UK it is currently 100,000 ECUs (equivalent to £70,000) then that business is required to register for VAT purposes in the UK.

Again, those businesses devoted to these areas are beyond the scope of this book and businesses devoted to that area should take professional advice or advice from Customs and Excise

Exempt supplies **[BT1.11]**

Under the VAT system currently operating in the UK, a number of supplies are designated as 'exempt'. These include:

- land;
- insurance;
- post;
- gaming;
- finance;
- education;
- health;
- burial;
- representative bodies;
- sport;
- art;
- fund raising; and
- culture.

If a business supplies only goods which are exempt then it cannot normally (except for insurance and finance) register for VAT purposes. If, however, a business supplies goods some of which are exempt and some of which are not exempt but are taxable (whether at the standard, reduced or zero rate) then that may be a case of partial exemption to which special rules apply.

Again, those businesses devoted to these areas are beyond the scope of this book and businesses devoted to that area should take professional advice or advice from Customs and Excise

Zero rated supplies **[BT1.12]**

Under the VAT system in the UK, a number of supplies are charged at a

VAT rate which is 0% and these are known as 'zero-rated supplies'. If the taxable turnover of a business exceeds the threshold but the business supplies only goods which are zero-rated then it is possible for the business to apply to Customs and Excise for exemption from registration.

If, however, a business supplies goods some of which are zero-rated and some of which are charged at the other rates then this will not be possible unless it can be demonstrated that input VAT will normally exceed output VAT.

Business making taxable supplies in the UK and Isle of Man [BT1.13]

Where a business makes taxable supplies within the UK and the Isle of Man, then the value of those supplies is known as the 'taxable turnover'. When the taxable turnover reaches a certain threshold figure defined in the legislation then that business becomes a 'taxable person' which must, compulsorily, register for VAT purposes. An application to register voluntarily may also be made.

For most businesses, trading in the UK and Isle of Man, therefore, where voluntary registration is not being sought, registration for VAT purposes will involve keeping the taxable turnover of the business under review to determine whether the threshold has been reached at which registration for VAT purposes must be made.

Compulsory registration [BT1.14]

Any entity can be registered for VAT purposes. If the entity seeking registration has previously been registered for VAT purposes then this is something of which Customs and Excise ought to be informed, as if they have had difficulties in the collection of VAT from that entity before then they are entitled to seek security by way of a guarantee or payment in advance.

Note, however, that where a business has been purchased as a going concern then special rules may apply and instead of applying for registration anew, the existing VAT Registration Number (if any) of the business may be assumed by the new owners.

Where the business is a new business then the registration will be a new registration in the name of that business. It is important, however, to appreciate that registration is effectively personal. Thus, an individual registered for VAT as a sole trader who has several trades will not be given a separate VAT Registration for each trade but instead will be given a single VAT Registration and will be expected to bring all of his or her trades under that registration. The same principle applies to limited companies which will be expected to bring all of their trades under the one registration. Of course, because they are separate legal entities it is possible for an individual to have one VAT Registration as a sole trader and another VAT registration for the Personal Service Company in which that individual happens to be involved, but the important point to appreciate is that all of an entity's trades require to be taken together to determine taxable turnover and that registration cannot be avoided by the same entity seeking to divide its business into a number of small trades.

Timing of registration [BT1.15]

The UK legislation (*Value Added Tax Act 1994*) specifies the taxable turnover which is the threshold above which the entity requires as a then taxable person to register for the purposes of VAT. The legislation also provides that that threshold may be amended by Treasury Order. The Treasury Order currently in force specifies a turnover threshold of £ 52,000.

There are a number of complex provisions which define what 'turnover' is for various classes of business (e.g. the travel business). For most varieties of business, however, 'turnover' will be the total value of all business supplied in the UK or the Isle of Man which would be the subject of VAT at either the standard or the zero rate. Any exempt supplies and sales of capital assets are excluded. Effectively, 'turnover' will in the case of most businesses be the total sales of the business.

The rules for registration require that a business considers the taxable supplies which it has made in the last 12 months and thinks that it will make in the next 30 days.

The business must register for VAT purposes if:

- at the end of any month, the total value of taxable supplies made by the business in the last 12 months or less is more than the threshold (currently £52,000); or
- at any time the business expects the value of its taxable supplies to be more than the current threshold in the next 30 days alone.

There is, however, a fail-safe procedure whereby if in any month the taxable turnover of the business for the last 12 months has exceeded the threshold but the business can prove to Customs and Excise that the taxable turnover will not exceed £50,000 in the next 12 months, then the business will not be required to register for VAT purposes.

Note that the business is still required, within 30 days of the end of that month, to notify the local VAT Business Advice Centre (not the Registration Office) that the limit has been reached but the business is not required to send VAT Form 1 to the Registration Office and register although clearly, should the taxable turnover increase, it may be necessary to do that later.

Note that penalties apply for a failure on the part of a business to register when it should have.

Application for compulsory registration is made on VAT Form 1.

Example 1

Taxable supplies in last 12 months reaching the VAT threshold

Date on which supplies exceeded threshold	31 August
Date by which Form VAT 1 must be submitted	30 September
Date on which registration effective	1 October

Example 2

Taxable supplies estimated to exceed the threshold in the next 30 days

Date on which supplies estimated to exceed threshold	20 January
Date by which Form VAT 1 must be submitted	21 February
Date on which registration effective	20 January

Example 3

Voluntary registration

Date on which application made for voluntary regulation	1 January
Date by which Form VAT 1 submitted	1 January
Date on which registration granted and effective	1 January

Checklist [BT1.16]

Voluntary registration

- ✓ Written reasons for voluntary registration.
- ✓ Form VAT 1.
- ✓ Details of computer used (if applicable).
- ✓ Details of other address for correspondence (if applicable).
- ✓ Application for return periods to match the company's year-end (if applicable).
- ✓ Intimation of adoption of Cash Accounting Scheme (if selected).

Compulsory registration

- ✓ Form VAT 1
- ✓ Details of computer used (if applicable).
- ✓ Details of other address for correspondence (if applicable).
- ✓ Application for return periods to match the company's year-end (if applicable).
- ✓ Intimation of adoption of Cash Accounting Scheme (if selected).

What should happen next?

Within three weeks of sending VAT Form 1 to the appropriate VAT Registration Office (not the Local Office) then a reply should be received from that office and if no reply is received then (bearing in mind that the registration date may already be running with all that that entails) you should check the position with that office.

Once the Registration Office has checked the details on the application form, they will advise the business that it has been registered for VAT purposes and issue a formal Certificate of Registration showing the registration details including the identity of the business registered and the VAT number issued to that business. The business will also receive notification at the same time of the dates upon which it must make its VAT Returns.

Upon registration, Customs and Excise will also send the business a number of booklets which fully explain the basic VAT rules and procedures and a (free) choice of a 'welcome to VAT' video, a private meeting in the Local Office, or an opportunity to attend a seminar on VAT, after which ignorance of the VAT rules and procedures will be no excuse! That business must thenceforth comply with all the complex rules of the VAT regime.

BT2 – PAYE, NIC and Benefits

Introduction [BT2.1]

Personal Service Companies should adopt a planned, pre-determined and fixed remuneration strategy. PAYE, NIC and benefits are potentially one of the most difficult areas for such companies.

Where those individuals behind the Personal Service Company fall into the habit of treating the assets of the company (a separate legal and taxation entity) as their own, then they are likely to face extensive compliance requirements at the end of the year.

Where, however, a policy of strict separation between the company and the individuals behind it is observed then a considerable relaxation of the administrative burden of compliance can sometimes be achieved.

The problems in this area have now been compounded by IR35. If the company believes that it is likely to fail the IR35 Test, it may be prudent for the company to make provision from the outset for the deduction of the appropriate amount of PAYE and NIC.

PAYE [BT2.2]

Consideration should be given to the remuneration strategy for all those who are going to hold an office or employment within the company.

Remuneration strategy will need to be decided on for:

- the principal person (shareholder/director) within the company who is, in the main, providing the personal services;
- any others providing support who are to be involved in the company as directors or employees; and
- genuine employees?

In addition, a decision will need to be made as to whether pay is to be fixed or variable involving bonuses or profit-related pay.

Benefits [BT2.3]

Consideration should also be given to the benefits strategy for all of those who are going to hold an office or employment within the company.

- Is a policy to be adopted whereby no benefits are received or any benefits received are reimbursed with the result that the company operates in a relatively trouble-free manner as a stand-alone entity?
- Is a policy to be adopted whereby the maximum benefits are to be obtained reflecting the close relationship between the company and those who work in the company but costing and requiring considerable administrative effort in identifying, reporting and accounting for the private element of those benefits?
- Is a benefits package to be constructed so as to attract employees to work for the company?
- Are benefits to be fixed or flexible?

There are now some benefits which are taxed in the hands of all employees no matter what their earnings. However, for those employees who are designated as higher-paid and for those who hold the office of director, a separate expenses and benefits regime operates.

NIC [BT2.4]

By and large National Insurance Contributions (NIC) will be applied automatically in light of the decisions arrived at above.

The categorisation of National Insurance [BT2.5]

Liability to NIC depends upon residence (decided in the same manner as for general taxation) and the class of contribution into which the contributor falls.

National Insurance is regulated by the *Social Security Contributions and Benefits Act 1992* and supporting Regulations which group national insurance contributions into categories as follows:

Class 1	Contributions payable by employed earners and those who pay their earnings
Class 1A	Contributions payable in respect of benefits in kind
Class 1B	Contributions payable in PAYE settlement agreement situations
Class 2	Contributions payable by self-employed earners
Class 3	Contributions paid voluntarily in order to make up benefit entitlements
Class 4	Contributions payable by self-employed earners

Class 1 **[BT2.6]**

Class 1 contributions are earnings-related levied on the earnings of 'employed earners' and must be paid at a specified rate by an employer and an employee when specified earnings limits are reached.

There are separate provisions relating to contracting in and contracting out.

Children under 16 and their employers pay no contributions.

The reduced rate applies to married women or widows with a valid certificate of election.

Men over 65 and women over 60 pay no primary contributions though employers still pay the secondary contribution at the usual rate.

Employees must pay Class 1 contributions if their earnings reach the lower earnings limit (LEL). Employee's primary contributions are paid on all earnings up to an upper earnings limit. Employer's secondary contributions are paid on all of an employee's earnings above a specified earnings threshold.

Interest is chargeable on late payments.

Class 1A **[BT2.7]**

Employers (but not employees) have, since 5 April 1991, been required to pay contributions on an annual basis at a specified rate in respect of cars or fuel provided for the private use of directors and higher earning employees.

From 6 April 2000, the Class 1A charge has been extended by the *Child Support, Pensions and Social Security Act 2000* to cover most benefits.

Interest is payable on late payments

Class 1B **[BT2.8]**

Employers have, since 6 April 1999, been required to pay contributions on the amount of emoluments chargeable to Class 1 or Class 1A in a PAYE Settlement at a specified rate.

Class 2 **[BT2.9]**

Self-employed persons pay these contributions at a flat rate. Exemptions are available.

Class 3 **[BT2.10]**

This is a flat rate which can be paid voluntarily. This will often be done to satisfy the contribution requirements for certain benefits.

Class 4 **[BT2.11]**

Self-employed persons whose profits or gains are over a certain amount require to pay contributions at a specified rate between lower earnings limits and upper earnings limits.

Dispensations [BT2.12]

The way in which a company structures its affairs, including its benefits policy, clearly influences the amount of administration. Some companies might involve a large number of benefits and need to spend time properly recording these. Others might have little or no benefits in which case the reporting procedures for benefits becomes something of an administrative burden. To cope with this latter situation, the Inland Revenue have introduced – but only for higher-paid employees and directors reporting under Form P11D – a procedure known as a 'dispensation'.

Where the incidence of expenses and benefits would clearly involve no extra tax liability, then it is open to an employer to apply to the Inland Revenue for a dispensation. Once granted, a dispensation relieves the employer of the burden of reporting expenses and benefits on Form P11D.

Furthermore, it normally follows from the granting of a dispensation that the employer no longer need operate the PAYE system for tax and NIC system in relation to those expenses. Moreover, the granting of a dispensation normally means that those higher-paid employees and directors need not include those expenses and benefits in their tax assessments, PAYE codes, or tax returns.

In addition, expenses and benefits covered by a dispensation are excluded in the calculation of the remuneration threshold (currently £8,500 for 2000) to determine whether an employee is a higher-paid employee who needs to return a P11D at all.

Kinds of benefits and expenses covered [BT2.13]

A dispensation applies to specific expenses and benefits and, therefore, round sum allowances (where the employee is not called upon to account for individual expenses) are excluded.

Beyond that, most expenses and benefits (unless excluded – see **BT2.14** below) can be covered by a dispensation and, by way of example only, the Inland Revenue have indicated that a dispensation can cover:

- reasonable scale rate payments for travelling and subsistence;
- entertaining;
- subscriptions to professional bodies or learned societies;

- non-cash vouchers; and
- credit-tokens.

Kinds of benefits and expenses excluded [BT2.14]

The Inland Revenue have indicated, by way of example, certain expenses and benefits which will not be covered by a dispensation, including:

- company cars;
- company vans;
- medical insurance; and
- beneficial loans.

Despite being excluded, the reporting of these benefits can be eased by approaching the Inland Revenue for permission to report the expenses and benefits information on lists.

Requirements [BT2.15]

Dispensations are granted at the discretion of the Inspector of Taxes who will look in particular at the control over expenses operated by the employer.

Accordingly, as noted at **BT2.13** above, any system of round sum allowances being operated by the employer will be excluded and only a system which the expenses are individually authorised and accounted for will be considered.

The Inspector will be looking for a system where expenses claims are independently checked and authorised within the company and, where possible, receipts go with the claims. Beyond that, the Inspector will want to be satisfied that no extra tax would be payable by the employees on the expenses or benefits provided by the employer.

Application [BT2.16]

Dispensations for expenses and benefits in general are applied for by completing Form P11DX but travel and subsistence expenses now have their own Form 490(DIS).

It may be of assistance for a company to have a written procedure for handling expenses and to produce that with the form.

Ambit of a dispensation [BT2.17]

A dispensation is not confined to the start of a tax year and can apply from any point in time.

The ambit of a dispensation clearly only covers the circumstances for which the dispensation has been issued, the employees specified and the expenses specified. In the event of a change in any of the circumstances under which the dispensation was granted, then the Inland Revenue must be informed.

Dispensations are reviewed from time-to-time and may be revoked by written notice in which case Form P11Ds would require to be completed in that respect thereafter.

PAYE settlements [BT2.18]

Where the incidence of expenses and benefits is open to simplification, then an employer may apply to the Inland Revenue for a 'PAYE settlement' which will allow the employer to make a single annual payment. Once granted, a PAYE settlement is a voluntary agreement between the taxpayer and the Inland Revenue under which the employer agrees in a single annual payment to meet:

- the tax payable on certain expenses and benefits given to employees; and
- Class 1B National Insurance Contributions on those expenses and benefits.

It normally follows from the granting of a PAYE settlement that the employer no longer need:

- operate the PAYE system for tax and NIC in relation to those expenses;
- include the items covered in a Form P9D or P11D; nor
- to assess any liability to Class 1 or Class 1A NIC.

Moreover, the granting of a dispensation normally means that those employees need not include those expenses and benefits in their tax assessments, PAYE codes, or tax returns.

Kinds of benefits and expenses covered [BT2.19]

PAYE settlements are aimed at expenses and benefits which are so irregular or so small or so difficult to divide amongst the individual employees affected (e.g. shared bus, chiropodists etc.) that the full operation of the PAYE system in relation to them is unreasonable.

Most expenses and benefits of that type (unless excluded – see **BT2.20** below) can be covered by a PAYE settlement and, by way of example only, the Inland Revenue have indicated that a PAYE settlement can cover items such as:

- long service awards;
- incentive awards;
- late night taxi fares;
- personal incidental expenses;
- some entertainment and gifts to employees;
- company vans;
- company cars which are pooled;
- sports and recreation expenses;
- telephone accounts;
- spouse accompanying an employee abroad;
- some relocation expenses;
- overseas conferences;
- occasional use of company assets; and
- gifts.

Kinds of benefits and expenses excluded [BT2.20]

The Inland Revenue have indicated, by way of example, certain expenses and benefits which will not be covered by a PAYE settlement, including:

- round sum allowances;
- cash payments of wages to employees or casual workers;
- company cars;
- car fuel;
- accommodation; and
- beneficial loans.

Requirements for a dispensation [BT2.21]

PAYE settlements are granted at the discretion of the Inspector of Taxes and one of the areas which an Inspector will consider to be the most important will be the nature of the expenses and benefits themselves.

As already noted, any system of round sum allowances being operated by the Employer will be excluded and only a system which the expenses are individually authorised and accounted for will be considered.

Application [BT2.22]

There is no specific form for use in applying for a PAYE settlement. The company or its accountant simply writes to the company's District Inspector of Taxes explaining that the company would like to agree a PAYE settlement.

The letter should specify the expenses and benefits to which the company would like the PAYE settlement applied.

The Inspector of Taxes will consider the matter and, if satisfied, agree what is to be included. An agreement will then be formally signed as a permanent record.

It is possible to apply:

- before the beginning of the tax year to which the PAYE settlement applies;
- during the tax year; or
- after the end of the tax year but for items which would otherwise have to be put on the P11D the time limit is no later than 6 July following the tax year to which the PAYE settlement is to relate.

Calculation of tax payable [BT2.23]

In order to calculate the tax payable, the company will have to consider the:

- value of the expenses and benefits involved;
- number of employees receiving those expenses and benefits; and

- rate of tax to be applied (which is grossed up to take account of the effective marginal rates of tax of the employees involved).

Example

PSC Ltd employs 3 people – a director; a higher-paid and higher tax rate employee and a lower-paid and basic tax rate employee. PSC Ltd pays £5,000 for a box at Wimbledon which is open to all employees.

The tax payable might be calculated as follows.

Lower-paid and basic rate tax employees
1/3 * £5,000 = £1,667
Grossed up: 1,667 * 100 = £2,165
100 - 23
Basic rate tax thereon 2,165 * 23% = £498

Directors, higher-paid and higher tax rate employees
2/3 * £5,000 = £3,333
Grossed up: 3,333 * 100 = £5,555
100 - 40
Higher rate tax thereon 5,555 * 40% = 2,222

Calculation of total tax payable under PAYE settlement: **£2,720**

Calculation of the NIC payable [BT2.24]

With effect from 6 April 1999, NIC are aligned with, and treated in the same way as, tax for the purposes of a PAYE settlement.

A new class of NIC, Class 1B, was introduced by *Social Security Act 1998, section 53* with effect from that date and so far as PAYE settlements are concerned, any Class 1B NIC may be dealt with in a single annual payment in much the same way as tax.

Emoluments would have been chargeable emoluments for Class 1B purposes if they would have been liable to Class 1 or Class 1A contributions and on those chargeable emoluments grossed up for tax purposes, Class 1B NIC are payable at a rate equal to the rate of secondary contributions.

Example

Value of the item normally giving rise to Class A NIC: £5,000

Total tax payable under PAYE settlement
Lower rate taxpayers £2,165
Higher rate taxpayers £5,555
£7,720
£12,720

Class 1B Charge £12,720 @ 12.2% = £1,551.64

Agreement of the Inspector of Taxes [BT2.25]

The figures for tax and NIC will be agreed and finalised with the Inspector of Taxes. The company will also be told where and when to pay. Reconsideration or an appeal is possible if the amount cannot be agreed.

The company will then pay that sum to the Inland Revenue in a single annual payment. This can be paid at any time during the year but no later than 19 October following the year to which the PAYE settlement relates. Interest will be due on late payments.

The company will then no longer require to operate the PAYE system on that benefit and will no longer need to record that benefit on the Forms P35, P14, P9D or P11D.

Although not keeping those records, the company will still need to keep:

- the same records as those kept for accounting purposes in relation to the items covered by a PAYE settlement;
- where it cannot be ascertained which employee receives which part of the benefit, records will need to be kept of the:
    - overall cost of the benefit in question,
    - applicability of Class 1 NIC to the benefit,
    - number of employees receiving the benefit, and
    - tax rates of those employees.

Records must be retained for a period of three years.

Ambit of a PAYE settlement [BT2.26]

The ambit of a PAYE settlement clearly only covers the circumstances for which the PAYE settlement has been issued, the employees specified and the expenses specified.

In the event of a change in any of the circumstances under which the PAYE settlement was granted then the Inland Revenue must be informed.

PAYE Settlements are annual agreements and have to be renewed each year.

Registration for PAYE, NIC and benefits purposes [BT2.27]

The procedure, when a business is about to pay someone for the first time, is now to telephone the New Employer's Support Initiative on: 0845 6070 143 whereupon an employer's reference number will be issued to the business and a new employer's starter pack sent to the business.

The importance of compliance [BT2.28]

The proper operation of the PAYE, NIC and benefits procedures has now been transformed into a complex and onerous task.

As an employer, the company should appreciate that registration carries with it the obligation to meet certain requirements and that a system of enforcement involving interest and penalties exists to ensure compliance. Companies would therefore be well advised to ensure at the outset that they have in place systems which correctly operate PAYE, NIC and benefits. A number of organisations now specialise in providing such a service.

Professional advisers may provide such a service or may themselves carry out a review of the adequacy of the company's own procedures.

BT3 – Corporation Tax

Introduction [BT3.1]

It is a simple fact of commercial life that heavy expenditure can be incurred in setting up a business before any revenue is accrued. Where this expenditure is for the benefit of the business and for the purpose of generating that revenue, it is only sensible that that expenditure should be offset against that revenue before the resulting profit is calculated and taxed.

This involves carrying that expenditure forward against later revenue and there are a number of considerations involved.

Expenditure incurred by the company [BT3.2]

The Inland Revenue operate the principle that pre-trading expenditure incurred by a person other than the eventual trader does not qualify. Accordingly, there is very little point in the individuals behind the company spending a great deal of money on the equipment required by the company because they will not be allowed to offset that expenditure against the later income of the company – a distinct and separate person in the eyes of the law.

It is only sensible, therefore, for the company – after incorporation but before trading – to incur all of the necessary early expenditure in the name of the company so that it can later be offset against the company's income. The way in which this is done involves a consideration of whether the expenditure is of a capital or a revenue nature.

The distinction between capital and revenue expenditure is a question of law. In essence, the distinction will in practice be drawn between expenditure on, say, an asset which is expected to have a life of several years in the business (capital) and expenditure the benefit of which is expected to be consumed in that year (revenue).

Pre-trading capital expenditure by the company [BT3.3]

Where the company incurs pre-trading capital expenditure then relief will be given through Capital Allowances. Again, it is only expenditure by and in the name of the company itself (adequately vouched) which counts and not any expenditure by the individuals behind the company.

Pre-trading revenue expenditure by the company [BT3.4]

Where the company incurs pre-trading revenue expenditure (i.e. not capital expenditure or company formation costs) then provided that the expenditure is of the sort which would be allowable as a deduction in computing trading profits once trading had commenced, it may be carried forward and treated as incurred on the first day of trading.

Thus, it is possible for a company, after incorporation, to spend several years expending money in building itself up to a position to commence trading and once trading does commence all of that expenditure, if qualifying, may be carried forward, treated as incurred on the first day of trading, and offset against future profits.

Again, it is only expenditure by and in the name of the company itself (adequately vouched) which counts and not any expenditure by the individuals behind the company.

Registration [BT3.5]

Formal registration to incur the offset of such expenditure is not necessary as once registration of the company for Corporation Tax purposes does take place, the Inland Revenue will be prepared to look back at the company's origins.

In practice, however, any such claim will be easier to process where voluntary disclosure has been made by the company to the Inland Revenue of its activities between incorporation and commencement of trading.

Example 1

Two individuals set up a Personal Service Company.

In January, out of redundancy money made available to them, the two individuals purchase a substantial amount of equipment goods and services which they feel they will need in their own names. No receipts are obtained from the suppliers.

In May, the company is both incorporated and commences trading.

At the end of its accounting period, one year later, the company seeks to offset against the revenue earned by the company the expenditure incurred on goods and services but the claim is disallowed by the Inland Revenue as having been incurred not by the company but by the two individuals who are separate persons.

Effectively, the individuals have had to bear the burden of the costs of setting up the company personally (not allowed as a deduction against the company) even though the supplies on which the expenditure was made were for the purposes of the company's trade.

Example 2

Two individuals decide to set up a Personal Service Company.

In January, the individuals incorporate PSC Limited. They arrange bank facilities for the company and all purchases of goods and services needed for the future business of the company are taken in the name of the company and a receipts addressed to the company are in each case obtained from the supplier.

In May, preparation has been completed and PSC Limited is ready to commence trading.

At the end of the following May, PSC Limited completes its accounts and company tax return in which the company offsets both Capital Allowances in respect of the capital expenditure made in its own name and trading expenditure in respect of the revenue expenditure made in its own name thereby allowing the company to obtain the benefit of that expenditure.

Registration with the Inland Revenue for the purposes of Corporation Tax has now become largely automated in that the Inland Revenue receive details of the registration at Companies House of all new companies and automatically send such companies an inquiry form. This will also intimate to each company the Inland Revenue Office dealing with its Corporation Tax affairs.

The responsibility for the administration of the Inland Revenue generally (of which Corporation Tax is an internal branch) in the UK is placed in the hands of the Commissioners of the Inland Revenue.

There are a number of Inland Revenue Offices spread throughout the country. Some Offices are Enquiry Centres (they can be found in the local telephone book under 'Inland Revenue') which deal with enquiries generally and some general aspects of Corporation Tax. There are also a number of Offices dedicated to Corporation Tax in each area to which any specific enquiries on Corporation Tax should be made. It is to this office that the company should submit its Company Tax Return.

The ruling legislation affecting Corporation Tax is *Income and Corporation Taxes Act 1988* now supported by *Finance Act 1998*. It is also necessary to take into account *Capital Gains Act 1992*; *Capital Allowances Act 1990*; *Taxes Management Act 1970* and indeed a wide range of other legislation, case law and practice.

Procedure [BT3.6]

Either automatically as a result of registration on the Register of Companies or by request, the Inland Revenue will send out Form (CT41G (Manual) Corporation Tax. New Company Details.

The Form will show the name, address, telephone number and reference number of the District dealing with the Corporation Tax affairs of the company.

Obligation to register [BT3.7]

As earlier noted, it is a combination of UK residence and a source of income arising which brings companies within the charge to Corporation Tax. The obligation to disclose this fact rests on the company.

A company which is chargeable to tax for an accounting period and has not received a notice requiring a company Tax Return, must give notice to the Inland Revenue that it is so chargeable. The notice must be given within twelve months from the end of the accounting period.

What should happen next? [BT3.8]

The Corporation Tax system is largely driven by the company Tax Return. Once the Inland Revenue are aware that the company is chargeable to Corporation Tax then steps will be taken to issue the company with a formal Notice requiring the company to make a company Tax Return and that will place the company within the computerised system for the administration of Corporation Tax.

Part C

RUNNING A PERSONAL SERVICE COMPANY

Introduction

Running a company has never been an entirely easy task and it is not a particularly easy task today. The administrative burden of 'red tape' and taxation (the latest addition to which, so far as Personal Service Companies are concerned, is IR35) arises constantly as one of the major complaints of small and medium-sized companies who say that the burden is now such that it interferes with their productivity. That does indeed appear to be the case with only tentative steps are now being taken to put forward proposals for improving the position. If the intention is serious about developing the knowledge-based sector as a new area of the economy for Britain then it would seem important to reform the system so as to allow companies in the sector to operate easily and without any undue administrative burden.

As things stand at present, however, the administrative burden must be met and overcome and it is important for those involved in Personal Service Companies to appreciate that unless they can clearly identify some form of exemption or exception applying to their category of company then they are, in the eyes of the law, under exactly the same obligations as those which apply to any other private limited company.

The hurdles which a private limited company must surmount are not inconsiderable and nor – with the advent of IR35 – are the hurdles which face a Personal Service Company. The hurdles are such, in fact, that as has been emphasised throughout this book, a company of any sort (and particularly a Personal Service Company) must be made to *really* work in order to justify the effort involved in overcoming all the hurdles although it should perhaps be added that if that can be done successfully then the benefits will far outweigh the difficulties.

In theory – as in every fully developed commercial country – it ought to be possible for a Personal Service Company to overcome all of the administrative burdens itself. That is the case in the United Kingdom, although perhaps only in strict theory, and as will be seen from this section what is involved administratively is such a blend of legislation, precedent, and practice that it may require the involvement of a spouse or partner to concentrate upon this aspect of the company's affairs and the involvement of professional advisers, if not essential, will at least greatly assist the successful running of a Personal Service Company.

Having reached the decision to use a Personal Service Company as the commercial vehicle for self-employment and having successfully started up such a company, we consider in this section what is involved in running a Personal Service Company.

So far as law is concerned, we consider the role of the company secretary and the role of the directors; consider the manner in which the company is controlled; and the manner in which the legal structure of the company is thereafter maintained.

So far as management is concerned, we consider the nature of the contracts which Personal Service Companies enter into (the life-blood of their industry) and then the IR35 Test as it relates to those contracts. We consider also the administrative burden which is imposed upon companies in the form of the various returns which it is now incumbent upon a company to make.

So far as taxation is concerned, it is important to appreciate at the outset that a company incorporating and a company trading are distinct concepts. Just because a company has been incorporated, that does not automatically mean (although it may do) that that company has commenced trading. Instead, the decision by a Personal Service Company to commence trading should be a separate and distinct decision. We consider that decision in relation to the various taxes and then the taxes themselves – including, in relation to PAYE and NIC where it has its effect, the new rules relating to IR35.

Law

In relation to companies generally, it is important to appreciate the distinction between the directors of a company and the shareholders of a company. This is most marked where the directors are not shareholders and simply represent the professional management of the company while the shareholders own the company but take no part in the management of the company. However, even where the same individual is both a shareholder and a director it is important to appreciate that in the eyes of the law that individual is performing separate duties (colloquially known as 'wearing different hats') where acting in those different offices of shareholder and director.

In general, the shareholders delegate the task of managing the affairs of the company to a Board of directors (how ever many directors – even just one – there may actually be on the Board). That delegation is quite extensive and covers the whole business affairs of the company (including the issue of shares). Shareholders, on the other hand, exercise control over the Board of directors by having the power to appoint and dismiss directors. Shareholders also ultimately control the company through General Meeting. Nor is the structure of a company set in stone and it is open to the shareholders of a company to make significant changes to its structure.

Accordingly, the manner in which a company is, in law, run can be likened to a cascading effect. Many of the administrative tasks will be undertaken by the company secretary; these will be overseen by the Board of directors who will also manage the company generally; this in turn will be overseen by the shareholders who have the power to control the company and that whole legal structure can also be changed by the shareholders. In this section, it is proposed to consider each of these aspects in turn as they relate to a Personal Service Company.

CL1 – The Role of the Company Secretary

Introduction [CL1.1]

Together, the directors and secretary of a company are collectively known as the 'officers' of the company. As such, they collectively have responsibility for the running of the company.

Having said that, however, a distinction has traditionally been drawn between the functions of directors and the functions of secretaries. In general, the former are traditionally seen as being more executive while the latter are seen as being more administrative.

Powers [CL1.2]

The *Companies Acts* do not assign any specific rights or powers to company secretaries. However, it is possible that the Articles of Association of a particular company may assign them specific rights and powers.

Qualifications are not, at present, required in order to be the company secretary of a private limited company or a Personal Service Company.

The company secretary is expected to perform the general administrative duties. Many, if not most, of the official documents of a company can be signed by either or both the director(s) and the company secretary.

Duties [CL1.3]

The *Companies Acts* do not assign any specific duties to company secretaries. However, it is possible that the Articles of Association of a particular company may assign specific duties to them.

Traditionally the company secretary's duties will include the following.

Ensuring that the records of the company are properly filed at Companies House [CL1.4]

Companies are required to deliver to Companies House an Annual Return which is aimed at ensuring that the information about the company held on file at Companies House is up-to-date and correct.

The proper completion of the Annual Return has traditionally been regarded as the task of the company secretary (although one which the directors are required to properly oversee). Completion and submission of the Forms necessary to effect any changes has also, on a similar basis, traditionally been seen as the task of the company secretary.

Maintaining the Registers [CL1.5]

Companies are required by statute to maintain various Registers and to hold these open for inspection. A company can also maintain a number of Registers voluntarily. It has traditionally been regarded as the duty of the company secretary to maintain these Registers.

Controlling the meetings [CL1.6]

The company secretary traditionally plays a major role in controlling both shareholders' and directors' meetings.

A company secretary should be aware of the:

- circumstances in which such meetings may be called and ensure that it is competent to do so;
- notice required for any matter which it is proposed to deal with at the meeting and ensure that the correct amount of notice has been given;
- persons entitled to notice of such meetings and ensure that notice is sent to all those entitled;
- quorum requirements for such meetings and ensure that those are being complied with; and
- practices for the proper conduct of meetings and ensure that these are complied with.

It has also been traditionally regarded as the duty of the company secretary to take, check, confirm, have signed, and record the minutes of the meetings.

Year-end functions [CL1.7]

Many of the most important functions of a company (Annual Returns, Forms, accounts, and the like) take place at the year-end.

Most of these functions are so important that they might best be regarded as the direct responsibility of the directors (who bear the primary legal responsibility) but in practice many directors delegate or share these functions with the company secretary.

Company contracts and the company seal (if any) [CL1.8]

Companies are no longer legally required to have a company seal. Where a company chooses to do so, however, then the custody and use of that seal has traditionally been regarded as being the duty of the company secretary.

Even single member companies have to have another individual as the company secretary. Where the company has no seal and a document is regarded as being of such importance that a single signature is not enough, then the signature of the company secretary may also be called into service.

Executive functions [CL1.9]

A company secretary whose duties are defined as being purely administrative and who discharges those duties properly has little to fear.

However, where a company secretary allows their function to exceed the administrative and become executive then they should be aware that they may be exposing themselves to potential liability particularly in relation to those areas where the officers of a company may be held liable.

CL2 – The Role of Directors

Introduction [CL2.1]

A director is 'any person occupying the position of a director, by whatever name called'.

The law, for obvious reasons, prefers to adopt an approach whereby all of those who perform the *function* of directors are caught rather than an approach under which formal title or methods of appointment are definitive. That will apply to Personal Service Companies.

It should be appreciated that neither the failure to register directors with Companies House nor the failure to give an individual the formal title of director prevent any individual undertaking a director's functions from having the obligations, duties and responsibilities which the position of director involves. Indeed, one of the most significant developments in this area of the law in recent years has been the creation and development of the concept known as the 'shadow director' (see **CL2.9** below).

Categories [CL2.2]

The law itself recognises only one category of director (which includes shadow directors). Commerce, however, is very keen to categorise directors. It is not beyond the bounds of possibility that the category of director involved might be of significance where the actions called for from the 'reasonable director' are under examination but in general all of these categories of director are in law considered in the same manner.

Non-executive directors [CL2.3]

The concept of a non-executive director is one which has existed for some time. The concept has, however, grown to prominence in recent years as Corporate Governance has come under examination by a number of committees (namely Greenbury, Cadbury and Hampel).

Essentially, the theory is that non-executive directors do not have any executive responsibilities in the company. They have, therefore, a measure of independence and objectivity which allows them to assist the company to come to better and more proper decisions in 'grey areas'. They are normally remunerated by way of fees.

Now virtually a necessity for public companies offering their shares to the public, the concept is nevertheless not without relevance to private companies.

Executive directors **[CL2.4]**

Executive directors are, self-evidently, those who hold executive office in the company and are usually remunerated as such.

Executive directors are normally formally appointed and filed as such at Companies House and will often have a further executive description (e.g. director of advertising).

There are various categories or description of executive director, including the following.

Chairman/President **[CL2.5]**

The positions of Chairman and President has grown not through law but through practice in public companies who offer their shares to the public. The Chairman/President often makes a (non-mandatory) statement at the outset of the financial statements detailing the achievements of the company over the year. They are often non-executive and sit on the Boards of several companies.

Of importance to Stock Exchanges, this position is of little importance to private companies (although for administrative purposes, every meeting should have a Chairman).

Managing Director/Chief Executive Officer **[CL2.6]**

The positions of Managing Director and Chief Executive Officer have grown not through law but through practice in public companies who offer their shares to the public. Whereas the Chairman/President was in effect a figurehead, it is upon the shoulders of the holder of this executive office that the full responsibility for the performance of the company usually rests. Effectively, he or she leads the Board although they can, of course, be out-voted.

Of importance to Stock Exchanges, this position is of less importance to private companies (although for administrative purposes, someone should lead the other directors – if there are any).

Ordinary directors [CL2.7]

The remaining directors, if any, will be ordinary directors. It is important for them to appreciate, however, that although the contents of any individual report being made by any individual director may not be directly relevant to them, they are nevertheless collectively responsible for its contents as a Board.

Nominee directors [CL2.8]

Those who lend money to a company or who are otherwise closely associated with the developments of a company often like to appoint a nominee director to attend the Board meeting and look out for their interests.

Such individuals normally require to accept and consent to formal appointment as directors – in which case they will be in exactly the same position as any other director – failing which they might be in danger of being considered shadow directors.

Shadow directors [CL2.9]

A 'shadow director' is a person 'in accordance with whose directions or instructions the directors of the company are accustomed to act'.

Accordingly, without ever having acquired the formal title of director and without ever having gone through the formal process of appointment, where an individual is in a position to give directions or instructions in accordance with which the directors of the company are accustomed to act then that individual is likely in law to be regarded as a director of that company and to have all of the legal requirements applied to them.

The *Companies Acts* and recent company law cases are peppered with reference to 'shadow directors' and the concept is one which is taken seriously and which is growing. Indeed, in one recent case a company which owed a great deal of money to a bank and which was in financial difficulties found itself closely following the directions of the bank in an effort to trade out of its difficulties and the bank then found itself in danger of being designated a 'shadow director' of the company.

IR35 point [CL2.10]

While not strictly a factor in the IR35 Test, it perhaps bears mentioning that a Personal Service Company with only one client and one director is intuitively more likely to be regarded as employment. On the other hand, a Personal Service Company with a varied Board serving a number of clients is more likely to be intuitively regarded as self-employed.

Qualifications [CL2.11]

There are at present no qualifications necessary to become a director of a company. The UK currently relies upon the publication of such sanctions (usually disqualification) as are applied, in order to encourage others to meet the required standards as director.

Another company and, where it is a separate legal person such as in Scotland, a partnership can be the director of a company.

The Institute of Directors has, however, recently introduced a number of training courses although these are aimed mostly at the larger companies.

Disqualifications [CL2.12]

The following are disqualified from acting as directors:

- those who have been disqualified under legislation;
- those who are bankrupt – although permission of the courts to do so is possible and, indeed, has become more prevalent in recent years; and

- those who have been made subject to a court order – insolvency, fraudulent trading, wrongful trading, persistent late filing of company documents and other actions can result in a court of law issuing an order, usually for a specified period, that the person involved may not act as a director of a company, although it is possible to apply to the court to amend or vary the order and this too appears to be more prevalent in recent years.

Service contracts [CL2.13]

It is quite common for executive directors to enter into contracts which regulate their powers, duties, responsibilities and remuneration *vis-à-vis* the company (including restrictive covenants) and these, although essentially no different from any other contract of employment, are known as service contracts.

This is usual where the director is divorced from the company and is essentially providing professional management. It is less common where owner/managed companies are concerned.

Where a service contract does exist then *section 318* of the *Companies Act 1985* provides that where not reduced to writing, its terms must be set out in a Memorandum and held, open for inspection by members, at the Registered Office of the company. *Section 319* of the *Companies Act 1985* also provides that no service contract is to exceed a term of five years unless approved by the company in general meeting.

So far as appointment is concerned, formal service contracts will generally be unnecessary for Personal Service Companies and such companies should simply appoint such directors as suit the individual circumstances of the company.

Remuneration [CL2.14]

1985 Table A usually provides that, for holding the office of director, the directors of the company are entitled to such remuneration (usually described as 'fees') as the shareholders may, by ordinary resolution, determine. Without this provision in the Articles, directors would not, as fiduciaries, be entitled to any remuneration from the company. The Articles often also provide that the Board has the power to appoint one of their number to an executive position and fix their remuneration (usually described as 'salary'). In doing so, the directors are under a duty to act in good faith and in the best interests of the company. The remuneration of directors is, therefore, flexible.

In practice, the company by ordinary resolution usually votes the directors a basic salary and then at the end of the year, when the performance of the company over the year can be assessed, further entitlement in the form of a bonus or dividend may be approved by the company in general meeting.

The effect of IR35 is, of course, to carry the potential to alter the equation of shareholder/directors' remuneration so far as PAYE and NIC are concerned.

At whatever level it is arrived at, the remuneration of directors requires to have the PAYE and NIC systems properly operated on it. The remuneration of directors in particular (as distinguished from other employees) has come under increasing restriction and scrutiny in recent years.

Benefits are now a major consideration for directors. These now increasingly impinge on the PAYE and NIC systems and Form P11D must be returned by the company each year showing the expenses and benefits paid by the company to its directors.

Pensions are also an increasingly important area and the manner in which the company can be used, with maximum tax relief, to provide for the future of the shareholder/directors is a matter upon which the advice of a person duly authorised to give such advice must now be taken.

IR35 point **[CL2.15]**

So far as remuneration is concerned, it was, undoubtedly, the actions of a few which encouraged the introduction of IR35. An irresponsible minority adopted a practice of paying themselves a salary of less than £8,500 and taking the rest of their net income by way of dividend thereby virtually by-passing the NIC system altogether. The responsible majority drew a reasonable salary upon which they made the appropriate NIC before drawing any net balance out of the company by way of dividend. As a result of the introduction of the legislation implementing IR35 the choice has been taken out of the matter at least so far as those contracts deemed to be 'relevant engagements' are concerned.

It is undeniable that for the smaller Personal Service Company, IR35 offers a potent threat. With a responsible attitude and careful planning this should not be insurmountable but great care will require to be exercised and a degree of flexibility in the area of remuneration should be obtained.

Giving powers to directors [CL2.16]

Directors exercise their powers as a Board. The practice tends to be that individual directors carry out investigations and make recommendations which the Board (if there is one) as a whole then accepts or rejects.

The powers of the directors come from the Articles of Association. In strict theory, where powers are delegated to a Board then that Board in turn requires specific authority before it can delegate its powers. In practice, however, the Articles usually provide for that.

For example, *1985 Table A, Article 72* provides that:

> 'The directors may delegate any of their powers to any committee consisting of one or more directors. They may also delegate to any managing director or any director holding any other executive office such of their powers as they consider desirable to be exercised by him. Any such delegation may be made subject to any conditions the directors may impose, and either collaterally with or to the exclusion of their own powers and may be revoked or altered. Subject to any such conditions, the proceedings of a committee with two or more members shall be governed by the articles regulating the proceedings of directors so far as they are capable of applying.'

and 1985 *Table A, Article 71* provides that:

> 'The directors may, by power of attorney or otherwise, appoint any person to be the agent of the company for such purposes and on such conditions as they determine, including authority for the agent to delegate all or any of his powers.'

Companies commonly designate a director as having a specific function (e.g. Director of Finance, Director of Technology or Director of Sales etc.). The authority given to these individual directors within their remit is usually loosely expressed but ultimate authority rests with the Board as a whole.

A sole director performs, of course, all of the functions but where there is more than one director it is generally advisable to have regular (perhaps monthly) meetings at which issues are called together and formally decided.

The internal aspect of the directors exceeding their powers [CL2.17]

Where a company has a diverse administration and one element of that administration or a member of the company feels that what is proposed is outside the powers of the company then they are still quite at liberty to raise that issue within the company or at law using the doctrine of '*ultra vires*'. The directors may be personally liable in such circumstances.

The external aspect of the directors exceeding their powers [CL2.18]

So far as third parties dealing with the company are concerned, however, the 'teeth' of the *ultra vires* doctrine have been withdrawn by legislation.

Third parties no longer need to seek out the Memorandum and Articles of Association of a company to satisfy themselves that any transaction with the company will be within the powers of the company and valid. Instead, transactions with third parties acting in good faith will be valid even where the company has in fact exceeded its stated powers.

In certain circumstances directors can become personally liable to third parties – see **CL2.75–CL2.91** below.

The inter-relationship of directors' powers and duties [CL2.19]

Simply having the *prima facie* power to do something may not be enough if it conflicts with the duties of the directors.

For example, a company which had traded successfully for many years with a loyal staff decided to close down. As a reward to the staff, it was proposed to make payment of a capital sum to each member of staff. While the directors might technically have had the power to make payment of capital sums, a shareholder raised an action seeking a declaration that the proposal was not in accordance with the duty of the directors to act *bona fide* in the interests of the company itself.

The *Companies Acts* were changed shortly after that case and the concept of redundancy was also introduced shortly afterwards but the case does illustrate the complexities which can surround the issue of directors' powers.

Specific powers [CL2.20]

Bank accounts and cheques [CL2.21]

One of the specific powers which the directors have is control of the operation of the company's bank account and the directors (usually two) are normally the signatories on the company's cheques.

Banks usually require a formal Board minute opening the bank account and appointing the signatories.

It is important that the name of the company appears on the face of the cheques because if it does not so appear then the director signing may be held to be personally liable on the cheque.

Borrowing [CL2.22]

Some consider that the power of the directors to borrow money on behalf of the company is a power which would be implied as incidental to the objects of the company.

In most instances, however, the Memorandum of Association will specifically give the directors the power to borrow money on behalf of the company. The power to grant security for the borrowings over the assets of the company will usually also be provided for in the Memorandum. In practice, substantial borrowings are unlikely to be given without security and security is unlikely to be taken by the funder unless the power both to borrow and give security is in the Memorandum.

Shares [CL2.23]

Although the total authorised share capital is a matter within the control of the shareholders, the actual allotment and issue of the shares which have been authorised is normally a power which is given to the directors.

Dividends [CL2.24]

The directors normally have the power to declare a dividend.The normal procedure is for the directors to recommend a dividend in their report which the shareholders then vote on at the AGM.

The issue of dividends is also controlled by the *Companies Acts* and can only be made out of'profits available for the purpose' (*CA 1985, s263*).

Board meeting minutes [CL2.25]

There is, of course, no legal requirement to have a Board as such.A sole director can perfectly competently manage the affairs of a company. However, administratively speaking it is strongly advisable even for that one individual to have a meeting with a reasonable degree of formality and to keep minutes.

The minutes of a directors' meeting are, of course, confidential. However, extracts of those minutes can be produced or the meeting and its minutes can be confined to a specific topic.

In the event of an IR35 Test, the ability to produce minutes dealing with the matters in issue might be more of an indicator of self-employment than in the case of a company forced to admit that it has never held a directors' meeting.

Directors' duties [CL2.26]

In accepting appointment as a directors of a company, an individual immediately assumes a large number of varied duties. Ignorance of the law relating to such duties will, of course, be no excuse but in fact many of these duties arise under the common law and may not be immediately clear.

Small companies in which the shareholders and directors are the same individuals often assume that they in fact owe no duties as directors since any duties owed would be to themselves as shareholders. That is, however, an erroneous assumption.

The first area in which the directors will assume duties is under the Articles of Association because that is where the duties of the directors are set out. Directors will then owe a number of general and specific fiduciary duties arising under the common law.

In addition, an increasing number of statutes – primarily the *Companies Acts* but also various other statutes – will impose duties upon directors. Furthermore, directors increasingly owe duties to creditors, employees, customers, and indeed to the community generally.

No company – not even a single member Personal Service Company – is an island unto itself. Those involved are sometimes not brought face to face with their duties until some sort of investigation is underway or some dispute arises internally within the company. That does not mean, of course, that these duties have not previously existed and a preferable course for the directors of such companies is to be aware of and observe throughout the duties which are incumbent upon them.

The duties of directors are largely neutral so far as any IR35 Test is concerned other than to the extent that their proper performance point to self-employment.

Duties arising under the constitution of the company **[CL2.27]**

The most obvious written source of the duties of a director will be found in the constitution of the company – the Memorandum of Association and the Articles of Association. As such, every director ought to have an up-to-date copy of these documents in their possession.

The Memorandum will set out the powers which the company itself has. The Articles of Association will set out the duties which have been given to the directors. It is within the confines of that constitution that the directors should discharge their duties in managing the affairs of the company.

Sometimes, the constitution of the company has not kept pace with those developments. The consequences of this are potentially serious. A company is an artificial person and in the eyes of the law that artificial person can only competently do what it has been authorised to do.

Duties arising under common law – general [CL2.28]

The common law imposes a general duty upon directors to act with reasonable skill and care.

'Skill' might be described as any special abilities to be expected from the directors concerned (in which a distinction may be drawn between professional executive directors and amateur non-executive directors). 'Care' is a recognised legal concept and is represented by the pains which a reasonable man or woman would take in the handling of their own affairs.

For many years, the litmus test for the common law general duty of skill and care was to be found in *Re City Equitable Fire Insurance Co [1925] Ch 407.*

In that case, Romer J said:

> '...a director need not exhibit in the performance of his duties a greater degree of skill than may reasonably be expected from a person of his knowledge and experience. A director of a life insurance company ...does not guarantee that he has the skill of an actuary of a physician. A director is not bound to give continuous attention to the affairs of his company. His duties are of an intermittent nature to be performed at periodical board meetings. He is not, however, bound to attend such meetings, though he ought to attend whenever he is reasonably able to do so...In respect of duties that, having regard to the exigencies of business and the articles...may properly be left to some official, a director is, in the absence of grounds for suspicion, justified in trusting that official.'

Those words have been described as an 'amateurs charter'. They were, however, written in 1925, and they relate to the conditions of the time when gentlemen acted as what we might now describe as non-executive directors. It would be unsafe for an executive director to rely upon that definition today.

The *City Equitable* decision has not been fully replaced but recent decisions have held, for example, that by not reading a proposal before signing it, a director had breached the duty and while it has been held that the expertise to be expected from a director is much less extensive in a small company in a modest way of business with simple accounting procedures and equipment than in a large company with sophisticated procedures, the point was firmly made that in both instances certain minimum standards have to be attained. Those 'minimum standards' are slowly being tightened up by the courts in practice.

Any remedy lies in the hands of the company itself so that the practical consequences of any breach of duty might depend upon where control of the company rests. Nevertheless, if it came to the crunch, the other members (if there are any in a majority) could cause the company to take legal proceedings based upon a breach of this duty. The consequences could involve personal liability on the part of the directors involved.

Accordingly, directors will no longer be able to claim lack of expertise. Certain minimum standards are now expected of all those assuming the post of director on an executive basis and such directors are under a general common law duty to exercise reasonable skill and care.

Duties arising under common law – fiduciary

[CL2.29]

The position of a director is a difficult one to categorise in law. To some extent, the director is:

- an agent of the company;
- a trustee of the company; and
- an employee of the company.

For one reason or another, however, no single one of these descriptions fully covers the office of director. What directors do have, however, in the eyes of the law, is an obligation to look after the affairs of the company and out of that obligation the common law has, over a number of years, recognised a number of fiduciary duties which apply to directors.

Duty to act honestly **[CL2.30]**

A director is under a common law fiduciary duty to act honestly. This does not mean to act honestly in a financial sense, which is a given, but has a more sophisticated legal meaning calling for the director to act with good faith and probity.

Duty to act in good faith in the interests of the company **[CL2.31]**

A director must act in good faith in the best interests of the company.

For example, where, upon assuming office in poor health, a director arranged for the company to purchase insurance which provided generous benefits to his widow in the event of his death. The insurance contract was held not to be in the best interests of the company and was reduced.

Clearly, therefore, even though they might have the necessary powers, directors are not entitled to act solely in their own interests but must always act in the best interests of the company. This issue often arises in situations such as the value at which assets of the company should be disposed of to one of its directors and the level of directors' remuneration.

Just because a transaction incidentally benefits a director, however, that does not mean that it is automatically not in the best interests of the company.

The courts have made it clear that they will not substitute, with hindsight, their own assessment of what was in the best interests of the company but will instead seek to arrive at a determination of what would have been, at the time, commercially considered to be the best interests of the company.

Duty to exercise their powers for a proper and not a collateral purpose **[CL2.32]**

This duty can best be illustrated by examples.

For example, the directors of a company issuing shares to five additional shareholders in order to secure votes in favour of the directors' own appointments, or the directors issuing more shares not to raise capital but in order to forestall a takeover bid would be likely to be regarded as for collateral purposes.

Clearly, there was a collateral objective in these cases in which it was held that the powers were not being exercised by the directors for their proper purposes.

Duty not to allow conflicts of interest **[CL2.33]**

A director is under a duty not to allow their interests to conflict with those of the company. This is a fundamental duty which arises directly from the nature of being a fiduciary.

This rule requires directors not to put themselves in the position where there is an actual or potential conflict between their interests and those of the company.

However, a conflict will be permitted provided that it is fully disclosed and approved in either the Articles of Association or by the company in general meeting. Many small companies, especially those where the members and directors are the same individuals, adjust their Articles of Association to allow for this.

Duty not to compete **[CL2.34]**

A director is under a common law fiduciary duty not to compete with the company. Thus, directors should ensure that they do not find themselves in a situation where they are called upon to decide which company should take advantage of a commercial opportunity and that in practice makes it difficult, if not impossible, for the same individual to sit as a director on the Boards of two companies which are in direct competition.

Duty not to make secret profits **[CL2.35]**

Should a commercial opportunity arise relating to the business of the company which the company itself decides not to take up then it is a breach of duty for directors to take up that opportunity individually and make a secret profit.

It may, however, be possible for the director to disclose an interest and obtain the approval of the company in general meeting to do so.

Duty in respect of the assets of the company **[CL2.36]**

The assets of a company belong to that company which is a separate legal entity. As a fiduciary, a director is under a duty to protect those assets.

Thus the directors must ensure that the assets of the company are not given away, misapplied, lost or become unidentifiable.

Duties arising under statute **[CL2.37]**

At numerous stages, the *Companies Acts* impose duties (often supported by sanctions) upon directors. Each director should therefore have access to a copy of these Acts. Numerous other statutes impose duties and create liability for directors in areas such as:

- financial services;
- health and safety;
- employment;
- environment;
- data protection; and
- product liability.

Much depends on the nature of the company's individual business. Ignorance of the law is not an excuse. Accordingly, directors should, with their professional advisers, identify the legislation which applies to their business.

Duties owed to others **[CL2.38]**

Traditionally, directors have owed their duties more to the company and less to the individual shareholders and others.

That position is, however, gradually being changed. Increasingly, duties on the part of directors are being recognised in relation to others.

Creditors **[CL2.39]**

In general, the interests of the shareholders as a whole outweighs the interests of the creditors as a whole. At least, while the company is solvent.

It is now considered, however, that as soon as a company borders upon insolvency then that position changes and in certain circumstances companies now owe duties to creditors.

Most of these duties arise from recent legislation relating to trading while insolvent (on which see **CL2.81–CL2.83** below). Thus, where there is no reasonable prospect of the company trading out of its difficulties, the directors of the company must have regard to the interests of its creditors in preference to the interests of its shareholders.

Employees **[CL2.40]**

Traditionally, the directors had regard to the best interests of the company, as an entity, alone.

However, the *Companies Acts* have altered that position with a direction that the directors of a company must include the interests of employees in their deliberations. The legislation does not require that the interests of the employees be given any priority or indeed influence their decisions and it is unenforceable by employees individually. However, it is the duty of directors to take the interests of employees into account.

In what is considered by some to be a blizzard of red tape, however, a raft of recent indigestible legislation has imposed numerous duties on employers regarding employees (e.g. maximum hours, part-time workers, maternity leave and the like) and where the employer is a company these devolve to the directors.

Customers **[CL2.41]**

There is no recognised duty which directors owe to customers. Clearly, however, it is in the best interests of the company to have regard to the interests of their customers.

Customers will enforce any interests they have through their contracts. However, as part of that enforcement process the position might be reached wherein the extent to which a company has met its obligations may come to be examined. Reports can emanate from such investigations and from those reports the individuals concerned can be disqualified from acting as directors of a company for a period of time (see **CL2.92** below).

The community [CL2.42]

There is no recognised duty which directors owe to the community. Any such obligations tend to be enforced indirectly through environmental legislation.

However, in the common market the interests of the community as a whole receives much more recognition. Some European countries require, for example, a 'two-tier' Board of management upon which employees receive representation by legislative right and who require to give regard to the wider interests of the community.

Although not represented, to any great extent, in the UK at present, these considerations are likely to be a continuing development flowing from membership of the EC.

Board of directors' meetings [CL2.43]

In contrast to the regulation of shareholders' general meetings, which are fairly closely circumscribed, the way in which the Board's meetings are regulated is more informal.

If such meetings are controlled at all then they will be controlled through the Articles of Association. If there is no provision in the Articles then such meetings should be conducted just as any other executive meeting would be. If there is specific provision in the Articles (and sometimes, especially when funders, particularly venture capitalists, are involved quite complex provisions are introduced) then reference will require to be made to the specific provisions for such meetings. In most cases, however, companies simply adopt *1985 Table A* without modification.

Where a company is being examined to see whether or not it contravenes the legislation introduced to implement IR35, then the minutes of Board meetings are quite likely to become an important factor. Where the company has only one client and has never called or recorded a meeting to regulate the business of the company in relation to that sole client then that contract is more likely to be regarded as a contract of service and of employment. However, where it is being suggested that the company has, under contracts for services, regulated more than one client on a self-employed basis, then (couched in terms which the company will not mind others later having sight of) the best evidence of that fact is likely to be the minutes of meetings of the Board regulating those clients and their different businesses.

The need for meetings and the use of resolutions

[CL2.44]

Instead of having a meeting of the Board, some Articles permit the directors to reach a decision by means of a written resolution.

1985 Table A, Article 93 so permits by providing:

> 'A resolution in writing signed by all the directors entitled to receive notice of a meeting of directors or of a committee of directors shall be as valid and effectual as if it had been passed at a meeting of directors or (as the case may be) a committee of directors duly convened and held and may consist of several documents in the like form each signed by one or more directors; but a resolution signed by an alternate director need not also be signed by his appointer and, if it is signed by a director who has appointed an alternate director, it need not be signed by the alternate director in that capacity.'

Frequency of meetings **[CL2.45]**

1985 Table A, Article 88 provides that (subject to any other Article provisions) the directors may regulate their proceedings as they think fit which means that they may hold meetings of the Board as frequently or as infrequently as they feel is necessary.

It would be unusual for the Board of directors not to meet at least once a year and indeed it would have to so meet in order to discharge its duties in relation to the company's accounts. Other formal matters such as the issue of shares or approval of the transfer of shares will also require a formal meeting. Concluding and executing contracts of importance to the company will also often require a formal meeting.

As earlier noted, much administration can be delegated but best practice calls for regular meetings of the Board (perhaps quarterly or monthly depending upon the volume of business) and the date of the next meeting should be fixed at the conclusion of the last meeting.

Calling a meeting **[CL2.46]**

1985 Table A, Article 88 provides that a director may, and the company secretary at the request of a director shall, call a meeting of the Board.

Notice of meeting **[CL2.47]**

Formal notice of such a meeting should be given to all the directors of the company even where it is known that a director is unlikely to attend. *1985 Table A, Article 88* provides, however, that it shall not be necessary to give notice of a meeting to a director who is absent from the UK.

Quorum **[CL2.48]**

1985 Table A, Article 89 provides that the directors may fix the necessary quorum for the transaction of business in the meeting of the Board. However, if the directors fail to fix any other number then *Article 88* provides that the quorum shall be two.

If the company is running a system which allows for an absent director to appoint an alternate director, then *Article 88* specifically provides that where the person appointed as the alternate is present, but his appointor is not, then that person may be counted in the quorum.

If a director is not entitled to vote (for example, by having an interest – see **CL2.51** below) then *Article 95* provides that that director shall not be counted in the quorum although *Article 96* allows this provision to be relaxed or suspended by ordinary resolution.

If the number of directors present falls below the quorum then the directors (or sole director) may continue to act in terms of *Article 90* but only for the purpose of filling vacancies in the Board or for the purpose of calling a general meeting of the shareholders.

In the event of difficulty in gathering a quorum some Articles (including *1985 Table A*) allow directors to appoint an alternate director in their place. Should obtaining a quorum be anticipated to be a recurring problem then the Articles could be amended to specifically allow, for example, meetings by telephone, fax or e-mail.

The conduct of the meeting **[CL2.49]**

1985 Table A, Article 91 provides that the Board may appoint one of their number to be the Chairman of the Board and may at any time remove the Chairman from that office.

Article 91 also provides that unless unwilling to do so, the director so appointed to act as Chairman shall preside at every meeting of the Board at which he is present.

Article 91 further provides that if:

> '...there is no director holding that office, or if the director holding it is unwilling to preside or is not present within five minutes after the time appointed for the meeting, the directors present may appoint one of their number to be chairman of the meeting.'

Making decisions **[CL2.50]**

1985 Table A, Article 88 provides that questions arising at a meeting shall be decided by a majority of votes with, in the case of an even number of votes, the Chairman of the meeting being given a second (or casting) vote.

The company may be running a system which allows an alternate director to be appointed in place of an absent director. If so, then *Article 88* specifically provides that the person appointed as the alternate, if already a director, may cast two votes (i.e. their own vote as director and that as the alternate director).

Decisions at meetings where a director has an interest **[CL2.51]**

1985 Table A, Article 94 provides that – except as otherwise provided in the Articles – a director shall not vote at a meeting or on a resolution on any matter in which that director has (directly or indirectly) any material interest or duty which conflicts or may conflict with the interests of the company.

That rule does not apply to resolutions relating to:

- the giving of guarantees, securities, or indemnities in respect of money lent to or in respect of obligations incurred, for the benefit of the company;
- the giving of guarantees, securities, or indemnities in respect of an obligation for the benefit of the company for which a director has assumed responsibility;
- the subscribing or agreeing to subscribe for any shares, debentures or other securities of the company; or
- a retirement benefit scheme of a type approved by the Inland Revenue.

Article 94 also provides that the interests of persons connected with the director and alternates appointed by the director are to be treated as the interests of that director.

A director who, under this provision, is not entitled to vote may not be counted in the quorum present at the meeting (*Article 95*).

However, *Article 96* allows the company, by ordinary resolution, to suspend or relax, generally or in relation to a particular matter, any provision in the Articles prohibiting a director from voting at a meeting.

Although the above exceptions will cover many conflicts of interest, such a provisions is often considered irksome in small private companies who modify the Article to allow directors to disclose their interest and then vote.

Decisions concerning the appointment of directors **[CL2.52]**

1985 Table A, Article 97 provides that if two or more directors are being considered for appointment at the same time, the proposals may be divided and each director shall be counted as quorum and entitled to vote in respect of any decision except that relating to his own appointment.

Validity of the decisions made at the meeting **[CL2.53]**

A decision arrived at by the Board, a committee of directors or a sole director, may appear to be valid. Afterwards, it may be discovered that some defect (in the appointment of any of the directors, or that any of them were disqualified from holding office, or had vacated office, or were not entitled to vote as directors) exists in the decision. *Article 92* provides in such circumstances the decision will remain as a valid decision notwithstanding the defect.

Note that this exception does not apply to any failure on the part of a director to disclose an interest.

The directors' report [CL2.54]

The shareholders of a company entrust the management of the business of the company to the directors.

At the end of the year, the directors report to the shareholders about their stewardship of the company's affairs by way of the directors' report (*CA 1985, s234*).

Formal requirements [CL2.55]

Section 234A of the *Companies Act 1985*, requires that the Directors' Report is approved by the Board and is signed by a director or by the company secretary. Every copy of the Report which is laid before the company in general meeting (or otherwise sent, circulated, published or issued) must state the name of the person who signed on behalf of the Board. In the event of a copy of the Directors' Report being filed with Companies House then that copy must be signed by a director or the company secretary.

Contents [CL2.56]

For a normal company to which full reporting requirements apply, the Directors' Report is required to contain the following.

- Changes in the company's activities or directors of the company.
- Significant changes in asset values – including any significant differences between the market value of such assets and the amount at which they are included in the balance sheet.
- Directors' interests in shares or debentures of the company.
- Other matters listed under the *Companies Act 1985, Schedule 7*:

- likely future developments of the business of the company;
- company acquiring its own shares;
- information as to employees;
- charitable and political gifts;
- liability insurance effected for officers or employees of the company;
- disabled employees; and
- policy and practice on the payment of creditors.

Exemptions **[CL2.57]**

Small companies (on which see **CM7.6**) are entitled to certain exemptions and it is important to distinguish what, in relation to the directors' report, goes to the members and what to Companies House.

Members **[CL2.58]**

So far as members are concerned, the normal requirements of the *Companies Acts* in relation to the Directors' Report are restricted by *Companies Act 1985, section 246* which provides that where a company qualifies as small in relation to a financial year then:

> '**246(4)** The directors' report for the year need not give the information required by–
> (a) section 234(1)(a) and (b) (fair review of business and amount to be paid as dividend);
> (b) paragraph 1(2) of Schedule 7 (statement of market value of fixed assets where substantially different from balance sheet amount);
> (c) paragraph 6 of Schedule 7 (miscellaneous disclosures); or
> (d) paragraph 11 of Schedule 7 (employee involvement).'

Companies House **[CL2.59]**

Under *Companies Act 1985, section 246(5)(b)*, notwithstanding anything in *CA 1985, s242(1)*, the directors of the company need not deliver a copy of the directors' report for the year to Companies House.

Re-appointment of directors [CL2.60]

Directors usually retire by rotation and come up for re-appointment every three years.

1985 Table A, Article 73 provides:

> 'At the first Annual General Meeting all the directors shall retire from office, and at every subsequent Annual General Meeting one-third of the directors who are subject to retirement by rotation or, if their number is not three or a multiple of three, the number nearest to one-third shall retire from office; but, if there is only one director who is subject to retirement by rotation, he shall retire.'

Article 74 et seq. then go on to make further and more detailed provision about the retirement and re-appointment of directors.

In companies where the directors and the shareholders are the same individuals, the requirement for retirement by rotation and re-appointment is generally regarded as an unnecessary administrative burden and the Articles are frequently amended to delete such requirements.

Resignation of directors [CL2.61]

Having appointed the first or replacement directors, a director is at liberty to resign at any time. However, resignation rarely features in small Personal Service Companies where the shareholders and directors are the same individuals and, of course, not at all where they are the same single individual.

Where resignation does arise in such companies, however, it often signifies a breakdown of some sort in which all of the activities of the company, its rights and duties, and the way in which it has performed these come to be looked at very closely indeed.

Grounds [CL2.62]

A director might be under a moral duty to attempt to correct any wrongs which in the eyes of that director are taking place but should that not be possible then the major protection which a director has against incurring liability is to resign.

Procedure for resignation [CL2.63]

A director wishing to resign should intimate the resignation in writing to the company. The company secretary should have the director(s) sign Form 288B which is then filed with Companies House.

The resigning director should ensure that this is done.

The removal of directors [CL2.64]

The removal of a director is usually a difficult process requiring professional advice and regard has to be had to both the Articles of Association and the *Companies Acts*.

Removal of a director rarely features in Small Personal Service Companies where the shareholders and directors are the same individuals and, of course, not at all where they are the same single individual.

However, where removal does arise in such companies, it often signifies a breakdown of some sort in which all of the activities of the company, its rights and duties, and the way in which it has performed these come to be looked at very closely indeed. Professional advice should be sought at the earliest possible stage.

The Articles [CL2.65]

1985 Table A, Article 81 provides:

> 'The office of director shall be vacated if–
>
> (a) he ceases to be a director by virtue of any provision of the Act or he becomes prohibited by law from being a director; or
>
> (b) he becomes bankrupt or makes any arrangement or composition with his creditors generally; or
>
> (c) he is, or may be, suffering from mental disorder and either–

- (i) he is admitted to hospital in pursuance of an application for admission for treatment under the Mental Health Act 1983 or, in Scotland, an application for admission under the Mental Health (Scotland) Act 1960,or
- (ii) an order is made by a court having jurisdiction (whether in the United Kingdom or elsewhere) in matters concerning mental disorder for his detention or for the appointment of a receiver, curator bonis or other person to exercise powers with respect to his property or affairs; or

(d) he resigns his office by notice to the company; or

(e) he shall for more than six consecutive months have been absent without permission of the directors from meetings of directors held during that period and the directors resolve that his office be vacated.'

A specific provision in a set of Articles of Association that a director may not be removed is unlikely to be regarded as lawful.

Companies Acts [CL2.66]

Notwithstanding whatever is in the Articles, the shareholders may, by ordinary resolution remove a director (*CA 1985, s303*).

Section 304 of the *Companies Act 1985* gives the director being removed a right to be heard. The director may insist upon his or her objections being circulated to members and may be entitled to be heard at a meeting called for the purpose.

Areas of special consideration for directors [CL2.67]

By virtue of the nature of their office, the activities of directors come in for special consideration in a number of areas which are considered below.

Shares [CL2.68]

Directors are required to notify the company, within five days, if they acquire or cease to have an 'interest' in the shares or debentures of the company.

A director's 'interest' includes that of their spouse or children under the age of majority.

Share options [CL2.69]

Options acquired by a director to buy shares in the company (often known as 'put' options or 'call' options or a combination of the two) are subject to a specific prohibition (*CA 1985, s323*).

Insider dealing [CL2.70]

Dealing in the shares of a company on the basis of 'inside' information is considered to distort the market and is heavily frowned upon. It has now been made the subject of a specific criminal offence (*Criminal Justice Act 1993*).

Loans [CL2.71]

While loans by a shareholder/director to his or her company are relatively unobjectionable, loans by the company to a director are objectionable. As a result of a number of abuses in the 1970s, legislation was introduced broadly prohibiting companies making loans to directors.

Companies Act 1985, section 330 provides, with various exceptions, that a company may not, in relation to a director of that company (or a related group of companies):

- make a loan;
- enter into a guarantee; or
- provide any security.

The exceptions broadly are:

- there is a *de minimus* cut-off point of £5,000 and only provisions made which exceed £5,000 are caught by the prohibition; and
- a company may in effect make a loan to a director by advancing funds to meet expenditure to be incurred for the purpose of enabling the director to perform his or her duties for the company.

  However, to come within this exception:

- prior approval must be given by the company in general meeting or on condition that if approval is not given before the next AGM, any provision made will be discharged within six months; and
- the aggregate amount provided does not exceed a set limit (currently £10,000).

Transactions **[CL2.72]**

Substantial property transactions **[CL2.73]**

Regardless of what the Articles of Association provide, *section 320* of the *Companies Act 1985* provides that, with a number of exceptions, a company and its directors may not enter into what are known as 'substantial property transactions' without the prior approval of the shareholders in general meeting on pain of the transaction being voidable (i.e. capable of being reduced) at the instance of the company (with the director liable to account for any gain made).

'Substantial property transactions' are the lesser of assets having a value (according to Y2K figures) in excess of:

- £5,000; or
- 10% of the company's net asset value (by reference to the last accounts failing which the share capital).

The exceptions (for Y2K) broadly are:

- a *de minimus* limit for transactions below £1,000 (regardless of net asset value); and
- where the value of the asset is less than £50,000 or 10% on net asset value.

Other transactions **[CL2.74]**

In order to control the behaviour of directors, *Companies Act 1985, Part X* provides for an increasing number of prohibitions and disclosures such as:

- prohibition on tax-free payments to directors;
- compensation for loss of office to be disclosed;
- payments made to a director in relation to takeovers to be disclosed;

- service contracts in excess of five years to have prior approval and to be disclosed.

The liability of directors to third parties [CL2.75]

Directors primarily owe their duties to the company as a whole and for any breach of their duties their resulting liability is to the company (whose wishes will be directed by those with control of the company or in the case of insolvency, any insolvency practitioner).

However, there are circumstances in which, notwithstanding the principle of limited liability, directors can become liable *personally*.

The directors of Personal Service Companies are probably less exposed to the possibility of personal liability than many other types of trading company. However, the possibility is there and it is a real one and therefore care should be taken and full insurance carried.

In the event of an IR35 Test resulting in a finding that there is a 'relevant engagement' which is not the subject of an appeal and a payment is 'deemed' then a failure to pay the relevant PAYE and NIC in time could result in interest and penalties and ultimately personal liability on the part of the directors.

Criminal liability [CL2.76]

The limited liability of a company offers no protection against criminal liability.

International offences [CL2.77]

The vast majority of criminal offences require intention on the part of the perpetrator. If, therefore, a director forms the intention of committing a criminal act, then it is stating the obvious to say that the director will be personally liable and that the limited liability of the company will be of no avail even where the intentional act was performed in the best interests of the company.

Strict liability offences **[CL2.78]**

An increasing number of offences involve strict liability (i.e. it is no defence that there was no intention to commit the offence). Some of these apply to the company itself. Traditionally, however, the directors have by statute been held personally liable for such transgressions and it will be of no avail to say that whatever was done was done in the best interests of the company.

Company legislation offences **[CL2.79]**

A raft of *Companies Acts* provisions, on the basis that it is the directors who control the actions of the company, expose the directors to the personal liability of a fine for non-compliance.

Taxation legislation offences **[CL2.80]**

Similarly, a raft of taxation legislation provisions, on the basis that it is the directors who control the actions of the company, expose the directors to the personal liability of a fine for non-compliance.

Insolvency legislation **[CL2.81]**

Personal Service Companies are in a better position than many other types of trading company. Whereas other trading companies often need to speculate (which carries the possibility of failure and insolvency), Personal Service Companies should have a reasonable idea in advance of what their likely income is going to be so that they can match their expenditure and thus avoid insolvency.

However, if an assessment of PAYE and NIC which has been made under the legislation introducing IR35 is not paid, then the insolvency of the company is one of the enforcement options open to the Inland Revenue.

Wrongful trading **[CL2.82]**

The *Insolvency Acts* have introduced the concept of wrongful trading, which requires the directors to keep the financial affairs of their company under review and when the stage is reached where the company is not going to be able to trade out of its difficulties then the company should cease trading. Continuing to trade in those circumstances will be deemed 'wrongful trading' for which the directors may be asked to contribute personally.

This only applies where the company does actually go into insolvent liquidation.

The procedure is that the liquidator asks the court to declare that the directors are liable to make a contribution to the assets of the company.

There is a defence available that the directors have taken all necessary steps to minimise any potential loss to the company's creditors.

In relation to the financial stage which the company had reached and the necessary steps to minimise the loss to creditors, the court has regard to the general knowledge, skill and experience that may reasonably be expected of a person carrying out the same functions as are carried out by that director in relation to the company, and the general knowledge, skill and experience that that director actually has. The extent to which the management obligations of running the company have been complied with will be a relevant factor.

Fraudulent trading **[CL2.83]**

The *Insolvency Acts* have also introduced the concept of fraudulent trading, the concept of which is that if in the course of a winding up of a company it appears that the business of the company has been carried on with the intent to defraud the company's creditors or for any other fraudulent purpose.

The procedure is that the liquidator asks the court to declare that the directors are liable to make a contribution to the assets of the company.

Civil liability **[CL2.84]**

Negligence 'tort' or 'delect' **[CL2.85]**

The general rule is that company itself is 'vicariously liable' for the actions of an employee in the course of their employment. However, there are circumstances where the directors can be held personally liable.

Contract **[CL2.86]**

The general rule is that where a director enters into a contract as the agent of, and on behalf of, a company then the liability on the contract is that of the company alone and the director is not personally liable.

It is no longer necessary for the other contracting party to satisfy themselves that the director concerned had the necessary authority to so contract and the company can no longer avoid liability on that basis.

However, in order to achieve that protection from personal liability, the director must make it clear that the contract is being entered into on behalf of the company. This is normally done by putting the words 'for and on behalf of PSC Ltd' before the signature of the director or otherwise making that clear when contracting. A failure to do so can make the director personally liable.

The use of company notepaper, commercial paper or cheques without the name of the company on them can all result in the personal liability of the directors signing.

Relief from liability **[CL2.87]**

There is an understandable reluctance on the part of directors to 'stick their neck out' on behalf of the company unless the company gives them some form of comfort and protection.

There is much which can be done in this area although it is a tricky area.

Ratification **[CL2.88]**

Where a director has made a transgression in a minor civil matter then most companies will ratify the actions of the director and assume liability therefor. Ratification is achieved by putting the whole details of the matter and the proposal for ratification before the shareholders by way of ordinary resolution at a general meeting.

Indemnification **[CL2.89]**

It is clearly tempting for directors to ask the company to insert in any contract which they have between them or in the Articles of Association themselves, some sort of general indemnity clause under which the company will hold the director indemnified against all liability of whatsoever nature which the director incurs on behalf of the company.

However, such a general exclusion clause is prohibited by legislation (although not, apparently, an agreement agreeing to reimburse a director in respect of costs incurred by him or her personally where the director is 'acquitted').

Settlement **[CL2.90]**

In practice, such situations often result in a settlement being reached with all parties involved in the course of which the director concerned incurs no personal liability. Provided that it is in the best interests of the company to so settle and the settlement has the necessary agreements then such settlements are not in principle illegal.

Since the shareholders and directors are often the same individuals (or are known to each other) in Personal Service Companies, settlements are normally easy to achieve.

Insurance **[CL2.91]**

It is now possible to obtain directors' indemnity insurance. However, its terms are complex and restrictive.

It is not possible, however, to obtain insurance against the financial consequences of failing the IR35 Test. It is, however, (where there is no conflict of interest) possible to obtain insurance against the cost of fighting an IR35 assessment properly and this is recommended.

Directors' disqualification **[CL2.92]**

The relevant legislation is now to be found in the *Company Directors Disqualification Act 1986*.

Disqualification can arise from a number of circumstances including where:

- a person is convicted of an indictable offence in connection with the promotion, formation, management, or liquidation of a company;
- a person is in persistent default of his duties under the *Companies Acts* to file documents with the Registrar of Companies;
- there has been wrongful trading;
- there has been fraudulent trading;
- the person is shown to be unfit to be involved in the management of a company which might involve:
    - any misfeasance or breach of any fiduciary or other duty by the director in relation to the company;
    - any misapplication or retention of company funds or property;
    - failure to comply with the requirements to maintain proper accounting records and registers and to prepare and to submit annual returns;
    - in cases of insolvency, the extent of the directors' responsibility for such insolvency; or
    - failing to prepare the statement of affairs following upon receivership or liquidation.

Insolvency practitioners are under an obligation to report what they find in their investigations. However, only the Secretary of State or persons authorised by him can apply for disqualification. A section of the DTI is devoted to the task.

The courts have shown a willingness to adjust or cancel such orders. While an order for disqualification exists, however, the person subject to the disqualification commits a criminal offence if they attempt to become involved in the promotion or flotation of companies or become a director of any company.

CL3 – Controlling the Company

Introduction [CL3.1]

The shareholders control the company. The control of a company is determined by the *Companies Act 1985* and the Articles of Association.

Formal matters which require a decision of the shareholders [CL3.2]

Companies Act 1985 provide, in several areas usually related to the constitution of the company, that the approval of the shareholders to the extent of a specified percentage must be obtained.

It is open for the Articles of Association, if suitably amended, to specify that other areas also require the approval of shareholders in a stated percentage (this is often done by venture capitalists as a condition of their lending).

In relation to any major matter being considered, regard should be had to both *Companies Act 1985* and the Articles to see whether the matter requires a shareholders' meeting and approval and, if so, to what extent.

The following are *examples* of matters normally requiring a shareholders' meeting.

- Alteration of the Memorandum of Association.
- Alteration of objects.
- Alteration of the company's name.
- Increase or reduction of share capital.
- Alteration of the Articles of Association.
- Authority re allotment of shares.
- Acquisition by the company of its own shares.
- Annual matters such as:
  - approval of the Accounts, Directors Report and Auditors Report;

- approval of any dividend;
- appointment or removal of directors;
- appointment or removal of auditors
- remuneration of auditors and directors; and
- exemption from audit.

Types of shareholders' meeting [CL3.3]

There is a procedure now whereby the decisions of shareholders can be arrived at by written resolutions. There are essentially two types of shareholders' meeting:

- the Annual General Meeting (AGM) which is held once a year to conduct the formal business of the company; and
- Extraordinary General Meetings (EGM) which can be called at short notice during the year to deal with any urgent formal matters.

Annual General Meetings [CL3.4]

A company need not hold an AGM in the year of incorporation or the following year *provided* that the first AGM is held within eighteen months of the date on incorporation. Thereafter, every company must hold an AGM in each calendar year (except where an elective resolution has been passed overriding this and no more than 15 months must elapse between each AGM (*CA 1985, s366*).

Notice of an AGM [CL3.5]

An AGM requires at least 21 days' clear notice (*CA 1985, s369*) and the company secretary should arrange for notice to be given to:

- all members of the company;
- the directors; and
- the auditors (if any).

Article 39 of *1985 Table A* provides that accidental failure to give notice to a member shall not, of itself, invalidate the meeting (although legal action could later be taken).

Notice must be in writing and detail:

- date, time and place of the meeting;
- the business of the meeting;
- any resolutions to be proposed; and
- details of proxy procedure.

Note, however, that all members entitled to attend and vote at such a meeting may consent in writing to shorter notice.

Resolutions of members at AGMs **[CL3.6]**

Under *Companies Act 1985, sections 376* and *377* allow certain members to give the company written notice of any resolution which the member proposes to move at the next AGM.

In addition, the member has the right to circulate to the members a statement (of not more than one thousand words) with respect to the proposed resolution.The procedure to be followed, including payment of the expenses of the company, is specified in the Act including protection against abuse.

Extraordinary General Meetings **[CL3.7]**

In principle an EGM may be called at any time (unless the Articles provide otherwise). It will either be 'convened' or 'requisitioned'.

An EGM is 'convened' when a number of directors join together and, usually at a Board Meeting, instruct the company secretary to arrange such a meeting. Directors will normally do so upon the request of a shareholder.

Where, however, co-operation is not forthcoming from the directors, shareholders (where they represent more than 10% of the voting share capital of the company) can 'requisition' an EGM by delivering a document known as a 'requisition' to the Registered Office of the company (*CA 1985, s368*).The directors then have 21 days from that date to instruct the company secretary to arrange such a meeting, failing which the requisitioning shareholders may themselves instruct the company secretary to arrange such a meeting and recover any expenses incurred in so doing.

The company secretary does not alone have the power to arrange such a meeting and must be duly authorised to do so by one or other of the above methods.

Notice of Extraordinary Meetings [CL3.8]

The notice for an EGM depends upon the type of resolution (see **CL3.9** below) will be involved at the meeting. Some resolutions require special notice of 28 days. A special resolution requires at least 21 days' clear notice whilst an ordinary resolution requires at least 14 days' clear notice.

The company secretary should arrange for notice to be given to:

- all members of the company;
- the directors; and
- the auditors (if any).

Article 39 of *1985 Table A* provides that accidental failure to give notice to a member shall not, of itself, invalidate the meeting (although legal action could later be taken).

Notice must be in writing and detail:

- date, time and place of the meeting;
- the business of the meeting;
- any resolutions to be proposed; and
- details of proxy procedure.

Note, however, that members holding a certain percentage of the voting share capital issued (usually not less than 95% but sometimes reducible to 90%) may consent to an EGM being called at shorter notice.

Resolutions [CL3.9]

Special notice resolutions [CL3.10]

Certain events are considered so significant that *Companies Act 1985* provides for special notice for resolutions concerning them.

In the case of private limited companies these are:

- a resolution to remove a director (*CA 1985, s303*); and
- a resolution to remove an auditor or appoint an auditor other than that retiring (*CA 1985, s391A*).

Such resolutions must be lodged with Companies' House.

The period of notice for such resolutions (which cannot be reduced) is 28 days.

Special resolutions [CL3.11]

Certain events are designated in the Companies Acts to require the approval of at least 75% of the votes. These are special resolutions and they must be lodged with Companies House.

The period of notice for such resolutions (unless reduced – see **CL3.8** above) is 21 days.

Elective resolutions [CL3.12]

Companies Act 1989, section 116 introduced a new provision into *CA 1985, s379A* called elective resolutions.

Elective resolutions require the consent of *all* members entitled to vote. The notice must state the terms of the resolution and the fact that it is an elective resolution. Such resolutions must be lodged with Companies House. Once agreed, an elective resolution can be revoked by a simple ordinary resolution.

Essentially, in an attempt to make life easier for private (as opposed to public) companies elective resolutions allow the company to elect to dispense with certain provisions of the *Companies Acts*, as detailed below.

Annual General Meetings [CL3.13]

Companies may, before 30 September in any year, pass an elective resolution dispensing with the need to hold an AGM in that year or in any subsequent year until the elective resolution is either revoked or ceases to have effect.

However, any member may require that an AGM be held by giving notice to that effect to the company not later than three months prior to the end of the year.

Laying of Accounts **[CL3.14]**

A company must prepare proper Accounts for its members. Companies may, at any time not less than 28 days before the end of the period allowed for delivery of the accounts to Companies House, pass an elective resolution dispensing with the need to *lay* the accounts before the members in general meeting in that year or in any subsequent year until the elective resolution is either revoked or ceases to have effect. Instead the Accounts and reports will be *sent* to the members. However, any member may require that the accounts be laid before an AGM.

Auditors **[CL3.15]**

Where the company chooses to have auditors, an elective resolution can be passed to dispense with the need for the auditors to be re-elected annually.

Allotment of shares by directors **[CL3.16]**

The authority of the directors to allot shares could formerly run for a period not longer than five years (*CA 1985, s80*) but an elective resolution may now be passed giving the directors such authority for any, even an indefinite, period.

Extraordinary General Meetings **[CL3.17]**

An elective resolution can be passed reducing the percentage of shareholders' consent to short notice for an EGM from 95% but not below 90%.

Extraordinary resolutions **[CL3.18]**

Extraordinary resolutions require the approval of at least 75% of the votes.

The period of notice for such resolutions (unless reduced) is 14 days. Such resolutions must be lodged with Companies House.

Ordinary resolutions [CL3.19]

Ordinary resolutions require 50% approval.

Such resolutions do not normally require to be lodged with Companies House (except those altering the terms of the Memorandum of Association).

The period of notice for such resolutions (unless reduced) is 14 days.

Resolution	Notice	Majority	Companies House Filing
Special Notice	28 days	75%	Yes
Special	21 days*	75%	Yes
Elective	21 days*	100%	Yes
Extraordinary	14 days*	75%	Yes
Ordinary	14 days*	50%	No**

* This period of notice may be reduced if the requirements for shortening are met.
**Except where altering the Memorandum of Association.

Written resolutions [CL3.20]

Companies Act 1989, section 113 introduced into *CA 1985, ss381* and *382* a procedure whereby – except in relation to the AGM – any matter which could be dealt with by the company in general meeting may be done without such a meeting and without notice provided that all of the members entitled to attend and vote at such a meeting sign a written resolution.

This procedure can be used for all types of resolution except those which the *Companies Acts* specify as requiring special notice. Note also that additional requirements arise where the company has auditors who are also entitled to notice.

Such written resolutions are as effective as resolutions passed at general meetings. A copy of the signed written resolution must be kept in the same way as the minutes of meetings and, if necessary, filed with Companies House.

Proxies [CL3.21]

In the case of a company having a share capital, *Companies Act 1985, section 372* provides that every notice must contain a statement that a member entitled to attend and vote is entitled to appoint one or more proxies to attend and, on a poll, to vote instead of the member and that a proxy need not be a member of the company.

While such a proxy may vote generally, they may not vote on a show of hands (with the single exception of a show of hands on the demand for a poll).

The appointment of a proxy must be in writing and lodged with the Registrar of Companies at least 48 hours prior to the meeting.

Representatives [CL3.22]

It sometimes happens that a shareholder is in fact a company. *Companies Act 1985, section 375* allows such a shareholder to appoint a 'representative'. Any such representative is entitled to the same powers as an individual member including the right to vote. No prior lodging of written authorisation is required by a representative.

Quorums [CL3.23]

A meeting needs a quorum (throughout the meeting) in order to be properly constituted.

Section 370(4) of the *Companies Act 1985* formerly provided that (unless the Articles of Association provide otherwise) any two members personally present constitute a quorum, although provision is now also made for single member companies.

In the case of a single member company, it would be prudent to amend the Articles in line with these regulations.

Voting [CL3.24]

The meeting will be presided over by a Chairman.

During the meeting voting is normally done on a show of hands (although proxies cannot participate in these).

It is possible for those present (in the form of the Chairman or any two members or any member holding more than 10% of the issued shares) to demand a poll upon which a vote by a show of hands (at which proxies can vote) will be taken.

In the event of a poll, a formal count is taken with each member normally having a vote for every share held.

Recording [CL3.25]

Companies Act 1985, sections 382 and *383* provide for the keeping of minutes of proceedings of all general meetings, board meetings and managers' meetings (where applicable). The company secretary or some other person is normally appointed to keep the minutes of the meeting.

After the meeting, the minutes are normally typed up, checked and signed by the Chairman. Any resolutions required to be filed with Companies House are so filed.

The minutes are to be kept at the Registered Office and must be made available for inspection (and, on production of a fee, copied) by any member.

Simplifying the procedure [CL3.26]

It is an identifiable feature of practice that where the shareholders and directors of a small private company are the same individuals (as is often the case in Personal Service Companies), then some of the formalities tend to be ignored. A major casualty of this tendency has been the formal AGM.

Proposals are being examined at the moment to make the AGM easier by, for example, having the AGM in the form of an E-mail conference. However, an AGM remains a legal requirement at present and is likely to remain so in the future no matter what form reforms allow it to take.

In the past, a failure to observe that legal requirement has had little in the way of practical consequences. That, however, may change as a result of the legislation and a failure by a Personal Service Company to observe the legal requirements relating to meetings could well turn out to be one of the factors relied upon by the Inland Revenue in relation to the employment/self-employment test.

CL4 – Maintaining the Legal Structure of the Company

Altering the Memorandum of Association [CL4.1]

The Memorandum of Association is one of the documents which makes up the constitution of a company (the other is the Articles of Association) and while the Articles of Association essentially regulate affairs within the company, the Memorandum of Association is the document which essentially regulates the relationship of the company with those outside the company.

Indeed, so important and fundamental is the Memorandum of Association to the constitution of a company that the *Companies Act 1985, section 2(7)* prohibits the alteration of any of the conditions contained in the Memorandum except in accordance with that Act.

Of course, the conditions which at the time of incorporation suit a company as regards its relationship with the outside world may not necessarily remain those which suit a company as it develops and therefore, although a fundamental and important document, there has to be a procedure for altering the Memorandum of Association. The procedures for altering the main sections of the Memorandum are considered below.

The name of the company [CL4.2]

A company is entitled to change its name either by written resolution of *all* its members or by a special resolution (*CA 1985, s28*).

This special resolution must be sent to the Registrar of Companies within 15 days of it being passed together with the appropriate fee (currently £10).

The change of name will be valid once the Registrar of Companies has issued a Certificate of Incorporation on change of name.

Compulsory change **[CL4.3]**

Where a company has achieved registration of a name which, upon reflection, in the opinion of the Secretary of State is the same as or too like a name:

- appearing at the time of the registration in the registrar's index of company names; or
- which should have appeared in that index at that time,

then *Companies Act 1985, section 28(2)* empowers the Secretary of State, in writing, within twelve months of that time, to direct the company to change its name within such period as he may specify or extend.

Where a company has achieved registration of a name and it later appears to the Secretary of State that misleading information has been given for the purpose of a company's registration with a particular name, or that undertakings or assurances have been given for that purpose and have not been fulfilled, then *Companies Act 1985, section 28(3)* empowers the Secretary of State to direct the company in writing within five years of the date of registration, to change its name within such period as he may specify or extend.

Under *Companies Act 1985, section 26* any officer who fails to comply with a direction of the Secretary of State made under *section 28* is liable to a fine and, for continued contravention, to a daily default fine (*CA 1985, s28(5)*).

CA 1985, s28 **[CL4.4]**

The change of name by a company is regulated by *Companies Act 1985, section 28*.

Special rules apply in the case of companies seeking an exemption from using the word 'limited' but for most other companies *section 28* provides that a company may change its name by special resolution.

Where a company changes its name then *section 28(6)* goes on to direct that the Registrar of Companies shall (subject to the prohibition of registration of certain names contained in *CA 1985, s26*) enter the new name on the register in place of the former name, and shall issue a Certificate of Incorporation altered to meet the circumstances of the case. The change of name has effect from the date on which the altered certificate is issued. Note that the Registered Number of the company does not change.

Companies Act 1985, section 28(7) also provides that a change of name by a company under this section does not affect any rights or obligations of the company or render defective any legal proceedings by or against it. In addition, any legal proceedings that might have been continued or commenced against it under its former name may be continued or commenced against it under its new name.

Consequential changes **[CL4.5]**

Certain consequential actions must be taken following the change of a company name.

- Change the company name displayed outside all company offices.
- Notify company bankers, auditors, accountants, solicitors etc.
- Change company notepaper.
- Change company invoices, order forms etc.
- Change company bank account details.
- Amend all other stock of company documentation including the Memorandum and Articles of Association.

The objects of the company **[CL4.6]**

A company is entitled to change the objects for which it has been formed and this may be done by way of special resolution (*CA 1985, s4*). This special resolution must be sent to the Registrar of Companies within 21 days of it being passed.

Note that within 21 days of the date of the passing of the special resolution the holders of the remaining 15% of the membership (provided that they have not consented to or voted for the amendment) may apply to the courts to have the alteration cancelled (*CA 1985, s5*). Any such objection should be notified to Companies House forthwith.

Where the special resolution has been filed with the Registrar of Companies then this objection should also be filed with the Registrar.

Under *Companies Act 1985, section 6(3)*:

> 'If a company makes default in giving notice or delivering any document to the registrar of companies as required by [s6(3)(1)], the company and every officer of it who is in default is liable to a fine and, for continued contravention, to a daily default fine.'

The Registered Office [CL4.7]

In the Memorandum of Association it is only necessary to specify the country in which the company is registered. It is not competent for a company to seek to place its new Registered Office outside the country of incorporation (for which the only solution at present is re-incorporation in that other country).

Within that country, however, a company is entitled to change its Registered Office with very little formality (*CA 1985, s287*).

This change must be intimated to the Registrar of Companies on Form 287.

Under *Companies Act 1985, section 348(2)*:

> 'If a company does not paint or affix its name as required [in s348(1)], the company and every officer of it who is in default is liable to a fine; and if a company does not keep its name painted or affixed as so required, the company and every officer of it who is in default is liable to a fine and, for continued contravention, to a daily default fine.'

Under *Companies Act 1985, section 351*, failure to mention in legible characters in all business letters and order forms of the company, the address of the registered office will result in the company and any officer that has authorised it being liable to a fine.

The liability of the company [CL4.8]

The liability of a company requires to be either limited (by shares or by guarantee) or unlimited and this status will, in the first instance, be fixed by this clause when the company is incorporated. That status can, however, to a certain extent be altered.

So far as companies of limited liability are concerned, there is no provision in the *Companies Acts* for a company limited by shares to change its status to a company limited by guarantee or for a company limited by guarantee to change its status to a company limited by shares. There is, however, provision for a company to change its liability between limited and unlimited and vice versa.

A company whose liability is limited can change itself into a company whose liability is unlimited with the written consent of all the members of the company and a statutory declaration to that effect by the directors of the company (*CA 1985, s49*). An undated copy of the Memorandum of Association must be sent to the Registrar of Companies together with the appropriate fee (currently £20).

A company whose liability is unlimited can change itself into a company whose liability is limited by means of a special resolution ((which requires the approval of 75% of its members) which should also state whether the limitation is to be by way of shares or guarantee (*CA 1985, s51*). An undated copy of the Memorandum of Association must be sent to the Registrar of Companies together with the appropriate fee (currently £20).

The share capital of the company [CL4.9]

The authorised (or 'nominal') share capital of the company (and the number of shares that sum is divided into) will be fixed by this clause when the company is incorporated. However, provided that the Articles of Association give the company the power to do so then the capital of the company can to some extent be altered.

Shares can be:

- increased – by ordinary resolution which, together with Form 123 must be lodged with the Registrar within 15 days (*CA 1985, s121*);
- divided or subdivided – by way of ordinary resolution which, together with Form 122 must be lodged with the Registrar within one month (*CA 1985, s121*);
- consolidated – by way of ordinary resolution which, together with Form 122 must be lodged with the Registrar within one month (*CA 1985, s121*);
- redeemed or cancelled – by way of ordinary resolution which, together with Form 122 must be lodged with the Registrar within one month (*CA 1985, s121*);
- converted or re-converted from stock – by way of ordinary resolution which, together with Form 122 must be lodged with the Registrar within one month (*CA 1985, s121*).

- reduced – by way of a special resolution (*CA 1985, s135*) which, once approved by the courts, a copy of the court order must be lodged with the Registrar within one month.

The subscribers of the company **[CL4.10]**

The names of the subscribers cannot be altered.

Intimation **[CL4.11]**

As might be expected, given the fundamental importance of the Memorandum of Association, any changes thereto require to be intimated.

As indicated above, any changes to the Memorandum of Association require to be intimated to the Registrar of Companies. Furthermore, *Companies Act 1985, section 18*, further requires that a copy of the Memorandum suitably altered to reflect the change should be sent to the Registrar of Companies.

A company and any officer in default of *CA 1985, s18* shall be liable to a fine.

Under *Companies Act 1985, section 711(1)(b)*, the Registrar must publish in the Gazette:

> '...any document making or evidencing an alteration in a company's memorandum or articles'

and accordingly upon receipt the Registrar will intimate for the company concerned the date of receipt and a description of the document.

Members of the company are, of course, likely to have received intimation as part of the procedure for change and further intimation in the publication in the Gazette and therefore intimation to them is not required. *Companies Act 1985, section 20* provides however, that once a change has been made, anyone (including members – *CA 1985, s19(1)*) who requests a copy of the company's Memorandum of Association will be sent a copy which reflects the changes.

A failure to properly intimate any such changes can have certain legal consequences for the company (*CA 1985, s42*) in that a company may not rely as against 'other persons', upon the happening of certain events (defined to include changes in the Memorandum of Association) if those events have not been officially notified.

Subsequent issue or allotment of shares [CL4.12]

A company will often have made an initial issue or 'allotment' of shares upon incorporation or very shortly after the first Board Meeting and the shareholding pattern (including control of the company) will have been set for the company then and for the foreseeable future.

It may happen, however, that a company later wishes to alter that shareholding pattern by issuing more shares. In these circumstances, as well as the usual considerations, a number of new consideration arise which were not there during the initial allotment of shares. Principally these are due to the fact that those who received their shares in the initial allotment may now have a number of entrenched rights which the company must be careful not to interfere with when making any subsequent allocation of shares.

Therefore, when contemplating the subsequent allocation of shares by a company the company secretary must consider:

- authorised share capital of the company;
- authority of the directors to issue shares; and
- rights of existing shareholders.

The importance of observing these requirements, apart from a desire to follow the law and to do things correctly, lies in the fact that in the event of any subsequent disputes arising in the company those holding shares in relation to which these procedures have not been followed then a court could later disqualify them as shareholders.

The authorised share capital of the company [CL4.13]

In a subsequent allotment of shares the first step the company secretary will need to take is to examine the Memorandum of Association to see what the *authorised* (sometimes also called the 'nominal') share capital of the company is. The total allotment (both initial and subsequent) must not exceed the total authorised share capital (although it is possible, if necessary, to later alter the Memorandum of Association so as to vary the authorised share capital of the company – see **CL4.9** above).

The authority of directors to issue shares [CL4.14]

Having ascertained that the proposed subsequent allotment is within the total limit of the authorised share capital of the company, the company secretary should then check that the directors have the authority to make the proposed allotment of shares.

This is not a power which the directors automatically have in law. Indeed, *Companies Act 1985, section 80* specifically provides that the directors may *not* issue 'relevant securities' (a term which includes any shares) unless authorised to do so. Accordingly, the company secretary must check that the directors have the power to issue shares, a power which can be given either under the Articles of Association or by way of an ordinary resolution passed by the company in general meeting.

The standard *1985 Table A* Articles do not give this power to the directors and therefore a modification is often made in order to do so. However, under *Companies Act 1985, section 80*, such authority given in the Articles must state the maximum period of the authority which must not exceed five years.

It may be that although the directors had the power to make an initial allotment of shares that power, if more than five years old, has lapsed and in which case will be required to be renewed.

The rights of existing shareholders [CL4.15]

Where it is decided to issue more shares later in the life of the company and at a time when the company already has existing shareholders then clearly those existing shareholders have rights and expectations which they do not wish to see disturbed.

> Example
>
> A company has an authorised share capital of £1,000 divided into 1,000 ordinary shares of £1 each. If, 2 shares were issued on incorporation and 98 issued after the first Board meeting in circumstances in which shareholder A has 55 ordinary shares. Clearly, in those circumstances by holding 55% of the issued share capital, shareholder A effectively controls the company through having, at any vote, a majority of the issued shares.

However, were the directors decide to issue another 100 shares and to allot them all to shareholder B (who, say, already held 2 shares) then the total number issued shares would be 200 of which shareholder A would hold 55 and shareholder B would hold 101, effectively giving shareholder B control (51%) of the company through having, at any vote, a majority of the issued shares. Clearly, shareholder A might not be happy about having what he saw as his right to control the company usurped and losing control of the company in this way and there are a number of circumstances in which that situation is controlled.

1985 Table A, if adopted in its original form, does not specifically cater for this situation. However, under *Companies Act 1985, sections 89–96* gives existing shareholders what are known as 'pre-emptive' rights.

Section 89 provides that a company proposing to allot ' equity securities' (defined in *s94* to include shares) must offer them to existing shareholders on a pre-emptive basis.

Section 90 specifies the method of communication of the pre-emption offer to the existing shareholders.

Many private companies, however, prefer not to rely on the *Companies Acts* and prefer instead to make their own arrangements.

It is in fact possible when the company is giving the directors the power to issue shares, either in the Articles or by way of ordinary resolution, to include within that power the right to ignore pre-emptive rights altogether. This right is expressly recognised by *section 89(1)*.

Most private companies, however, prefer to modify their Articles of Association instead, so as to include specific pre-emptive rights which are even stricter. For example, the modified Articles might provide:

> 'Any new shares which the company proposes to issue shall first be offered by notice (i.e. in writing) to the existing members of the public in proportion (as nearly as fractions will allow) to the number of existing shares respectively held by them.
>
> The notice must specify the number of shares offered and the period (being not less than 14 days) within which the offer, if not accepted, will be deemed to be declined. The notice shall further invite each member to state in his or her

reply the number of additional shares (if any) in excess of their proportional shares which they desire to purchase.

If all the members do not take up their proportional entitlement in full then any shares not so accepted will be used to satisfy the requests (if any) for additional shares in proportion (as nearly as fractions will allow) to the number of shares already held by them, provided that no member shall be obliged to take more shares than they have applied for.

Where any shares cannot be issued without using fractions then those shares shall be offered to existing members in that class by lots drawn as the directors see fit. Any shares not taken up in accordance with the foregoing shall be under the control of the directors provided that they shall not be disposed of to allotees on terms more favourable than the terms offered to the existing members.'

Checklist **[CL4.16]**

1. Check Memorandum of Association for the authorised share capital of the company.

Does the amount of further share capital which the Board meeting has now decided to issue exceed the total authorised share capital of the company?

If the answer is YES:
Arrange for the Memorandum of Association to be altered to increase the authorised share capital of the company. Note that in the event of the authorised share capital of a company being increased, a copy of that resolution and Form 123 must reach Companies House within 15 days of it being passed.

If the answer is NO:
Proceed to point 2.

2. Check the Articles of Association for the power on the part of directors to issue the company's authorised share capital.

Do the Articles currently give the Directors a valid power to issue more of the Authorised Share Capital of the Company?

If the answer is YES:
Proceed to point 3.

If the answer is NO:
Arrange for a general meeting of the company to be held at which an ordinary resolution will be tabled giving the directors the power to issue the shares. Note that the any ordinary resolution giving, varying, revoking, or renewing an authority to allot shares must be delivered to Companies House within 15 days of being passed.

3. Check the application of pre-emptive rights under either the Articles of Association or, if there is no specific provision there, under the Companies Act 1985 sections 89–96.

Have the new shares first been offered in writing in the appropriate manner to the existing shareholders?

If the answer is YES:
Proceed to the procedure for the subsequent issue or allotment of shares.

If the answer is NO:
The company secretary must ensure that this is now done properly and that the pre-emptive rights are respected.

Procedure [CL4.17]

A company is not required to keep a register of the shares issued or allotted but companies may nevertheless find it convenient to do so.

For any subsequent issue of shares (in exactly the same way as any initial issue of shares) the relationship between a member and the company in which they hold shares is essentially one of contract (albeit a contract heavily influenced by terms implied by statutes such as the *Companies Act 1985*). Technically, therefore (although this is often not observed in practice in the case of small private companies) the contract should be arrived at in the usual manner of offer and acceptance with, in the case of England and Wales, consideration.

See further allotment of shares at **CL4.12** above.

Transfer of issued shares [CL4.18]

After the desired shareholding pattern of the company has been set and the shares have been issued either initially or subsequently, events may later lead to some persons leaving the company and other persons joining the company. Where those persons are, or are to become, shareholders then a transfer of shares by purchase and sale or gift may be needed.

Just as in the issue or subsequent allotment of shares (see **CL4.12** and **CL4.17** above), those involved in a private company are usually anxious to control the transfer of shares so that they do not arrive at a situation where an unknown and perhaps hostile person is a shareholder in their company.

The transfer of property requires a proper instrument of transfer. Although a variety of forms can be used, since the transfer of shares is a transfer of property the transaction is subject to stamp duty and, therefore, a Stock Transfer Form which covers the aspects of both the transfer and the stamp duty at one and the same time will usually be used.

Restrictions on transfer [CL4.19]

The transfer of shares is dealt with in *1985 Table A* by *Articles 23–28.*

> **Article 23**
> The instrument of transfer may be in any usual form or in any other form which the directors may approve and shall be executed by or on behalf of the transferor and, unless the share is fully paid, by or on behalf of the transferee.
>
> **Article 24**
> The directors may refuse to register the transfer of a share which is not fully paid to a person of whom they do not approve and they may refuse to register the transfer of a share on which the company has a lien.
>
> They may also refuse to register a transfer unless–
> (a) it is lodged at the office or at such other place as the directors may appoint and is accompanied by the certificate for the shares to which it relates and such other evidence as the directors may reasonably require to show the right of the transferor to make the transfer;

(b) it is in respect of only one class of shares; and
(c) it is in favour of more than four transferees

Article 25
If the directors refuse to register a transfer of a share, they shall within two months after the date on which the transfer was lodged with the company send to the transferee notice of the refusal.

Article 26
The registration of transfers of shares or of transfers of any class of shares may be suspended at such times and for such periods (not exceeding thirty days in any year) as the directors may determine.

Article 27
No fee shall be charged for the registration of any instrument of transfer or other document relating to or affecting the title to any share.

Article 28
The company shall be entitled to retain any instrument of transfer which is registered, but any instrument of transfer which the directors refuse to register shall be returned to the person lodging it when notice of the refusal is given.

Checklist **[CL4.20]**

✓ Following receipt of the consideration (if any) the transferor gives the transferee a signed Stock Transfer Form and the Share Certificate(s).

✓ The transferee pays the stamp duty in respect of the Stock Transfer Form (currently, at a rate of 50p per £100) within 30 days of the Form's execution of the Form. In certain circumstances, certain transactions may by subject to a rate of duty as adjudicated upon by the Inland Revenue Stamp Office, at a fixed rate of 50p or may be exempt. (Note that there are penalties for non-compliance).

✓ The transferee presents the Stock Transfer Form (stamped or certified) together with the Share Certificate they have been given to the company secretary and request a transfer and issue of a new Share Certificate in their name.

✓ The company secretary checks the Articles to see if there are any special provisions relating to the transfer of shares and if so whether these have been complied with. If it is not then the transfer will be refused and the transferee will be advised of this fact.

- ✓ The company secretary checks that the Share Certificate presented is valid. If it is not then the transfer will be refused and the transferee will be advised of this fact.
- ✓ The company secretary will check that the Stock Transfer Form in the correct form. If it is not then the transfer will be refused and the transferee will be advised of this fact.
- ✓ The company secretary must ensure that any further requirements under the Articles (such as that any transfer requires the approval of the directors who are entitled to refuse any transfers that exists in *1985 Table A*) are complied with.

Management

Having started up and established a Personal Service Company, the next task – largely the responsibility of the appointed directors regardless of who the individual shareholders are – is to see to the proper running of that Personal Service Company.

For Personal Service Companies, their most important task (whether for income or expenditure) relates to their contracts – the life-blood of a Personal Service Company. We therefore consider first in this section the manner in which a Personal Service Company might go about contracting.

The contracts of a Personal Service Company have, however, been given a certain added piquancy by the introduction of the legislation implementing IR35 which in the first instance concentrates upon the contracts of Personal Service Companies to determine whether or not those contracts are 'relevant engagements'.

Having, over the year, entered into its contracts (whether for income or expenditure) the Personal Service Company is required to draw a balance and produce a set of accounts. The Personal Service Company is also required to make a number of returns and in that respect the administrative burden upon Personal Service Companies (in common with all other private limited companies) is at present a weighty one. We consider that burden, in outline, in this section.

CM1 – Commencing Trading

Introduction [CM1.1]

Commencing trading is often, after suitable preparations have been made, the subject of a conscious decision. It may or may not involve the first signing of a contract by the company but it will certainly involve the first implementation of a contract by the company. However, the precise point in time at which trading commences can sometimes be surprisingly difficult to identify. For example, what the taxpayer might interpret as a preparatory capital transaction the Revenue or the courts might interpret as trading.

The courts have developed a number of tests or 'badges' of trade which are considered below.

In addition, identifying the correct point of trading can have important ramifications in relation to the individual taxes involved and we consider this point below generally as regards VAT, PAYE, NIC, benefits, and Corporation Tax.

Furthermore, whereas once a company commenced trading and that was an end of that consideration, for Personal Service Companies the advent of the legislation implementing IR35 has meant that in future the concept of commencing trading must be addressed by such companies not just generally but *in relation to each and every contract.*

This, the IR35 Test, is the main impact of the legislation and is considered in detail at **Chapter CM3** below.

It is important to appreciate the distinction between a company incorporating and a company trading.

When a company incorporates, that means the company is in existence (defined by registration) but it does not mean that the company is trading. Such companies are known as dormant companies. A dormant company is a company which has not carried out a trade or business throughout the accounting period concerned. In practice, the dormant status of a company will be looked at as a matter of common-sense and a significant factor applied in practice is that it has no income (Inland Revenue

Corporation Tax Manual CT 3059). It can often be a practical advantage to incorporate a company and in the name of that company perform all the pre-trading tasks necessary before the company begins to trade.

For tax purposes, it is the concept of the company *trading*, rather than the company incorporating, which is the significant event. For example, a company beginning to trade is defined (*Income and Corporation Taxes Act 1988, section 12*) as the beginning of an accounting period and it is also the point in time under Corporation Tax self-assessment at which a UK company falls under an obligation to make disclosure to the Inland Revenue.

Trade has been defined, in a somewhat tautologous way, as 'every trade, manufacture, adventure or concern in the nature of trade' but just when a trade comes into existence has, however, generated a number of cases for sole traders, partnerships and companies alike. It is often claimed that whatever has been done was a capital transaction, a one-off event, or in the nature of a hobby. As a result, the cases have established what are known as the 'badges of trade' any one of which will be recognised as pointing towards the existence of a trade. These are:

- the subject matter of the transaction;
- the period of ownership of the asset;
- the frequency of the transactions;
- any supplementary work;
- the circumstances of any realisation; and
- the motive for the transaction.

In days gone by, considerable attention was devoted to the commencement of trading for tax purposes but under modern conditions circumstances are largely neutral as to the date for the commencement of trading and the completion of an accounting period twelve months later.

In most trading situations, for most companies, it will be entirely apparent when trading begins – it will often be the occasion of a small celebration. In the case of a Personal Service Company, the moment that trading begins will probably be regarded as the first day on which the company begins working for and earning from the client.

A company can, in fact, have more than one trade where its activities are sufficiently different from each other. Thus, a Personal Service Company which, for example, essentially provides coding and provides that in many different ways to many different clients will have only one trade but if that company also built and sold computer hardware then that might be regarded as a separate trade. As is apparent from the company Tax Return, the expenses of one trade may be offset only against the profits of that trade and keeping the accounting of the two trades separate often becomes so complicated that in practice it is better to have two companies for the two trades.

Commencing trading for the first time is an important consideration for most companies. In particular, those companies will want to ensure that the systems which they have spent time building up begin to operate at the same time as trading commences.

VAT is a special case in this respect. The company might have voluntarily registered for the purposes of VAT (and the VAT on pre-trading expenditure picked up) in which case it is important for the company to ensure that the system is working for VAT to be carried forward and charged on its very first sales as trading commences. A failure to do so may mean that the company itself has to pay the VAT element to Customs & Excise even where that VAT element has not been recovered from the client.

Where the company is not registered for VAT then it is a question of watching in order to ascertain the point in time at which the turnover threshold which requires compulsory registration for the purposes of VAT is passed. A failure to do so can result in the company being liable for back-tax, interest and penalties.

PAYE, NIC and benefits will also be a consideration in this respect. It is possible that the directors have been paying themselves a salary during the preparation period. If so, the systems should be in force and it is a question of carrying them forward. It is possible, however, that an employee is being taken on as trading commences or that the directors only begin to pay themselves as trading commences.

If so, then it is important that the systems are in place and operating properly from the outset. This area is now very (perhaps unnecessarily) complicated. The company should have a clear and defined remuneration package in relation to which benefits are identified, the PAYE system applied and the NIC system operated. A failure to do so can again result in back-tax, interest and penalties.

Corporation Tax will also be a major consideration for companies. It is important that all income and expenditure is properly dealt with from the commencement of trading and that the systems to allow that to happen are in place. Again, if upon a review any discrepancies are discovered then back-tax, interest and penalties can result.

VAT [CM1.2]

Voluntary registration for VAT purposes may already have taken place in which case the business will already:

- be registered for VAT purposes;
- have been supplied with a VAT Number;
- have incorporated that VAT Number on its VAT invoices; and
- be well placed to meet its legal obligation of charging, collecting and accounting for VAT.

However, if voluntary registration has not been applied for, then VAT is something which has to be watched in the early stages of the business as registration approaches. The point to watch, however, is the point at which the registration threshold is passed because if the company does not register and charge the customer VAT at that point then not only do penalties exist for the failure to meet this obligation to register but the business may itself become liable for the VAT element. Thus, if Customs and Excise were later to discover that a business has not in fact charged its customers VAT from the correct registration date then they will expect the business to pay that missing VAT (with penalties).

Note that the VAT in question will still be demanded from the business even though the customer has not paid the VAT to the business.

To cater for this situation a 30-day delay has been built into the system.

Example

Taxable supplies reaching the figure of £52,000.

Date upon which supplies exceeded threshold of £52,000	Date by which Form VAT 1 must be submitted	Date upon which registration is effective
31 August	30 September	1 October

Accordingly, on passing the threshold on 31 August the business has until 1 October to get its systems in place and charge its customers VAT.

Corporation Tax [CM1.3]

Commencing trading is less of a problem in relation to Corporation Tax. It will be appreciated that Corporation Tax is assessed by reference to accounting period and one of the criterion (*ICTA 1988, s12*) for determining the commencement of an accounting period for Corporation Tax purposes is whenever the company first comes within the charge to UK Corporation Tax which in turn is an event recognised by starting to trade.

Accordingly, when a Personal Service Company makes the positive decision to commence trading in the UK, then that company (if it does not already do so) will fall within the charge to UK Corporation Tax and an accounting period (by reference to which Corporation Tax will be self-assessed and charged) will have begun.

PAYE, NIC and benefits [CM1.4]

At or about the time that trading commences, the remuneration of those administering the trading is likely to start in earnest.

The company must be prepared to administer the PAYE, NIC and benefits systems. This is now a complicated (perhaps unnecessarily so) matter. Some benefits require to be included in gross pay, others have to have NIC applied to them, and the benefits themselves and the basis for their taxation require to be dealt with.

Benefits are more of a danger for small companies (where members and directors are the same individuals) than for larger companies. The reason for this is that because the few individuals behind the small company tend to regard the company as their own they also tend to regard the assets of the company (a separate legal entity) as their own without fully appreciating the extent to which these are in law regarded as benefits which are subject to taxation.

A compliance review which discovers the taking of numerous benefits without considering the taxation requirements is likely to have most unpleasant consequences. Personal Service Companies may be at particular risk in that respect.

It is for that reason that it is suggested Personal Service Companies adopt – at the outset when they commence trading – a clear and defined remuneration package for the employees (including directors) of the company. This involves the following.

Benefits [CM1.5]

The company must be aware of what benefits are taxable and which of these benefits apply to the remuneration package adopted by the company.

The periodical and year-end requirements of those benefits must be appreciated from the outset and the ultimate responsibility for this rests with the directors.

PAYE [CM1.6]

Some benefits require to be included in gross pay. In any event, gross pay for all employees and directors must be identified from the outset and the PAYE system properly applied.

The company must have a system for dealing with this from the commencement and the ultimate responsibility is that of the directors.

NIC [CM1.7]

The NIC system now applies, in different ways, to both emoluments and benefits and must be applied properly from the outset.

The company must have a system for dealing with this from the commencement and the ultimate responsibility is that of the directors.

CM2 – Contracts

Introduction [CM2.1]

Having commenced trading, a Personal Service Company is likely to do so by signing and them implementing a contract. In general, a Personal Service Company is likely to either contract direct with the client or contract with an agency who in turn will contract with the client.

It remains to be seen whether any difference in approach by the Inland Revenue is detected as between Personal Service Companies contracting with agencies and Personal Service Companies contracting directly with a client.

Contracts between Personal Service Companies and agencies tend to be in the standard form of the agency with little choice given to the Personal Service Company by way of adjustment to the contract or its method of execution.

As a result of the legislation implementing IR35, the contracts of Personal Service Companies are likely to be examined much more closely then ever before. Furthermore, in relation to the IR35 Test, the number of clients, and therefore the number of contracts, is likely to be of major importance.

It is suggested that even where one of the individuals connected with the company provides personal services only for one half-day a week, that that activity be treated as a contract of the company (with VAT applied) and is formally entered into and treated as such. So far as the IR35 Test is concerned, to do such a seemingly small thing might sometimes have consequences in favour of the company which outweighs its apparent significance.

Accordingly, it is recommended that Personal Service Companies pay a great deal more attention to their contracts than they might hitherto have done, and that these contracts be attended with an increasing level of formality and be carefully preserved.

Indeed, it may be prudent for the company to adopt a Register of Contracts so that, should the issue be raised in an IR35 Test, the contracts of the company can be produced neatly tabulated and cross-referenced. Such a step might just later save a Personal Service Company a great deal of time and money.

Contract law [CM2.2]

A large number of legal textbooks have been written on the topic of contract law. It is probably also a subject which takes up as much court time as any other. Nor is it a subject which remains immutable in that contract law tends to evolve with modern commercial conditions.

Despite all that, however, while a contract might be difficult to define in precise terms, it tends to be something which you recognise when you see one. Common-sense goes a long way in contracting. Nevertheless, in matters of importance, independent professional advice should always be taken where possible and the purpose of this section is to set out in outline the main contractual principles applying to Personal Service Contracts so that those involved might better understand the objectives which they are trying to reach with their professional advisers.

No matter where it is entered into, a contract may be reduced to the situation where parties reach agreement on the essential features of their transaction. Different legal systems might have additional requirements but almost all would accept that that, in essence, is what a contract is.

Intention to create legal relations [CM2.3]

Not all agreements result in legal contracts but a general presumption that the parties intend to create a legal contract in business or commercial situations will apply.

The parties [CM2.4]

It should be noted that where the other parties are interested in securing personal services then they might be less concerned about whether those personal services come from the individual or the individual's company. It might, however (and under IR35 is increasingly likely to be) a matter of importance to the individual.

Accordingly, if it is desired that the contract be taken in the name of a Personal Service Company then any piece of paper which is signed should record not the individual but the Personal Service Company as the party to the contract.

The agreement [CM2.5]

Although it has its limitations, contracts are usually analysed in terms of agreement and that in turn usually requires an analysis of offer and acceptance. The position can become complicated when there are a series of counter-offers but essentially when an acceptance meets an offer then a contract arises.

Consideration might be summarised as a benefit gained or detriment suffered by either of the parties. In practice, it is not hard to find in commercial situations so that although it does represent a legal distinction it does not amount to much of a practical distinction.

Offer [CM2.6]

An offer must first of all be distinguished from an invitation to treat – the suggestion that someone is 'interested' is more likely to be regarded as an invitation to treat because the key feature of an offer is that it contemplates acceptance. An offer must be sufficiently definite so as to be capable of acceptance. Having said that, these are only presumptions and in certain circumstances an offer can be made, without words, by implication.

Another essential feature of an offer is that it is communicated – by act or deed – to the party to whom it is made. If complying with the requirement that it contemplates acceptance then, unless qualified in some way, the offer is out there for acceptance unless revoked or withdrawn before acceptance.

Acceptance [CM2.7]

An acceptance, like an offer, must be clear and definite but if unqualified will amount to assent to the offer and may constitute a contract. In practice, many apparent acceptances contain new terms or alter the terms of the offer or are qualified in some other manner which prevents them being an unqualified acceptance and instead makes them a counter-offer (itself inviting acceptance).

Like an offer, an acceptance must be communicated and although silence does not constitute acceptance this may be done by word or deed. An acceptance can in general be withdrawn before it is communicated but once communicated in an unqualified form may constitute a contract.

The battle of the forms [CM2.8]

A particular difficulty increasingly encountered in business in the area of offer and acceptance is what is known as the 'battle of the forms'. Essentially, this arises where all of the parties are using standard pre-printed contracts or conditions so that when exchanged some of their terms are incompatible.

The law in this area is subject to change but the general approach might be described as one where if the parties are satisfied they contracted then the courts will try to glean therefrom the terms of their agreement which might in practice mean the terms of the last form which was communicated and accepted without objection. Again, this is a matter which requires professional advice.

Additional requirements [CM2.9]

It is always necessary to also have regard to where the contract is being made. A complex code of law known as 'private international law' is used to determine where a contract was made and the point can sometimes be of significance. For example, if both parties had premises in Scotland, were meeting in Scotland, and were discussing a contract which required to be carried out in Scotland then (in the absence of any express provision to the contrary) the contract might be regarded as made in Scotland with the contract law of Scotland to apply to that contract.

Where, however, both parties had premises in England, were meeting in England, and were discussing a contract which required to be carried out in England then (in the absence of any express provision to the contrary) the contract might be regarded as made in England with the contract law of England to apply to that contract as the proper law of that contract. England does, in fact, have further requirements and the above would not necessarily be sufficient to constitute a valid contract in England unless there was also what is known as 'consideration'.

A number of European Community and United Nations initiatives are aimed at eliminating or reducing the distinctions relating to the formation of contracts in various countries. Such distinctions are becoming less significant but they do still exist which is one of the reasons why professional advice is advisable.

The formalities [CM2.10]

Under the laws of England and Wales, Scotland or Northern Ireland, provided that the essential requirements above have been met, very little (and, indeed, increasingly less) in the way of formality is required to constitute a contract, even by companies.

So far as companies are concerned, the first question to be addressed is the *substantive* authority to enter into a contract. This normally takes the form of an authorisation from the Board of directors which may be delegated by the Board to the individual director involved. This area, known as the rule of *ultra vires*, used to be an area of difficulty in practice but as a result of a number of recent reforms while disinterested members (if there are any) may raise internally any issue about a lack of substantive authority to enter into a contract, third parties or members of the public entering in good faith into contracts with companies are now protected.

Although it is a matter upon which, again, professional advice should be taken, as a general principle a company can contract in exactly the same manner as an individual. Thus, a person representing a company can enter into a contract with another person by conduct, orally, by a memo, by a letter, by a formal written document or by a deed and all are likely to be equally valid.

So far as companies are concerned, it was formerly a *requirement* that *all* companies have a common seal and for those transactions for which formality was prescribed it was formerly a *requirement* that companies use their common seal. This requirement no longer exists, although a company may still choose to have a common seal if it so wishes.

Where a company has chosen not to have a common seal then documents which are by law required to be executed as deeds may be executed by a company simply having two directors or a director and the company secretary signing the document and expressing in any form of words that it is being executed by the company. If the document additionally makes it clear that it is intended to be a deed then it has effect as a deed on its delivery and it is presumed unless the contrary is shown that the document was delivered upon it being executed.

Accordingly, the result is a dual system whereby if a company is called upon to formally execute a contract then it may do so either in the formal manner prescribed by law for companies or by using the common seal of the company where it has one.

The *Contracts (Rights of Third Parties) Act 1999* recently introduced into the law of England and Wales (such rights were recognised at common law in Scotland) is likely to have far-reaching effects.

So far as Personal Service Companies are concerned who might be dealing with a client through an Agency, the new legislation might turn out to be of considerable significance.

Contracts abroad [CM2.11]

A company which requires to transact business in foreign countries may (for England & Wales but not Scotland), under the *Companies Act 1985, sections 38* and *39*, use a facsimile of its common seal abroad or under its common seal empower others to execute deeds there on behalf of the company.

Under *CA 1985*, a Scottish company can, without any requirement for formality, authorise others to execute abroad on behalf of the company.

If a Personal Service Company envisages any business abroad, therefore, then that is another reason to adopt the use of the common seal.

Commercial paper [CM2.12]

Failure to disclose the company name on commercial papers (which are essentially contracts) can result in personal liability arising on the part of signatories.

If, therefore, a director or a company secretary (or indeed anyone else purporting to act on behalf of the company, e.g. an agent) signs a piece of commercial paper which does *not* mention the company name, then the person signing may be personally liable on that commercial paper.

Data Protection Act 1998 [CM2.13]

Different contracts will have different considerations but in many instances circumstances may arise under which the Personal Service Company should obtain a copy of and an appreciation of the terms of the *Data Protection Act 1998* in relation to its contracts.

Personal Service Company contracts [CM2.14]

A consideration of the specific terms of typical Personal Service Contracts is beyond the scope of this book. However, the following clauses are typically included.

Definitions	Although not strictly part of the contract itself, this section (often seen in England and Wales but less often in Scotland) deserves careful study as it will be used to interpret any ambiguities. It might also cover the scope of the contract and the severability of any terms.
Engagement	This will state the parties and the nature of the engagement and should be carefully checked.
The term	This will state the term or length of the engagement or how that is to be arrived at.
Transfer, assignability	The ability of either party to transfer or assign the benefit of the contract will often be covered.
Obligations of the client	This will state the obligations of the client and will clearly be a major if not vital consideration in any IR35 Test.
Obligations	This will state the obligations of the Personal Service Company and will clearly be a major if not vital consideration in any IR35 Test.

Location	This might become an important clause
Fees, expenses, tax and payment	Clearly another important section.
Confidentiality	This will be a matter of importance to the client and its ambit and significance should be carefully studied and appreciated by all of those in the Personal Service Company
Intellectual property rights	This section will be more important in some contracts than others.
Liability and insurance	This is a crucial clause and it is important that those those behind the company do not sign away its limited liability rights which is one of its few remaining advantages. One of the key methods of preserving that is by providing sufficient insurance cover to satisfy the client.
Enticement	Where the Personal Service Company has employees then this might be a useful clause.
Default, termination	Where a default clause is included its terms must be carefully studied and appreciated and understood in advance. Few contracts of this type run to plan and so any termination provisions must be similarly appreciated.
Governing law	This is a vital clause for there is little point in one party contracting on the basis of what they understand their position to be if a different law is to apply which may produce different results. This clause will also determine where and under what legal system the rights and obligations of the parties can be enforced. Under modern conditions some provisions for Alternative Dispute Resolution is usually included also.
Schedules	The above terms will often be standard on the part of the client or the Personal Service Company and a Schedule is added covering the specific terms applying to any individual projects.

Variation of the contract [CM2.15]

A major difficulty in practice is a tendency on the part of the parties to modify their contract verbally as it progresses without recording that modification in the same manner as the contract itself was recorded. This is something to be avoided.

Policy for executing contracts [CM2.16]

It is advisable for companies to adopt a policy for the execution of the company's contracts. This might involve:

- designated persons as signatories;
- designated methods (with or without seals); and
- a designated method of recording (perhaps a Register of Contracts).

For Personal Service Companies which have only a single member, the position is more complicated. It might be easier in practice for such companies to adopt the use of a common seal. Otherwise, the company secretary, whoever that might be, may have to be involved in the execution of all formal contracts. Note that where a private limited company which has only one member enters into a contract (other than in the ordinary course of business) with that member then the company is obliged (*CA 1985, s41*) to ensure that either the contract is in writing or its terms are recorded in a written memorandum or in the minutes of the first Board of directors meeting held after that contract was entered into. A failure to do so will not affect the validity of the contract itself but may expose the officers of the company to a fine.

For Personal Service Companies which have more than one member and more than one director then the best course of action might be to meet with the company's professional advisers and establish a policy and practice in relation to contracts. There is no reason why a seal should not be used and its use offers certain convenience and advantages. Otherwise two of the directors or a director and company secretary would be formally authorised to sign all the contracts of the company. The contracts of the Personal Service Company formally executed in the agreed manner could be entered in a Register of Contracts and carefully preserved ready to be easily produced in the event of an IR35 Test being called for.

It is important that those involved in Personal Service Companies have an appreciation of what is involved should the company wish, for example, to enter into a transaction relating to land.

Clearly, however, in the majority of cases the contracts entered into by Personal Service Companies will *not* fall into the category of contract which in either England and Wales or Scotland require to be executed with formality.

Nevertheless, just because these contracts do not in law *require* formality of execution does not mean that these contracts cannot be executed by Personal Service Companies and their clients with a degree of solemnity. Such contracts are, after all, the life-blood of a Personal Service Companies and are now of increasing importance. As suggested, a policy for the execution and preservation of the contracts of a Personal Service Company ought to be arrived at.

Contracting directly with the client [CM2.17]

Negotiating a successful contract is an art-form. It is rare that the parties negotiating a contract will meet on a completely equal basis. In the case of Personal Service Companies, only rarely will a Personal Service Company with a pressing need for work meet a client with a pressing need for services.

Ascertaining in advance the strengths and weaknesses of the position and negotiating to a satisfactory conclusion is, as mentioned, an art-form acquired mostly through experience. In many cases, however, having got beyond that stage, there will be a broad meeting of minds between the client and the Personal Service Company. All that remains is to put that broad agreement down in writing in the form of a contract. It is at this stage that the individuals behind a Personal Service Company can create for themselves a lot of advantages or a lot of disadvantages, especially from the point of view of taxation.

In implementing the legislation following on from IR35, the Inland Revenue has already made it very clear that it will not be enough for the client and the individual behind the Personal Service Company to agree between them that the contract between the client and the Personal Service Company will be a contract 'for services' (i.e. self-employment) and not a contract 'of service' (i.e. employment).

While clearly the declared agreement and intention of the parties will be a factor in distinguishing those two categories of employment and self-employment for taxation purposes, the Inland Revenue have made it clear that that factor will only be taken into account where the other factors are neutral. It is, therefore, the other factors which will be largely determinative of whether, under the legislation following IR35, this particular Personal Service Company is taxed as self-employed or employed.

Those factors will be established and reflected in the contract made at this stage and if, therefore, those individuals representing the Personal Service Company take care at this stage to ensure that the contract between the Personal Service Company and the client reflects their true intention then that effort is likely to be rewarded when the time comes for the taxation of the Personal Service Company to be considered.

Whose contract? **[CM2.18]**

Many meetings of the sort mentioned above end with someone saying something along the lines of 'Well, if that is all agreed, shall we have someone put it down in the form of a contract for our signature?' In those circumstances if you can make that 'someone' you (as the individual representing the Personal Service Company) and if your Personal Service Company has a standard form of contract which it has had drawn up for such purposes (and which clearly reflects the desires and intentions of the Personal Service Company) then that will be very advantageous because not only will that fact of itself be a factor pointing to self-employment but what the Personal Service Company has constructed within its standard form contract are likely to be – if that is both the intention and the actuality – factors pointing to self-employment.

Of course, the suggestion that you (as the individual representing the Personal Service Company) draft the contract for the approval of the parties is likely to meet with resistance from the client because they will require to have your draft contract checked by their legal department and they much prefer the easier task of revising their own standard form contract the terms of which they know well rather than the harder task of revising the terms of a contract which they have never seen before. Just who gets to draft the contract is likely to depend upon the relative strength of the parties' bargaining positions but, as indicated above, it is worth pushing for that privilege whenever possible.

Even where the meeting does not grant you the privilege of drafting the contract, it cannot deny you the privilege of revising the contract. Here many Personal Service Companies have drafted standard terms and conditions which they seek to have inserted into the contract en bloc. This, of course, inevitably leads to a conflict (known as the 'battle of the forms' – see **CM2.8** above) between the terms sought to be inserted into the contract by the client and those sought to be inserted into the contract by the Personal Service Company. Indeed, the draft contract is likely to have a clause aimed at preventing such a situation and ensuring the agreement of the parties on signature to their terms taking precedence over any other terms and conditions sought to be inserted.

Even where it does not prove possible for the Personal Service Company to insert the terms it considers important by some standard format it will still prove possible for the Personal Service Company to revise the draft contract presented to them clause by clause. In that respect those negotiating on behalf of a Personal Service Company may wish to bear the following in mind.

Overall position of the client **[CM2.19]**

The client usually wishes to avoid employing the individual supplying the services as an 'employee' with all that that entails. However, the client would quite like to have the individual providing the services (through the commercial vehicle of a Personal Service Company) working exclusively for them, under their control at all times, on their premises throughout, using their equipment, and subject to a number of other terms and conditions (such as excluding substitution).

Overall position of the Personal Service Company **[CM2.20]**

If the Personal Service Company is genuine about being self-employed then it will want to be treated as such with all that that entails. Therefore, the Personal Service Company would quite like:

- to take on work for other clients;
- for they themselves to control the work in question;
- to use their own expensively acquired equipment;
- to work on their own equipment in their own premises, and
- to include or avoid a number of other terms and conditions (such as allowing for substitution).

Negotiating to the end position **[CM2.21]**

The end position arrived at in the contract might be anywhere on the spectrum between the overall position of the client and that of the

Personal Service Company and the end result is likely to depend, as indicated, upon negotiation. For example, those experienced in negotiation are often good at concealing their weakness and in some circumstances although a client might normally insist upon personal service workers being on their premises and although the client's standard contract may provide for that, the client finds themselves in a position where they are not truly bothered where the work is done so long as it is done properly and on time. In those circumstances, the Personal Service Company might secure agreement on a term that the work will be carried out within the premises of the Personal Service Company.

As stated, that might not truly bother the client on this occasion but it might mean a lot to the Personal Service Company as regards the manner in which the company is taxed.

Taxation relevant factors to take into account at the contracting stage **[CM2.22]**

Length of engagement **[CM2.23]**

Short-term contracts are a feature of the world of Personal Service Companies. For the purpose of distinguishing between employment and self-employment, a series of short-term contracts for different clients will be a strong indicator of self-employment.

However, regularly working for the same client could be regarded as a single and continuing contract of employment and even in the case of a series of short contracts or an initial short contract followed by longer contracts, it may be the overall length of the engagement which is considered rather than the length of the individual contracts. Work recorded as being that of the Personal Service Company which has been done for other clients during gap periods or at weekends will be well worthwhile for its importance as a factor indicating the self-employed nature of the Personal Service Company. Also, the Personal Service Company should ensure that any contradictory standard terms are, if possible, removed from the contract.

Exclusivity **[CM2.24]**

The fact that a Personal Service Company works frequently for the same client is not, of itself, likely to be determinative of the distinction between employment and self-employment. However, The fact that a Personal Service Company works for one client is, of itself, likely to be determinative of the distinction between employment and self-employment. Accordingly, a Personal Service Company should ensure that any exclusivity terms are, if possible, removed from the contract. Work recorded as being that of the Personal Service Company which has been done for other clients during gap periods or at weekends will be well worthwhile for its importance as a factor indicating the self-employed nature of the Personal Service Company.

Control – part and parcel of the organisation **[CM2.25]**

This is not a determinative feature for the distinction between employment and self-employment. For example, a ship's captain or a consultant brain surgeon will be an employee even though in the discharge of their functions they are not subject to the direct control of those who employ them. Nevertheless, this is likely in many cases to be a strong factor in making the distinction between employment and self-employment.

For example, if the terms of the agreement simply provide that the Personal Service Company will perform a specific (end-result) task at a specific time for a specific price then that will be a strong pointer towards self-employment.

For example, if the terms of the agreement simply provide that the named individual sent by the Personal Service Company will be directed by a team leader who can assign the individual to any task at any time then that will be a strong pointer towards employment.

However, if the position in question is somewhere inbetween then some effort should go into having the contract reflect the intention and the actuality of the parties. The more that an individual from the Personal Service Company spends all of his or her time within the premises of the client and effectively becomes 'part and parcel' of that organisation the more that will reflect employment.

The more the individual concerned is seen as an independent contractor outwith the organisation the more that will reflect self-employment. In particular, from the point of view of the Personal Service Company, no standard terms or conditions should be left hanging in the contract where they oppose or do not in fact reflect the true intention of the parties.

The right to use a substitute or helper on the task **[CM2.26]**

This is likely in many cases to be a significant factor in making the distinction between employment and self-employment.

For example, if the terms of the agreement simply provide that the Personal Service Company will provide a specified individual only who is not permitted to delegate then that will be a strong pointer towards employment.

For example, if the client has sufficient confidence in the Personal Service Company to feel that any individual employed by that company would be of a sufficient standard to do the job in question then that will be a strong pointer towards self-employment.

However, if the position in question is somewhere inbetween then some effort should go into having the contract reflect the intention and the actuality of the parties and in particular, from the point of view of the Personal Service Company, no standard terms or conditions should be left hanging in the contract where they oppose or do not in fact reflect the true intention of the parties.

Provision of equipment **[CM2.27]**

Many jobs can be performed equally well using the equipment of the client that of the Personal Service Company. Where it involves adding value to an asset of the client then the client may be reluctant to allow any of those assets out of their premises but sufficiently strongly-worded confidentiality terms can often overcome such objections. This aspect may not, therefore, matter too much to the client but it can matter a great deal to the Personal Service Company. To be truly and effectively self-employed a Personal Service Company should have its own equipment and should be using that equipment. The presence of that factor is a strong pointer to self-employment. The absence of that factor is a strong pointer towards employment.

Accordingly, if it is not a critical matter for the client some effort by the Personal Service Company should be put into allowing the work to be done within their own premises and on the expensive equipment which they have purchased for the purpose. Again, care should be taken that no standard terms or conditions are be left hanging in the contract where they oppose or do not in fact reflect the true intention of the parties.

Financial considerations [CM2.28]

This is also likely to be a significant factor in determining the distinction between employment and self-employment. A Personal Service Company which has no assets, does not arrange for any training, and relies totally on what it needs being provided by the client who pays the company an hourly rate is in danger of being treated as employed. A Personal Service Company which purchases equipment, arranges training for its employees, and then goes out into the market seeking (and risking) a financial return on that investment is more likely to be regarded as self-employed. Fixed price contracts will also be a strong indicator of self-employment. The Personal Service Company should keep a careful record of its income and expenditure in this respect and always be in a position to demonstrate how sound management such as working more effectively or reducing expenditure would produce the opportunity to make a profit as this would be an indicator of self-employment. Again clear out of the contract any standard terms or conditions which oppose or do not reflect this aspect.

Right of dismissal [CM2.29]

Where the contract provides that neither party has the right to terminate the contract (other than the common law right following a breach of contract) then this will be largely a neutral factor for it is considered common to have such terms in short-term contracts whether in employment or self-employment.

Employee benefits [CM2.30]

Employees often have a contractual entitlement to expenses, sick pay, holiday pay; pensions and the like, while independent contractors or the self-employed working for a client do not have such contractual entitlements. This factor is not necessarily determinative, however, as short-term contracts for employees often exclude such benefits.

Agencies [CM2.31]

Agencies appear to be a natural development in service industries. To some extent, the rise of agencies in the new technology industries appears to have been encouraged by tax considerations of the very nature which IR35 is now addressing.

When employers in the new technology industries made the shift from long-term contracts to short-term contracts those employers soon discovered that joining and leaving was considerably more trouble-free where those involved were not designated as 'employees'. It was also discovered that if not designated as employees then certain advantages in terms of PAYE and NIC accrued to the employers.

The Revenue authorities were not, of course, slow to respond to such a development and upon a finding that some of these workers were indeed employees, some employers found themselves having to pay back-tax (which they had not deducted from the employee) together with interest and penalties. For employers, therefore, the distinction between employment and self-employment assumed importance and some Personal Service Companies developed at that time as an emphatic (through the use of a separate legal personality) declaration of self-employment.

Rather than deal with these uncertain issues, however, many employers simply introduced a rule against direct engagement in favour of engagement through agencies only. The Revenue authorities were not, of course, slow to respond to such a development either and upon a finding that some of these workers were indeed 'employees', some agencies found themselves having to pay back-tax (which they had not deducted from the employee) together with interest and penalties. For agencies, therefore, the distinction between employment and self-employment also assumed importance and more Personal Service Companies developed at that time as an emphatic (through the use of a separate legal personality) declaration of self-employment.

Some agencies will only enter into engagements if the person providing the personal services agrees to become an employee of the agency (who will then operate the PAYE and NIC system in respect of their remuneration). Some agencies will only enter into engagements if the person providing the personal services agrees to be self-employed as an independent contractor (usually in the form of a Personal Service Company).

It remains to be seen what the attitude of the Inland Revenue will be in practice as regards the contracts which Personal Service Companies have with or through agencies. From the manner in which the legislation has been revised and is now structured, however, it is now clear that the problem is *not* now that of the agency but is that of the Personal Service Company alone.

The advantage of agencies is, of course, that they can get the work (often through having the exclusive ear of the employers). They therefore provide much in the way of what a Personal Service Company needs in terms of marketing and contracts but they do so, of course, at a cost and in a relatively inflexible manner. Clearly, if the Inland Revenue designate a particular class or type of agency contract to be a 'relevant engagement' for the purposes of IR35, then there will not be a lot which a Personal Service Company will be able to do about that other than perhaps face up to that fact.

Much will, of course, depend upon the agencies involved. Employment agencies are now regulated in the UK. The original legislation is the *Employment Agencies Act 1973* which empowers the Secretary of State to make regulations to secure the proper conduct of employment agencies and employment businesses and to protect the interests of persons availing themselves of the services of such agencies and businesses. This has now been amended by the *Employment Relations Act 1999* and a comprehensive body of regulations exist in the UK controlling the activities of employment agencies.

CM3 – The IR35 Contract Test

Introduction [CM3.1]

IR35 has dealt a severe – some would even argue fatal – blow to certain of the Personal Service Companies in the UK. While undoubtedly a serious consideration, another way of looking at the situation is, however, simply to view IR35 as the latest in a number of hurdles which all Personal Service Companies face.

The view taken in this book is that in relation to any IR35 Test being undertaken, it is likely (as the Inland Revenue concede in their booklet on supplying services), that the number of clients which a Personal Service Company has may be relevant to the decision whether the work being undertaken under the contract being tested is as an employee or as a self-employed person. Thus, the IR35 Test may lead on to a consideration of the employment/self-employment test and that in turn may lead to a consideration of the way in which the Personal Service Company has contracted, recorded its sales, dealt with its income, filed its Accounts and Returns and complied with all the corporate formalities.

In short the application of IR35 in practice may come down to little more than one facet of an overall examination of the way in which a Personal Service Company is being run – is the company (and its contracts) being run as a form of disguised employment on the back of an envelope with little or no regard for corporate formalities or is the company (and its contracts) being properly run on a self-employed basis with due regard for all the corporate formalities.

The extent of the problem [CM3.2]

With the advent of IR35, however, the basis upon which trading is being undertaken is something which a Personal Service Company is going to have to address not just when the company commences trading but *on every occasion upon which a new contract is being taken out.*

As companies now fall generally under a self-assessment regime it is for the companies concerned to assess their own tax and if nothing is done in the interim then it may not be until a review is carried out several years later that the IR35 Test is considered by the Inland Revenue in relation to a number of contracts for a number of years. It remains to be seen what approach to enforcement is adopted by the Inland Revenue but the overall consequences could be significant for the Personal Service Company concerned. Indeed, it has been suggested that some companies will bow to the new tax rules in relation to all their contracts while other companies will move abroad in an attempt to avoid the new tax rules altogether. Either of these would be an extreme solution but the practical effect of IR35 remains to be seen.

The contract itself [CM3.3]

As noted, any consideration of the IR35 rules is likely to be initiated by a consideration of the contract in question itself. Under the legislation implementing IR35, the Inland Revenue will have the right to examine each and every contract which a Personal Service Company has and apply the IR35 Test to those contracts. A quick 'litmus test' likely to be used by the Inland Revenue for the immediate interpretation of contracts.

Those contracts which fail the IR35 Test are to be called 'relevant engagements' while all those which pass the IR35 Test are to be called 'non-relevant engagements'.

It perhaps bears mentioning at this stage, however, that no single factor determines the outcome of the employment/self-employment test and therefore, although possibly a factor, the current rewriting of contracts by agencies is unlikely of itself to be determinative. Some contracts will fall clearly into one category or the other. Other contracts may fall into a 'grey area' in which it may be a matter of opinion as to whether or not the engagement is a relevant or non-relevant one. It is in these 'grey areas' that resort may need to be had to the wider employment/self-employment test.

The nature of the employment/self-employment test [CM3.4]

This is not, in fact, a new test devised for the purposes of IR35 alone. Instead, it is a long-standing test which has existed and which has been used for some time to determine the distinction between employment and self-employment generally.

The difficulty with the employment/self-employment test is that it is not a numeric test which applies in an easily anticipated black-and-white manner. Instead, the test involves opinion and the application of professional judgment. That means, in practice, that the same set of facts could result in a number of different opinions.

The running of the company generally [CM3.5]

It perhaps bears mentioning at this stage that in the event of a contest of opinion in relation to a contract falling into one of the 'grey areas', the way in which the Personal Service Company has itself been run may very well turn out to be a relevant, indeed crucial, consideration.

For example, a Personal Service Company which, in addition to its main contract, has a number of small contracts which have been properly minuted and entered into contractually, had vat properly applied, are properly recorded as sales of the company, are deposited as receipts of the company, appear in the Accounts of the company and are properly reflected in the company Returns, stands a good chance of being regarded as self-employed in a non-relevant engagement.

On the other hand, a Personal Service Company which in addition to its main contract makes vague reference to a few other small jobs which have not been minuted, have not been entered into contractually, have not had vat applied, were treated as those of the individual and have not been recorded as sales of the company, do not appear in the bank account of the company which has produced no Accounts or Returns and is in default in relation to its corporate obligations is much more likely to be regarded as a form of disguised employment and a relevant engagement.

The Inland Revenue opinion [CM3.6]

The Inland Revenue has already indicated in relation this whole area that, for existing contracts only, they are prepared to give a written opinion on the outcome of the IR35 Test upon that contract for the purposes of the new tax rules.

Such a facility goes some way to countering criticism that in some instances it may only be several years down the road (with decisions as to the status of the contract made and expenditure incurred accordingly) that the Inland Revenue come to examine the contracts in question.

This facility opens up the possibility of the Personal Service Company having all existing contracts tested by the Inland Revenue and, in the light of the outcome, it would be able to tailor its response. If the contract failed the IR35 Test in the opinion of the Inland Revenue then the Personal Service Company could restrict its expenditure in relation to that contract and ensure that the necessary PAYE and NIC were paid on time. If the contract passed the IR35 Test in the opinion of the Inland Revenue then the Personal Service Company could proceed in its normal manner as regards expenditure, PAYE and NIC. This facility is clearly more advantageous to Personal Service Companies which have several contracts and which are able to absorb an adverse finding that a contract is a relevant engagement. The position is more serious for Personal Service Companies with only one contract where an adverse finding might not only make the company loss-making but might call into question the very viability of continuing as a Personal Service Company at all – in effect, a life-or-death opinion.

Another difficulty about this facility is its application to contracts which fall into the grey area. The Inland Revenue can, of course, only give an opinion upon the facts which are placed before it and if the Personal Service Company does not introduce all of the relevant facts then the Inland Revenue can hardly be faulted for their opinion.

The matter is, at the end of the day, a matter of opinion. Further, it is in relation not to a purely tax matter but to a wider judicial test. Views are likely to change in the light of experience but it may in fact transpire that in practice the judicial application of the employment/self-employment test to the IR35 position may be different from that envisaged by the Inland Revenue. It may well turn out to be the case that the true application of the employment/self-employment test is wider than that currently suggested by the Inland Revenue at least in their booklet, although the advice given by them is likely to change with experience once the test comes into effect.

For 'grey areas' the opinion of the Inland Revenue is, of course, as they themselves would concede, only one opinion (albeit one which commands respect). That opinion offers certainty but it also – in a matter which may be essential to the very continued existence of the Personal Service Company – has the practical effect of shifting the initiative to the Inland Revenue and the taxpayer must either abide by the opinion given or seek to mark an appeal against it.

The taxpayer's opinion [CM3.7]

Under the tax system which operates in this country, there is no obligation (although the advantages of so doing have been indicated above) to seek a ruling or determination from the Inland Revenue in advance. Taxpayers (supported by professional advisors or others) are entitled to their own opinion.

This is, of course, one of the areas where professional advice is generally considered advantageous. Those professionals who practice in the area will be familiar with the precedents in relation to the IR35 Test and the essential facts which bear upon them and accordingly are well placed to present a good opinion.

One of the difficulties in practice for Personal Service Companies is likely to be the cost, where necessary, of establishing and supporting such an opinion.

This is where insurance comes in. With the benefit of adequate insurance, a Personal Service Company is in a better position to support its opinion in relation to a matter which may be of supreme importance to its continued existence.

The possibility of an appeal [CM3.8]

As noted above, the opinions of the taxpayer, the Inland Revenue and the company's professional advisers may differ in regard to the employment/self-employment test. In practice, however, further discussion can often narrow any differences between opinions. However, should that not prove possible then an independent appeal is available where experienced Commissioners can settle such differences.

The judicial approach [CM3.9]

The employment/self-employment test stems from the Schedular approach to taxation adopted in the UK. Within the UK, taxation is assessed, and has been since its re-introduction in modern form in 1842, on the basis of Schedules. Tax is charged in respect of all property, profits or gains respectively described or comprised in the Schedules marked A, B, C, D and E, contained in the first Schedule to this Act and in accordance with the Rules respectively applicable to those Schedules.

Each of the Schedules has a particular aim or purpose (e.g. Schedule A, relates to the taxation of property) and, therefore, the rules applicable to each Schedule are quite radically different and are aimed at helping to achieve the taxation aim or objective of the Schedule. For that reason, it is important to establish into which Schedule a particular source of income falls.

The Inland Revenue also regard it as important for the practical reason (doubtless based upon experience) that for those brought under Schedule E the employer must deduct tax at source and remit that tax to the Inland Revenue whereas under Schedule D the obligation to pay tax rests upon the taxpayer whose compliance the Inland Revenue then has to ensure.

One area of particular difficulty is that relating to 'employment' and the distinction between Schedule D (self-employment) and Schedule E (employment). A person might receive income under a contract 'for services' (self-employment and therefore Schedule D) or under a contract 'of service' (employment and therefore Schedule E).

Case law **[CM3.10]**

The earliest cases relate, of course, to master and servant where a 'servant' was defined as 'a person employed by another person or body of persons to work under direction for wages' and the early test was simply and solely whether the person in question was 'under direction'. In modern employment conditions of employer and employee (although still technically sometimes referred to as master and servant) the concept of 'direction' has been replaced by the concept of 'control'. Furthermore, under modern conditions 'control' is no longer the sole test but is simply one of a number of tests which must be examined.

In *Bank voor Handel en Scheepvaart NV v Slatford [1952] 2 All E R 956* Denning LJ said:

> 'I would observe the test of being a servant does not rest nowdays on submission to orders. It depends on whether the person is part and parcel of the organisation.'

In *Zuijus v Wirth Brothers Pty Ltd [1954] 93 CLR 561* LJ said:

'What matters is lawful authority to command, so far as there is scope for it. And there must always be some room for it, if only in incidental and collateral matters.'

The Ready Mixed Concrete case **[CM3.11]**

Both of the above considerations were adopted and expanded by MacKenna J in the case of *Ready Mixed Concrete (South East) Ltd v Minister of Pensions & National Insurance [1968] 1 All E R 433.* This case involved a person who owned his own lorry and was engaged by a company to deliver concrete to the customers of the company. Was that person self-employed or an employee of the company?

MacKenna J held that a contract 'of service' (i.e. employment) existed if the following three conditions were fulfilled.

- The servant agrees that in consideration of a wage or other remuneration he will provide his own work and skill in the performance of some service for his master. This condition did not, the judge felt, call for comment other than that remuneration was a requirement which had to be present.
- He agrees, expressly or impliedly, that in the performance of that service he will be subject to the other's control in a sufficient degree to make that other master. Under this condition 'control', the judge felt, includes the power of deciding the thing to be done, the way in which it shall be done, the means to be employed in doing it, the time when, and the place where it shall be done. All these aspects of control must be considered in deciding whether the right exists in a sufficient degree to make one party the master and the other his servant.
- The other provisions of the contract are consistent with its being a contract of service. This condition, the Judge felt, was the important one and he gave five examples to explain what he meant by provisions inconsistent with the nature of a contract of service.
    - A contract obliges one party to build for the other, providing at his own expense the necessary plant and materials. This is not a contract of service, even though the builder may be obliged to use his own labour only and to accept a high degree of control, it is a building contract. It is not a contract to serve another for a wage, but a contract to produce a thing (or a result) for a price.
    - A contract obliges one party to carry another's goods, providing at his own expense everything needed for performance. This is not a contract of service it is a contract of carriage.

- A contract obliges a labourer to work for a builder, providing some simple tools, and to accept the builder's control. Notwithstanding the obligation to provide the tools, the contract is one of service. That obligation is not inconsistent with the nature of a contract of service. It is not a sufficiently important matter to affect the substance of the contract.
- A contract obliges one party to work for the other, accepting his control, and to provide his own transport. This is still a contract of service. Transport, in this example is incidental to the main purpose of the contract.
- A contract provides both that one party shall work for the other subject to the other's control, and also that he shall sell him his land. The first part of the instrument is no less a contract of service because the second part imposes obligations of a different kind.

In other words, while an obligation to do work subject to the other party's control is a necessary, though not always a sufficient, condition of a contract of service. If the provisions of the contract as a whole are inconsistent with its being a contract of service, it will be some other kind of contract.

The Market Investigations Case **[CM3.12]**

In the same year, the matter was considered again (with Canadian American and British authorities) in the case of *Market Investigations Ltd v Ministry of Social Security [1968] 3 All ER 732* where Cooke J said:

> 'The observations of Lord Wright, of Denning LJ and of the judges of the Supreme Court in the USA suggest that the fundamental test to be applied is this:
>
> "Is the person who has engaged himself to perform these services performing them as a person in business on his own account? If the answer to that question is "Yes" then the contract is a contract for services. If the answer is "No" then the contract is a contract of service. No exhaustive list has been compiled and perhaps no exhaustive list can be compiled of considerations which are relevant in determining that question, nor can strict rules be laid down as to the relative weight which the various considerations should carry in particular cases. The most that can be said is that control will no doubt have to be considered, although it can no longer be regarded as the sole determining

factor; and that factors, which may be of importance, are such matters as whether the man performing the services provides his own equipment, whether he hires his own helpers, what degree of financial risk he takes, what degree of responsibility for investment and management he has, and whether and how far he has an opportunity of profiting from sound management in the performance of his task".'

The test set out above – working out where the line is to be drawn between a person undertaking to provide merely labour and a person undertaking to provide a service which the other person requires albeit that his labour is a major component of that service by considering and weighting the various factors which go to answering the question whether that person is 'in business on his own account' is probably the current test for the distinction between employment and self-employment *generally.*

Inland Revenue Guidance **[CM3.13]**

Following the decision in *Market Investigations Ltd v Ministry of Social Security [1968] 3 All ER 732*, the Inland Revenue issued guidance (IR56) on the matter. The Inland Revenue begin by saying that the distinction between employment and self-employment is something to be decided in a commonsense way and go on to list the factors tending to indicate upon which side of the line an individual case will fall.

Factors pointing towards self-employment are said to be:

- Whether the individual has the final say in how the business is run.
- Whether the individual risks his own money in the business
- Whether the individual is responsible for meeting losses as well as enjoying profits.
- Whether the individual provides the major items of equipment that are needed,
- Whether the individual is free to hire other persons on terms of his own choice to do the work which he has undertaken to perform, and, if so, whether he pays that person out of his own pocket.
- Whether the individual has to correct unsatisfactory work in his own time and at his own expense.

If an affirmative answer can be given to all of the above questions then the individual concerned will have a strong case for self-employment.

Factors pointing towards employment are said to be:

- Whether the individual has to do the work personally rather than hire someone else to do the work.
- Whether someone can tell the individual at any time what to do or when or how to do the work.
- Whether the individual is paid by the hour, the week or the month and whether overtime is paid.
- Whether the individual works set hours or a given numbers of hours per week or month.
- Whether the individual works at the premises of the person the individual is working for or at a place or places that they decide.

If an affirmative answer can be given to any of the above questions then the Inland Revenue is likely to regard the individual as employed.

The test is the same for both Income Tax (IR56) and National Insurance (NI39) and the Government has indicated that once an individual's status has been established with one of these authorities then that decision will be accepted by the other.

Businesses without premises, stock etc. **[CM3.14]**

While the *Market Investigations* case (see **CM3.12** above) and the resulting Inland Revenue Guidance (see **CM3.13** above) probably represent the current test for the distinction between employment and self-employment *generally*, even the Inland Revenue concede that the *Market Investigations* test may not be as relevant to professional people who conduct their businesses without the usual business trappings of premises, stock and the like and another whole series of cases have emerged in this area and in particular in the area where an individual apparently self-employed takes on a number of other short-term contracts which it might be argued are employments.

Davies v Braithwaite **[CM3.15]**

In *Davies v Braithwaite 18TC 198* an actress who was generally self-employed entered into a contract to perform as an actress in the USA for a few weeks.

Tax law at that time was that if self-employed (Schedule D) then UK tax had to be paid on USA earnings along with all her other earnings in the usual way whereas if employed then UK tax was only payable on USA earnings when these were remitted to the UK.

The actress contended that her USA contract was an employment taxable (on a remittance basis) under Schedule E. The Inland Revenue argued that the USA contract was merely an incident of her normal self-employment as an actress and was taxable under Schedule D. Finding for the Inland Revenue Rowlett J said:

> 'it seems to me that where one finds a method of earning a livelihood which does not contemplate the obtaining of a post and staying in it, but essentially contemplates a series of engagements and moving from one to the other – and in the case of an actor's or actresses's life it certainly involves going from one to the other and not going on playing one part for the rest of his or her life, but in obtaining first one engagement and then another, and a whole series of them – then each of the engagements could not be considered an employment, but is a mere engagement in the course of exercising a profession.'

Fall v Hitchen **[CM3.16]**

In *Fall v Hitchen 49 TC 433* a ballet dancer who would generally be regarded as self-employed entered into a contract (a British Actor's Equity Association standard form of contract) to perform at a theatre in England for six months. The ballet dancer (following *Davies v Braithwaite*) argued that these earnings were self-employment falling to be assessed under Schedule D. The Inland Revenue argued that they fell to be assessed as employment under Schedule E. The judge, for reasons which are not entirely clear, agreed with the Inland Revenue.

McGowan and West **[CM3.17]**

Given the contradictory nature of the decisions in *Davies v Braithwaite* and *Fall v Hitchen*, Equity arranged for two cases relating to their members Alex McCowan and Sam West to be taken before a Special Commissioner who (finding on the facts that both members were self-employed) indicated that in his opinion the above cases were not contradictory but dealt with different situations. The Inland Revenue did not appeal that decision to a Court of Law but instead issued an extra-statutory concession (no longer in effect) to Equity indicating that those Equity members already taxed under Schedule D would continue to be so but that any new Equity members would be taxed under Schedule E as regards any word entered into a standard Equity contract.

Lorimer **[CM3.18]**

As well as Equity, the Inland Revenue had a look at behind-the-camera film workers. Again, an Extra Statutory Concession (no longer in effect) was introduced which applied to certain specified 'grades' of person. A Mr Ian Lorimer, whose 'grade' as a Film Technician was not listed on that concession and who not being a member of Equity or other representative organisation, was unable to afford full representation) took his own case all the way from the Commissioners to the Court of Appeal in the case of *Hall v Lorimer [1994] STC 23.* The facts of the case – in which the Inland Revenue contended that Mr Lorimer had had 580 'engagements' over 4 years – were set out ('with admirable thoroughness and clarity') in some detail in the case stated and the issue in law for the Court of Appeal was whether on those facts the contract in question was one 'of service' or 'for services'.

In considering the test for that, the Court of Appeal – perhaps somewhat surprisingly – cast doubt upon whether the approach adopted in the *Market Investigations* case was necessarily the best approach in the circumstances which faced the court here. Nolan LJ, delivering the opinion of the court, indicating that:

> 'In cases of this sort there is no single path to a correct decision. An approach which suits the facts and arguments of one case may be unhelpful in another.'

As a general approach, however, Nolan LJ quoted with approval the opinion of Mummery J to the effect:

> 'In order to decide whether a person carries on business on his own account it is necessary to consider many different aspects of that person's work activity. This is not a mechanical exercise of running through items on a check list to see whether they are present in, or absent from, a given situation. The object of the exercise is to paint a picture from the accumulation of detail. The overall effect can only be appreciated by standing back from the detailed picture which has been painted, by viewing it from a distance and by making an informed, considered, qualitative appreciation of the whole...Not all details are of equal weight or importance in any given situation. The details may also vary in importance from one situation to another. [It is] impossible in a field where a very large number of factors have to be weighted to gain any real assistance by

> looking at the facts of another case and comparing them one by one to see what facts are common, what are different and what particular weight is given by another tribunal to the common facts. The facts as a whole must be looked at, and a factor which may be compelling in one case in the light of the facts of that case may not be compelling in the context of another case.'

Nolan LJ specifically held the case of *Davies v Braithwaite* to be good law and went on to say that he found the distinctions drawn (in the *Ready Mixed Concrete* and *Market Investigations* cases) between an employee selling his labour and a contractor selling the product of his labour very hard to apply in the case of a professional man. Nolan LJ went on to say:

> 'Surely the self-employed barrister advising in his chambers or the doctor advising in his surgery is selling his skill and labour and not its product. If the scene shifts to the court or to the operating theatre can the client or patient really be said to be buying the product which may be disastrous in spite of the best efforts of the advocate or the surgeon...Again, the question, whether the individual is in business on his own account, though often helpful, may be of little assistance in the case of one carrying on a profession or vocation. A self-employed author working from home or an actor or singer may earn his living without any of the normal trappings of a business. For my part I would suggest there is much to be said in these cases for bearing in mind the traditional contrast between a servant and an independent contractor... It is, I think, in any event plain that Cooke J was not intending to lay down an all-purpose definition of employment. For example, his test does not mention the duration of the particular engagement or the number of people by whom the individual is engaged.'

Much that was said by Nolan LJ on behalf of the Court of Appeal is of the utmost importance albeit obiter dicta (indirect authority) in that the Court of Appeal found Mr Lorimar to be self-employed on *Edwards v Bairstow* principles i.e. that it was not a decision that a reasonable Tribunal properly instructed in the law could have reached. The Inland Revenue did not appeal the case further to the House of Lords.

Nevertheless, the Inland Revenue seem to have taken on board what was said in the *Hall v Lorimer* case. The Inland Revenue have also concluded that the *Market Investigations* test may not be very relevant to professional people who conduct their occupations without the usual trappings of business such as stock, premises, and equipment.

The Inland Revenue have indicated that such engagements may need to be looked at in the light of the additional factors such as:

- exposure to bad debts and the amount of time spent on organising, obtaining or carrying out the work;
- the length of the individual engagement; and
- the number of other persons for whom similar work is performed.

The Inland Revenue have indicated that independence may be a useful factor in such cases and that the Inland Revenue will also look at whether the individual's services require the exercise of rare skill and judgment, the worker is engaged for a specific task, the worker incurs substantial unreimbursed expenditure in obtaining organising and carrying out engagements requiring visits to various sites, whether there is a risk of delayed payment and bad debts, and the extent to which the worker is able to influence pay.

O'Kelly **[CM3.19]**

The variety of factors to be considered in such cases raises an important practical point. The question of the test of employment/self-employment is likely in practice to be raised by the Inland Revenue with the taxpayer. The taxpayer, if not in agreement, should muster for that difference of opinion, as many factors in favour of self-employment as are genuinely available. If agreement cannot be reached then the taxpayer has an appeal to the Commissioners where, again, the taxpayer should muster as many factors in favour of self-employment as are genuinely available. The reason that it is important to do that is that these factors form the basis of any decision and if not available cannot be considered by the Commissioners or, on further appeal, any subsequent court of law. Their importance at that stage has been indicated by Sir John Donaldson MR in *O'Kelly v Turnhouse Forte plc [1983] 3 All E R 456* when he said:

> 'The test to be applied in identifying whether a contract is one of employment or for services is a pure question of law and so is its application to the facts. But it is for the tribunal of fact not only to find those facts but to assess them qualitatively and within limits, which are indefinable in the abstract, those findings and that assessment will dictate the correct legal answer. In the familiar phrase, it is all a question of fact and degree. It is only if the weight given to a particular factor shows a self-misdirection in law that an appellate court with limited jurisdiction can interfere' (i.e. the application of the *Edwards v Bairstow* principle).

Lee Ting Sang **[CM3.20]**

An example of the application of such facts can be seen in the Privy Council case of *Lee Ting Sang v Chung Chi-Keung & Another [1900] 2 WLR 1173.* Lee Ting Sang was a stonemason working for a subcontractor who provided him with his tools. After noting in passing that despite a plethora of authorities (the best of which, they agreed with the Hong Kong Court of Appeal, was that of Cooke J) the courts have not been able to devise a single test that will conclusively point to the distinction (between employment and self-employment) in all cases, the Privy Council turned to consider the facts, again noting in passing that it must now be taken to be firmly established that such questions of fact are to be regarded by an appellate court as determined by the trial court, as follows:

> 'It is true that he was not supervised in his work, but this is not surprising, he was a skilled man and he had been told the beams upon which he was to work and the depth to which they were to be cut and his work was measured to see that he achieved that result. There was no question of him being called upon to exercise any skill or judgement as to which beams required chipping or the depth that they were to be cut. He was simply told what to do and left to get on with it...The picture emerges of a skilled artisan, earning his living by working for more than one employer as an employee and not as a small businessman venturing into business on his own as an independent contractor with all its attendant risks. The applicant ran no risk whatsoever save that of being unable to find unemployment which is, of course, a risk faced by casual employees who move from one job to another...'.

On those facts, the Privy Council reversed the decision of the Court of Appeal in Hong Kong holding that those facts:

> '...point out so clearly to the existence of a contract of service that the finding that the applicant was working as an independent contractor was .. a view of the facts which could not reasonably be entertained and is to be regarded as an error of law'.

The *Lee Ting Sang* case was in fact a case involving the area of industrial injuries law (although the employment/self-employment test is substantially the same in all the areas of law in which it arises). The Inland Revenue often cite the *Lee Ting Sang* case although some Commissioners have suggested that as an authority it is so remote that its persuasive value is limited.

Clearly, those who provide personal services offer a level of skill or expertise which is akin to that of a professional. There is also the complication that they have chosen to do so using the commercial vehicle and separate legal entity of a limited liability company. The Inland Revenue Schedule E Manual states:

> 'To avoid PAYE many [film, video, television and radio workers] in Schedule E Grades have set up limited companies. Normally the worker is the major shareholder and a director. It is alleged that the service company supplies the services of the individual to [the production company]. An examination of many such cases has shown that such arrangements often fail.'

One of the reasons why such arrangements often fail is that upon examination the individual concerned is not operating the company in a proper manner. It is clearly vital in such circumstances, therefore, that a proper Board of directors is constituted which meets regularly and records its decision properly. Another of the reasons why such arrangements often fail is that upon examination the individual concerned or his company has signed a contract which has all of the factors of employment (e.g. that the client still has to pay the Service Company when the individual concerned is sick) and none of the factors of self-employment.

Clearly, therefore, for Personal Service Companies any contract between the client and a Personal Service Company is going to become of vital importance. That will apply equally, if not more so, where an agency intervenes.

Narich Pty Ltd **[CM3.21]**

The importance of the contract was emphasised by the Privy Council in the case of *Narich Pty Ltd v Commissioners of Payroll Tax [1984] ICR 286* Lord Brandon said:

> 'The first principle is that, subject to one exception, where there is a written contract between the parties whose relationship is in issue, a court is confined, in determining the nature of that relationship, to a consideration of the terms, express or implied, of that contract in the light of the circumstances surrounding the making of it; and it is not entitled to consider also the manner in which the parties subsequently acted in pursuance of such contract. The one exception to that rule is that, where the subsequent conduct of the parties can be shown

> to have amounted to an agreed addition to, or modification of, the original written contract, such conduct may be considered and taken into account by the court.'

Although only one factor to be considered in the test, the actual contract between the client and the Personal Service Company is clearly going to be a very important factor. It will not do, however, simply to draw up a list of the factors pointing to self-employment and insert them in the contract. Such a contract would clearly not be a genuine commercial agreement arrived at by parties negotiating at arm's length and would be likely for that reason to attract even closer scrutiny from the Inland Revenue.

Specialeyes **[CM3.22]**

An example of the importance of the contract and the application of the factors can be seen in the Special Commissioners case of *Specialeyes (Optical Services) Ltd Taxation, 4 July 1991.*

Specialeyes (Optical Services) Ltd traded through a nationwide chain of shops in which they offered eye examinations by opticians. These opticians had only one client (Specialeyes); received a fixed fee for each eye test performed out of which a remittance was made by the optician to Specialeyes to cover the use of its premises and equipment; were responsible for their own professional indemnity insurance; and could stipulate their hours. The approach taken by the Special Commissioners appears to have been influence by the formal terms of the contract; the fact that in relation to the factor of control, that of the client was limited in that it was only be negotiation and agreement that the branch and the time of attendance by the optician was agreed; and the fact that they did not consider the opticians to the 'part and parcel' of Specialeyes' organisation. The Special Commissioners found that the opticians were self-employed. The Inland Revenue did not appeal.

Where there is a formal contract, such as in the above example, the Court is confined to construing that written contract although that is unlikely be the only factor in the determination of the test. Where no formal contract exists the remit of the Court will be that much wider.

Stevenson Jordan and Massey **[CM3.23]**

It will be appreciated from the above that no single factor is ever likely to provide the determinative answer to the employment/self-employment test.

The real problem in relation to 'employment' – which has existed for some time – is whether a contract is *of service* (in which case it is taxed under Schedule E) or *for services* (in which case it is taxed under Schedule D). The distinction can be quite difficult to draw in practice. Lord Denning rather neatly encapsulated the problem in his own inimicable style when he refused to attempt to formulate a legal definition of the distinction but instead stated (in *Stevenson Jordan & Harrison Ltd v McDonald & Evans [1952] 1 TLR 101* and again in *Massey v Crown Life Assurance Co [1978] 2 All E R 576*):

> 'It is often easy to recognise a contract of service when you see it but difficult to say where the difference lies. A ship's master, a chauffeur and a reporter on the staff of a newspaper are all employed under a contract of service; but a ship's pilot, a taxi-man and a newspaper contributor are employed under a contract for services.'

It will always depend upon a proper consideration of all of the surrounding circumstances.

Inland Revenue approach to the test in relation to Personal Service Companies [CM3.24]

On 10 November 1999 the Inland Revenue placed on its website a draft guidance paper on the application of employment status rules to service company workers. That was then discussed at two meetings with representatives of professional bodies and service company workers resulting in the final version which was published in the Inland Revenue's Tax Bulletin of 7 February 2000.

Whether a worker would have been an employee if engaged directly by the client depends on a range of factors. However, the final decision is not reached by adding up the number of factors pointing towards employment and comparing that result with the number pointing towards self-employment. The courts have specifically rejected that approach. In *Hall v Lorimer* Mummery J made the following comment which was quoted by Nolan LJ in the Court of Appeal:

> 'In order to decide whether a person carries on business on

> his own account it is necessary to consider many different aspects of that person's work activity. This is not a mechanical exercise of running through a checklist to see whether they are present in, or absent from, a given situation...It is a matter of evaluation of the overall effect, which is not necessarily the same as the sum total of all the individual details. Not all details are of equal weight or importance in any given situation. The details may also vary in importance from one situation to another.'

When the detailed facts have been established, the right approach is to stand back and look at the picture as a whole, to see if the overall effect is that of a person in business on his own account or a person working as an employee in somebody else's business. If the evidence is evenly balanced the intention of the parties may then decide the issue (*Massey v Crown Life Insurance Co*).

Establishing the facts [CM3.25]

In deciding whether a worker would have been an employee if engaged directly by the client, it is firstly necessary to establish the terms and conditions of the engagement. In a simple case involving one intermediary (e.g. where a worker works through a service company) these will normally be established mainly from the contract between the client and the intermediary. It is that contract that will usually reflect the terms that would have applied had the worker been engaged directly by the client. The contract may be written, oral or implied or a mixture of all three.

Having established the terms and conditions, it is then necessary to consider any surrounding facts that may be relevant e.g. whether the worker has other clients and a business organisation. In this context other contracts the company has under which the worker's services are supplied and any business organisation of the company which is relevant to the supply of the worker's services will be taken into account as relevant surrounding facts.

Deciding employment status [CM3.26]

There is no statutory definition of 'employment'. However, the question of employment status has come before the courts on numerous occasions. The approach taken by the courts has been to identify factors which help to determine if a particular contract is a 'contract of service' (employment) or a 'contract for services' (self-employment). The relevant factors are considered below.

Control **[CM3.27]**

A worker will not be an employee unless there is a right to exercise 'control' over the worker. This may be a right to control 'what' work is done, 'where' or 'when' it is done or 'how' it is done. Actual control of this sort is not important – it is the right of control that is important.

Where a client has the right to determine 'how' the work is done this is a strong pointer to employment. But it is not an essential feature of employment. Many 'experts' who are employees are not necessarily subject to such control (for example, ship's captain, consultant brain surgeon etc.).

Equally a right to determine 'what' work is carried out is a strong pointer to employment. It will normally be a feature whenever a client needs a worker to undertake whatever tasks are required at any particular time or where the worker is required to work as part of a co-ordinated team.

A working relationship which involves no control at all is unlikely to be an employment (*Ready Mixed Concrete (South East Ltd) v Minister of Pensions and National Insurance (1968) 2 QB 497*).

The right to get a substitute or helper to do the job **[CM3.28]**

Personal service is an essential element of a contract of employment. A person who has the freedom to choose whether to do the job himself or hire someone else to do it for him, or who can hire someone else to provide substantial help is probably self-employed (*Austrian Mutual Provident Society v Chaplin (1978) 18 ALR 385* and *Express and Echo Publications Ltd v Tanton (1999) IRLR 367*). However, this must be viewed in the context of the arrangements overall.

For example, a worker may choose to pay a helper to take phone messages and deal with invoicing and general book-keeping work for the intermediary. However, this would not be directly relevant when considering an engagement where the worker is engaged to lay bricks for a client.

Provision of equipment **[CM3.29]**

A self-employed contractor generally provides whatever equipment is needed to do the job (though in many trades, such as carpentry, it is common for employees, as well as self-employed workers, to provide their own hand tools). The provision of significant equipment (and/or materials) which are fundamental to the engagement is of particular importance. For example, where an IT consultant is engaged to undertake a specific piece of work and must work exclusively at home using the worker's own computer equipment that will be a strong pointer to self-employment. However, where a worker is provided with office space and computer equipment that points to employment. The fact that a worker might occasionally choose to do some of the work at home using his or her own computer does not change that (many employees do just that) (*Ready Mixed Concrete (South East) Ltd v Minister of Pensions and National Insurance*).

Financial risk **[CM3.30]**

An individual who risks their own money by, for example, buying assets needed for the job and bearing the running costs and paying for overheads and large quantities of materials, is almost certainly self-employed. Financial risk could also take the form of quoting a fixed price for a job with the consequent risk of bearing the additional cost if the job overruns.

Another example of a financial risk is where a skilled worker incurs significant amounts of expenditure on training to provide himself with a skill which he uses in subsequent engagements. This can be treated in the same way as investment in equipment to be used in a trade, as a pointer to self-employment, if there is a risk that the investment would not be covered from income from future engagements (*Market Investigations Ltd v The Minister of Social Security (1968) 2 QB 173*).

Basis of payment **[CM3.31]**

Employees tend to be paid a fixed wage or salary by the week or month and often qualify for additional payments such as overtime, long service bonus or profit share. Independent contractors, on the other hand, tend to be paid a fixed sum for a particular job. Payment 'by the piece' (where the worker is paid according to the amount of work actually done) or by commission can be a feature of both employment and self-employment.

Opportunity to profit from sound management [CM3.32]

A person whose profit or loss depends on his capacity to reduce overheads and organise his work effectively may well be self-employed (*Market Investigations Ltd v The Minister of Social Security*). People who are paid by the job will often be in this position.

Part and parcel of the organisation [CM3.33]

Establishing whether a person becomes 'part and parcel' of a client's organisation can be a useful indicator in some situations. For example, someone taken on to manage a client's staff will normally be seen as part and parcel of the client's organisation and is likely to be an employee.

Right of dismissal [CM3.34]

A right to terminate an engagement by giving notice of a specified length is a common feature of employment. It is less common in a contract for services which usually ends only on completion of the task or if the terms of the contract are breached.

Employee benefits [CM3.35]

Employees are often entitled to sick pay, holiday pay, pensions, expenses and so on. However, the absence of those features does not necessarily mean that the worker is self-employed – especially in the case of short-term engagements where such payments would not normally feature.

Length of engagement [CM3.36]

Long periods working for one engager may be typical of an employment but are not conclusive. It is still necessary to consider all the terms and conditions of each engagement. Regular working for the same engager may indicate that there is a single and continuing contract of employment

(*Nethermere (St Neots) Ltd v Gardiner (1984) ICR 612*). Where an engagement is covered by a series of short contracts, or an initial short contract subsequently extended for a longer period, it is the length of the engagement that is relevant, rather than the length of each contract.

Personal factors **[CM3.37]**

In deciding a person's employment status it may sometimes be necessary to take into account factors which are personal to the worker and which have little to do with the terms of the particular engagement being considered. For example, if a skilled worker works for a number of clients throughout the year and has a business-like approach to obtaining his engagements (perhaps involving expenditure on office accommodation, office equipment, etc.) this will point towards self-employment (*Hall v Lorimer 66 TC 349*). Personal factors will usually carry weight in the case of an unskilled worker, where other factors such as the high level of control exercised by the contractor are likely to be conclusive of employment.

Intention **[CM3.38]**

It is the reality of the relationship that matters. It is not enough to call a person 'self-employed' if all the terms and conditions of the engagement point towards employment. However, if other factors are neutral the intention of the parties will then be the decisive factor in deciding employment status (*Massey v Crown Life Insurance Co (1978) ICR 590*).

CM4 – Administration of a Personal Service Company

Introduction [CM4.1]

In this section, it is intended to cover – in outline – the legal obligations which are imposed upon a Personal Service Company and which (often under the sanction of penalties) have to be met and observed. These are divided into sections as follows.

VAT [CM4.2]

The turnover of most Personal Service Companies is likely to (or ought to) exceed the turnover threshold beyond which registration for the purposes of VAT is compulsory. The principal obligation of a Personal Service Company in that respect is to maintain a proper VAT account and then from that to make proper VAT Returns.

The Accounts [CM4.3]

All Personal Service Companies will require to produce Accounts. However, the extent to which they do so may vary. The turnover of most Personal Service Companies is likely to be such that an audit of the Accounts will no longer be compulsory. However, there remain many circumstances in which an audit of the Accounts may be beneficial or even demanded of a Personal Service Company.

Accordingly, there is for Personal Service Companies an element of choice so far as the Accounts are concerned and a number of exemptions or exceptions may be applied. Thus, a Personal Service Company could choose to produce a full set of Financial Statements for the year with an Audit Report and a Directors' Report. Alternatively, a Personal Service Company could take advantage of the exceptions and exemptions and produce a much more restricted set of Financial Statements for the year without, for example, an Audit Report.

What there is no alleviation for at present, however, is the nature of those accounts. While it might appear as an unduly onerous requirement for a Personal Service Company where the directors reporting to the shareholders are effectively reporting to themselves, it nevertheless remains a legal obligation to produce those accounts to stipulated standards.

From that standard-set basis, those Financial Statements should be laid before or sent to the members of the company in full although so far as the Accounts which require to be placed with Companies House for public consumption are concerned, considerable exemptions and restrictions are available.

Corporation Tax [CM4.4]

For companies in general, including Personal Service Companies, the position has recently changed to one of self-assessment. Personal Service Companies are now required to produce a company Tax Return (which will be based upon their Accounts) and assess their own Corporation Tax.

Company matters [CM4.5]

The price of limited liability is publicity and amongst other things Personal Service Companies will require to present an Annual Return to Companies House each year.

PAYE, NIC and benefits [CM4.6]

Personal Service Companies will have employees, if only the directors of the company themselves. For such remuneration as they vote themselves, the appropriate amount of PAYE and NIC will require to be calculated, deducted, accounted for and returned.

By far the biggest bugbear for Personal Service Companies today, however, is going to be ascertaining and returning the benefits relating to the company. From minor and sensible beginnings the legislation relating to benefits has grown to an unintelligible morass which is generally accepted to now amount to an unreasonable burden. Nevertheless, (and subject to quite severe penalties) this is a matter which all Personal Service Companies will require to meet and address by properly making the appropriate returns.

CM5 – VAT Return

Introduction [CM5.1]

The nature of VAT is considered below, the manner in which both input and output are calculated, and the way in which a VAT Account is arrived at. So far as the administration of a Personal Service Company is concerned, however, its principal obligation will be to produce from that VAT Account a VAT Return (see **p315** below). In this Chapter, we consider what is involved in completing and filing the company's VAT Return.

Preparing the VAT Return [CM5.2]

Box 1 [CM5.3]

In this box should be inserted the VAT due on sales and purchases.

Remember to *include* any:

- supplies to staff;
- sales of business assets;
- private motoring element;
- hire or loan of goods to someone else;
- postal imports (other than by datapost) with a value < £2000;
- services upon which the 'reverse charge' procedure is applied;
- gifts in excess of £10;
- things taken in part-exchange;
- things taken out of the business for private use;
- commission received for selling for someone else;
- self-supplies;
- other (sideline) taxable business income; and
- supplies of goods to unregistered customers in EC.

Remember to *adjust for* any:

- VAT on credit notes issued by you to your customers;
- VAT overdeclared/underdeclared in previous returns < £2000; and
- amounts already assessed by Customs and Excise.

Box 2 **[CM5.4]**

In this box should be inserted the VAT due from you on acquisitions of goods from other EC Member States.

Box 3 **[CM5.5]**

In this box should be inserted the total output VAT due from you. This is the sum of Box 1 and Box 2.

Box 4 **[CM5.6]**

In this box should be inserted the total input VAT due to you. This includes VAT you have paid on imports, on services obtained under the reverse charge procedure, on acquisitions from EC Member States, and on qualifying purchases made within the UK.

Remember to *exclude*:

- cars where there is private motoring;
- business entertainment;
- purchases for purely private or personal use;
- purchases for non-business activities; and
- accommodation for directors of companies.

Remember to *include*:

- input tax on acquisitions from EC Member States;
- input tax on services being dealt with as a 'reverse charge';
- input tax claimed back as bad debt relief;
- any credit notes issued by suppliers;
- any adjustments for amounts declared overpayments by C & E;
- any adjustments for amounts owed by C & E; and
- any underdeclarations/overdeclarations < £2000.

Box 5 **[CM5.7]**

In this box should be inserted the net VAT either due from you to Customs and Excise or due by Customs and Excise to you. This is the difference between Box 3 and Box 4.

Box 6 **[CM5.8]**

In this box should be inserted the total value of sales and all other outputs excluding any VAT.

Note – take off any credits but do not take off any cash discounts.

Note – any item included for Box 8 should be included in this Box also.

Remember to *include* any:

- standard-rated supplies (including road fuel scale charges);
- supplies to VAT registered traders in EC Member States;
- supplies to non-VAT registered traders in EC Member States;
- zero-rated supplies (including any exports);
- exempt supplies;
- other business income;
- 'reverse charge' transactions;
- supplies outwith the scope of UK VAT;
- deposits for which an invoice has been issued;
- goods transferred to another EC Member State; and
- EC supplies made on a sale or return basis.

Remember to *exclude*:

- any VAT itself;
- wages and salaries received;
- PAYE and NIC received;
- money paid into of the business;
- any loans received;
- any gifts of money received;
- any dividends received;
- any insurance claims received;
- Stock Exchange dealings; and
- any income which by not being for consideration is outside VAT.

Box 7 **[CM5.9]**

In this box should be inserted the total value of any purchases and all other inputs, excluding any VAT.

These should include all imports, all acquisitions from EC Member States and all 'reverse charge' transactions.

Note – take off any credits but do not take off any cash discounts.

Note – anything included in Box 9 should be included in this Box.

Remember to *exclude*:-

- any VAT itself;
- wages and salaries paid out;
- PAYE and NIC paid out;
- money taken out of the business;
- any loans made;
- any gifts of money made;
- any dividends paid;
- any insurance claims;
- Stock Exchange dealings;
- MOT certificates;
- motor vehicle licence duty; and
- Local Authority Rates.

Box 8 **[CM5.10]**

In this box should be inserted the total value of all supplies of goods and related services, excluding any VAT, to other EC Member States.

This is a control box used for statistics and enforcement of VAT in the EC.

Note – any entry in this box should also be included in Box 6.

Box 9 **[CM5.11]**

In this box should be inserted the total value of all acquisitions of goods and related services, excluding any VAT, from other EC Member States.

This is a control box used for statistics and enforcement of VAT in the EC.

Note – any entry in this box should also be included in Box 7.

Form VAT100

HM Customs and Excise

Value Added Tax Return
For the period
to

For Official Use

Registration Number | Period

You could be liable to a financial penalty if your completed return and all the VAT payable are not received by the due date.

Due date :

For official use DOR only

Fold | Here

Before you fill in this form please read the notes on the back and the VAT leaflet *"Filling in your VAT return"*. Fill in all boxes clearly in ink, and write 'none' where necessary. Don't put in a dash or leave any box blank. If there are no pence write "**00**" in the pence column. Do not enter more than one amount in any box.

For official use

		£	p
VAT due in this period on **sales** and other outputs	1		
VAT due in this period on **acquisitions** from other **EC Member States**	2		
Total VAT due **(the sum of boxes 1 and 2)**	3		
VAT reclaimed in this period on **purchases** and other inputs (including acquisitions from the EC)	4		
Net VAT to be paid to Customs or reclaimed by you (Difference between boxes 3 and 4)	5		
Total value of **sales** and all other outputs excluding any VAT. **Include your box 8 figure**	6		00
Total value of **purchases** and all other inputs excluding any VAT. **Include your box 9 figure**	7		00
Total value of all **supplies** of goods and related services, excluding any VAT, to other **EC Member States**	8		00
Total Value of all **acquisitions** of goods and related services, excluding any VAT, from other **EC Member States**	9		00

Retail schemes. If you have used any of the schemes in the period covered by this return, enter the relevant letter(s) in this box

If youare exclosing a payment please tick this box

DECLARATION: You, or someone on your behalf, must sign below.

I, ...declare that the
(Full name of signatory in BLOCK LETTERS)
information given above is true and complete

Signature ....Date.................................19...........

A False declaration can result in prosecution

VAT 100 (Full) PCU (June 1996)

Form VAT100 – continued

Notes

These notes and the VAT leaflet *Filling your VAT Return* will help you fill in this form. You may also need to refer to other VAT notices and leaflets.

If you need help or advice please contact your local VAT office.

If you are using the 'cash accounting scheme', the amount of VAT due and deductible are for payments you actually receive and make, and not on invoices you receive and send out.

If you put **minus figures** in boxes 1 to 3, or are entering a sum **DUE** to Customs in box 4, please enclose the figure in brackets.

Amounts not declared correctly on previous returns

1. If any of your previous returns declared too much or too little VAT that has not yet been accounted for, you can correct the position using boxes 1 and 4 for net amounts of **£2000 or less.**

2. If the net amount is **over £2000**, tell your local VAT office immediately. Don't include the amount on this return.

If you do not follow these instructions you could be liable to a financial penalty.

How to pay your VAT

Cross all cheques and postal orders "AC Payee Only" make them payable to "HM Customs and Excise" and put a line through any spaces on the "pay" line.

In your own interest do not send notes, coins, or uncrossed postal orders by post.

If you wish to pay by credit transfer, ask your local VAT office. Pre-printed booklets of credit transfer slips will be sent to you.

Please write your VAT registration number on the back of all cheques and bank giro credit slips.

Where to send this return

You must make sure your completed form and any VAT payable are received by the 'due date' (shown over the page) by:

The Controller
VAT Central Unit
HM Customs and Excise
21 Victoria Avenue
Southend-on-Sea X
SS99 1AA

Complaints

The Adjudicator reviews complaints not settled to your satisfaction by Customs. The recommendations of the Adjudicator are independent and the service is free. It covers complaints not general enquiries. [Telephone the Adjudicator on 0171 930 2292]

Box 1

Show the VAT due on all goods and services you supplied in this period

Box 2

Show the VAT due (but not paid) on all goods and related services you acquired inthis period from other EC Member States

Box 3

Show the total amount of the VAT due ie the sum of boxes 1 and 2. This is your total **Output** tax.

Box 4

Show the amount of VAT deductible on any business purchases including acquisitions of goods and related services from other EC Member States. This is your **Input** tax.

Box 5

If this amount is under £1, you need not send any payment, nor will any repayment be made to you, but you must still fill in this form and send it to the VAT Central Unit.

Boxes 6 and 7

In box 6 show the value excluding VAT of your total outputs (supplies of goods and services). Include zero rated, exempt outputs and EC supplies from box 8.

In box 7 show the value excluding VAT of all your inputs (purchases of goods and services). Include zero rated exempt inputs and EC acquisitions from box 9.

Boxes 8 and 9

EC TRADE ONLY

Use these boxes if you have supplied goods to or acquired goods from another EC Member State. Include related services such as transport costs where these form part of the invoice or contract price. The figures should exclude VAT.

The other EC Member States are: Belgium, Denmark, France, Germany, Greece, Netherlands, Ireland, Italy, Luxembourg, Portugal, Spain, Austria, Finland and Sweden.

You must tell your local VAT office about any changes in your business circumstances (including changes of address).

VAT 100 (Full) Reverse (06/96)

Printed in the UK for HM Customs and Excise by McCorquodale Confidential Print

CM6 – Requirements Relating to Accounts

Company requirements for accounts [CM6.1]

The nature of a company's accounts are prescribed by law.

The *Companies Act 1985* (as amended by the *Companies Act 1989*) distinguishes between what it calls 'consolidated accounts' (the accounts of a group of several companies drawn together) and 'individual accounts' (the accounts of a company standing alone).

For individual accounts, *Companies Act 1985, section 226(1)* imposes a duty upon the directors of every company to prepare for each financial year of the company:

- a balance sheet as at the last day of the year; and
- a profit and loss account.

The overriding requirement in relation to those accounts is contained in *CA 1985, s226(2)* (underline added for emphasis):

> 'The balance sheet shall give a true and fair view of the state of affairs of the company as at the end of the financial year; and the profit and loss account shall give a true and fair view of the profit or loss of the company for the financial year.'

CA 1985 then goes on to specify the form and content which those individual accounts shall take. This is done in two ways – there are what might be called the full requirements and there also, in the case of companies who are able to bring themselves under one of the exemptions, more restricted requirements.

The full requirements [CM6.2]

Companies Act 1985, section 226(3) states that:

> 'A company's individual accounts shall comply with the

> provisions of Schedule 4 as to the form and content of the balance sheet and profit and loss account and additional information to be provided by way of notes to the accounts.'

However, *CA 1985* recognises that those requirements as to form and content may not alone be enough to achieve the required objective of a true and fair view and therefore goes on to adjust that position in two material respects.

Firstly, it is recognised that where the form and content provided for is not sufficient to achieve a true and fair view then something more may be required. *Companies Act 1985, section 226(4)* states that:

> 'Where compliance with the provisions of that Schedule [4], and the other provisions of this Act as to the matters to be included in a company's individual accounts or in notes to those accounts, would not be sufficient to give a true and fair view, the necessary additional information shall be given in the accounts or in a note to them'.

Secondly, it is recognised that strict adherence to form and content may still not produce a true and fair view and therefore (in what is known as a 'true and fair override') *Companies Act 1985, section 226(5)* permits a departure:

> 'If in special circumstances compliance with any of those provisions is inconsistent with the requirement to give a true and fair view, the directors shall depart from that provision to the extent necessary to give a true and fair view.
>
> Particulars of any such departure, the reasons for it, and its effect shall be given in a note to the accounts'.

Approval and signing of the accounts [CM6.3]

The directors must approve and sign the prepared accounts.

Companies Act 1985, section 233 provides that:

> '(1) A company's annual accounts shall be approved by the board of directors and signed on behalf of the board by a director of the company.
> (2) The signature shall be on the company's balance sheet.

(3) Every copy of the balance sheet which is laid before the company in general meeting, or which is otherwise circulated, published or issued, shall state the name of the person who signed the balance sheet on behalf of the board.

Under *Companies Act 1985, section 233*:

'(5) If annual accounts are approved which do not comply with the requirements of this Act, every director of the company who is party to their approval and who knows that they do not comply or is reckless as to whether they comply is guilty of an offence and liable to a fine.
For this purpose every director of the company at the time the accounts are approved shall be taken to be a party to their approval unless he shows that he took all reasonable steps to prevent their being approved.

(6) If a copy of the balance sheet–
  (a) is laid before the company, or otherwise circulated, published or issued, without the Balance Sheet having been signed as required by this section or without the required statement of the signatory's name being included, or
  (b) is delivered to the registrar without being signed as required by this section,

the company and every officer of it who is in default is guilty of an offence and liable to a fine.

Directors' report [CM6.4]

Companies Act 1985, section 234 provides that:

'(1) The directors of a company shall for each financial year prepare a report–
  (a) containing a fair review of the development of the business of the company during the financial year and of their position at the end of it, and
  (b) stating the amount (if any) which they recommend should be paid as dividend…

(2) The report shall state the names of the persons who, at any time during the financial year, were directors of the company, and the principal activities of the company…in the course of the year and any significant change in those activities in the year.'

Companies Act 1985 also specifies what, for both public and private companies together, shall be disclosed in the Directors' Report. This is done in two ways – there are what might be called the full requirements and there are also, in the case of companies who are able to bring themselves under one of the exemptions (see **CM7.6** below), more restricted requirements.

The full requirements [CM6.5]

Companies Act 1985, section 234(3) provides:

> 'The report shall also comply with Schedule 7 as regards the disclosure of the matters mentioned there'.

Companies Act1985, section 234(4) notes that:

> 'In Schedule 7–
> Part I relates to matters of a general nature, including changes in asset values, directors' shareholdings and other interests and contributions for political and charitable purposes,
> Part II relates to the acquisition by a company of its own shares or a charge on them,
> Part III relates to the employment, training and advancement of disabled persons,
> . . .
> Part V relates to the involvement of employees in the affairs, policy and performance of the company,
> Part VI relates to the company's policy and practice on the payment of creditors.'

Under *Companies Act 1985, section 234*:

> '(5) In the case of any failure to comply with the provisions of this Part as to the preparation of a directors' report and the contents of the report, every person who was a director of the company immediately before the end of the period for laying and delivering accounts and reports for the financial year in question is guilty of an offence and liable to a fine.
>
> (6) In proceedings against a person for an offence under this section it is a defence for him to prove that he took all reasonable steps for securing compliance with the requirements in question.'

Approval of the directors' report [CM6.6]

Companies Act 1985, section 234A provides:

> '(1) The directors' report shall be approved by the board of directors and signed on behalf of the board by a director or the secretary of the company.
>
> (2) Every copy of the directors' report which is laid before the company in general meeting, or which is otherwise circulated, published or issued, shall state the name of the person who signed it on behalf of the board.'

Under *Companies Act 1985, section 234A*:

> '(4) If a copy of the directors' report–
>
> (a) is laid before the company, or otherwise circulated, published or issued, without the report having been signed as required by this section or without the required statement of the signatory's name being included, or
>
> (b) is delivered to the registrar without being signed as required by this section,
>
> the company and every officer of it who is in default is guilty of an offence and liable to a fine.'

The auditors' report [CM6.7]

The audit of a company's accounts is, under present circumstances, virtually optional in that for those companies able to bring themselves within the definition of the *Companies Act 1985 (Audit Exemption) Regulations 1994* (*SI 1994/1935*) (which will be most companies) an audit is no longer a legal requirement.

An audit may nevertheless remain a practical requirement in that bankers, funders, some clients and the like (including 10% of the shareholders) may (and often do) make it a requirement of their involvement that the company's accounts be audited.

Note also that any applicable exemption has to be expressly claimed and that where that is not done then the normal requirements of the *Companies Acts* will apply.

Under *Companies Act 1985, section 236*:

> '(4) if a copy of the auditors' report–
> (a) is laid before the company, or otherwise circulated, published or issued, without the required statement of the auditors' names, or
> (b) is delivered to the registrar without the required statement of the auditors' names or without being signed as required by this section,
>
> the company and every officer of it who is in default is guilty of an offence and liable to a fine.'

The full audit requirements [CM6.8]

Companies Act 1985, sections 235 and *236* provide:

> **'235.**
>
> (1) A company's auditors shall make a report to the company's members on all annual accounts of the company of which copies are to be laid before the company in general meeting during their tenure of office.
>
> (2) The auditors' report shall state whether in the auditors' opinion the annual accounts have been properly prepared in accordance with this Act, and in particular whether a true and fair view is given–
> (a) in the case of an individual balance sheet, of the state of affairs of the company as at the end of the financial year,
> (b) in the case of an individual profit and loss account, of the profit or loss of the company for the financial year,...
>
> (3) The auditors shall consider whether the information given in the directors' report for the financial year for which the annual accounts are prepared is consistent with those accounts; and if they are of opinion that it is not they shall state that fact in their report.
>
> **236.**
>
> (1) The auditors' report shall state the names of the auditors and be signed by them.
>
> (2) Every copy of the auditors' report which is laid before

the company in general meeting, or which is otherwise circulated, published, or issued, shall state the names of the auditors.

(3) The copy of the auditors' report which is delivered to the registrar shall state the names of the auditors and be signed by them…

(5) References in this section to signature by the auditors are, where the office of auditor is held by a body corporate or partnership, to signature in the name of the body corporate or partnership by a person authorised to sign on its behalf.

Publication of the accounts and reports to members [CM6.9]

The directors must publish the accounts and the directors' report to the members. There are essentially two methods by which this can be done.

It is open to the shareholders to pass an elective resolution to the effect that instead of the accounts being *laid* before the members, the accounts shall be *sent* to the members.

Where no such elective resolution is in force, then a general meeting will need to be held. The *Companies Act 1985* provides that every company shall in each year hold an Annual General Meeting (AGM) in addition to any other meetings in that year, and shall specify the meeting as such in the notices calling it. It is customary for the accounts to be laid by the directors of the company before the members at the AGM. However, all that is legally required is that there is a general meeting during the financial year at which the accounts and reports for that financial year can be laid before the members.

Companies Act 1985, section 238(1) provides:

> 'A copy of the company's annual accounts, together with a copy of the directors' report for that financial year and of the auditors' report on those accounts, shall be sent to–
> (a) every member of the company,
> (b) every holder of the company's debentures, and
> (c) every person who is entitled to receive notice of general meetings…'

Companies Act 1985, section 238(2) provides that:

> 'Copies need not be sent–
> (a) to a person who is not entitled to receive notices of general meetings and of whose address the company is unaware, or
> (b) to more than one of the joint holders of shares or debentures none of whom is entitled to receive such notices, or
> (c) in the case of joint holders of shares or debentures some of whom are, and some not, entitled to receive such notices, to those who are not so entitled.'

Under *Companies Act 1985, section 238(5)*:

> 'If default is made in complying with [s238], the company and every officer of it who is in default is guilty of an offence and liable to a fine.'

Time limit for publication [CM6.10]

The accounts and the directors' report shall be sent not less than 21 days *before* the date of the general meeting at which copies of those documents are to be laid in accordance with *CA 1985, s241*.

However, *Companies Act 1985, section 238(4)* provides that if copies are sent less than 21 days before the date of the general meeting they shall, notwithstanding that fact, be deemed to have been duly sent if it is so agreed by all of the members entitled to attend and vote at the general meeting. Failure to adhere to these time limits will result in the company and every officer of it who is in default is guilty of an offence being liable to a fine (*CA 1985, s238(5)*).

Laying of accounts and the reports [CM6.11]

Under *Companies Act 1985, section 241(1)*:

> 'The directors of a company shall in respect of each financial year lay before the company in general meeting copies of the company's annual accounts, the directors' report and the auditors' report on those accounts.'

Under *Companies Act 1985, section 241(2)*:

> 'If the requirements of [s241(1)] are not complied with before the end of the period allowed for laying and delivering accounts and reports, every person who immediately before the end of that period was a director of the company is guilty of an offence and liable to a fine and, for continued contravention, to a daily default fine.'

Time limit **[CM6.12]**

Under *Companies Act 1985, section 244* the period allowed in the *Companies Acts* for laying and delivering accounts and reports is as follows.

(1) *Normally*

For a private company, ten months after the end of the relevant accounting reference period (*CA 1985, s244(1)(a)*). 'Relevant accounting reference period' means the accounting reference period by reference to which the financial year for the accounts in question was determined (*CA 1985, s244(6)*).

(2) *The company's first period*

If the relevant accounting reference period is the company's first and is a period of more than twelve months, the period allowed is whichever last expires of:

- ten months or seven months, as the case may be, from the first anniversary of the incorporation of the company; or
- three months from the end of the accounting reference period.

(3) *Companies with interests outside the UK, Channel Islands and Isle of Man*

Where a company carries on business, or has interests, outside the UK, the Channel Islands, and the Isle of Man, the directors may, in respect of any financial year, give to the Registrar before the end of the period allowed in (1) or (2) above, a notice in the prescribed form–

- stating that the company so carries on business or has such interests, and
- claiming a three month extension of the period allowed for laying and delivering accounts and reports and upon such a notice being given the period is extended accordingly.

(4) *Company altering its Accounting Reference Date*

If the relevant accounting period is treated as shortened by virtue of a notice given by the company under *CA 1985, s225* (alteration of Accounting Reference Date), the period allowed for laying and delivering accounts is that applicable in accordance with the above provisions or three months from the date of the notice under that section, whichever last expires.

(5) *Extension by the Secretary of State*

If for any special reason the Secretary of State thinks fit he may, on an application made before the expiry of the period otherwise allowed, by notice in writing to a company extend that period by such further period as may be specified in the notice.

Right to demand copies of accounts and reports [CM6.13]

Companies Act 1985, section 239 provides:

> '(1) Any member of a company and any holder of a company's debentures is entitled to be furnished, on demand and without charge, with a copy of the company's last annual accounts and directors' report and a copy of the auditors' report on those accounts.
>
> (2) The entitlement under this section is to a single copy of those documents, but that is in addition to any copy to which a person may be entitled under section 238.'

Under *Companies Act 1985, section 239*:

> '(3) If a demand under this section is not complied with within seven days, the company and every officer of it who is in default is guilty of an offence and liable to a fine and, for continuing contravention, to a daily default fine.
>
> (4) If in proceedings for such an offence the issue arises whether a person had already been furnished with a copy of the relevant document under this section, it is for the defendant to prove that he had.'

Publication of the accounts to Companies House [CM6.14]

Once publication of the accounts, the directors' report and the auditors' report has been made to the members, publication of these documents should then be made to Companies House.

Again, a difference arises between what might be called the full requirements and, in the case of companies able to bring themselves under one of the exemptions (see **CM7.6** below), more restricted requirements.

The full requirements [CM6.15]

Under *Companies Act 1985, section 242*:

> '(1) The directors of a company shall in respect of each financial year deliver to the registrar a copy of the company's annual accounts together with a copy of the directors' report for that year and a copy of the auditors' report on those accounts.'

Under *Companies Act 1985, section 242(2)*:

> 'If the requirements of [s242(1)] are not complied with before the end of the period allowed for laying and delivering accounts and reports, every person who immediately before the end of that period was a director of the company is guilty of an offence and liable to a fine and, for continued contravention, to a daily default fine.'

In addition, under *Companies Act 1985, section 242*:

> (3) Further, if the directors of the company fail to make good the default within 14 days after the service of a notice on them requiring compliance, the court may on the application of any member or creditor of the company or of the registrar, make an order directing the directors (or any of them) to make good the default within such time as may be specified in the order.

The court's order may provide that all costs of and incidental to the application shall be borne by the directors.

(4) It is a defence for a person charged with an offence under this section to prove that he took all reasonable steps for securing that the requirements of [s242(1)] would be complied with before the end of the period allowed for laying and delivering accounts and reports.

(5) It is not a defence in any proceedings under this section to prove that any documents in question were not in fact prepared as required by this Part.'

Under *Companies Act 1985, section 242A*:

'(1) Where the requirements of section 242(1) are not complied with before the end of the period allowed for laying and delivering accounts and reports, the company is liable to a civil penalty.
This is in addition to any liability of the directors under section 242.

(2) The amount of the penalty is determined by reference to the length of the period between the end of the period allowed for laying and delivering accounts and reports and the day on which the requirements are complied with, and whether the company is a public or a private company, as follows–

Length of period	*Penalty for Private Companies*
More than 3 months	£100
More than 3 months but not more than 6 months	£250
More than 6 months but not more than 12 months	£500
More than 12 months	£1,000

(3) The penalty may be recovered by the registrar and shall be paid by him into the Consolidated Fund.

(4) It is not a defence in proceedings under this section to prove that the documents in question were not in fact prepared as required by this Part.'

The restricted requirements [CM6.16]

Under *Companies Act 1985, section 246*:

'(1) Subject to section 247A, this section applies where a company qualifies as a small company in relation to a financial year.

(2) If the company's individual accounts for the year–
- (a) comply with the provisions of Schedule 8, or
- (b) fail to comply with those provisions only in so far as they comply instead with one or more corresponding provisions of Schedule 4,

they need not comply with the provisions or, as the case may be, the remaining provisions of Schedule 4; and where advantage is taken of this subsection, references in section 226 to compliance with the provisions of Schedule 4 shall be construed accordingly.

(3) The company's individual accounts for the year–
- (a) may give the total of the aggregates required by paragraphs (a), (c) and (d) of paragraph 1(1) of Schedule 6 (emoluments and other benefits etc. of directors) instead of giving those aggregates individually; and
- (b) need not give the information required by–
  - (i) paragraph 4 of Schedule 5 (financial years of subsidiary undertakings);
  - (ii) paragraph 1(2)(b) of Schedule 6 (numbers of directors exercising share options and receiving shares under long term incentive schemes);
  - (iii) paragraph 2 of Schedule 6 (details of highest paid director's emoluments etc); or
  - (iv) paragraph 7 of Schedule 6 (excess retirement benefits of directors and past directors).]

(4) The directors' report for the year need not give the information required by–
- (a) section 234(1)(a) and (b) (fair review of business and amount to be paid as dividend);
- (b) paragraph 1(2) of Schedule 7 (statement of market value of fixed assets where substantially different from balance sheet amount);
- (c) paragraph 6 of Schedule 7 (miscellaneous disclosures); or
- (d) paragraph 11 of Schedule 7 (employee involvement).

(5) Notwithstanding anything in section 242(1), the directors of the company need not deliver to the registrar any of the following, namely–
- (a) a copy of the company's profit and loss account for the year;
- (b) a copy of the directors' report for the year; and
- (c) if they deliver a copy of a balance sheet drawn up as at the last day of the year which complies with the requirements

of Schedule 8A, a copy of the company's balance sheet drawn up as at that day.

(6) Neither a copy of the company's accounts for the year delivered to the registrar under section 242(1), nor a copy of a balance sheet delivered to the registrar under subsection (5)(c), need give the information required by–
  (a) paragraph 4 of Schedule 5 (financial years of subsidiary undertakings);
  (b) paragraph 6 of Schedule 5 (shares of company held by subsidiary undertakings);
  (c) Part I of Schedule 6 (directors' and chairman's emoluments, pensions and compensation for loss of office); or
  (d) section 390A(3) (amount of auditors' remuneration).

(7) The provisions of section 233 as to the signing of the copy of the balance sheet delivered to the registrar apply to a copy of a balance sheet delivered under subsection (5)(c).

(8) Subject to subsection (9), each of the following, namely–
  (a) accounts prepared in accordance with subsection (2) or (3),
  (b) a report prepared in accordance with subsection (4), and
  (c) a copy of accounts delivered to the registrar in accordance with subsection (5) or (6),

shall contain a statement in a prominent position on the balance sheet, in the report or, as the case may be, on the copy of the balance sheet, above the signature required by section 233, 234A or subsection (7), that they are prepared in accordance with the special provisions of this Part relating to small companies.

(9) Subsection (8) does not apply where the directors of the company have taken advantage of the exemption from audit conferred by section 249AA (dormant companies).'

Under *CA 1985, section 247A*:

'(1) Nothing in section 246 or 246A shall apply where–
  (a) the company is, or was at any time within the financial year to which the accounts relate–
  (i) ...
  (ii) a banking or insurance company, or
  (iii) an authorised person under the Financial Services Act 1986; or
  (b) the company is, or was at any time during that year, a member of an ineligible group [defined in s247A(2)].

CM7 – Application of the Accounts Requirements

Introduction [CM7.1]

The requirements relating to the accounts of a company are set out in **Chapter CM6**.

These requirements, effectively amounting to a duty of disclosure which balances the right of limited liability, are essential requirements of the *Companies Acts* and no concession is in principle made simply, for example, because the individual reporting as the sole director is the same individual being reported to as the sole member. The requirements of the *Companies Acts* are legal requirements which in principle apply to *all* companies registered as companies under those Acts.

Having said that, it has been increasingly recognised over recent years that while many, indeed the majority, of the provisions in the *Companies Acts* are aimed at protecting those dealing with companies whose shares are offered to the public the entirety of these requirements can be seen as excessive in the case of small private companies which do not offer their shares to the public which we consider below in relation to the application of the requirements.

Accounting Reference Date [CM7.2]

The obligation to produce accounts (*CA 1985, s226*) is related to the financial year of the company.

Companies Act 1985, section 223 then determines what a financial year is and it does so by reference to accounting reference periods.

> '223(2)[A company's] first financial year begins with the first day of its first accounting reference period and ends with the last day of that period or such other date, not more than seven days before or after the end of that period, as the directors may determine.

223(3) Subsequent financial years begin with the day immediately following the end of the company's previous financial year and end with the last day of its next accounting reference period or such other date, not more than seven days before or after the end of that period, as the directors may determine'.

'Accounting reference periods' are (under *CA 1985, s224*) determined by reference to the 'accounting reference date' as follows.

'224(2) A company may, at any time before the end of the period of nine months beginning with the date of its incorporation, by notice in the prescribed form given to the registrar specify its accounting reference date, that is, the date on which its accounting reference period ends in each calendar year.

224(3) Failing such notice, a company's accounting reference date is–…

(b) in the case of a company incorporated after [1st April 1990], the last day of the month in which the anniversary of its incorporation falls.

224(4) A company's first accounting reference period is the period of more than six months, but not more than 18 months, beginning with the date of its incorporation and ending with its accounting reference date.

224(5) [The company's] subsequent accounting reference periods are successive periods of twelve months beginning immediately after the end of the previous accounting reference period and ending with its accounting reference date.

224(6) This section has effect subject to the provisions of section 225 relating to the alteration of accounting reference dates and the consequences of such alteration.

225(1) A company may by notice in the prescribed form given to the registrar specify a new accounting reference date having effect in relation to–

(a) the company's current accounting reference period and subsequent periods…

225(2) …

225(3) The notice shall state whether the current...accounting reference period–

(a) is to be shortened, so as to come to an end on the first occasion on which the new accounting reference date falls or fell after the beginning of the period, or

(b) is to be extended, so as to come to an end on the second occasion on which that date falls or fell after the beginning of the period.

225(4) A notice under subsection (1) stating that the current... accounting reference period is to be extended is ineffective...if given less than five years after the end of an earlier accounting reference period of the company which was extended by virtue of this section...

225(6) An accounting reference period may not in any case, unless an administration order is in force under Part II of the Insolvency Act 1986, be extended so as to exceed 18 months and a notice under this section is ineffective if the current ... accounting reference period as extended in accordance with the notice would exceed that limit.'

On incorporation [CM7.3]

Accordingly, if after incorporation the company takes no action during the nine-month period then its accounting reference date will be the last day on the month on which the anniversary of its incorporation falls and that will determine both the company's accounting reference period and its financial year (with the directors given a leeway either side of not more than seven days).

If the company takes the option during the nine months to specify its own accounting reference date then the first accounting reference period, beginning with the date of incorporation, must be not less than six months and not more than eighteen months.

Subsequent financial years [CM7.4]

Subsequent financial years will begin with the day following the end of the previous financial year for the accounting reference period forming the next financial year and so on (again with the directors given a leeway either side of not more than seven days).

If the company so wishes, it can later adjust its accounting reference period but only within the limits specified in *CA 1985, s225* (see **CM7.2** above). This cannot be done retrospectively and can only be done once in any five year period.

An overview of the financial statements of a company [CM7.5]

A full set of financial statements for a private limited company is likely to consist of:

- Directors' Report (see **CL2.54** above);
- Profit and Loss Account;
- Balance Sheet;
- Statement of Source and Application of Funds;
- Notes to the Accounts; and
- Audit Report.

The exemptions [CM7.6]

The *Companies Acts (Accounts of Small and Medium-sized Companies and Minor Accounting Amendments) Regulations 1997 (SI 1997/220)* provide for the exemption from accounting requirements.

Disentitlements [CM7.7]

Certain companies cannot receive exemptions no matter what their size (*CA 1985, s247A(1)*) and these include:

- public companies;
- banking companies;
- insurance companies;
- companies authorised under the *Financial Services Act 1986*; and
- companies which are members of a group which is ineligible by any members being:
  - able to issue share or debentures to the public;
  - an authorised business under *Banking Act 1987*;
  - an insurance company; or
  - an authorised person under *Financial Services Act 1986.*

Medium-sized companies [CM7.8]

The definition of a medium-sized company involves:

Turnover not exceeding	£11,200,000
Balance Sheet total	£ 5,600,000
Average Number Employees	250

Small companies [CM7.9]

The definition of a small-sized company involves:

Turnover not exceeding	£2,800,000
Balance Sheet total	£ 1,400,000
Average Number Employees	50

and where the following conditions are met.

A company qualifies as a small-sized company for a financial year if it satisfies any *two* of the following three conditions during that year:

1. The amount of the turnover did not exceed (currently £2,000,000).
2. The balance sheet total* did not exceed (currently £975,000).
3. The average number of employees did not exceed (currently 50).

Turnover [CM7.10]

Turnover receives its generally accepted meaning. However, for the purposes of these provisions may be applied proportionately. Thus, if a company produced accounts for a period of only 10 months then for that company the turnover threshold would be £1,666,666 (i.e. 10/12ths of £2,000,000)

Average number of employees [CM7.11]

The average number of employees means the average number of persons employed by the company in the financial year determined on a weekly basis.

The method of calculation prescribed (*CA 1985, Sch 4, para 56(2)(3)*) is to add up those defined as employed for each week and then divide that by the number of weeks in the year.

Balance Sheet total **[CM7.12]**

The balance sheet total is in effect the gross assets of the company but is defined by reference to the format of Accounts which the *Companies Act* requires a company to produce of which there are two.

Format 1
The balance sheet total is the aggregate of the amounts shown under:

A Called up share capital not paid;
B Fixed assets;
C Current assets; and
D Pre-payments and accrued income.

Format 2
The balance sheet total is the aggregate of the amounts shown under the heading 'Assets'.

The application of the concession **[CM7.13]**

The concession has been designed (for administrative ease) to apply in a cascading manner.

In its first financial year, a company which satisfied two of the conditions bringing the company within the definition of a small-sized company will be entitled to deliver to the Registrar of Companies abbreviated financial statements.

In subsequent financial years, a company which satisfied two of the conditions bringing the company within the definition of a small-sized company *in both the preceding year* *<u>and</u>* *that year* will be entitled to deliver to the Registrar of Companies abbreviated financial statements.

In subsequent financial years, a company which satisfied two of the conditions bringing the company within the definition of a small-sized company *in the preceding year* *<u>but not</u>* *that year* will still be entitled to deliver to the Registrar of Companies abbreviated financial statements for that year.

In subsequent financial years, a company which has not satisfied two of the conditions bringing the company within the definition of a small-sized company *in the preceding year* *<u>but has</u>* satisfied two of the conditions bringing the company within the definition of a small-sized company *in that year* will be entitled to continue deliver to the Registrar of Companies abbreviated financial statements for that year.

In subsequent financial years, a company which has not satisfied two of the conditions bringing the company within the definition of a small-sized company *in the preceding year or in that year* will no longer be entitled to continue deliver to the Registrar of Companies abbreviated financial statements for that year.

Directors' Reports [CM7.14]

The full requirements for Directors' Reports are as follows.

- Fair review of business development.*
- Dividends.*
- Directors' names.
- The company's principal activities.
- Significant changes in fixed assets.*
- Directors' interests in shares or loans.
- Political and charitable gifts.
- Post Balance Sheets.*
- Likely future developments.*
- Research and development.*
- Acquisition of own shares.
- Employee information.
- Employment of disabled persons.
- Health, safety and welfare at work.
- Employee involvement.*
- Average number of employees.

Where the small companies' exemption applies, then the Directors' Report need *not* disclose those entries listed above that are marked with an asterisk. However, if advantage is to be taken of these exemptions then that fact must be stated in the Directors' Report.

The company's accounts [CM7.15]

So far as the accounts of a company are concerned, the position has become more complex with something of a schism opening up as regards the approach which may be adopted by large companies and by medium and small-sized companies.

The full and proper approach, which requires to be adopted by large companies involves the accounting records of the company (which may already have been utilised for the management accounts of the company) being converted into a full set of accounts (complying with the Generally Accepted Accounting Principles (GAAP) for the UK) which are audited and then placed before the members and lodged with the Registrar of Companies. After the appropriate adjustments have been made to those accounts they may then also be used to complete the company's Tax Return which will in turn by the Inland Revenue (who will be relying upon the above process) to determine the taxation liability of the company.

The lesser approach, which may be adopted by medium and small-sized companies, still requires those companies to have accounting records. Those records need not be used for management purposes (although it is clearly advisable to do so) and may not require to be audited. A set of accounts must still be placed before the members (which ought to comply with the relevantly applicable Generally Accepted Accounting Principles (GAAP) for the UK) but only a restricted form of accounts requires to be lodged with the Registrar of the Companies. Again, after the appropriate adjustments have been made to those accounts they may then also be used to complete the company's Tax Return which will in turn by the Inland Revenue (who will be relying upon the above process) to determine the taxation liability of the company.

Clearly, where the ownership and control of the company are in the hands of the same individuals there is a temptation to save time and money by avoiding an audit and producing only the minimum required in the way of accounts. However, it may be found in practice that if the proper accepted accounting principles (audited or unaudited) – which generally involves the use of an accountant – have not been applied in the preparation of the accounts then (particularly where there is no involvement of a properly qualified accountant) the Inland Revenue may be less willing to rely upon those accounts for the purposes of determining the taxation liability of the company and may insist upon having a closer look at the accounting records of the company. In practice, also, where the company borrows to fund a project the funders or bankers may insist upon an audit.

Accordingly, it is a simple facet of commercial life in practice that, no matter what the strict minimum legal requirements might be, it will be advantageous for small companies to follow as closely as time, money and circumstances permit the normal procedures for the preparation and presentation of the company's accounts.

In the event of the Inland Revenue choosing to examine your company in order to determine whether or not the requirements of the legislation implementing IR35 have been met, the form of the company's accounts might well turn out to be a factor.

A company which has only one client and which records the income from that client and any subsequent expenditure on the back of an envelope is more likely to be regarded as akin to a contract of service in employment whereas a company with a number of clients producing full and proper accounts would be more likely to be regarded as providing contracts for services on a self-employed basis.

Time limits for preparation [CM7.16]

Section 226 of the *Companies Act 1985* imposes upon the directors of a company the duty to prepare a balance sheet and a profit and loss account for each financial year of the company. The first financial year of a company begins on the date of incorporation and ends on the accounting reference date.

Upon incorporation a company is given a deemed accounting reference date (the last day of the month which is the anniversary of the date of incorporation). The company is at liberty during the nine months following incorporation to change that accounting reference date to one more suitable to the company but if no alteration is made then after the expiry of that period, the accounting reference date of the company is deemed to be that given to the company upon incorporation.

The auditing requirement [CM7.17]

Auditing is an extremely complex concept. The purpose of auditing, its nature, and the relationship between auditing and accountancy are extremely etheral concepts. In consequence, over many years a 'perception gap' appears to have opened up between what might be called the public's expectations of what an audit is intended to achieve and what might be called the profession's expectations of what an audit is intended to achieve. In recent years, however, a great deal of work has gone into defining more closely these expectations and closing the gap or at least raising the understanding of its nature.

For larger public companies, particularly those who offer their shares to the public on a recognised stock exchange, the concept of auditing remains fundamental. It is, quite simply, as well as being a statutory requirement, an indispensable requirement for a listing and the right to offer shares to the public. The creation of the Auditing Practices Board and publication of Statements of Auditing Standards has gone some way towards defining more closely what is expected by way of an audit and any failure in that respect has led to increasing negligence claims against auditors which has in turn led to a drive for auditors to themselves achieve limited liability either through the concept of a limited liability company or a limited liability partnership.

Dispensing with the annual requirements **[CM7.18]**

Where the company accounts are still to be audited, the administrative burden has been eased in a number of ways.

Election to dispense with the obligation to lay accounts before members annually **[CM7.19]**

Where a private company has elected in accordance with *section 252* of the *Companies Act 1985* to dispense with the laying of accounts then there are special provisions for the appointment of the auditors.

In the case of the first auditors for a new company which has made such an election, *Companies Act 1985, section 385A* allows the directors to appoint the auditors whom failing the company is to make an appointment in general meeting.

In the case of existing auditors for existing companies which has made such an election the auditors must be appointed by the company in a General Meeting held within 28 days of the Accounts for the previous year being sent to the members and the auditors so appointed will hold office until the next date upon which the appointment of auditors falls due.

Election to dispense with the obligation to appoint auditors annually **[CM7.20]**

Private companies can also pass an elective resolution under *Companies Act 1985, section 379A* to dispense with the obligation to appoint auditors annually, in which case the existing auditors will, so long as the election continues, be deemed to have been re-appointed unless a resolution is passed ending the appointment or the company falls dormant.

The current legislation on auditing is to be found in *SI 1997/936* which applies an exemption.The exemptions do not apply to public companies, banking companies, small charitable companies, or companies which are persons authorised under the financial services legislation.

However, for those companies not excluded from the exemption, where:

- the annual turnover does not exceed £350,000; or
- the balance sheet totals do not exceed £1,400,000

then the company is excluded from the requirement to file an audit certificate.

The exemption can, however, be disapplied where 10% or more of the Members (Shareholders) of the company demand a full statutory audit.

Where the exemption is applied for then in place of the audit certain additional requirements are imposed on the directors.The directors need to make a Statement on the Balance Sheet to the effect:

- that advantage has been taken of the exemption provisions; and
- expressly acknowledges the responsibility of the directors to:
    - ensure that proper accounting records are kept by the company; and
    - prepare accounts which comply with the *Companies Act 1985;*

  and give a true and fair view of the state of affairs on the company at the end of its financial year-end and of its profit and loss for the period.

The exemption [CM7.21]

For medium and small-sized companies, however, particularly those whose shares are not offered to the public, the need to have a full statutory audit has been the subject of debate for a number of years. As a result, while it remains possible for companies to have their accounts audited voluntarily (often a requirement imposed by Banks), successive Chancellors of the Exchequer have both introduced a threshold below which the requirement for a full statutory audit was removed and then steadily increased that threshold.This process was begun in 1994 which introduced a threshold below which companies were permitted to replace the full audit report with a compilation report which was effectively an independent accountant's report on whether a company's accounts correctly reflected its accounting records. In 1997 the process was continued by raising the threshold generally and also introducing a lower threshold below which not even a compilation report was required. More recently, the *Companies Act 1985 (Audit Exemptions) (Amendment) Regulations 2000* have increased the threshold for exemption from the audit requirement to £1 million.

CM8 – The Company Tax Return

Introduction [CM8.1]

It is necessary and indeed vital to account properly for Corporation Tax. This involves the company making a Tax Return.

Previously (under a system known as Pay-and-File) it was the responsibility of the Inspector of Taxes to issue an Assessment. However, under the system which is now in force (for accounting periods ending on or after 1 July 1999) the system has been changed to one of Corporation Tax self- assessment.

Notification of chargeability [CM8.2]

Although the Inland Revenue have procedures for tracing the existence of companies they may not be aware of when a company is chargeable to Corporation Tax for an accounting period.

Accordingly, the obligation is imposed (under the *Finance Act 1998, Sch 18, para 2(1)*) on the company to give notice to the Inland Revenue that it is chargeable to Corporation Tax within twelve months of the end of the company's accounting period. There are penalties for a failure to do this (*Finance Act 1998, Sch 18, para 2(3)*) although it is provided that the penalty will not exceed the tax payable for the period.

Notice to deliver a return [CM8.3]

Once aware of, or notified of, the chargeability to Corporation Tax of a company the Inland Revenue are empowered to (*Finance Act 1998, Sch 18, para 3(1)*) and normally will issue a formal notice (Form CT603) requiring the company to deliver a company Tax Return. This notice must specify the period for which the Return is required (usually twelve calendar months).

The period specified by the Inland Revenue might cover more than one accounting period of the company and in these circumstances a company Tax Return is required for every accounting period ending in the period specified by the Inland Revenue.

Example

A Ltd was incorporated on 1 July 2000. On becoming aware of, or being notified of that fact, the Inland Revenue are likely to issue a Form CT603 requiring the company to deliver a company Tax Return for the period 1 July 2000 to 30 June 2001.

A Ltd had commenced trading on 1 January 2001, specified its accounting period as 31 December, and planned to make up its first accounts for a twelve month period ending on 31 December 2001. As no accounting period ended in that period specified by the Inland Revenue, A Ltd would make a nil company Tax Return to the Inland Revenue for that period.

The Inland Revenue are likely to later issue a further Form CT603 requiring the company to deliver a company Tax Return for the period 1 July 2001 to 30 June 2002.

As the accounting period ended 31 December 2001 ended in this period specified by the Inland Revenue, A Ltd would make or 'file' a full company Tax Return to the Inland Revenue.

The deadline for making or 'filing' a company Tax Return [CM8.4]

A company is, as we have seen, assessed to Corporation Tax by reference to the total profits it has received during its accounting period. The accounting period is therefore very important as it fixes, amongst other things, the deadline within which the company Tax Return must be filed. Accordingly, there are specific rules determining for companies when their accounting periods begin and end.

When accounting periods begin [CM8.5]

An accounting period will begin when the company first becomes chargeable to corporation tax which might be when:

- the company first becomes resident in the UK;
- the company first acquires a source of income (e.g. interest); and
- the company commences trading.

As soon as one accounting period ends (on which see below) another accounting period begins

When accounting periods end **[CM8.6]**

An accounting period can never exceed twelve months and in these circumstances an accounting period comes to an end on the date upon which the company makes up its accounts

There are special rules where a company:

- ceases to be chargeable to any Corporation Tax;
- ceases to trade;
- is wound up; or
- ceases to be resident in the UK.

In light of the above requirements, the deadline for the filing by a company of its company Tax Return (and a number of returns may be required) is related to the period of account i.e. the period for which the company makes up its accounts.

Example 1

A Ltd commences trading on 1 January 2001 and makes up its accounts to 31 December 2001.

A Form CT603 was issued by the Inland Revenue requiring the company to deliver a company Tax Return for a period 1 July 2001 to 30 June 2002.

The deadline for the company to submit its company Tax Return would be 31 December 2002.

For later periods of account, a distinction is drawn between those which are not longer than 18 months and those which are longer than 18 months.

Where the company's accounting period does not exceed 18 months then although two returns will be required – one for 12 months and one for 6 months – the deadline for filing the company's Tax Return is twelve months from the end of the company's accounting period. (*FA 1998, Sch 18, para 14(1(d).*)

Example 2

A Ltd commences trading on 1 January 2001 and makes up its accounts to 30 June 2002.

A Form CT603 was issued by the Inland Revenue requiring the company to deliver a company Tax Return for a period 1 July 2001 to 30 June 2002.

Two returns will be required from the company – one for the 12 month period 1 January 2001 to 31 December 2001 and one for the period 1 January 2002 to 30 June 2002.

The deadline for the company to submit both of these in its company Tax Return would be 30 June 2003.

Where the company's accounting period does exceed 18 months then although again several returns will be required, the deadline for filing the company's Tax Return is thirty months from the beginning of the period. (*FA 1998, Sch 18, para 14(1(d).*)

Example 3

A Ltd commences trading on 1 January 2001 and makes up its accounts to 31 March 2003.

A Form CT603 was issued by the Inland Revenue requiring the company to deliver a company Tax Return for a period 1 July 2002 to 30 June 2003.

Three returns will be required from the company – one for the 12 month period 1 January 2001 to 31 December 2001; one for the 12 month period 1 January 2002 to 31 December 2003; and one for the period 1 January 2003 to 31 March 2003.

The deadline for the company to submit all of these in its company Tax Return would be 30 June 2003.

In other cases, the deadline for filing the company's Tax Return is three months from the date of the notice to deliver a Return. (*FA 1998 Sch 18 para 14(1)(d).*)

The return must be delivered to the Inland Revenue by the filing date. It is advisable for a company to retain evidence of timeous delivery. Due to the non-standard nature of such returns the electronic lodgement system is not at present available.

The form of the company's Tax Return [CM8.7]

Under *Finance Act 1998, Sch 18, para 3(1)*, the Inland Revenue can prescribe in the notice requiring a company Tax Return from the company such information, accounts, statements and reports, relevant to the Corporation Tax liability or applicability of the *Tax Acts* in relation to the company. Accordingly, the Inland Revenue may require particular types of information in the case of Personal Service Companies.

The basic company Tax Return consists of a core Return Form (Form CT 600) together with such other supplementary pages as the Inland Revenue may direct.

Payment [CM8.8]

In future, the payment of Corporation Tax will be determined by the level of profits. 'Large' companies (currently defined as having profits in excess of £1.5 million), are required to pay Corporation Tax on a quarterly basis.

Companies which are not 'large' will pay Corporation Tax by reference to their accounting periods and company Tax Returns which by law must include a self assessment of the Corporation Tax payable in relation to that Return which normally has to be paid within 9 months and 1 day after the end of the accounting period.

CM9 – Company Matters – The Annual Return

Introduction [CM9.1]

In addition to delivering Accounts and reports to Companies House, every company also requires to deliver to Companies House an annual return each year.

Under *Companies Act 1985, section 363*:

> (1) Every company shall deliver to the registrar successive annual returns each of which is made up to a date not later than the date which is from time to time the company's 'return date', that is–
> (a) the anniversary of the company's incorporation, or
> (b) if the company's last return delivered in accordance with this Chapter was made up to a different date, the anniversary of that date.
>
> (2) Each return shall–
> (a) be in the prescribed form,
> (b) contain the information required by or under the following provisions of this Chapter, and
> (c) be signed by a director or the secretary of the company;
>
> and it shall be delivered to the registrar within 28 days after the date to which it is made up.

Section 364 deals with the contents of the annual return in general. *Section 364A* deals with the contents of the annual return as it relates to particulars of the share capital and shareholders. *Section 365* allows the Secretary of State to make further regulations.

In fact, the current practice is for Companies House to issue automatically what is known as a 'shuttle' annual return (Form 363s), the sections of which cover the above-mentioned requirements and which companies have simply to complete and return.

Under *Companies Act 1985, section 363*:

'(3) If a company fails to deliver an annual return in accordance with this Chapter before the end of the period of 28 days after a return date, the company is guilty of an offence and liable to a fine and, in the case of continued contravention, to a daily default fine.
The contravention continues until such time as an annual return made up to that return date and complying with the requirements of [s363(2)] (except as to date of delivery) is delivered by the company to the registrar.

(4) Where a company is guilty of an offence under [s363(3)], every director or secretary of the company is similarly liable unless he shows that he took all reasonable steps to avoid the commission or continuation of the offence.'

The *Companies Acts* oblige every company to make an Annual Return to Companies House and it is, in fact, a criminal offence not to do so for which the directors and the company secretary can be prosecuted.

Formerly, it was something of a strain for Companies to remember the due date for their Annual Return, obtain the Form, complete the Form, and file it with Companies House within the required period. Today, matters are made a little easier by Companies House automatically issuing an Annual Return to the company about two weeks before the Annual Return is due to be made up.

Companies House enters on the Form the information about the company presently held on its file at Companies House so that the company has merely to notify any changes or confirm that the Form is correct and return it.

Name of the company [CM9.2]

The company name will normally remain unchanged and it is simply a matter of ensuring that the Annual Return has been issued in the correct name of the company, failing which Companies House should be advised.

Registered Number of the company [CM9.3]

This is the principal means of identification of a company and remains unchanged even after a change of name. It is simply a matter of ensuring that the Annual Return has been issued using the correct Registered Number, failing which Companies House should be advised.

Company type [CM9.4]

The type of company (e.g. whether private or public) should be entered in this Form. Although the type of company can be changed that cannot be done by means of this Form and is the subject of a separate procedure. No changes should be entered here unless and until any such change has been effected.

The Registered Office [CM9.5]

The situation of the company's Registered Office is a vital piece of information and this Form seeks to confirm the current situation.

The address where the Registers of the company are kept if not at the Registered Office [CM9.6]

It will often be convenient to keep all of the Registers which a company must maintain at the Registered Office of the Company. There is, however, no obligation to do so and some of the Registers may be kept elsewhere. In order that they can be consulted, however, it is necessary to know where they are being kept and this Form seeks to elicit that information.

The principal activities of the company [CM9.7]

Companies House seeks to apply the UK Standard Industrial Classification (SIC 92) Codes for this purpose.

Name and address of the company secretary [CM9.8]

This will often be unchanged and can be marked accordingly. Where changes have taken place, however, then the correct details should be entered.

Directors' details [CM9.9]

The name, address, date of birth, nationality and business occupation of the directors will often be unchanged and can be marked accordingly. Where changes have taken place, however, then the correct details should be entered.

Date to which the Annual Return is made up [CM9.10]

This is the date to which it is certified the information contained in the Annual Return is correct.

The nominal value of the issued share capital [CM9.11]

This will normally be unchanged but changes can be made and should be notified.

Names and addresses of members and number and type of shares held [CM9.12]

A company's share capital will often remain unchanged for substantial periods of time. The 'shuttle' Annual Return allows for this but a 'full list' of members must be made on the first annual return after incorporation and every third annual return thereafter.

The Annual Return asks for details as to the:

- name of the class of each type of share;
- total nominal value of such shares as at the date of the Annual Return;
- total number of shares issued to shareholders as at the date of the Annual Return.

Date for the Annual Return [CM9.13]

The formal date for an Annual Return, known as its made-up date, is usually the anniversary of the incorporation of the company or the made-up date of the previous annual return registered at Companies House.

The Annual Return must be delivered to Companies House within 28 days of the made-up date given on the Form.

Taxation

In this section, we consider the application of the principles of taxation insofar as they can be applied to Personal Service Companies in particular and we also consider the new tax rules relating to IR35 before concluding with a consideration of the means by which all taxation disputes (including those relating to IR35) which cannot be resolved amicably will be settled – by way of appeal.

Value Added Tax

VAT applies to the supply of goods and services. Personal Service Companies are, of course, concerned mainly with the supply of services but such companies are unlikely to be free from a consideration also of the rules relating to goods.

Corporation Tax

Corporation Tax is likely to be worked out, by way of self-assessment, for Personal Service Companies in much the same way as for other trading Private Limited Companies. One distinguishing feature, however, the effects of which will require to be worked out in practice, is the consequences of failing the IR35 Test. A Personal Service Company will, of course, wish to offset any tax and NIC on any deemed payments against profits for Corporation Tax purposes. It is possible to accrue salary, tax and NIC for directors in the company Accounts but to be an allowable deduction these must be paid within a period of nine months. What the position is going to be in relation to Corporation Tax where the Inland Revenue come along several years later and on a finding of 'relevant engagements' deem payments for several years is, as noted, something which has yet to be worked out in practice.

PAYE, NIC and benefits
For any private limited company this area of taxation is now (unnecessarily) a veritable minefield. It is, however, perhaps potentially more dangerous for Personal Service Companies (especially those involving only one or two people) than for other types of company because a failure to maintain a rigid distinction (as often happens) between the assets of the company and the assets of the individual has the practical result of most assets becoming a potential benefit.

IR35
In this section we consider the likely effect of the legislation implementing IR35 so far as appears likely as presently advised.

Appeals
The final resort for any taxation dispute with the Inland Revenue (including IR35) is by way of an appeal to the Commissioners and in this final section we consider what is involved in that.

CT1 – VAT

Introduction [CT1.1]

One of the consequences of receiving a high level of income as a self-employed trader (in whatever capacity) is becoming a 'taxable person' and being obliged to register for, charge, offset, return and account for VAT.

Effectively, the trader is acting as an unpaid tax collector for the Government as the incidence of VAT makes its way up the chain of production to the ultimate consumer which is where the incidence of VAT rests. Experience has shown that a tendency to treat VAT monies in hand as those of the trading entity can lead to that entity's downfall. A more prudent approach is to regard VAT monies as the monies of the Government which is just passing through the entity rather than belonging to it.

The company must ensure that:

- the VAT system applying to the particular business of the trading entity must be understood and applied correctly;
- output VAT is charged correctly;
- input VAT is offset correctly;
- a VAT account is maintained;
- a proper VAT Return is made;
- the payment of VAT is made; and
- proper records are kept and retained.

The whole VAT system is underpinned by a system of VAT enforcement which has a reputation for firm but fair enforcement. There is also an appeals system.

Output VAT [CT1.2]

The main supply made by Personal Service Companies is that of personal services to clients and/or agencies. In the main, therefore, so far as output VAT is concerned, a Personal Service Company will be concentrating on where and when those personal services are supplied to the clients/agencies. A particular set of VAT rules apply to the supply of services.

It is, however, important for Personal Service Companies to appreciate that they have registered for VAT purposes not just in relation to the provision of services but in relation to the VAT system as a whole.

Thus, should a Personal Service Company which normally provides services decide to sell some assets owned by the company, it is important to appreciate both that the sale of those assets will also be subject to VAT and that a different set of rules may apply in ascertaining the VAT payable thereon.

The charging provision [CT1.3]

Section 4 of the *Value Added Tax Act 1994* requires businesses in the UK to charge VAT. This provision revolves around the concept of 'taxable supplies'. Essentially, VAT must be charged where supplies (of services or goods) are made:

- which are taxable (i.e. not exempt);
- by a taxable person;
- in the course of the furtherance of business; and
- in the UK or the Isle of Man;

Supply [CT1.4]

Even though the concept of 'taxable supplies' is central to the system of VAT, that concept is not particularly closely defined in the legislation. *Section 5(2)(a)* of the *Value Added Tax Act 1994* defines 'supply' as:

> '…all forms of supply, but not anything done otherwise than for consideration'.

Clearly, this is a very wide and open-ended definition and it may be that it has deliberately been made so in order to perform a 'catch-all' function for VAT purposes.

The word 'supply' has been judicially described as a word having the 'widest import'. In interpretation the word will be given its ordinary meaning by the courts but clearly it is wide enough to cover the provision of virtually all services and goods, qualified only by the need for there to be consideration.

Consideration **[CT1.5]**

The qualification of the need for consideration is clearly aimed at confining the system of VAT to transactions of a business nature. Again, the term 'consideration' has not been closely defined for the purposes of VAT but perhaps it does not require to be so defined because the concept of consideration which will apply for VAT purposes will be exactly the same concept of consideration which applies elsewhere (such as in the law of contract) in determining transactions of a business nature.

In relation to the law of contract, for example, the term 'consideration' is fundamental to the law of England and Wales (although not a requirement in Scotland) where its meaning has, over the years, been interpreted as meaning *anything* (i.e. not just money) provided in exchange for something else where one is conditional upon the other.

However, there are some references to 'consideration' in the VAT literature which may help to confine the definition in practice. For example, the *Second VAT Directive* states:

> 'The expression "consideration" means everything received in return for the supply of goods or the provision of services, including incidental expenses (packing, transport, insurance etc.) that is to say not only the cash amounts charged, but also, for example, the value of goods received in exchange or, in the case of goods or services supplied by order of a public authority, the amount of the compensation received.'

This specific VAT definition of 'consideration' was not in fact repeated in the *Sixth VAT Directive* (although it might, by implication, be incorporated and applied there in the same way). The *Sixth Directive* does, however, define 'taxable amount' as:

> '...everything which constitutes the consideration which has been or is to be obtained by the supplier from the purchaser, the customer or a third party for such supplies including subsidies directly linked to the price of such supplies'.

Like 'supply' the term 'consideration' is of the widest import but the above does perhaps offer some guidance as to the manner in which the term 'consideration' is likely to be interpreted for VAT purposes.

De minimis gifts **[CT1.6]**

In the application of the definitions of 'supply' and 'consideration', Customs and Excise operate a tightly-controlled disregard for *de minimis* (minor) items such as gifts made for business reasons, provided that they are not part of a series of succession of gifts to the same person and provided their value (excluding VAT) is below a certain level (currently £15).

'Supply' and 'consideration' are widely defined. In practice, therefore, there is likely to be very little in the way of the application of personal services by a Personal Service Company (other than that specifically excluded as *de minimus*) which will not be a 'consideration' and therefore a 'supply' chargeable to VAT.

Example

PSC1 Ltd provides a particular form of computing service. PSC2 Ltd provides another particular form of computing services. Both companies come to an arrangement whereby certain computing services will be provided by PSC1 Ltd to PSC2 Ltd in exchange for which PSC2 Ltd will provide certain other computing services to PSC1 Ltd. No money changes hands between the companies.

Even though no money has changed hands between the companies, the exchange of services with one being conditional on the other is likely to be interpreted as 'consideration'. This will make the computing services a 'supply' for VAT purposes and exposes the companies to VAT penalties if they do not properly charge and account for VAT thereon.

Therefore each company would be required to:

- calculate the market value of their services;
- provide proper invoices thereon; and
- charge and collect the relevant VAT.

Services **[CT1.7]**

While 'taxable supplies' is the concept around which the VAT system revolves, the concept of supply is in fact divided into the supply of goods and services. It is clearly in the area of 'services' that a Personal Service Company will be concerned but in fact the definition of 'services' applied is where there is anything which is not a supply of goods but is done for consideration.

However, VAT Guide (Notice 700) provides guidance on what might constitute a 'supply of services':

> '*Supplies of services*
>
> You supply services if you do something, other than supplying goods, for a consideration. A consideration is any form of payment in money or in kind, including anything which is itself a supply.
>
> You also supply services if you:
>
> - lend goods to someone for use outside your business
> - hire goods to someone
> - provide goods from someone else's materials
> - use goods owned by the business outside the business
> - agree, for a consideration, to refrain from doing something; and
> - agree to grant, assign, or surrender a right for consideration.'

Example

PSC Limited exceeds the turnover threshold and is registered for VAT purposes. PSC Limited agrees to design a web page for R Limited at an agreed monthly sum of money (the 'consideration').

This clearly a 'supply' of services for which PSC Limited should issue a formal VAT invoice to R Limited each month.

Goods [CT1.8]

Even though a Personal Service Company might set out to only provide personal services (which by definition would involve the company in, for VAT purposes, the supply of services), should that Personal Service Company decide to sell some of the company assets then not only does the company require to charge VAT on the sale of those assets but it requires to do so under the rules relating to the supply of goods. It is, therefore, necessary for a Personal Service Company to be aware of the rules relating to the supply of goods also.

A supply of goods and charge to VAT arises where the property in goods is transferred:

- by sale;
- under an agreement for the sale of the goods; or
- transferred under agreements which expressly contemplate that the property will pass some time in the future.

VAT Guide (Notice 700) provides guidance.

> '*Supplies of goods*
> You supply goods if you pass the exclusive ownership of goods to another person.
>
> You also supply goods if you:
>
> - transfer them under an agreement such as a hire-purchase agreement (but not if you transfer such an agreement itself);
> - provide water or any form of power, heat, refrigeration or ventilation (but not if you hire out equipment which does this);
> - supply a major interest in land or a lease exceeding 21 years;
> - transfer goods permanently out of the business for your private use.
>
> You do *not* make a supply if you provide goods (such as overalls or goods) to employees solely for the purpose of their employment and make no charge.'

Example

PSC Limited exceeds the turnover threshold and is registered for VAT purposes. PSC Limited normally supplies services to R Limited for which PSC Limited issues a VAT invoice to R Limited each month.

PSC Limited decides to replace its computer system. PSC Limited advertises its old computer in a magazine and reaches an agreement to sell that computer to a reader. Title or ownership of the computer will be transferred by PSC Limited to the reader purchasing the computer by a bill of sale.

From the point of view of PSC Limited, which is registered for VAT purposes, that is a supply of goods for which PSC Limited must charge and account for VAT.

In practice, there is little objection to PSC Limited quoting a single figure to the reader as the price of the computer but a failure on the part of PSC Limited to record and account for the VAT element of that price would be an offence and could result in penalties being imposed on PSC Limited.

Exempt supplies **[CT1.9]**

The UK currently operates a system whereby certain supplies are exempt from VAT.

Examples of 'exempt supplies' include:

- selling, leasing and letting land (but not garages, parking spaces, or holiday accommodation);
- insurance;
- betting, gambling and lotteries (but not fruit machines);
- providing credit;
- certain education and training;
- the services of doctors and dentists (but not others such as osteopaths); and
- certain services from undertakers.

Note that exempt supplies should be distinguished from zero-rated supplies which are taxable supplies on which the rate is currently 0% in the UK.

A business which supplies only exempt supplies is unlikely to be allowed to register for VAT purposes. A business exceeding the turnover threshold which provides supplies some of which are taxable and some of which are exempt should charge output VAT on its taxable supplies and should *not* charge output VAT on its exempt supplies (equally, that business may recover input VAT (see **CT1.42** below) on expenses incurred in providing taxable supplies but may *not* recover input VAT on expenses incurred in providing exempt supplies).

It is unlikely (unless involved education and training) that a Personal Service Company will be involved in exempt supplies.

Taxable person [CT1.10]

The charging provision (see **CT1.3** above) revolves around the concept of taxable supplies by a taxable person. A 'taxable person' is defined as one who is (or is required to be) registered for VAT which in turn depends upon the threshold turnover currently in operation (Yr 2000, £52,000).

The regulations define when the threshold is passed. There is also a special provision dealing with a business only temporarily exceeding the threshold. It is possible for a business to exceed the threshold in one period and then to fall back below the threshold in another. That would require registration and then de-registration but it could in fact give rise to the situation where a business became a taxable person and then ceased to become a taxable person.

Accordingly, a business which is not a taxable person need have nothing to do with the VAT system (although they can do so voluntarily if they so wish). A business which becomes a taxable person should immediately turn its attention to its obligations under the VAT system (and the applicable date from which to do that may precede and will not necessarily be the date of registration). A business which ceases to become a taxable person is (subject to the cessation provisions) no longer entitled to charge VAT and should cease to do so.

A Personal Service Company is likely to be a taxable person and, indeed, if not exceeding the current threshold should perhaps consider the wisdom of continuing to trade using the commercial vehicle of a limited liability company.

It is possible that in the event of gaps arising in the demand for its personal services a company might dip above and below the threshold which would make the company a taxable person. In practice, however, repeated registration and de-registration is something to be avoided if possible.

In the course of the furtherance of the business [CT1.11]

In order to be subject to VAT, the taxable person must provide the taxable supplies in the course of the furtherance of business.

'Business' receives a very wide interpretation under the VAT system and essentially includes, for these purposes, any means by which a company receives income.

The consideration that it be in the course of the furtherance of business applies in two main respects.

Firstly, in the (perhaps unlikely) event of a Personal Service Company having a non-business activity then it should not charge output VAT on that non-business activity (and, equally, should not seek to offset input VAT on goods and services acquired for that non-business activity).

Secondly, it is vital to appreciate that it is the 'person' (be it sole trader, partnership or limited company or other) and not the business which is registered for VAT purposes and accordingly, it is necessary to look for VAT purposes not just at the business which happens to have exceeded the VAT threshold but all of the activities of the registered person.

Example

PSC Limited is a company providing specialist engineering supplies to the oil industry. It has a turnover of over £1,000,000 and is registered for VAT purposes.

Out of retained profits the company buys a number of empty commercial properties which the company lets out as shops and regards as a separate matter unrelated its main oil business the income of which is £5,000 per annum.

The income from the separate business of letting shops is at £5,000, below the threshold for registration for VAT purposes but because registration is not by business but by person the company is obliged to charge VAT on its property letting and will be liable to penalties should the company fail to do so.

Supplies made in the UK or the Isle of Man [CT1.12]

The UK consists of Great Britain, Northern Ireland and the waters within 12 nautical miles of their coastlines. It does not include the Channel Islands and The Isle of Man. However, the Isle of Man (under its own Manx legislation) has brought itself within the UK VAT system.

Supply of services [CT1.13]

Having determined the incidence of output VAT and that that output VAT is chargeable, consideration will then have to be had to the place of supply and the time of supply.

Place of supply [CT1.14]

Traditional taxes (such as Corporation Tax) are charged on the basis of the person's residence and a person whose residence falls within a particular jurisdiction is taxed within that jurisdiction on all their activities no matter where in the world those activities take place.

Value Added Tax, however, operates in a different manner and is essentially a transactional tax. Accordingly, the place of supply (i.e. where the transaction is deemed to have taken place) is of particular importance to VAT and indeed determines the application of that tax.

The basic approach for the supply of services is to look not where the services are located but where the supplier 'belongs'.

The place of 'belonging' is, however, examined for each supply of services and therefore it is possible for a person to belong to one country for the purposes of the supply of one service and to belong to another country for the purposes of the supply of another service. The basic rule (although special rules have been evolved for special categories of services) is that services are treated as being supplied at the place where the supplier belongs.

A person 'belongs' to the place where they have their business or other fixed 'establishment'. This will normally be their base failing which their permanent address or residence but where a person has more than one establishment they belong to the location of the establishment most directly concerned with the particular supply. This definition applies both to the person supplying the services and, where applicable under the special rules, applies to determine where the customer belongs.

Special rules have been evolved for:

- passenger transport;
- intra-EC transport;
- the hiring of means of transport;
- land and property;

- cultural, artistic, sporting, scientific, educational, entertainment or similar activities;
- intermediary services – intermediaries who make arrangements for the supply (not merely facilitating the making of such supplies) of services such as stockbroking, insurance broking, patent copyright licences, trade-marks and similar services, advertising services and the like;
- telecommunications services – services relating to the transmission, emission, or reception of signals, writing, images and sounds or information of any nature by wire, radio, optical or other electro-magnetic systems, including the transfer or assignment of the right to use capacity for such transmission, emission or reception; and
- 'intellectual' services – services of consultants, engineers, consultancy bureaux, lawyers, accountants and similar services, data processing and provision of information.

Intermediary, telecommunications and 'intellectual' services are treated as being provided where the *customer* belongs. Personal Service Companies are likely to be involved more with services of the 'intellectual' services type than the other types of services. For other types of Personal Service Company not falling within this category, the place of supply will be where the *company* belongs.

'Intellectual' exception **[CT1.15]**

A Personal Service Company falling within the 'intellectual' exception should not charge output VAT in relation to a transaction for the supply of services where the customer belongs outside the EC. Following the creation of the single market, a Personal Service Company falling within the 'intellectual' exception is entitled to zero-rate the supply of services where the customer belongs within the EC.

All taxable Personal Service Companies, even those falling within the 'intellectual' exception, are required to charge output VAT in relation to a transaction for the supply of services where the customer belongs inside the UK or Isle of Man.

Time of supply of services **[CT1.16]**

The time when a supply of services is treated as taking place is known as the 'tax point'. There are two types of tax point in existence – the basic tax point and the actual tax point. Rules exist to determine which is applicable.

There are also two main accounting systems in operation – the traditional accounting system where VAT must be accounted for on the basis of invoices issued and the cash accounting system where VAT must be accounted for on the basis of invoices paid.

The traditional accounting system **[CT1.17]**

In the supply of services, the basic tax point is the date when the service is performed and normally that will be the date upon which all the work except invoicing is completed.

However, the basic tax point is overridden by the actual tax point where:

- *before* the basic tax point is reached, either payment is received or a VAT invoice is issued in which case the date that the first of these happens takes over as the actual tax point; or
- *after* the basic tax point is reached, the business issues a VAT invoice within 14 days of that date in which case the date of the invoice becomes the actual tax point.

A business must account for VAT on tax points occurring within the tax period (usually a quarter for which a VAT return is being made) under consideration.

The cash accounting system **[CT1.18]**

Under the cash accounting scheme, the tax point will be the point in time at which the VAT invoice for the services is paid.

Supply of goods **[CT1.19]**

As noted at **CT1.8** above, a company set up as a Personal Service Company might still find itself concerned with the supply of goods.

Place of supply **[CT1.20]**

So far as the supply of goods is concerned, the basic approach is to look not at where the parties are located but where the goods are located. The basic rule is that goods are treated as being supplied at the place where the goods are situated when they are dispatched or, if not dispatched, at the place where the goods are situated when they are supplied. Accordingly, the place of supply is the place where the goods first become identified with the particular supply (*Value Added Tax Act 1994, section 7*).

The *Sixth Directive, Article 8* and *Value Added Tax Act 1994, section 7* specify special rules for the supply of goods in some circumstances, namely:

- installed or assembled goods;
- distance selling of goods;
- importing and exporting goods where the distance selling rules do not apply; and
- supply of goods not removed from or to the UK.

Installed or assembled goods **[CT1.21]**

Where goods are being installed or assembled, the place of supply is taken as being the place at which the installation or assembly takes place.

Distance selling of goods **[CT1.22]**

People who are not registered for VAT may shop around (generally by mail order) to buy goods at the lowest possible rate of VAT and this is known as 'distance selling'.

Special rules have been introduced to cover the sale of goods in this way and if you are registered for VAT in any Member State and involved in distance selling to non-VAT registered persons in another Member State then you might well be required to register for VAT and should take advice on the matter.

Importing goods **[CT1.23]**

If the company imports goods into the UK for selling onto a customer then much depends upon the manner in which this is done. If a non-EC customer imports the goods then the place of supply is not the EC. If the company imports the goods from outside the EC, then the place of supply is the UK. If the company removes goods into the UK from another Member State then the place of supply is *not* in the UK. The seller – if able to produce the customer's VAT Number can zero-rate the supply and the buyer in the UK will pay VAT on their 'acquisition' – later treated as input tax in their VAT account).

Exporting goods **[CT1.24]**

If goods are exported to elsewhere in the EC, the place of supply is in the UK. If goods are exported to a place outside the EC, the place of supply is in the UK.

Supply of goods not removed from or to the UK **[CT1.25]**

Where the supply of goods does not involve the removal of the goods from or to the UK then it will depend where the goods are situated when they are supplied. If the goods are outside the UK when supplied then the place of supply is outside the UK. If the goods are inside the UK when supplied, then the place of supply is in the UK.

Example

PSC Limited, a company resident in the UK, owns computer A situated in the USA and computer B situated in the UK. The company sells both computers.

For VAT purposes, since computer A was outside the UK when allocated to supply, computer A is treated as being the supply of goods situated *outside* the UK (on which output VAT should not be charged). For VAT purposes, since computer B was inside the UK when allocated to supply, computer B is treated as being the supply of goods situated *within* the UK (on which output VAT should be charged).

Time of supply **[CT1.26]**

The time of supply will vary according to whether the traditional accounting system or the cash accounting system is being used.

The traditional accounting system [CT1.27]

The 'basic tax point' for goods is the date upon which the goods are sent to the customer or the customer takes them away, or, if neither sent nor taken (e.g. built on site) the date upon which the goods are made available to the customer. However, the basic tax point is overridden if an 'actual tax point' is created by:

- the issuance of a VAT invoice or the receipt of payment *before* the basic tax point; or
- the issuance of a VAT invoice up to 14 days *after* the basic tax point (provided that prior to that date payment has not been received or any form of invoice issued).

It will be appreciated from the above that for goods, time of supply is the *earliest* of the date upon which supply is actually made (the 'basic tax point') and the date upon which a VAT invoice is issued or payment is received (the 'actual tax point') with the exception of the 14 day rule.

The 14 day rule (a rule which can be applied by Customs & Excise under penalties for non-observance) assists accounting procedures in that rather than using a variable basic tax point a business may (provided that it is within 14 days of the basic tax point) use the fixed date of an accounting run of invoices. It is possible to differentiate between supplies for this purpose where agreement to do so is reached with Customs & Excise. It is possible, if more convenient to the business, to agree with Customs & Excise a period other than 14 days.

For exceptional categories of goods reference must be made to any special provisions relating to time of payment.

The cash accounting system [CT1.28]

Under this system the tax point for the supply of goods will be the date upon which the goods are paid for.

Taxable supplies [CT1.29]

Output VAT is the VAT due on the 'taxable supplies' which, as a taxable person, the business makes to its customers.

It is important to appreciate, as already noted, that anything the business does in the course of or in the furtherance of its business – not just the things that the business does in the course of its normal trade or profession or in the course of providing its normal services – can be a taxable supply.

However, some supplies are exempt (see **CT1.9** above).

The tax value of the supply [CT1.30]

The 'tax value' or 'taxable amount' is the value or amount upon which VAT is charged.

The value or amount of a supply is generally what the company is given in exchange for the supply and this is called the 'consideration'. There are a number of rules which determine exactly what the consideration is.

Wholly in money [CT1.31]

If the consideration given in exchange for a supply is wholly an amount of money, which will usually be the case, then the value or amount is that sum of money. That sum of money is, technically speaking, defined to include the VAT element and therefore for the avoidance of doubt it is generally advisable to always provide quotations as exclusive of VAT with the VAT element separately quoted and added.

Unconditional discounts [CT1.32]

If you offer a customer an unconditional discount and the customer pays that unconditional discounted amount then the value or amount is that discounted amount.

Prompt payment discounts [CT1.33]

If you offer a discount for prompt payment then the value or amount is that discounted amount, regardless of whether or not the customer in fact takes up the offer.

Contingent discounts **[CT1.34]**

If you offer a discount subject to some condition (e.g. that more goods are purchased later) then the value or amount is the full amount and if the condition is later fulfilled and a discount applied the matter can be adjusted by way of a credit note.

Not wholly in money **[CT1.35]**

If the consideration given in exchange for a supply is not in money (e.g. as in barter) or is partly in money and partly in something else then the value or amount is the monetary equivalent of the consideration. Again, that monetary equivalent is, technically speaking, defined to include the VAT element and therefore for the avoidance of doubt it is generally advisable to always specifically provide that quotations not wholly in money are exclusive of VAT with the VAT element separately quoted and added and provided to be payable by the customer (otherwise the VAT element will require to be paid by the supplier).

Expressed in a foreign currency **[CT1.36]**

The value or amount must always be expressed in Sterling for VAT purposes. Accordingly, if expressed in a foreign currency then a conversion to Sterling must be made. There are alternative ways to do this (either for all supplies or for classes of supplies). A company can opt to use the period rate of exchange published by Customs and Excise for customs purposes (which option cannot thereafter be changed without permission) failing which the company must use the UK market selling rate at the time of supply (of which the rate published in national newspapers for that day will be acceptable evidence) although it is also possible to apply in writing to Customs and Excise for the use of a rate or method of determining a rate not covered by either of the above but which could be used for commercial purposes.

Excise duty **[CT1.37]**

If goods are supplied subject to excise duty, the value or amount includes the duty.

Special rules [CT1.38]

There are special rules covering:

- packaging;
- delivery charges;
- second-hand goods;
- exchange units;
- samples;
- gifts;
- payphones;
- loss of goods; and
- cancellations and the like.

Private use [CT1.39]

If you or your family, friends or employees use goods belonging to the company for private use (e.g. cars, road fuel, or services) with no consideration, then you are deemed to make a taxable supply the amount or value of which is the full cost to the business of making them available.

VAT rate [CT1.40]

There are currently three rates of VAT.

standard rate	17.5 %	which applies to most supplies
reduced rate	8%	which applies to certain supplies of fuel and power
zero rate	0%	which applies to the undernoted items

Zero-rated items include the following.

Group 1	Food (Leaflet 701/14)
Group 2	Sewerage and Water (Leaflet 701/16)
Group 3	Books (Leaflet 701/10)

Group 4	Talking Books (Leaflet 701/1)
Group 5	Construction of Buildings (Leaflet 708/2)
Group 6	Protected Buildings (Leaflet 708/1)
Group 7	International services (Leaflet 741)
Group 8	Transport (Notice 744)
Group 9	Caravans & Houseboats (Leaflet 701/20)
Group 10	Gold (Leaflet 701/21)
Group 11	Bank Notes (Leaflet 701/29)
Group 12	Drug, medicine, aid for handicapped (Leaflet 701/7)
Group 13	Imports; Exports (Notice 700)
Group 14	Tax-free shops (Notice 700)
Group 15	Charities (Leaflet 701/1)
Group 16	Clothing & footwear (Leaflet 701/23)

Areas highlighted by Customs and Excise for particular consideration include:

- sales to employees;
- sales of business assets;
- hire or loan of assets to someone else;
- gifts of goods (in excess of £10);
- assets of the business taken for private use; and
- commission received for sales made on behalf of third parties.

Gifts with little value are ignored (see **CT1.6** above) but all other gifts of goods provided free of charge must have VAT accounted for. There is no charge to VAT if services are genuinely provided for free.

Credits [CT1.41]

Once a VAT invoice has been issued, circumstances sometimes arise under which a credit has to be given to the customer. It follows that that credit has to be reflected in the VAT records also and accordingly in the event of issuing a credit (whether for services or goods), businesses must reflect the VAT element of that credit in the VAT records of the business.

Input VAT [CT1.42]

The principles involved in the determination of input VAT are considered below but from the point of view of a Personal Service Company whereas output VAT is likely to involve a confined area (the supply of services), input VAT is likely to involve much wider considerations.

The amount of involvement with input VAT is likely to vary between Personal Service Companies but a busy company might be involved in obtaining goods and services from:

- outside the EC;
- within the EC; and/or
- within the UK and the Isle of Man.

A Personal Service Company may, therefore, need an awareness of the VAT principles applying to all of these areas.

Note also that a clear distinction must be maintained between business and non-business expenditure for the purposes of input VAT.

Input VAT is essentially the VAT which the company has been charged on the purchases and expenses which the company, as a taxable person, has incurred in the course of or furtherance of its business in producing the product, be it goods or services, which the company will in turn sell on with the addition of output VAT.

Input VAT is specifically defined in *Value Added Tax Act 1994, section 24*, as:

> '…"input tax", in relation to a taxable person, means the following tax, that is to say–
> (a) VAT on the supply to him of any goods or services;
> (b) VAT on the acquisition by him from another Member State of any goods; and
> (c) VAT paid or payable by him on the importation of any goods from a place outside the Member States,
> being (in each case) goods or services used or to be used for the purpose of any business carried on or to be carried on by him."

A number of considerations flow from this definition which restrict the application of input VAT which are considered below.

Taxable person **[CT1.43]**

It is necessary to be a 'taxable person' to be able to reclaim input VAT. A 'taxable person' is a person who is, or is required to be, registered for the purposes of VAT within the UK (*VATA 1994, s3*).

Therefore, a taxable person will be part of the VAT system and part of the chain in charging output VAT against which they will seek to offset input VAT.

A Personal Service Company which has not registered for the purposes of VAT will not be entitled to charge output VAT or offset input VAT and will essentially be a consumer and as such have to bear the burden of VAT.

As noted above, however, most Personal Service Companies whose turnover exceed the threshold will have been required to register for VAT purposes. They will therefore already be charging output VAT as a 'taxable person' and will be concerned in the recovery of input VAT.

For the purposes of any business carried on or to be carried on [CT1.44]

The difference between business and non-business activities is an important distinction for VAT purposes (input VAT can only be offset in relation to business activities). 'Business' has a very wide meaning for VAT purposes and is defined by the *Value Added Tax Act 1994, section 94* as the carrying on of a '...trade, profession and vocation'. Essentially, this concept will encompass any way in which a company makes its income.

Under the *Sixth VAT Directive*, 'economic activities' are defined as:

> '...producers, traders and persons supplying services including mining and agricultural activities and activities of the professions. The exploitation of tangible or intangible property for the purpose of obtaining income therefrom on a continuing basis shall also be considered an economic activity.'[

However, so far as offsetting the input VAT in relation to that business, it will be necessary for the company to be able to answer the question, 'Is this expense wholly for my business?' in the affirmative before it will be entitled to do so.

The company can only reclaim its own input VAT. Thus, if the company buys something for the business of the company then it may offset any input VAT incurred. If, however, the company buys something exclusively for the private use of its directors, employees, someone else, or for some other non-business purpose, then it is not permitted to reclaim or seek to offset the input VAT upon that expenditure.

There are a number of areas where Customs and Excise specifically disallow the reclaiming of input VAT.

A number of special rules exist and these are considered in more detail below.

Motoring expenses **[CT1.45]**

Input VAT on the *purchase* of a car (including fitted accessories and delivery charges) by a company is, in principle, wholly recoverable. However, if it is intended that there should be any non-business use of that car by a director or employee then *none* of the input VAT is recoverable.

Input VAT on the *hire* of a car by a company is, in principle, wholly recoverable. However, if it is intended that there should be any non-business use of that car by a director or employee then only 50% of the input VAT is recoverable.

Note that input VAT is not recoverable on fuel used for private motoring.

Business entertainment **[CT1.46]**

As a general rule, input VAT is not recoverable on the provision of business entertainment except for:

- reasonable staff entertainment costs;
- the provision of canteen facilities for staff;
- hotel and similar accommodation for business trips away; and
- actual business expenses (but not a flat rate for subsistence expenses).

Domestic accommodation **[CT1.47]**

If the business provides domestic accommodation for employees then any VAT incurred can be offset as input VAT. Directors, however, cannot recover VAT on expenses in connection with domestic accommodation supplied to them by the company (although they may be able to allocate a percentage if business meetings are in fact held there).

Other special rules [CT1.48]

There are also special rules relating to:

- purchasing businesses as a going concern;
- tour operators' margin schemes;
- goods sold under a second-hand scheme;
- certain articles (fitted furniture and appliances) installed in new buildings by builders; and
- assets transferred as a going concern.

If the company buys something partly for business use and partly for private use then it will be required to allocate the input VAT between the private element and the public element (reclaiming only the latter). There is no special method of apportionment but the calculation must be fair and reasonable and the company must, if asked, be able to justify the calculations to Customs and Excise.

Goods and services from outside the EC [CT1.49]

A company might source goods and services from *outside* the EC.

VAT is not only a tax on supplies but is also a tax on importation. Different rules apply to the importation of goods and services.

Goods [CT1.50]

When goods are imported into the UK from outside the EC then VAT is normally due on those goods at the same rate as would be applied had those goods been supplied in the UK. Customs Duty is likely to have been charged on those goods and VAT will be charged and collected alongside that duty. VAT is charged as if it were a duty of Customs and is payable at the same time as any Customs duty arising.

The regulations on imports from outside the EC are very specialised and beyond the scope of this book and is a matter upon which professional advice should be taken. Informal advice can often be obtained from any freight forwarders involved who are very experienced in the procedures and regulations involved. If goods are ordered over the internet to be sent by post then the *Postal Packets (Customs and Excise) Regulations 1986*

(*SI 1986/260*) will apply which prohibits goods being brought into the UK except in a parcel or packet which must have a customs declaration attached to it. The person sending the goods is likely to have been required to have made a declaration as to the contents of the parcel containing the goods and the importer will generally be called upon to pay both Duty and VAT at the same time.

It will be appreciated that, as might be expected from its nature and the reason for its existence, the EC is a Common Market and a Customs Union. That means that while there are no custom duty barriers amongst Member States but there is a common duty tariff against goods brought from outside into the EC and therefore the UK is imposing VAT on goods imported not in isolation but (albeit at a different rate of VAT) in common with the other Member States.

Input VAT (but not the duty) so paid may be reclaimed. So far as a Personal Service Company requiring to import goods from outside the EC is concerned, the main objective will be, wherever possible, to recover or offset as an input the tax paid and that in turn will depend upon ensuring that the documentation relating to matters such as the place of supply, the importer, and the payment of tax is all in the correct order.

Services **[CT1.51]**

Where services are received from outside the EC for use by a business registered for VAT purposes within the UK, then the position is slightly different from that relating to goods.

The person supplying the services will not be registered for VAT purposes and so will not be charging VAT (they may be charging their equivalent in the form of a sales tax but that is not recoverable under VAT rules or at all in the absence of a double-taxation agreement specifically covering that area).

No VAT is chargeable on the importation of those services.

Note, however, that although there is no input VAT on them, if a company receives for business purposes from outside the EC any of the services listed in *Value Added Tax Act 1994, Schedule 5* (see list below), then it is treated as if the company supplied those services and the company must account for output VAT on those services.

1. Transfers and assignments of copyright, patents, licences, trademarks etc.
2. Advertising services.
3. Services of consultants, engineers, consultancy bureaux, lawyers, accountants and other similar services, data processing and provision of information (excluding land).
4. Acceptance of any obligation to refrain from pursuing or exercising in whole or part, any business activity or any such rights as are referred to in 1 above.
5. Banking, financial and insurance services (including reinsurance but not including the provision of safe deposit facilities).
6. The supply of staff.
7. The letting on hire of goods other than means of transport.
8. The services rendered by one person to another in procuring for the other any of the services mentioned in 1 to 7 above.

Example

A company registered for VAT purposes in the UK obtains the services of a computer consultant in the USA who (for a fee, including Sales Tax for the State in which the consultant resides) sends over (down the line in real time) certain coding which the company incorporates into its services and in turn supplies to the client.

The Sales Tax is irrecoverable so far as VAT is concerned. No VAT is charged on the importation of those services.

Note, however, that since the consultancy services fall within *VATA 1994, Sch 5*, the company must treat those services as if the company had supplied them and account for output VAT on them.

Supplies acquired from a taxable person within the EC **[CT1.52]**

There are special rules (particularly after the abolition of border controls within the EC from 1 January 1993) relating to the incidence of VAT on goods and services acquired within the EC.

The general rule is that such goods and services are subject to VAT in the Member State to which they are dispatched. The person making the acquisition (unless falling within one of the exemptions – see **CM7.6** above) has to pay the VAT *at the time of acquisition*. That person can, if registered for VAT, claim the acquisition VAT which they have paid as an input on their VAT Return and then they in turn charge VAT on the goods and services which they go on to supply to their customers. The system is policed by requiring suppliers to provide periodic EC sales listings to their Member State to which the Member State of arrivals has access.

Example

PSC Limited, a company registered for VAT purposes in the UK orders for its business 500 special disks from a German company which is registered for VAT purposes in Germany. The German company, if (but only if) it can affix PSC Limited's VAT Registration Number to its invoice, can for VAT purposes zero-rate the supply of those disks (which allows it to recover in its Returns any VAT paid on the raw materials).

At the time of acquisition, PSC Limited will be required to pay acquisition VAT (at the standard UK rate (currently 17.5%). PSC Limited will then treat that acquisition VAT as an input in its next VAT return thereby reducing its VAT bill in the UK. When PSC Limited comes to utilise those disks in the provision of its services then it will charge its client VAT. In this way, the incidence of VAT is passed down the chain to the ultimate consumer which is where that tax is supposed to reside.

In general, under the *Value Added Tax Act 1994, section 10*, a business registered for VAT purposes in the UK which orders goods from elsewhere within the EC will have to pay acquisition VAT.

There are exceptions where the supplier in the EC Member State is making supplies to persons who are not a business or are not registered for VAT (although if the supplies are of sufficient quantities then this exemption may not apply). There are also exceptions where the goods in question are supplies of the type which are exempt (e.g. educational) or zero-rated (e.g. food). There are few other exceptions of relevance to a VAT-registered business such as a Personal Service Company.

The meaning of 'acquisition' **[CT1.53]**

The *Sixth VAT Directive* and *VATA 1994* define an 'acquisition' as arising where goods are removed from one Member State to another and the movement involves a supply by the person dispatching the goods.

Under this definition a company moving its goods from one Member State to another *for processing* is not treated as being involved in a supply but a company moving its goods from one Member State to another for other purposes is treated as being involved in a supply and is deemed to have made a supply in the Member State of dispatch and an acquisition in the Member State of acquisition (necessitating the payment of acquisition VAT). Some care should be exercised in the provision of a company's VAT Registration Number since its use by the supplier could result in the goods being deemed to have been acquired in the UK (and acquisition VAT payable) even if the goods are not physically within the UK.

Time of acquisition **[CT1.54]**

Under *VATA 1994, s12(1)*, the timing of an acquisition is defined as the earlier of:

- the fifteenth day of the month following that in which the goods are removed – i.e. despatched (referred to as 'the event'); and
- the date upon which the supplier issues an invoice.

It will be appreciated that as a result of this definition the point in time from which the obligation to pay acquisition VAT is calculated is divorced from the date upon which the supplier is paid for the goods. There are special rules relating to 'warehousing'.

Value of acquisition **[CT1.55]**

The value of the acquisition is defined as the value of the transaction under which it takes place. This will normally be the consideration involved in the transaction. There are, of course, anti-avoidance provisions relating to non-monetary considerations and the like and provisions relating to unusual circumstances such as gifts.

Reclaiming input VAT **[CT1.56]**

In general, input VAT may not be reclaimed unless it is vouched by a formal VAT invoice. Pro-forma invoices will not be acceptable as evidence for reclaiming input VAT. Import VAT certificates serve the same purpose as VAT invoices.

Only a registered person can issue a VAT invoice and penalties apply to any unauthorised issue. It is also an offence to receive an invoice from an unregistered person and knowingly use that invoice to reclaim VAT. If in doubt, the validity of VAT numbers (for anywhere in the UK or Isle of Man) can be checked at Local VAT Business Advice Centres.

Retention [CT1.57]

A record of all taxable supplies must be kept by taxable persons.

In particular, all invoices, certificates and the like relating to supplies (whether at the standard, reduced or zero rate) received for the business must be retained *and* kept in such a way that given the invoice date and the supplier's name, they can be easily produced to Customs and Excise.

The VAT account [CT1.58]

It is necessary to account properly for VAT. This involves, in the first place, keeping a proper VAT account and then, later, making a proper VAT return.

There are essentially two methods by which VAT may be accounted for – what might be termed the cash accounting scheme and the traditional accounting scheme. Whichever scheme is adopted must be reflected in the VAT account and then in the VAT return.

The business should keep a special book or ledger opening for VAT or use a computerised accounting system which provides for VAT.

It is recommended that at regular intervals the business makes up the VAT account by entering VAT payable and VAT deductible and any other relevant VAT entries (e.g. overdeclaration or underdeclaration).

There is no prescribed format and any account containing the essential information will be acceptable to Customs and Excise. The VAT account is likely to be inspected by Customs and Excise on any visits they make.

See **Appendix 7**.

The cash accounting scheme **[CT1.59]**

The cash accounting scheme, which is available provided that taxable turnover does not exceed a stipulated limit (currently £350,000), allows a business to account for all its transactions (both output and input) on the basis of payments received and made (as opposed to invoices issued and received).

It is not necessary to have the formal permission of Customs & Excise to operate the cash accounting scheme. The scheme can be operated from registration or it can be applied or disapplied as the business progresses but must be commenced at the beginning of a tax period.

There are a number of conditions which must be met:

- all VAT returns due have been sent to Customs & Excise;
- no VAT offences resulting in a conviction have been made in the last year;
- no offer to compound proceedings in connection with a VAT offence has been made;
- no penalty for evasion involving dishonest conduct has been imposed in the last year;
- no monies are owed to Customs & Excise (or arrangements are in place to clear it);
- no letter has been received from Customs & Excise denying use of the scheme; and
- the conditions for use of the scheme are complied with.

The scheme must be terminated where:

- the business cannot comply with the record keeping requirements;
- the business is convicted of a VAT offence;
- the business is assessed to a penalty for VAT evasion involving dishonesty;
- the business offers to compound proceedings for a VAT offence; Customs & Excise write denying use of the scheme; or
- the taxable turnover exceeds the threshold (currently £350,000) but note that there is a 25% tolerance built into the scheme which effectively brings the termination level up to £437,500.

Once the decision has been made to adopt the cash accounting scheme then that scheme must be used for *all* aspects of the business except:

- in relation to goods bought or sold under lease purchase, hire purchase, conditional sale or credit sale;

- in relation to goods imported or acquired from another EC Member State;
- where a VAT Invoice is issued but payment in full is not due within six months;
- where a VAT Invoice is issued in advance of making the supply or providing the goods.

There are a number of special rules for particular transactions including barter and part exchange.

The traditional accounting scheme [CT1.60]

Under the traditional accounting scheme, which will more closely match that being operated by the accounting system for the accounts themselves, VAT is accounted for in relation to VAT invoices issued and VAT invoices received.

The VAT return [CT1.61]

The company will be sent a VAT return for each of the tax periods established when registered for VAT which requires to be completed and returned. It is intended that the VAT information in the company's VAT account should be used to complete the VAT return onto which you should enter VAT payable and VAT deductible and any other relevant VAT entries (e.g. overdeclaration or underdeclaration). There is a prescribed format for the return and only that (unaltered) form will be acceptable.

VAT returns must be sent, together with payments due, to *arrive* (at the VAT Central Unit) by the date shown on the return (usually one month after the end of the tax period). A failure to do is likely to result not only in Customs & Excise making an assessment of the amount of VAT which, in their judgment, the company owes but also the imposition of as default surcharge.

Tax periods [CT1.62]

The period for which returns must be made are known as 'tax periods' or 'prescribed accounting period'. Usually, this is quarterly but it can be made monthly, annually, or for non-standard periods.

Annual **[CT1.63]**

Where a company has already been registered for VAT purposes for twelve months and the annual value of its taxable supplies (excluding VAT) is below a certain threshold (currently £300,000) then it is possible to apply to Customs & Excise to use an annual tax period.

Under this arrangement, for turnover between £100,000 and £300,000, based on an estimate of the amount of VAT likely to be due, nine monthly payments will be made by direct debit with a tenth balancing payment sent in with the Return within two months of the end of the year.

Under this arrangement, for turnover below £100,000 and the likely net VAT liability is *more than* £2,000 per annum, interim payments need only be made quarterly with a balancing payment sent in with the return within two months of the end of the year.

Under this arrangement, for turnover below £100,000 and the likely net vat liability is *less than* £2,000 per annum, no interim payments need be made with a payment sent in with the return within two months of the end of the year.

Quarterly **[CT1.64]**

To spread the flow of returns more evenly over the year, Customs & Excise use standard quarters:

- March, June, September, December;
- April, July, October, January; or
- May, August, November, February.

These will be allocated in turn to businesses registering, although it is possible to apply at the time of registration to be allocated a set of quarters one of which coincides with the year-end of the business (and simplifies the accounting).

Monthly **[CT1.65]**

It is possible to apply to Customs & Excise to have a monthly tax period in which case twelve returns will be sent each year.

Non-standard **[CT1.66]**

In the event of an accounting system not being in calendar months, it is possible to make an application to Customs & Excise to have the tax periods match the accounting periods of the business. If granted, a new VAT Registration Certificate with new VAT return periods will be issued.

Payment **[CT1.67]**

Where the VAT return shows that a payment of VAT is due by the taxpayer to Customs & Excise, then the taxpayer should enclose that payment with the VAT Return for that is the due date of payment.

Where the taxpayer has not done so then an extra payment (known as a surcharge) may need to be made following the issue by Customs & Excise of a formal surcharge liability notice. The surcharge currently ranges from £30 to a maximum of 15% of the VAT due.

Payment may be by cheque, postal order, or electronic means.

If electronic means are chosen (bank Giro Transfer, bankers automated clearing system, clearing house automated payment system) then application can be made to Customs & Excise for a further seven days in which to make the VAT Return and make payment.

Net payments of less than £1 may be disregarded.

Repayments **[CT1.68]**

Where the VAT Return shows that a repayment of VAT is due by Customs & Excise to the taxpayer then Customs & Excise will arrange for that repayment.

Customs & Excise prefer to make repayments using the bankers automated clearing system but will, if necessary, make repayment by payable order.

A supplement (the greater of £50 or 5% of the net repayment due) will be added to delayed repayments (usually where more than 30 days have elapsed after receipt of the VAT Return without the repayment being made). Note that in order to qualify for a supplement at all, the Return in question must have reached Customs & Excise by the due date for its submission.

Net repayments of less than £1 may be disregarded.

Enforcement [CT1.69]

Every system of taxation requires a system of enforcement but equally every system for the provision and enforcement of taxation requires a system to ensure that it operates fairly.

Customs and Excise operate centrally but there are also delegated regional Collectors of Customs and Excise. Various Local Offices (now known as VAT Business Advice Centres) deal with the day-to-day control of VAT. The address and telephone number of Local Offices are listed in local telephone books under 'Customs and Excise'.

VAT Officer visits [CT1.70]

It is likely that in the course of its business life a company will receive a visit from a VAT Officer. A mutually convenient appointment will normally be arranged (although unannounced visits are also possible) and for small businesses any initial visits are likely to be short.

The VAT Officer will:

- examine the premises;
- the methods adopted; and
- the records kept by the company.

During the visit, the VAT Officer ought to:

- give an indication of the length of the visit;
- discuss the various aspects of the business;
- examine the company's records of your business; and
- advise of any overpayments or underpayments.

At the end of the meeting the VAT Officer ought to discuss the review including any concerns that have arisen and what should be done in the future.

In an error has been found, the VAT Officer will describe the adjustments which it is proposed to make. Wherever possible, the VAT Officer will agree any adjustments with you but if you do not agree then the VAT Officer ought to inform you of your rights to review and appeal.

Should Customs & Excise discover, on a control visit or otherwise, that the business is not operating the VAT system by, for example:

- not registering for VAT purposes when required to do so;
- not making VAT returns; or
- not making correct returns,

or the like, then Customs & Excise are likely to move first to make up any VAT lost by means of the assessment system (see **CT1.88** ***et seq.*** below) and they are also likely, at the same time, to invoke the penalty procedures (see **CT1.72** below) open to them.

The VAT assessment system **[CT1.71]**

The normal procedure is for the taxable person to register, to calculate the net amount of VAT due and remit that to Customs & Excise. Where that fails to happen, Customs & Excise are given wide powers (supported by enforcement provisions) to make an assessment of the amount of VAT due.

Customs & Excise will, to the best of their judgment, assess the amount of VAT lost and will issue a demand for that sum to the taxable person in the form of a formal assessment.

The time limit for doing so, except in cases of dishonesty, is normally limited to the later of two years from the end of the prescribed accounting period and one year after facts sufficient to justify an assessment come to their knowledge, subject to an overall limit of three years from the end of the accounting period to which it relates.

The assessment issued will stipulate the period within which outstanding payment must be made. Failure to pay within that period will incur interest and penalties. If there are grounds to object to an assessment then firstly, the taxable person may ask Customs & Excise for a review failing which the taxable person may be able to appeal the assessment to the VAT and Duties Tribunal.

The penalty system **[CT1.72]**

When VAT was first introduced, because it was a new tax being brought in at a stage which in comparison with other established taxes was relatively recent (1973), the opportunity was taken to introduce strong enforcement procedures which relied heavily on criminal law. It was found in practice, however, that the high standard of proof (beyond reasonable doubt) required by the criminal law was making enforcement time-consuming, expensive, and difficult. A review of enforcement was carried out as a result of which a new system of civil penalties (using the civil standard of proof of balance of probabilities) was added and brought into effect by the *Finance Act 1985*.

When they feel that the circumstances merit it, Customs & Excise will issue a formal penalty assessment which will also contain details of any appeal available. This is either done by way of letter or Form VAT 291.

The onus then shifts to the taxable person to appeal the penalty assessment to the VAT and Duties Tribunal. As well as any defence on the merits of the case (if there is one) there is the defence of reasonable excuse and the penalty may be mitigated.

Reasonable excuse **[CT1.73]**

The term 'reasonable excuse' is not defined in the legislation. The matter is approached by Customs & Excise on the basis of what a reasonable business person would have done.

Customs & Excise have pointed to the following considerations as 'guidelines' which might be included within the definition of a reasonable excuse.

- Compassionate circumstances – e.g. where an individual who is totally responsible for running a small business and they or a member of their immediate family was seriously ill.
- Transfer of a business as a going concern in some circumstances.
- Doubts about the liability of suppliers – e.g. where the liability was and is in doubt and there is written evidence of an enquiry about liability.
- Uncertainty about status – where status was and is in doubt and there is written evidence of an enquiry about liability.

However, the legislation specifically *excludes* the following as a reasonable excuse:

- an inability to pay; or
- reliance upon another person to perform the task.

Mitigation [CT1.74]

Customs & Excise, and in some circumstances the VAT and Duties Tribunal, can mitigate any penalty issued after 27 July 1993. Mitigation can vary from 0% to 100%.

Customs & Excise have not issued guidelines on what may be included in mitigation but will consider matters such as complexity, compassionate circumstances, unforeseen events and the like. Customs & Excise will be able to mitigate the penalty on the basis of factors which fall short of a reasonable excuse but will require to be convinced that the application of the full penalty is not appropriate.

However, the legislation specifically *excludes* as mitigating factors:

- the fact that the trader acted in good faith;
- the fact that there has been no significant loss of VAT; or
- an inability to pay.

Circumstances in which penalties will be imposed [CT1.75]

The main circumstances in which penalties will be imposed are detailed below.

Late registration [CT1.76]

Upon reaching the designated turnover threshold a business becomes a taxable person and should register for the purposes of VAT. Failure to do so may result in a penalty being imposed.

The amount of the penalty is the greater of:

- £50; and

- a percentage* of the 'net VAT'** due to Customs & Excise between the date the business should have been registered and the date when either Customs & Excise became fully aware of the need for the business to become registered or received an application for registration by the business.

* the percentage is determined by the length of the delay involved as follows:

up to 9 months	5% of the VAT due
9-18 months	10% of the VAT due
over 18 months	15% of the VAT due

** net Vat is output VAT less input VAT.

The reasonable excuse defence applies to this penalty and mitigation is also possible.

Unauthorised issue of VAT invoices **[CT1.77]**

Where a person who is not registered for VAT purposes and who is not otherwise authorised to issue VAT invoices (such as an insolvency practitioner) issues an invoice in which VAT is purported to be included (whether or not the VAT is separately shown), then that person is liable to a penalty.

The amount of the penalty is the greater of:

- £50; and
- 15% of the purported VAT.

The reasonable excuse defence applies to this penalty and mitigation is also possible.

Failure to make records for VAT purposes **[CT1.78]**

A failure to make records for VAT purposes attracts a penalty. The amount of the penalty is a fixed daily rate. The basic rate is £5 per day while the breach continues. However, if there has been an earlier breach the daily rate is £10 and if more than one earlier breach £15.

This penalty is subject to a maximum of 100 times the daily amount.

The reasonable excuse defence applies to this penalty but mitigation is not.

Failure to furnish information and documents **[CT1.79]**

A failure to make records for VAT purposes attracts a penalty. However, this penalty cannot be imposed unless Customs & Excise have given the trader previous warning (within two years) concerning compliance with this requirement.

The amount of the penalty is a fixed daily rate. The basic rate is £5 per day while the breach continues. However, if there has been an earlier breach the daily rate is £10 and if more than one earlier breach £15. This penalty is subject to a maximum of 100 times the daily amount.

The reasonable excuse defence applies to this penalty but mitigation is not.

Failure to make a VAT return **[CT1.80]**

A failure to make a VAT return by the due date attracts a penalty. However, this penalty cannot be imposed unless Customs & Excise have given the trader previous warning (within two years) concerning compliance with this requirement.

The amount of the penalty is the greater of:

- the fixed daily rate (the basic rate is £5 per day while the breach continues, £10 if there has been an earlier breach £15 if more than one earlier breach); and
- the tax-geared percentage rate (this is based on the VAT shown in the return or if no return is made, the amount of VAT assessed by Customs & Excise).

The reasonable excuse defence applies to this penalty but mitigation is not.

Failure to pay the VAT due on a VAT return by the due date **[CT1.81]**

A failure to pay the VAT due on a VAT return by the due date attracts a penalty. However, this penalty cannot be imposed unless Customs & Excise have given the trader previous warning (within two years) concerning compliance with this requirement.

The amount of the penalty is the greater of:

- the fixed daily rate (the basic rate is £5 per day while the breach continues, £10 if there has been an earlier breach £15 if more than one earlier breach); or
- the tax-geared percentage rate (this is based on the VAT shown in the return or if no return is made, the amount of VAT assessed by Customs & Excise.

The reasonable excuse defence applies to this penalty but mitigation is not.

Misdeclarations **[CT1.82]**

For the VAT system to work properly there clearly has to be a system of penalties for misdeclarations.

There is no penalty if an error is discovered and disclosed voluntarily.

However, a penalty (which does not imply any dishonesty or any intention to evade VAT) will be imposed where there is a misdeclaration which in this context means a significant or repeated lack of care in preparing VAT returns.

The question of a possible misdeclaration is most likely to come up during a control visit and can be approached in the following way.

- *Errors* – adjustment may be agreed between the Customs & Excise Officer and the taxable person there and then.
- *Misdirection* – where a Customs and Excise Officer, with the full facts before them, has given a clear and unequivocal ruling on VAT in writing or, knowing the full facts, has misled a registered person

to that person's detriment, any assessment of VAT due will be based on the correct ruling only from the date the error was brought to the registered person's attention.

- *Misunderstanding* – Customs and Excise may exceptionally take no further action in respect of VAT undercharged by a registered person as a result of a genuine misunderstanding which does not concern anything clearly covered in guidance published by Customs & Excise or in specific instructions given to that registered person.

Otherwise, if a company underdeclares tax by:

- showing too little tax due on the VAT return;
- claiming a repayment which is too large on the VAT return; or
- failing to tell Customs and Excise within 30 days that a centrally issued assessment is too low,

then a misdeclaration penalty (which does not imply an intention to evade tax or dishonesty) may be imposed where the underdeclaration is:

- 30% or more of the VAT managed in the relevant period; or
- over £1 million.

Reasonable excuse and mitigation apply to this penalty

Where, however, there has been more than one misdeclaration so that the underdeclaration is one of a series which are:

- 10% or more of the VAT managed in the relevant period; or
- over £500,000.

then the company may be liable to a repeated misdeclaration penalty.

In addition to penalties, simple interest (calculated as a percentage of the VAT due and from the date the VAT ought to have been paid up to a maximum of three years) may be charged in order to effect commercial restitution. Unless agreed and paid at the time, an Assessment will be issued showing the amount of VAT due together with the amount of interest due on that VAT. A failure to pay that assessment within 30 days will result in a further interest charge.

Failure to notify cessation of taxable supplies **[CT1.83]**

A failure to notify cessation of taxable supplies for VAT purposes attracts a penalty. The amount of the penalty is a fixed daily rate. The basic rate is £5 per day while the breach continues. However, if there has been an earlier breach the daily rate is £10 and if more than one earlier breach £15.

This penalty is subject to a maximum of 100 times the daily amount.

The reasonable defence applies but mitigation does not.

Failure to retain records for six years **[CT1.84]**

A failure to retain records for six years attracts a fixed penalty of £500.

The reasonable excuse defence applies but mitigation does not.

Evasion **[CT1.85]**

All of the penalties for the circumstances detailed at **CT1.75 to CT1.84** above proceed on the basis that there is no dishonesty involved. Where, however, VAT has been dishonestly evaded, Customs and Excise may impose a penalty equal to that amount.

Again, however, Customs and Excise may, depending on the circumstances of the case, reduce the amount of penalty to take into account the extent to which co-operation was given to them in their investigation.

For aggravated or serious offences, Customs and Excise may take further proceedings. This might, depending upon the merits of the case, involve Customs and Excise (*CEMA 1979, s152*) accepting a financial settlement (known as 'compounding').

Alternatively, Customs and Excise may investigate the matter with a view to the institution of criminal proceedings and will generally do so if:

- a search warrant was used;
- the amount involved is £75,000 over three years;
- security was required but not provided;
- the offence is committed by professional advisers or prominent people;
- the evader is an undischarged bankrupt;
- there was a conspiracy or other criminal activity;
- a false VAT scheme was involved;

- there has been a previous compounding or deliberate intention to deceive; or
- there is an element of novelty or ingenuity in the offence capable of adoption by others.

System for ensuring that VAT operates in a fair manner [CT1.86]

So far as ensuring that the system operates fairly is concerned, it will be appreciated that VAT is a complex tax which deserves some concentration and effort by the taxable person. It is a simple fact of business life that if the business is seen to have adopted sensible systems and make returns correctly and on time then the business is unlikely to be greatly troubled by Customs and Excise. If, however, the Customs and Excise form the view that the business does not carry out these functions then the business is likely to come into more contact with them.

It is, therefore, in the interests of the business to:

- have a proper system in place for accounting for VAT;
- keep your records up-to-date;
- seek the advice of Customs and Excise if unsure; and
- advise Customs and Excise promptly of any changes to the business,

and provided that is done then the business should be able to rely upon the published Service Commitment of Customs & Excise.

There are procedures under which it is possible to ask Customs & Excise to review any decision made and these should (with professional assistance) be adopted. If agreement between the company and Customs & Excise cannot be reached, then an appeal can be made to the VAT and Duties Tribunal (an independent body) – see **CT1.88 *et seq.*** below.

The entitlements of the taxable person [CT1.87]

The rights or entitlements of the taxable person are contained in the Service Commitment of Customs & Excise (see Notice 700, page 1) under which they are committed to serving the needs of its customers by:

- acting fairly and impartially–
  - treat the company's affairs in strict confidence, within the law; and
  - want companies to pay or receive only the right amount due;
- communicating effectively with their customers by aiming to provide–
  - clear and simple forms and guidance; and
  - accurate and complete information in a helpful and appropriate way;
- providing good quality service by aiming to–
  - handle affairs promptly and accurately;
  - be accessible in ways that are convenient to its customers;
  - keep customers' costs to the minimum necessary;
  - take reasonable steps to meet special needs; and
  - be courteous and professional;
- take responsibility for their services by–
  - publishing annually their customer service aims and achievements;
  - listening to customers' comments and complaints in order to improve the service they offer;
- encouraging customers to help them by–
  - keeping accurate and up-to-date records;
  - letting them know if personal/business circumstances change;
  - giving them correct and complete information when they ask for it; and
  - making full payment at the correct time.

Review **[CT1.88]**

If Customs and Excise arrive at a decision with which you disagree then there are a number of steps which you can take, including seeking a review or appeal, although there may be time limits involved. Note, however, that any time-limits for an appeal against the decision (normally 30 days) should not be allowed to expire while the avenue of review is explored. It may be prudent to seek professional advice at this stage.

The procedure for review is to ask your Local VAT Office to reconsider that decision. Any further information or facts which may not have been fully taken into account may be brought forward at this stage.

It is the declared policy of Customs and Excise to explore locally all reasonable prospects for settling a dispute and to discuss or review a case even though an appeal may have been lodged and is running. Any *written* settlement arrived at by this means has the same force as a formal decision in an appeal.

Appeals **[CT1.89]**

Every assessment, formal decision and penalty issued by Customs & Excise ought to contain with it details of any appeal available.

Not every decision made by Customs and Excise carries a right of appeal but where a right of appeal is provided for then the VAT and Duties Tribunal has been established as an independent body which can hear and decide appeals by the taxpayer.

Time limits **[CT1.90]**

It is important to note that there is a time limit for appeals and a failure to observe these time limits may result in no appeal being available. The normal time limit is 30 days from the date of the decision being appealed.

Where negotiations or discussions have taken place then it is open to Customs & Excise to issue a letter extending the time for an appeal (usually by 21 days).

In the final event, it is possible for the person concerned to apply to the tribunal for an extension of time to make an appeal.

Procedure **[CT1.91]**

The procedure for an appeal is to complete a formal Notice of Appeal (which can be obtained from the Local Office or Tribunal) and send or fax that Notice directly to the Tribunal (*not* to any Customs & Excise Office). The decision appealed against must be referred to. Grounds of appeal must be briefly stated. The Notice must be signed by someone authorised to do so (e.g. a director or the company secretary). No fee is involved.

Appealable decisions **[CT1.92]**

An appeal will normally lie in relation to Customs and Excise decisions including those involving:

- refusal to allow registration;
- registration generally;
- cancellation/invalidation of registration;
- any requirement imposed in respect of computer invoicing;
- the amount of output tax chargeable in import; dispatch or supply;
- the amount of input tax which may be reclaimed;
- the value of goods or services supplied;
- a claim for repayment or bad debt;
- the requirement for security;
- the fact of an assessment;
- the amount of an assessment;
- default surcharges;
- the fact of a penalty;
- whether there was a reasonable excuse;
- the amount of the penalty; or
- the amount of interest/ repayment supplement.

Appeal requirements **[CT1.93]**

Different appeals have different requirements. Appeals which involve an amount of VAT such as against assessments or similar matter require to have the disputed tax paid or deposited with Customs & Excise before the appeal will be entertained by the tribunal. In cases where that would produce hardship, however, it is possible to ask Customs & Excise to waive that requirement failing which it is possible to apply to the tribunal to have the requirement waived.

Appeals which involve penalties do not have the requirement of payment as a precondition of appealing.

Subsequent procedure **[CT1.94]**

On receipt of the Notice of Appeal the tribunal staff will acknowledge the Notice. Where applicable, payment or deposit of VAT must be confirmed before the appeal will be allowed to proceed further. A preliminary hearing may be held in respect of leave to appeal late or waiver of payment of vat on the grounds of hardship. Otherwise, notification will be sent out of the date set down for the hearing before the tribunal.

The person making the appeal is known as the Appellant and they are entitled (indeed, strongly advised) to have a representative such as a barrister, accountant, solicitor, consultant or the like). They should make up, where required, a bundle of the documents produced in support of their appeal.

Customs & Excise are known as the Respondents. They are likely to be represented by a local solicitor which they use or by a solicitor employed directly within the Head Office of Customs & Excise. They will also make up a bundle, when required, of the documents produced in support of their decision.

The bundles should be exchanged so that each side is aware of the case for and against before the hearing.

The hearing **[CT1.95]**

The hearing will take place before a tribunal appointed by the Lord Chancellor. The Chairman, legally qualified, may sit alone or may sit with one or two members being either professionals (e.g. an accountant if the appeal involves accounts) or a layperson (if the appeal involves, for example, what a reasonable person might have done).

At present, appeals are divided into categories.

Category 1	– a penalty for tax evasion (dishonest conduct)
Category 2	– a default surcharge (late returns - for reasonable excuse only) – a penalty for misdeclaration or neglect – a late registration penalty – other penalties – mitigation
Category 3	– an assessment of tax – requirement to deposit security – any other decision

The precise procedure to be adopted at the hearing depends, to some extent, upon the category of appeal involved. In many cases, the law provides that the onus of proof is on the appellant. In some of the other more serious cases (e.g. Category 1) the onus of proof may remain on Customs & Excise. The hearing is said to be informal and it is likely that most Chairman will, at the outset of the hearing, establish the procedure to be followed by the parties.

The outcome **[CT1.96]**

The tribunal has a wide discretion to:

- allow the appeal against the decision;
- refuse the appeal against the decision; or
- vary the decision.

The tribunal also has the power in some cases to recognise that a reasonable excuse (see **CT1.73** above) existed or to mitigate the penalty (see **CT1.74** above).

A further appeal – on a point of law only – exists from the tribunal to the Courts of Law.

CT2 – Corporation Tax

Introduction [CT2.1]

In the application of Corporation Tax to a Personal Service Company it is important to bear in mind at the outset the important distinction between capital and revenue.

Capital [CT2.2]

The simple expenditure of capital on an asset likely to be of enduring benefit for the company will not of itself necessarily carry an entitlement to a capital allowance. Only expenditure which is 'qualifying' will carry the entitlement to a capital allowance and in this section it is proposed to consider the conditions which have to be satisfied before capital expenditure carries an entitlement to a capital allowance.

The main legislation covering capital allowances is the *Capital Allowances Act 1990* and subsequent *Finance Acts*.

How are capital allowances given? [CT2.3]

For companies, under self-assessment, capital allowances are treated as if they were a trading expense and deductible in computing Schedule D, Case I profits.

This is currently reflected in the company Tax Return. They may technically still need a claim but an entry in the Return is likely in practice to be treated by the Inland Revenue as a claim.

You start with the Accounts, strip out depreciation by adding it back and the calculate and claim the capital allowance to which you believe the company is entitled.

To deliver an incorrect return negligently or fraudulently attracts a penalty.

There is provision, in some circumstances, for amending a return within three months of becoming aware that the return was incorrect.

For what period are capital allowances given? [CT2.4]

Capital allowances are in theory given for a tax year (in the same way as Corporation Tax rates). However, in practice the basis period upon which capital allowances are calculated is generally synonymous with the accounting period of the company.

What 'expenditure' qualifies for capital allowances? [CT2.5]

The most important qualification which capital expenditure must have to qualify for capital allowances is that that expenditure has been incurred wholly and exclusively for the purposes of a trade

Capital allowances are normally given only for assets which the company acquires by the expenditure but there are exceptions to this rule.

For example, where several persons share in or contribute towards capital expenditure then if they all do so for trading purposes then they may all share the capital allowances. Thus, a qualifying equipment lessor could, in certain circumstances, make a joint election with a qualifying lessee for the purposes of claiming capital allowances over the asset leased. Another example is in the case of tenants. As earlier noted, where the terms of the lease oblige the tenant company to make expenditure on a attachments for a building which will remain with the building when they leave then provided they fall within the definitions in *Schedule A* of *CAA 1990* the tenant company will be able to claim capital allowances on the expenditure on those assets although it does not as a result own them. When the tenant company leaves those premises, however, then the appropriate adjustments will require to be made to the capital allowances calculation.

In a straightforward case, a company will order and pay for a capital asset within the accounting period. It sometimes happens, however, that the purchase contract is more complicated. In these circumstances, irrespective of any provision within the contract as to when the payment or payments require to be made, capital 'expenditure' will be treated for capital allowance purposes as incurred whenever the obligation to purchase becomes unconditional. There are, however, anti-avoidance provisions (*CAA 1990, s159*) aimed at the practice of manipulating payment dates so as to falsely accelerate entitlement to a capital allowance.

'Expenditure' for capital allowance purposes is aimed at the real expenditure of the claimant company.

If the company is registered for VAT purposes then the 'expenditure' is net of VAT (but if the company is not registered for VAT then VAT will be included in 'expenditure' for the purpose of capital allowances).

If the company is entitled to any subsidy or grant then 'expenditure' for capital allowance purposes is cost less any grants or subsidies (but if the grant subsequently becomes repayable then the Inland Revenue, by concession (ESC B49) will look at an adjustment to capital allowances in that respect).

Sometimes a third party will contribute to the capital expenditure of a company. If that third party does so for the purposes of a trade then that third party may be able to claim capital allowances in their own right. Such an asset is not 'pooled'.

What capital allowances are available? [CT2.6]

The rate of capital allowances and the assets to which they apply is an area very frequently adjusted in the *Finance Acts*. More recently, distinctions have started to be drawn between the various categories of company. There are at present two main categories of capital allowance available – First Year Allowances (FYA) and Writing Down Allowances (WDA).

The table below shows the current rates at which capital allowances are given.

Item		**FYA**	**WDA**	**Basis**
Plant and Machinery				
	(a)	100%		reducing balance
	(b)	40%		reducing balance
	(c)	50%	25%	reducing balance
Scientific Research		100%		n/a
Patent Rights			25%	reducing balance
Know-how			25%	reducing balance

Nature of the company [CT2.6]

It is now necessary to determine at the outset the nature of your business for certain capital allowances may now only be claimed by certain categories of business. In particular, First Year Allowances are now available only to small and medium-sized companies (SMEs). The definitions for these are contained in the *Companies Act 1985* and a small or medium-sized company is one which satisfies at least two of the following conditions:

- turnover does not exceed 11.2 million;
- assets do not exceed 5.6 million;
- number of staff does not exceed 250.

Clearly, therefore, virtually all Personal Service Companies will fall within the category of a small or medium-sized business.

Calculating capital allowances [CT2.7]

It will be appreciated that as a business goes through its working life it is likely to buy and sell a number of assets. The Writing Down Allowance is calculated on the balance of expenditure after acquisitions and disposals have been taken into account. Writing Down Allowances are then applied on a reducing balance basis to give the balance carried forward.

At this stage the difference between pooled and unpooled items will be appreciated. In the case of polled items adjustments are unlikely – in the unlikely event of disposals exceeding the balance on the pool then a balancing charge equal to the excess has to be made but no balancing allowances are to be made until the cessation of the business. In the case of unpooled items, any applicable balancing charge or a balancing allowance will be applied each year. Any applicable First Year Allowances will then be considered and applied.

The application of these calculations will result in a statement of the capital allowances claimed and the balances carried forward.

Capital gains [CT2.8]

There are a number of special rules which determine what the capital gains or losses are which are subject to Corporation Tax.

The basic approach **[CT2.9]**

The basic approach is to look at the matter over the whole period of the accounting period in question.Any capital gains and any capital losses in that period are established and offset so that a net chargeable gain/loss is established for the accounting period which is then entered on the company's tax return.

Net capital gain **[CT2.10]**

A net capital gain is *prima facie* subject to Corporation Tax but that tax can be reduced in a number of ways (e.g. if a company has been trading for a number of years then it might have accumulated a capital loss which it is carrying forward and that can be offset in the company's tax return).

Net capital loss **[CT2.11]**

A net capital loss can never be carried back and can (with very rare exceptions) never be offset against other profits arising in the accounting period.

However, a net capital loss can be carried forward and offset against any capital gains arising in the future.

Calculating capital gains **[CT2.12]**

As can be seen from the company's tax return, a number of other entries might reduce the Corporation Tax to be paid on any net capital gains.

In calculating capital gains it is necessary to establish the following factors:

- disposal proceeds;
- costs of disposal;
- acquisition cost;
- indexation allowance; and
- capital gain/loss.

Disposal proceeds **[CT2.13]**

In most cases the disposal proceeds will be the consideration paid in money terms for the asset (and there are special rules to cater for situations where the consideration is staggered, made conditional or deferred).

However, in certain circumstances the Inland Revenue is entitled to use the market value of the asset instead.

The most notable circumstance where this is done is where an asset of the company is sold or given to a shareholder/director/employee of the company. Since such a transaction is not at arm's length the Inland Revenue are entitled to disregard any agreed price stated and substitute instead the market value.

Costs of disposal **[CT2.14]**

The costs which can be offset against the disposal proceeds are defined in the *Capital Allowances Act 1990* and only these costs can be offset which are:

- valuation fees;
- advertising fees;
- selling agent (Estate Agent, auctioneer etc.) fees; and
- legal (selling) fees.

Acquisition cost **[CT2.15]**

The acquisition cost which can be offset against the disposal proceeds net of the costs of disposal is now a complicated situation and the figure to be inserted here can be arrived at in a number of ways.

In the first place, the acquisition value of the asset can be considered which is usually the consideration in money's worth paid for the asset together with any capital expenditure (but not revenue expenditure) incurred in maintaining the asset. If the asset was not purchased as such but was made, then the acquisition value of the asset can be taken as the cost of making up the asset together with any capital expenditure (but not revenue expenditure) incurred in maintaining the asset.

However, as a tax concession, the *Finance Act 1988* allowed for all assets held on 31 March 1982 to be 'rebased' which means that instead of the acquisition value arrived at in the first place above, the acquisition value can be deemed to be value of the asset as at 31 March 1982. There are essentially two ways in which a company can approach rebasing its assets.

In the second place, a company can make an election for the global rebasing of *all* its assets as at 31 March 1992. The election is a formal one which must (subject to Inland Revenue discretion) be made within two years of the end of the accounting period in which the company first makes a disposal after 31 March 1982. Whether or not the election is worthwhile will depend upon the individual assets owned by the company and the pattern of acquisitions and disposals. This election allows a company to use *solely* the 31 March 1982 rebased value as the acquisition value of the asset.

In the third place, if a global election is not made, then the company can decide for each individual asset whether to use the original acquisition cost of the asset or the deemed 31 March 1982 cost of the asset. The company must prepare both of these calculations which are then presented to the Inland Revenue (with the company's tax return) and compared. The lowest gain/loss may then be chosen by the company *except that* where one produces a gain and the other produces a loss then neither is deemed to apply and the Inland Revenue will apply a no gain/no loss ruling.

Indexation allowance **[CT2.16]**

Again as a tax concession, the *Finance Act 1988* allows for relief to be given to capital gains for the effect of inflation. Accordingly, in relation to 'relevant allowable expenditure' an indexation allowance based on the retail price index is allowed.

For the purposes of this calculation, the actual disposal proceeds (not reduced by the costs of disposal) and the acquisition cost (later of actual or rebased) is used and their Retail Price Index applied in the following formula:

$$\frac{RD - RI}{RI}$$

RD = Retail Price Index for actual disposal proceeds month
RI = Retail Price Index for later of:

- month acquisition cost actually incurred; and
- month of March 1982.

Assets of negligible value [CT2.17]

Where a company owns an asset which has fallen to a 'negligible value' then it is possible for the company to crystallise that situation into a capital loss.

The asset is deemed to have been sold at its negligible value (thereby creating a loss when measured against the cost of acquisition) and then to have been re-acquired by the company at the negligible value. Rebasing can apply but indexation (see **CT2.16** above) no longer applies to this procedure.

It is also possible to use that capital loss either in the accounting period in which that procedure is gone through or backdated to an earlier accounting period (not exceeding two years prior to the date that procedure is gone through).

Corporate debt [CT2.18]

If a company made a loan and needed to later write that loan off then that was formerly regarded as a capital loss. As from 1 April 1996, however, all such corporate debt ceased to fall within the capital gains tax regime.

Instead, if falling within the definition of 'qualifying corporate bonds' any such loss will be treated as a trading expense (and in the event of a gain as a trading profit under Schedule D).

Revenue [CT2.19]

A UK resident company with a source of income is chargeable to Corporation Tax on 'all its profits wherever arising' (*ICTA 1988, s8*) and this is administered through the company Tax Return.

In order to arrive at that 'profit' the company will normally take as its starting point the annual Accounts which it has prepared but a number of adjustments are necessary.

In the first place, the 'profit' for accounting purposes is not, in the UK, the 'profit' for taxation purposes and adjustments are necessary to convert one type of profit into the other. In the second place, while it sometimes will be the same, the 'accounting period' for accounting purposes will not necessarily be the 'accounting period' for taxation purposes and some adjustment may be necessary to reconcile the accounting periods.

A company's 'profits' for taxation purposes [CT2.20]

A UK resident company with a source of income is required to pay Corporation Tax on all its profits (income and capital gains less charges) wherever arising.

'Income' in the UK tax system is divided into mutually exclusive Schedules some of which are further sub-divided into Cases.

As already noted, Schedule E covers the income of those who are in employment. For those who are self-employed the other Schedules will apply and for companies that might include the following.

Schedule A		Profits from property
Schedule D		
	Case I	Profits from a trade
	Case II	Profits from a profession or vocation
	Case III	Interest received
	Case V	Foreign income
	Case VI	Miscellaneous income not taxed elsewhere

Various other categories of income are dealt with outwith this system – for example:

- interest received under deduction of tax;
- charges on income; and
- capital gains.

The result is that no matter how 'profit' might have been presented for accounting purposes, 'profit' for Corporation Tax purposes requires to be teased out and presented in the appropriate manner.

Schedule A [CT2.21]

Any income deriving from property or rights over land (e.g. rents, licences or any other income or receipts arising from the ownership of land) is subject to taxation under Schedule A.

So far as companies are concerned, from 1 April 1998 the concept of the 'Schedule A business' has been introduced which essentially means that instead of a prescriptive approach of defined receipts and defined deductions, the Schedule A income is regarded as a business in relation to which the calculation of profits is arrived at by treating the income and expenditure in much the same way as any other trade (on which see **CT2.22** below).

Schedule D [CT2.22]

Profits from which might be called 'business income' is taxed under Schedule D and this Schedule is divided into two Cases – Case I (in respect of any trade) and Case II (in respect of any profession or vocation).

The word 'trade' is incompletely defined to include:

> '…every trade, manufacture, adventure or concern in the nature of a trade.'

It is probably a mixed question of fact and law which the courts will consider in any individual case as to whether or not a trade exists.

The words 'profession' and 'vocation' are also incompletely defined, although very little, if anything, turns on the distinction between them. A 'profession' is regarded as requiring the application of intellectual skill while a 'vocation' is regarded as a calling.

Over the years the categorisation of activities as either a trade or a profession/ vocation has become settled and the distinction is now probably as much a matter of recognised practice as anything else.

Income [CT2.23]

All income, arrived at by generally accepted accounting principles, will fall into the definition of 'chargeable business assets' unless it is excluded by falling into one of the following excluded categories:

- VAT receipts;
- capital receipts;
- income already taxed by deduction at source; and
- income outside the scope of the trade or profession/vocation.

Activities which fall outside the trade or profession/vocation will not be charged to tax as a trade or profession/vocation and may not be entitled to have expenditure deducted therefrom in order to arrive at the profit concerned, but may be subject to taxation under another Schedule.

Expenditure **[CT2.24]**

Expenditure will fall into the definition of 'deductible expenses' and be excluded if it falls into one of the following excluded categories:

- VAT payments;
- capital payments; or
- expenditure subject to a specific statutory disallowance or restriction.

In arriving at a company's Schedule D, Case I profit, the only expenditure which will be treated as a deductible expense is that which satisfies the test of being wholly and exclusively incurred for the purposes of the company's trade.

Trading loans **[CT2.25]**

Previously, companies were taxed on any interest received (gross, without deduction of tax) under Schedule D, Case III and any interest paid was treated as a charge. However, in an attempt to mirror the accounting treatment of such transactions, with effect from 1 April 1996 a new approach has been adopted for companies under which loans of a trading nature will have all profits and losses charged or under Schedule D, Case I.

From 1 April 1996, all debts held and owed by companies which arise from the lending of money are to be known as 'loan relationships' and will include any money debt (in any currency) arising from a transaction for the lending of money. The debt does *not* have to be secured but it excludes shares and trade debtors and creditors.

The legislation reflects accounting principles and refers to 'credits' and 'debits'. Thus, qualifying loan interest received (credits) will be included in Schedule D, Case I income while qualifying interest paid (debits) will be included in Schedule D, Case I deductions. Interest will now be taxed and relieved under Schedule D only if they are arrived at under an authorised accounting method. Only two have been authorised – the accruals method and the mark-to-market method.

Under the accruals method, the normal method, interest will be taxed and relieved as it is accrued rather than as it is paid. Under the mark-to-market method, often used by investment companies, the loan is valued and restated each year with interest allocated as it becomes due and payable.

Example

On money deposited in the bank, PSC Limited has accrued interest of £5,000 (£4,000 paid). On money lent to PSC Limited by an enterprise company to construct an office, PSC Limited has incurred interest of £6,000 (£5,000 paid).

Previous treatment

Schedule D, Case I		
Schedule D, Case III		4,000
Less: charges on income		(5,000)
Profit chargeable to Corporation Tax		

Present treatment

Schedule D, Case I		
	Income	5,000
	Expenditure	(6,000)
Schedule D Case III		
Less: charges on income		
Profit chargeable to Corporation Tax		

The result is that no matter how 'trading profit' might have been presented for accounting purposes, 'trading profit' for Corporation Tax purposes requires to be teased out and presented in the appropriate manner so that only allowable income and expenditure is included in the calculation of Schedule D Case I profits. This is normally presented in the form of a Corporation Tax Adjustment of Profit.

Schedule D, Case III **[CT2.26]**

Schedule D, Case III charges to tax all interest of money, whether yearly or otherwise, or any annuity or other annual payment, whether such payment is payable in or outside of the UK, either as a charge on any property of the person paying the same by virtue of any deed or will or otherwise, or as a reservation out of it, or as a personal debt or obligation by virtue of any contract.

Previously, companies were taxed on any interest received (gross, without deduction of tax) under Schedule D, Case III. Companies will still be taxed under Schedule D, Case III in relation to any gross interest received which is of a non-trading nature. With effect from 1 April 1996, however, a new approach has been adopted for companies which have loans of a trading nature and that is to treat all profits and losses made on such trading loans by companies as income and subject them to taxation under Schedule D, Case I (see **CT2.25** above).

Schedule D, Case V **[CT2.27]**

Schedule D, Case V charges to tax income arising from foreign possessions. Generally, these will be dividends, royalties or the like and they fall to be taxed in the hands of the UK company under this Case *whether remitted or not.*

A UK company which decides to trade overseas will be taxed according to the way in which it carries out its operations.

Where the UK company trades abroad *only* then the income arising there may be taxable under Case V. Where the UK company trades *partly* in the UK and *partly* abroad (whether as a branch or not) then the income arising there may be taxable under Schedule D, Case I. Where the UK company sets up a subsidiary company then the income will be taxed only when remitted as a divided.

Taxation may also be incurred in the overseas country and Double Taxation Agreements may apply.

The position is complicated and beyond the scope of this book.

Schedule D, Case VI **[CT2.28]**

This is a 'catch-all' Case designed to sweep up any miscellaneous income not covered by any of the other Schedules or Cases. Examples are isolated insurance commissions, casual income, and the like. Note that gifts are excluded.

Charges on income **[CT2.29]**

Previously, interest paid by a company was separately dealt with here under the heading of charges on income. This has, of course, largely been superseded by the rules for 'loan relationships' introduced which now allow such payments to be deducted under Schedule D, Case I.

If not of a trading nature, however, any annual payments such as deeds of covenant, annuities and the like would require to be included here.

The system for ensuring enforcement of Corporation Tax [CT2.30]

Enquiries into company tax returns **[CT2.31]**

With effect from Accounting Periods ending 30 June 1999, companies are required to assess their own liability for Corporation Tax (i.e. self-assessment).

The self-assessment made by the company may in the first instance be accepted by the Inland Revenue. However, the Inland Revenue will (on a random basis as well as upon a basis with cause) select the returns made by various companies and may subject these to enquiry and this is likely to be the primary method by which Inspectors of Taxes will control Corporation Tax.

Time limits for enquiries **[CT2.32]**

The time limits for enquiries are set down as follows although different time limits apply where dishonesty is alleged.

Where a company files its tax return on time, the Inland Revenue may, within 12 months give notice that they intend to enquire into the return.

Where a company files its tax return late, the Inland Revenue may, before the end of the quarter day (quarter days are 31 January, 30 April, 31 July and 31 October) next following the first anniversary of the day the return was delivered, give notice that they intend to enquire into the return.

Where a company amends its tax return late, the Inland Revenue may, before the end of the quarter day next following the first anniversary of the day the return was amended, give notice that they intend to enquire into the return.

The scope of the enquiry **[CT2.33]**

Only one enquiry may be made into a return unless the company amends the return, in which case each amendment may be the subject of a separate enquiry.

An enquiry may cover anything contained in the return.

However, where an amendment is made by the company but the time limit for an enquiry into the return itself has passed, then the enquiry may only cover matters to which the amendment relates.

Notice to produce information **[CT2.34]**

Once notice of an enquiry has been issued, the Inland Revenue have the power to issue a notice (provided that it has a time limit of not less than 30 days) requiring the company to produce such documents and information as the Inland Revenue may reasonably require. Photocopies will generally suffice although the Inland Revenue have the power to call for originals.

An appeal may be marked against such a notice to the Commissioners although in this instance, any decision arrived at by the Commissioners is final and conclusive.

The right to issue this notice does not apply where the company has an appeal.

Amendment by the company during enquiry **[CT2.35]**

It is open to the company to amend its tax return during the course of an enquiry. That amendment may then itself form part of the enquiry. That amendment will, however, have no effect on the amount of Corporation Tax payable by the company until the enquiry is completed.

Amendment by the Revenue during enquiry [CT2.36]

The Inland Revenue may, by notice, amend a company's self-assessment during an enquiry in order to prevent tax loss.

Such an amendment by the Inland Revenue may be appealed by the company in the normal manner but such an appeal cannot be heard or determined until the enquiry has been completed.

Completion of enquiries [CT2.37]

There is no formal time-limit for the completion of an enquiry but it is open to a company to apply to the Commissioners for a direction that the Inland Revenue should issue a closure notice within a specified period.

The Commissioners are obliged to issue such a direction unless satisfied that the Inland Revenue has 'reasonable grounds' for not issuing a closure notice.

Closure of an enquiry [CT2.38]

An enquiry is formally ended by the issuance of a closure notice by the Inland Revenue. This will specify the conclusions of the Inland Revenue. The company then has 30 days to make amendments to the return in order to give effect to those conclusions.

Where a company fails, wholly or partly, to make any such amendments as the Inland Revenue considers necessary to give effect to an those conclusions within the period of 30 days and the Inland Revenue consider the return to be incorrect or incomplete, then the Revenue may, within a further 30 days, serve notice on the company, making such amendments as they consider appropriate.

The company may, within 30 days, appeal such a notice in the normal way.

The assessment system [CT2.39]

In most circumstances, Corporation Tax will be catered for under the new self-assessment procedures. Returns should be made, even if late, failing which the Inland Revenue may determine to the best of their information and belief the amount of tax due by the company.

In exceptional circumstances, however, where the tight definitions of 'fraud or negligence' is alleged, or it is alleged that on the basis of the information 'available' the Inland Revenue could not reasonably be expected to be aware of the circumstances, it is open to the Inland Revenue to make discovery assessments or discovery determinations.

Discovery assessments or determinations may not be made if any loss of tax is attributable to a mistake regarding the basis of the computation of liability made in accordance with the generally accepted practices prevailing at the time it was made.

Discovery assessments **[CT2.40]**

Where, following the issue of a notice for return, no return is delivered or delivered only partially, the Inland Revenue may after the filing date has passed determine the amount of tax payable by the company. No such determination may be issued more than five years after the date upon which the power to issue such a determination arose.

For most purposes (such as time limits, penalties and interest) such determinations will be treated as the equivalent of self-assessments. It can, in fact, be superseded by the company delivering a return and making a self-assessment.

Where the Inland Revenue discover that:

- an amount which ought to be assessed has not been assessed, or
- an assessment has become insufficient, or
- excessive relief has been given,

then the Inland Revenue may make a discovery assessment in such amount as they consider necessary to make good any loss of tax.

The sanction of the formal Board of the Inland Revenue is necessary where an adjustment to the return has been made and it is proposed to incorporate that adjustment into a discovery assessment.

The time limit for a discovery Assessment is six years after the end of the accounting period to which the assessment relates extended to twenty-one years in the case of fraudulent or negligent conduct.

Discovery determination **[CT2.41]**

Where the Inland Revenue discover that a company tax return for one period incorrectly states an amount that affects either the tax payable by that company in another period or the tax payable by another company, then the Inland Revenue may issue a discovery determination.

The sanction of the formal Board of the Inland Revenue is necessary where an adjustment to the return has been made and it is proposed to incorporate that adjustment into a discovery determination.

The time limit for a discovery determination is six years after the end of the accounting period to which the assessment relates extended to twenty-one years in the case of fraudulent or negligent conduct.

The penalty system **[CT2.42]**

Failure to give notice of chargeability **[CT2.43]**

Under the *Finance Act 1988, Schedule 18*:

> 'A company which–
> (a) is chargeable to tax for an accounting period, and
> (b) has not received a notice requiring a company tax return,
> must give notice within twelve months from the end of the accounting period to the Inland Revenue that it is so chargeable.'

Failure to do this will make the company liable to a penalty not exceeding the amount of tax payable (disregarding any relief available under *ICTA 1988, s419(4)* for repayment of loans etc.) for the accounting period in question that remains unpaid twelve months after the end of the period.

It is not yet clear how strictly these requirements are likely to be applied in isolation by the Inland Revenue. However, one effect of self-assessment for companies may be that for some the return made by them is likely to be accepted while for others (selected on a random basis) the return for that year is likely to be investigated closely.

As a result of that investigation the Inland Revenue might ask to see the underlying records for that and perhaps also for previous years. A failure on the part of the taxpayer to be able to produce adequate records at that stage would be likely to count against the taxpayer and may result in not only tax being sought but interest and penalties also. Since this will remain on the taxpayer's record, it is something to be avoided by keeping good records.

In the event of any dispute arising, the taxpayer company may seek to have the matter referred to the Commissioners for their decision. Here, the laws of evidence, strictly speaking, apply in relation to any documentation in issue.

Original documents are specifically required for:

- dividend vouchers (*ICTA 1988, s234*);
- subcontractor's certificates (*ICTA 1988, s566*);
- documents showing tax deducted or credited (*FA 1998, Sch 18, para 22(3)*); and
- claims outside a tax return (*TMA 1970, Sch 1A, para 2(a)*).

In other circumstances, the normal requirements have been relaxed and copies or optical images permitted (*FA 1998, Sch 18, para 22(1)* and *(2)*). The Inland Revenue is moving towards an electronic system and it may be possible in the future for everything to be done electronically but that position has not yet been reached.

The Inland Revenue generally operate a reasonable discretion and are subject to review by the Commissioners or the courts if they do not do so. Nevertheless, some system for maintaining record-keeping standards is necessary and this is provided for also. In the first place, if original records cannot be produced a fact may be proved by other available documentary evidence (e.g. duplicate copy bank statements from the bank).

A complete failure to comply with the record-keeping requirements carries a penalty of up to £3,000 (*FA 1998, Sch 18, para 23(1)*). In addition, a breach of *section 221* carries the possibility of imprisonment or a fine and every officer of the company who is in default is guilty of an offence unless he shows that he acted honestly and that in the circumstances in which the company's business was carried on, the default was excusable.

Record keeping **[CT2.44]**

A company which fails to comply with the record keeping requirements of *FA 1998, Sch 18, para 21* in relation to an accounting period is liable to a penalty not exceeding £3,000. However, no penalties are incurred:

- if the records which the company fails to keep or preserve are records which might have been needed only for the purposes of claims, elections, or notices not included in the return; or
- the records which the company fails to keep or preserve are statements in writing such as are mentioned in:
  - *ICTA 1988, s234(1)* (amount of qualifying distribution and tax credit); and
  - *ICTA 1988, s352(1)* (gross amount, tax deducted and actual amount paid in certain cases where payments are made under deduction of tax)

  provided by the company or person there mentioned whether after the making of a request or otherwise; and
- the Inland Revenue are satisfied that any facts which they reasonably require to be proved, and which would have been proved by the records, are proved by other documentary evidence furnished to them.

Failure to deliver a return within the time limit **[CT2.45]**

The close correlation between the Accounts of a company and the tax return of a company is, perhaps, illustrated by the fact that there is an excuse for late delivery of a return (avoiding the flat rate penalty) if:

- the period for which the return is required is one for which the company is required to deliver accounts under the *Companies Act 1985*, and
- the return is delivered no later than the last day for the delivery of those accounts to the Registrar of Companies.

Otherwise, a company which has had a notice to make a return and fails to deliver it by the filing date, may become liable to a flat-rate penalty of:

- £100 if delivered within three months of the filing date;
- £200 if delivered more than three months after the filing date; or
- if the returns for the two immediately preceding accounting returns were also late, then these flat rate penalties are extended to £500 and £1000 respectively.

Where a company's tax return is delivered later than 18 months after the end of the accounting period, a further tax-geared penalty may be due of:

- 10% if delivered within two years of the end of the period for which the return was required; or

- 20% if delivered after the two year period.

In the event of multiple tax-geared penalties being imposed they are capped to the largest of the individual penalties chargeable on that portion).

Incorrect or uncorrected returns **[CT2.46]**

A company which:

- fraudulently or negligently delivers a company tax return which is incorrect, or
- discovers that a company tax return delivered by it (neither fraudulently nor negligently) is incorrect and does not remedy the error without unreasonable delay,

is liable to a tax-related penalty of an amount up to but not exceeding the amount of tax understated being the difference between the actual amount of tax payable and the amount of tax payable (disregarding *ICTA 1988, s419(4)* – relief for repayment of loans).

Failure to produce information **[CT2.47]**

Where a notice to produce information is issued and the company fails to produce the documents or information called for in the notice, then the company may be subject to a penalty of:

- £30 per day where an Officer of the Board determines it under *TMA 1970, s100*;
- £150 per day where the Commissioners determine it under *TMA 1970, s100C*.

The entitlements of the company as a taxable person **[CT2.48]**

The rights or entitlements of the taxable person are contained in the Service Commitment of the Inland Revenue under which the Inland Revenue are committed to serving the needs of its customers.

CT3 – PAYE, NIC and Benefits

Introduction [CT3.1]

One of the consequences of having employees (which includes directors who are paid a salary by the company) is the requirement to have a system for identifying, recording, taxing, returning and accounting for PAYE, NIC and benefits.

Effectively, the business is acting as an unpaid tax collector for the Government which is keen, so far as possible, to have such taxes deducted at source.

Experience has shown that a tendency to treat tax and NIC deducted as monies of the business has led to the downfall of many businesses and a failure to remit and account for those monies (as well as being an offence and something which may attract interest and penalties) is often an indicator of approaching insolvency. A more prudent approach is to regard such deductions as monies of the Government not of the business and to treat them accordingly.

Even doing that, however, is likely to involve the business in a great deal of (unpaid) time and effort. The benefits system must be understood and applied correctly. The emoluments or gross pay of the employees must be understood and ascertained correctly. Proper calculations of the deductions for tax and NIC must be made. Proper records must be kept and retained. Proper returns must be made. The whole system is underpinned by an enforcement system which has a reputation for firm but fair enforcement although a system of appeals is also provided.

It is, of course, in this area of PAYE and NIC that the legislation implementing IR35 will 'bite' where the IR35 Test is failed and no appeal is marked.

Benefits [CT3.2]

In days gone by, the relationship between employer and employee was a relatively simple one in which the employer paid the employee a fair day's wage for a fair day's work which was then taxed in the hands of the employee. The position then became more complicated.

At an early stage, recognition was given to the fact that certain payments made by the employer to the employee for expenses incurred wholly, exclusively and necessarily in the course of employment should not be taxed. Later, during periods of high taxation, some employers began to remunerate their employees in part by the provision of a form of benefit and legislation was introduced to make these taxable. This tax is levied irrespective of the status or level of earnings of the employee and is payable periodically under PAYE by requiring such remuneration to be included in the calculation of the gross pay.

Still later, as a matter of policy, it was decided that certain benefits should be made subject to taxation. This tax is levied only on certain directors and higher-paid employees and is payable only at the end of the year. More recently, in the March 1999 Budget, the Chancellor of the Exchequer announced various changes to the system for the taxation of benefits which are being carried into effect in the *Child Support, Pensions and Social Security Act 2000*.

The result is that companies must now recognise the various types of benefits and to distinguish between them for the purposes of taxation. In particular, it will now be necessary to distinguish between those benefits which:

- are not taxable;
- require to be regarded as emoluments, included in gross pay, and accounted for under the PAYE system;
- require to be included on Form P11D with Class 1A NIC payable annually; and
- require simply to be included on Form P11D.

Benefits which are not taxable **[CT3.3]**

The following benefits, according to Inland Revenue Booklet BMSD 1/00, are not normally taxable.

- Accommodation, supplies or services (e.g. ordinary office equipment and accommodation, typists, messengers, stationery) provided for the employee in the employer's business premises and used by the employee solely in performing his or her duties (*ICTA 1988, s155(2)*).

- Free or subsidised meals provided on the employer's business premises, or in any canteen where meals are provided for the staff generally, or a ticket or token used to obtain such meals, if:
  - the meals are provided on a reasonable scale; and either all employees may obtain free or subsidised meals on a reasonable scale, whether on the employer's premises or elsewhere; or
  - the employer provides free or subsidised meal vouchers for staff for whom meals are not provided (this concession is restricted in the case of hotel, catering or similar businesses). (*ICTA 1988, s155(5)*.)
- Meal vouchers issued to employees provided that the vouchers are non-transferable, are used for meals only and the value of vouchers issued to the employees does not exceed 15p for each working day. (Note that this concession does not apply to any voucher not meeting the above rules.)
- Expenses incurred in the provision of any pension, annuity, lump sum, gratuity, or similar benefit to be given to the employee or any member of the employee's family or household on the employee's retirement or death. (Note that the cost of providing such benefits may in some circumstances be taxable under other provisions of the *Taxes Acts*.) (*ICTA 1988, s155(4)*.)
- The cost of necessary medical treatment abroad borne by the employer where an employee falls ill or suffers injury while away from the UK in the performance of his or her duties, and of providing insurance for the employee against the cost of such treatment. (*ICTA 1988, s155(6)*.)
- Places in nurseries or playschemes on premises made available by the employer or, if the employer runs the nursery or playscheme jointly with others, on premises made available by one or more of those others provided that the employer has some responsibility for managing and financing the provision of the care. (*ICTA 1988, s155A*.)
- The provision of living accommodation (including council tax) where:
  - it is necessary for the proper performance of the employee's duties that he or she should reside in the accommodation; or
  - the accommodation is provided for the better performance of the employee's duties and the employment is one of the kinds for which it is customary for employers to provide accommodation for the employee; or
  - there is a special threat to the employer's security, special security arrangements are in force and the employee resides in the accommodation as part of those arrangements.

  (Note that this concession does not apply to directors unless the director has no material interest and is a full-time working director.) (*ICTA 1988, s145(4)(5)*.)

- Certain travelling expenses of directors holding office as part of a professional practice (ESC A4).
- Reasonable travelling and subsistence expenses reimbursed to or borne on behalf of employees where, owing to the dislocation of public transport by strikes or other industrial action, employees occupy hotel or other overnight accommodation at or near their normal place of work, or incur extra costs in travelling to and from work (ESC A58).
- Assistance with the cost of travelling between home and work given to severely and permanently disabled persons incapable of using public transport because of their disability. (Note that this concession can also sometimes apply to the car and car fuel scale charges.) (ESC A59.)
- Travelling facilities provided between the mainland and offshore oil or gas rigs or platforms. And, where the timing of transport between the mainland and the rig make it necessary for employees to take overnight accommodation near the mainland departure point, subsistence expenses borne on behalf of or reimbursed to employees working on offshore oil or gas rigs or platforms. (ESC A65.)
- Costs met by an employer who is about to leave or has left within the previous year to enable the employee to attend certain courses of re-training intended to help the employee get another job. (Note that various conditions apply to this concession.) (*ICTA 1988, s588; Sch 29.*)
- Long service awards made to directors and employees as testimonials to mark long service, which take the form of tangible articles of reasonable cost or where the relevant period is not less than 20 years and no previous award has been made, of Shares in the employing company. (ESC A22.)
- Awards made to employees under suggestion schemes, where:
    - there is a formally constituted scheme open to all employees on equal terms;
    - the suggestion is outside the scope of the employee's normal duties;
    - awards are made directly to the employee and only after a decision to implement;
    - awards are based on the degree of improvement in efficiency/effectiveness;
    - the amount of the award does not exceed 50% of expected net financial benefit during first year of implementation, or 10% of expected net financial benefit over a period of up to five years subject to an overriding maximum of £5,000;
    - where a suggestion comes from several employees it is divided reasonably;
    - an 'encouragement' award of £25 or less may be made.

- The provision of a car or motorcycle parking place, or facilities for parking bicycles at or near the employee's place of work. (*ICTA 1988, ss141(6A); 143(1A); 155(1A).*)
- The provision of goodwill entertainment for an employee or a member of the employee's family or household. (Note that a number of conditions apply to the nature and cost of this concession.) (*ICTA 1988, ss41(6B); 142(3B);155(7).*)
- Certain gifts received by an employee where the:
  - gift consists of goods or a voucher or token only useable to obtain goods;
  - person making the gift is not connected to the employer or the employer;
  - gift is not made in recognition or anticipation of services in the employment;
  - gift has not been directly or indirectly procured by the employer;
  - the gift costs £150 or less;
  - total costs of all gifts by same donor to employee or household in tax year is £150 or less.

  (ESC A70.)
- The cost of transport (for up to 60 journeys a year) which an employer provides to take an employee home if either:
  - the employee is occasionally not regularly required to work late (9pm or later);
  - by the time the employee can go home, either public transport has ceased or it would not be reasonable to expect the employee to use it;
  - the employee normally travels to and from work in a car shared with other employees and due to unforeseen circumstances which could not reasonably have been anticipated, the employee cannot get home in the shared car.

  (ESC A66.)
- Annual Christmas parties or alternative functions of a similar nature which are open to staff generally and cost no more that £75 per head. (Note that only functions costing £75 or less will not be taxed.) (ESC A70B.)
- Sports facilities generally available to the employer's employees and members of their families and households. This does not apply to:
  - facilities available to the general public;
  - facilities associated with overnight or holiday accommodation;
  - facilities provided on domestic premises; or
  - mechanically propelled vehicles or cars, motor boats, aeroplanes

  (*ICTA 1988, s197G.*)
- The provision of a mobile telephone provided by an employer to an employee including any line rental and calls for that telephone paid directly by an employer unless all or any of these can be converted

into money by the employee. (Note that this concession does not apply to money or vouchers an employer pays an employee to use their own mobile telephone.) (*ICTA 1988, s155AA*.)

- The benefit to employees of travel between home and work in a works bus provided:
  - the bus has a seating capacity of 12 or more;
  - the bus service is available to all employees;
  - the main use of the service is travel between home/workplace/workplace or substantially the whole use of the service is by employees (and their children)

  (*ICTA 1988, s197AA*.)
- The benefit to employees of an employer subsidising a public transport bus/road service used by employees for travelling between home/workplace/workplace provided:
  - the service is available to all employees;
  - the terms for employees are not more favourable than for the public.

  (*ICTA 1988, s197AB*.)
- The benefit of bicycles and/or cyclists' safety equipment lent to employees (or vouchers to obtain these) provided:
  - such bicycles and equipment are available generally to employees;
  - the main use is between home/workplace/workplace.

  (*ICTA 1988, s197AC*.)
- Costs which an employer incurs like any other buyer, in connection with the purchase of an asset from an employee. (ESC A85.)
- Payment or reimbursement of expenditure on the provision of work-related training. (*ICTA 1988, s200B-D*.)
- The provision of removals expenses to employees. (*ICTA 1988 s191A;191B;Sch 11A*.)

All-employee benefits [CT3.4]

Certain benefits are specifically directed by legislation to be taxable irrespective of the level of earnings of the employee – i.e. benefits in relation to which all employees may be taxable. They include the following.

Living accommodation [CT3.5]

Where an employee or a member of that employee's family or household is provided with accommodation (such as a company house or a company flat) either rent-free or at a reduced rent then that employee (irrespective of his or her level of income) will normally be liable to taxation under Schedule E on the value of that benefit.

There is an exception to that rule where:

- it is necessary for the proper performance of the employee's duties that the employee resides in the accommodation;
- The accommodation is provided for the better performance of the duties of the employment and the employment is one in which it is customary for employers to provide their employees with accommodation; or
- there being a special threat to security, security arrangements are in force, and the accommodation is resided in by the employee as part of those security arrangements.

Vouchers **[CT3.6]**

Some employers provide their employees with vouchers. Much depends upon the form which these vouchers take.

Where the vouchers are cash vouchers (exchangeable for a sum of money not substantially less than their cost of provision) then the amounts for which they are capable of being exchanged are treated as emoluments upon which the PAYE system requires to be operated.

Where the vouchers are other than cash then the employee (irrespective of his or her level of income) will normally be liable to taxation under Schedule E on the value of that benefit.

Some vouchers (e.g. those for sports and recreation) are excluded.

Share schemes **[CT3.7]**

The general principle is that where shares are issued for nothing or at reduced prices to employees, then the employee (irrespective of his or her level of income) will normally be liable to taxation under Schedule E on the value of that benefit.

However, exceptions are made in the case of approved share option schemes, approved savings-related share option schemes, and the like.

Expenses [CT3.8]

The general principle is that the reimbursement by the employer to the employee of expenses incurred wholly, exclusively and necessarily in the performance of that employee's duties are not regarded as 'emoluments'. However, some employers adopt a policy of round sum allowances (in which the employee is not asked to account for every item of expenditure individually) and where these allowances are excessive so as to create an element of profit then the employee (irrespective of his or her level of income) will normally be liable to taxation under Schedule E on the value of that benefit.

Benefits for higher paid employees and directors [CT3.9]

For those falling into the category of 'higher-paid employees' or 'directors' a separate regime applies in relation to which different items are treated as benefits when received by persons falling into those categories. The two categories are usually treated together.

Higher paid employees [CT3.10]

ICTA 1988, section 167 provides that employees earning more than a specified threshold of earnings are to be treated as higher-rate employees. The threshold is currently £8,500.

In order to perform that calculation, all emoluments, expenses and benefits paid to the employee are taken into account (to determine the *rate* of pay, not the *amount* actually received to date) and the calculation is performed before any allowable expenses are deducted.

In practice, most employees will be higher paid unless a specific effort is made to bring an employee under the threshold.

Directors [CT3.11]

Being a director is a legal status and in theory the legislation covers shadow directors' (persons in accordance with whose instructions the directors of the company are accustomed to act). Those who are directors in a purely professional capacity (such as accountants or solicitors) are excluded.

Directors are excluded if they have no 'material interest' in the company ('material interest' is defined as being where a person together with any associates is able to control more than 5% of the ordinary share capital of the company or to receive more than 5% of the assets on liquidation) and are 'full-time working directors' (these are defined as being one who is required to devote substantially the whole of his or her time to the affairs of the company in a managerial or technical capacity). However, even if excluded under the above rules should the individual concerned be remunerated at a level above the threshold (currently £8,500) then that individual will be caught as a higher-paid employee (see **CT3.10** above).

The general charge [CT3.12]

There is a general charge to taxation in respect of any expenses or benefits paid by an employer to higher-paid employees or directors.

All expenses provided by an employer to a higher-paid employee or director are *deemed* (i.e. presumed) to have been paid by reason of the employment unless the contrary is proved.

As regards expenses, most sums paid by an employer to a higher-paid employee or director (with the sole exception of payments made in the course of domestic, family or personal relationships where they just happen to be employer and employee) will under the general charge be treated as emoluments and taxed under Schedule E.

As regards benefits, the full cost to the employer or the 'cash equivalent' of providing them will under the general charge be treated as emoluments and taxed under Schedule E.

Specific charges [CT3.13]

Quite apart from the general charge, certain benefits paid to higher-paid employees and directors are specifically charged to taxation under their own specific rules:

- company vehicles (company cars and company vans);

- car fuel;
- mileage allowances;
- beneficial loans;
- Income Tax for directors or employees notional earnings paid by the employer;
- scholarships; and
- shares acquired at an undervalue.

Specific exclusions [CT3.14]

Quite apart from the general charge, certain benefits paid to higher-paid employees and directors are specifically excluded from the charge to taxation under their own specific rules as follows:

- Accommodation where:
  - it is necessary for the proper performance of the employee's duties that the employee resides in the accommodation (this is not applicable to directors);
  - the accommodation is provided for the better performance of the duties of the employment and the employment is one in which it is customary for employers to provide their employees with accommodation (this is not applicable to directors);
  - there being a special threat to security, security arrangements are in force, and the accommodation is resided in by the employee as part of those security arrangements.
- Assets where:
  - computer equipment is lent free or at a reduced rate to the employee, as regards the first £500 of the annual benefit to the employee;
  - bicycles or bicycle safety equipment for employees commuting from home to work.
- Company vehicle parking facilities (at or near the workplace).
- Incidental personal overnight expenses (up to £5 per night in the UK).
- Lump sum/pension provided by the employer on the death of the employee.
- Meals provided by the employer (if for all staff).
- Mobile telephones (except private calls).
- Nurseries/playgroups/childcare provision by the employer (including shared provision).
- Sports and recreation provision (including shared provision).
- Transport such as bus services provided by the employer (including supported buses).

PAYE [CT3.15]

As noted above, different sources of income are taxed under different Schedules. For those who derive income from holding an 'office' (e.g. directors and company secretaries) or an 'employment' (i.e. a person under a contract of service) their income is charged to taxation under Schedule E.

Schedule E charges to taxation:

- emoluments from any office or employment;
- pensions; and
- any other income directed to be charged under Schedule E (for example, some benefits, some contributions by employers to retirement benefit schemes, some termination payments, and the like).

Schedule E is divided into three Cases:

- Case I – for persons resident and ordinarily resident in the UK (receipts basis);
- Case II – for persons not /ordinarily/resident but duties performed in the UK (receipts basis); and
- Case III – for persons resident in the UK receiving earnings in the UK (earnings basis).

Accordingly, all those who receive 'emoluments' from an office or employment in a company will have that income taxed in their hands under Schedule E.

Emoluments [CT3.16]

In respect of the emoluments of offices and employments, the *Taxes Management Act 1970*, the *Income Tax (Employments) Regulations 1993 (SI 1993/744)* and the *Income Tax (Employments) (Amendment) Regulations 1998 (SI 1998/2484)* require the employer to deduct tax at source by the operation of the system which is known as PAYE.

Emoluments are defined as 'all salaries, fees, wages, perquisites and profits whatsoever'. The word 'emoluments' receives a wide interpretation and a blend of legislation, precedent and practice has resulted in a number of inclusions and exclusions being recognised in its application. The category into which a payment falls will be determined not by the terms of the contract but by all the circumstances of the case.

Remuneration **[CT3.17]**

The largest and most obvious category is remuneration in the form of salary, wages, fees, commissions, bonuses or indeed any other form of remuneration paid by reason of employment or in return for acting as or being an employee.

Benefits **[CT3.18]**

It is important for companies to appreciate that over recent years legislation has directed that a number of benefits be treated as 'emoluments' which means that the company requires to include those benefits in the emoluments (i.e. gross pay) upon which they are operating the PAYE system (and also the NIC system).

Furthermore, in applying benefits to emoluments, different rules and a distinction falls to be drawn between:

- all employees;
- employees earning more than a specified amount (currently £8,500 p.a.); and
- directors.

(See **CT3.4–CT3.11** above.)

Rewards for future services **[CT3.19]**

Rewards for future services (colloquially known as 'golden hellos') are generally speaking taxable as emoluments although exceptions to this rule have been recognised.

Restrictive covenants **[CT3.20]**

Restrictive covenants (colloquially known as 'golden handcuffs') are generally taxable although, again, exceptions to this rule have been recognised.

Reduction in wages in return for benefits **[CT3.21]**

Attempts have been made to compensate employees with benefits in return for a reduction in wages which would bring them below the level of higher-earning employees (currently £8,500). The Inland Revenue (on the assumption that the benefits received could be converted into cash) assessed the employee on the amount by which the earnings were reduced.

Indirect remuneration from employers **[CT3.22]**

Attempts have been made to compensate employees indirectly by:

- giving the employee goods;
- discharging an obligation due by the employee; or
- paying a third party to provide goods or services to the employee.

The fact that such remuneration has arrived indirectly is irrelevant where it can be established that the remuneration was received in return for acting as or being an employee or officer.

Gifts **[CT3.23]**

Minor gifts of small value are likely to be disregarded but regular or substantial gifts which satisfy the test that they were received in return for acting as or being an employee or officer are likely to be taxable.

- awards for suggestions are specifically covered by the rules for benefits;
- an annual event for employees not exceeding £75 per head is disregarded; and
- as an extra-statutory concession, awards for long service are disregarded provided that they do not exceed £20 per year of service, the recipient has completed 20 years' service, and no similar awards have been made within the previous ten years.

Sickness, maternity and disability pay **[CT3.24]**

Statutory Sick Pay (SSP) and Statutory Maternity Pay (SMP) are taxable as emoluments under Schedule E as is any payment as sickness, maternity or disability pay which is the subject of a contractual arrangement with the employer.

Exclusions [CT3.25]

A number of categories are recognised as being excluded from 'emoluments' and therefore outwith the gross pay to which the PAYE system requires to be applied.

NICs [CT3.26]

As originally devised, the National Insurance Scheme was intended to provide a form of insurance to protect the population of the nation. However, matters have moved away from that notion. Although the entry 'National Insurance Fund' can be found within the Accounts of the Government, it does not operate as a stand-alone Fund in the accepted sense.

Social spending within the UK is massive but less and less of the funding for that spending comes from NIC. Instead, social spending is funded by general taxation to which NICs contribute. They are, in effect, another form of taxation. Despite this, NICs are – as many have discovered to their cost – vital in that they provide a gateway to a large number of the benefits provided. Unless the appropriate NICs are recorded as having been made, full benefits will not be payable.

Categorisation [CT3.27]

The appropriate NICs to be paid are divided into Classes and for Personal Service Companies the following will be relevant:

- Class 1;
- Class 1A; and
- Class 1B.

Class 1 [CT3.28]

Class 1 NICs are earnings-related and are based on an employed earner's employment. They are payable in two parts:

- Primary Contributions – paid by the employed earner; and
- Secondary Contributions – paid by the employer.

The procedure for primary contributions is to:

- establish the earnings period in question;
- establish the emoluments of gross pay of the employee, and
- compare that amount to the earnings limits and rates applicable ascertained from the tables supplied by the Revenue Authorities.

Secondary contributions are similarly aligned.

Class 1A **[CT3.29]**

Class 1A NICs were introduced in 1991 in relation to the income tax benefit arising on a higher-paid employee or director for the private use of employer-provided cars and fuel. It has since been expanded.

This contribution is based on cash equivalents of the benefit provided in the tax year and is payable once annually.

Class 1B **[CT3.30]**

Since 1996, it has been possible for employers to enter into PAYE Settlement Agreements which allow employers to account for the tax and contributions payable in respect of minor and irregular benefits.

CT4 – IR35

Introduction [CT4.1]

The concept of what is now generally known as IR35 was introduced on 9 March 1999 by an Inland Revenue Press Release.

There then followed a period of consultation which, in the opinion of the Tax Faculty of the ICAEW and various others, was not as full as it might have been. Nevertheless, the Government showed its determination in a Regulatory Impact Assessment and pressed on with the legislation.

The legislation is, in the main, in two parts – that relating to Income Tax and that relating to NICs.

Overall, much is clearly going to depend upon the way in which the legislation implementing IR35 is administered by the Inland Revenue in practice. If the (undeclared) objective is to drive certain groups back into direct employment then a robust administration can be expected. If the objective is merely, as declared, to distinguish disguised employment from self-employment then a more precise administration can be expected and IR35 will be something which a properly-run Personal Service Company will be able to cope with and survive.

Application of the legislation for Income Tax purposes [CT4.2]

The legislation implementing IR35, so far as Income Tax is concerned, is applied through *Schedule 12* of the *Finance Act 2000.*

Under FA 2000, Sch 12, para 1(1), that Schedule applies where:

> '(a) an individual ("the worker") personally performs, or is under an obligation personally to perform, services for the purposes of a business carried on by another person ("the client").

(b) the services are provided not under a contract directly between the client and the worker but under arrangements involving a third party ("the intermediary"), and

(c) the circumstances are such that, if the services were provided under a contract directly between the client and the worker, the worker would be regarded for income tax purposes as an employee of the client.

This is widely written and as further interpreted in the rest of *para 1* applies to intermediaries which are unincorporated bodies, partnerships and limited companies and includes local, public or government authorities.

Although initially directed at the terms of any contract under which the worker provides services to the client through an intermediary, the crux of the matter is clearly paragraph 1(1)(c) which in effect applies the employment/self-employment test (see **Chapter CM3** above).

The consequences of failing the test [CT4.3]

The consequences of failing the test, which results in the contract concerned being referred to as a 'relevant engagement', is that *FA 2000, Sch 12, para 2* will apply and the worker will be treated as receiving Schedule E income as follows:

'(1) If, in the case of an engagement to which this Schedule applies, in any tax year

(a) the conditions specified in paragraph 3, 4 or 5 are met in relation to the intermediary, and

(b) the worker, or an associate of the worker–

(i) receives from the intermediary, directly or indirectly, a payment or other benefit that is not chargeable to tax under Schedule E, or

(ii) has rights entitling him, or which in any circumstances would entitle him, to receive from the intermediary, directly or indirectly, any such payment or other benefit, the intermediary is treated as making to the worker in that year, and the worker is treated as receiving in that year, a payment chargeable to income tax under Schedule E ("the deemed Schedule E payment").

(2) The deemed Schedule E payment is treated as made at the end of the tax year, unless paragraph 12 applies (earlier

date of deemed payment in certain cases).

(3) A single payment is treated as made in respect of all engagements in relation to which the intermediary is treated as making a payment to the worker in the tax year.'

These are referred to in the Schedule as the 'relevant engagements' in relation to a deemed Schedule E payment.

The consequences of failing the test is not the immediate application of the fiscal legislation for further conditions of liability are applied. These are applied where the intermediary is a company, a partnership, or an individual.

So far as companies as intermediaries are concerned, the conditions of liability exclude associated companies of the client but otherwise apply where the payment or benefit referred to above in para 2(1)(b) is received or receivable by the worker directly from the intermediary and can reasonably be taken to represent remuneration for services provided by the worker to the client *or* the worker has a material interest in the intermediary.

A worker (and that includes 'associates' as defined in *FA 2000, Sch 12, para 19* where there is:

'(a) beneficial ownership of, or the ability to control, directly or through the medium of other companies or by any other indirect means, more than 5% of the ordinary share capital of the company; or

(b) possession of, or entitlement to acquire, rights entitling the holder to receive more than 5% of any distributions that may be made by the company; or

(c) where the company is a close company, possession of, or entitlement to acquire, rights that would in the event of the winding up of the company, or in any other circumstances, entitle the holder to receive more than 5% of the assets that would then be available for distribution among the participators [as defined in *ICTA 1988, s417(1)*].'

In other words, those who have failed the test but whose material interest in the company is less than 5% may not have the deemed Schedule E payment rules applied to them but even they may have those rules applied to them where they receive, or could receive, payments or benefits from the company which are not salary, but could reasonably be taken to represent payment for the services provided to the client.

Clearly, where the test is failed the vast majority will satisfy the conditions of liability.

The consequences where the conditions of liability are met [CT4.4]

Where the conditions of liability are met, the consequences in general are regarded as an end of tax year event.

There are, however, certain cases where an earlier date is specified for the deemed payment. These are detailed in *FA 2000, Sch 12, para 12.*

> 'Where the intermediary is a company and–
> (a) where the worker is a member of the company and ceases to be such a member,
> (b) where the worker holds an office (i.e. a director or company secretary) with the company and ceases to hold such office,
> (c) where the worker is employed by the company and ceases to be so employed
>
> then the deemed Schedule E payment is treated as having been made immediately before that event or, if there is more than one, immediately before the first of them.'

Otherwise, the deemed Schedule E payment is treated as made at the end of the tax year (*FA 2000, Sch 12, para 2(2)*) and all engagements are treated as being made in a single payment (*FA 2000, Sch 12, para 2(3)*).

The consequences where all the conditions are met [CT4.5]

Where all of the conditions are met then *FA 2000, Sch 12, para 7* lays down a nine-step process for the calculation of the deemed Schedule E payment as follows.

Step one

In respect of each of the contracts which the company has in that tax year, for those contracts which are 'relevant engagements' (i.e. have failed the test), establish the total amount of all payments and other benefits received by the company from the client, and reduce that amount by 5%

Step two

In respect of those 'relevant engagements' ,add the amount of any payments and other benefits received by the worker in that tax year otherwise than through the company and which are not chargeable to income tax under Schedule E but would have been so chargeable had the worker been an employee of the client (e.g where the client provides the worker directly with the use of a car).

Step three

Deduct the amount of any expenses met in that year by the intermediary that would have been deductible from the emoluments of the employment if the worker had been employed by the client and the expenses had been met by the worker out of those emoluments.

In other words, the intention of this legislation is to tax the worker as an employee, even through the worker operates through the intermediary of a company, and therefore in the same way as any other employee the Worker is permitted to deduct allowable or deductible expenses (i.e. those which meet the wholly, exclusively and *necessarily* test).

Step four

Deduct the amount of any capital allowances in respect of expenditure incurred by the company that could have been claimed by the worker under *section 27* of the *Capital Allowances Act 1990* (plant and machinery: extension of allowances to employments etc.) if the worker had been employed by the client and had incurred the expenditure.

Step five

Deduct any contributions made in that year for the benefit of the worker by the company to a scheme approved under *Chapter I* or *Chapter IV* of *Part XIV* of *ICTA 1988* that if made by an employer for the benefit of an employee would not be chargeable to income tax as income of the employee.

This does not apply to excess contributions made and later repaid.

Step six

Deduct the amount of any employer's NICs paid by the company for that year in respect of the worker.

Step seven

Deduct the amount of any payments or other benefits received in that tax year by the worker from the company:

- in respect of which the worker is chargeable to income tax under Schedule E, and
- which do not represent items in respect of which a deduction was made under step three.

If the result at this point is nil or a negative amount, there is no deemed Schedule E payment.

Step eight

Find the amount that together with the employer's NICs on it is equal to the amount resulting from step seven.

Step nine

The result is the amount of the deemed Schedule E payment.

Consequences for Personal Service Companies [CT4.6]

The consequences of failing the test is clearly going to be a substantial burden upon Personal Service Companies and their participants. The 'sting in the tail', however, (which may go some way towards justifying the position of those who say that the hidden objective of this legislation is to drive such participants out of their companies and back into employment) is that while the expenses which an employee would be allowed have been provided for, the *actual* expenditure which a Personal Service Company might have incurred in order to achieve the earnings it did are, for these purposes, disregarded in favour of a straight allowance of only 5%.

The result in practice for Small Personal Service Companies with only one contract which fails the test and becomes a 'relevant engagement' might will be that the tax (and NIC) burden imposed under these rules might, when added to the real expenditure already incurred, drive the Personal Service Company into a position of making losses which are irretrievable.

The application of the legislation for NIC purposes [CT4.7]

The legislation implementing IR35, so far as NICs are concerned, is applied through the *Social Security Contributions (Intermediaries) Regulations 2000* (*SI 2000/727*).

Under para 6(1), those Regulations apply where:

> '(a) an individual ("the worker") personally performs, or is under an obligation personally to perform, services for the purposes of a business carried on by another person ("the client").
> (b) the performance of those services by the worker is carried out, not under a contract directly between the client and the worker, but under arrangements involving an intermediary, and
> (c) the circumstances are such that, had the arrangements taken the form of a contract between the worker and the client, the worker would be regarded for the purposes of Parts I to V of the Contributions and Benefits Act as employed in employed earner's employment by the client.'

This paragraph is clearly in much the same terms as the legislation relating to Income Tax (see **CT4.2** above) although here *para 2* goes on to provide that *para 1(b)* above has effect irrespective of whether or not:

> '(a) there exists a contract between the client and the worker, or
> (b) the worker is the holder of an office with the client.'

This legislation is also widely written and applies to intermediaries which are unincorporated bodies, partnerships and limited companies.

Although initially directed at the terms of any contract under which the worker provides services to the client through an intermediary, the crux of the matter is clearly *para 6(1)(c)* which in effect applies the employment/self-employment test.

The consequences of failing the test [CT4.8]

The consequences of failing the test, which would make these Regulations apply, is that:

> '(a) the worker is treated, for the purposes of Parts I to V of the Contributions and Benefits Act, and in relation to the amount deriving from relevant payments and relevant benefits that is calculated in accordance with regulation 7 ("the worker's attributable earnings"), as employed in employed earner's employment by the intermediary, and
>
> (b) the intermediary, whether or not he fulfils the conditions prescribed under section 1(6)(a) of the Contributions and Benefits Act for secondary contributors, is treated for those purposes as the secondary contributor in respect of the worker's attributable earnings, and Parts I to V have effect accordingly.'

This legislation was clearly intended to match that relating to income tax but it remains to be seen in practice how closely they tie in.

Where the intermediary is a company the conditions (*para 5(2)*) are that:

> '(a) the intermediary is not an associated company of the client, within the meaning of section 416 of the Taxes Act, by reason of the intermediary and the client both being under the control of the worker, or under the control of the worker and another person; and
>
> (b) either–
>
> (i) the worker has a material interest in the intermediary, or
>
> (ii) the payment or benefit is received or receivable by the worker directly from the intermediary, and can reasonably be taken to represent remuneration for services provided by the worker to the client.

Under *para 5(3)*, a worker is treated as having a material interest in a company for the purposes of *para 5(2)(a)* above if:

> '(a) the worker, alone or with one or more associates of his, or

(b) an associate of the worker, with or without other such associates, has a material interest in the company.'

For these purposes, a material interest means:

'(a) beneficial ownership of, or the ability to control, directly or through the medium of other companies or by any other indirect means, more than 5% of the ordinary share capital of the company; or
(b) possession of, or entitlement to acquire, rights entitling the holder to receive more than 5% of any distributions that may be made by the company; or
(c) where the company is a close company (as defined in s414 and 415 of the Taxes Act), possession of, or entitlement to acquire, rights that would in the event of the winding up of the company, or in any other circumstances, entitle the holder to receive more than 5% of the assets that would then be available for distribution among the participators [as defined in *ICTA 1988, s417(1)*].'

The consequences where the conditions of liability are met [CT4.9]

Where the conditions of liability are met, the consequences in general are regarded as a single payment of the worker's attributable earnings made by the intermediary on the 5 April in the tax year concerned.

There are, however, certain cases where an earlier date is specified for the deemed payment. These are detailed in *para 8(5)* as being:

'Where the intermediary is a company and:
(a) where the worker is a member of the company and ceases to be such a member,
(b) where the worker holds an office (i.e. director or secretary) with the company and ceases to hold such office,
(c) where the worker is employed by the company and ceases to be so employed then the deemed payment is treated as having been made immediately before that event or, if there is more than one, immediately before the first of them.'

The consequences where all the conditions are met [CT4.10]

Where all of the conditions are met then *para* 7 lays down a nine-step process for the calculation of the deemed Schedule E payment as follows.

Step one

Find the total amount of all payments and benefits received by the intermediary in that year under the arrangements and reduce that amount by 5 per cent.

Step two

Add the amount of any payments and benefits received by the worker in that year under the arrangements, otherwise than from the intermediary, that:

- are not chargeable to income tax under Schedule E, and
- would be so chargeable if the worker were employed by the client.

Step three

Deduct the amount of any expenses met in that year by the intermediary that would have been deductible from the emoluments of the employment if the worker had been employed by the client and the expenses had been met by the worker out of those emoluments.

In other words, the intention of this legislation also is to tax the worker as an employee, even through the worker operates through the intermediary of a company, and therefore in the same way as any other employee the worker is permitted to deduct allowable or deductible expenses (i.e. those which meet the wholly, exclusively and *necessarily* test).

Step four

Deduct the amount of any capital allowances in respect of expenditure incurred by the company that could have been claimed by the worker under *section 27* of the *Capital Allowances Act 1990* (plant and machinery:

extension of allowances to employments etc.) if the worker had been employed by the client and had incurred the expenditure.

Step five

Deduct any contributions made in that year for the benefit of the worker by the company to a scheme approved under *Chapter I* or *Chapter IV* of *Part XIV* of *ICTA 1988* that if made by an employer for the benefit of an employee would not be chargeable to income tax as income of the employee.

This does not apply to excess contributions made and later repaid.

Step six

Deduct the amount of secondary Class 1 contributions and Class 1A contributions paid by the intermediary for that year in respect of the earnings of the worker.

Step seven

Deduct:

- the amount of any payments made by the intermediary to the worker in that year that constitute remuneration derived from the worker's employment by that intermediary including, where the intermediary is a body corporate and the worker is a director of that body corporate, payments treated as remuneration derived from that employment by virtue of *regulation 17A* of the *Contributions Regulations* (payments to directors to be treated as earnings), but excluding payments which represent items in respect of which a deduction was made under step three; and
- the amount of any benefits provided by the intermediary to the worker in that year, being benefits that constitute amounts of emoluments in respect of which Class 1A contributions are payable, but excluding any benefits which represent items in respect of which a deduction was made under step three.

If the result at this point is nil or a negative amount, there is no worker's attributable earnings for that year.

Step eight

Find the amount that, together with the amount of the secondary Class 1 contributions payable in respect of it, is equal to the amount resulting from step seven (if that amount is a *positive* amount).

Step nine

The result is the amount of the worker's attributable earnings for that year.

The application of the legislation overall [CT4.11]

The clear intention of the legislation is that in relation to IR35 the Income Tax and national insurance provisions should work together under the existing system.

That is likely to mean, in practice, that the payment of tax and NIC in relation to any 'deemed payment' where a 'relevant engagement' is found will require to be made on the normal payment date under the system (i.e. by 19 April following the year-end).

Representations have already been made by practitioners to the effect that that is a very tight deadline for a matter such as this and in response the Inland Revenue have already made it clear that they are prepared to accept estimates and payments to account provided that it is made clear to the Collector of Taxes that this is what is being done.

As with most taxation legislation, there is scope for adjustment in individual cases. For example, there may be room for negotiation in relation to what expenses *would* have been allowable as a deduction by an employee and provision has been made (including a measure of discretion to the Inland Revenue) to prevent double taxation.

All of these areas will become clearer with practice but the main battle-ground is clearly going to be the employment/self-employment test and whether or not a 'relevant engagement' exists in the first place.

The consequences for both eventualities are considered below.

Consequences for different Personal Service Companies [CT4.12]

The major effect of the legislation implementing IR35 is clearly going to be in the area of PAYE and NIC. Most Personal Service Companies are likely to be operating PAYE and NIC in any event in relation to any salaries paid to shareholder/directors to cover their basic living expenses.

The major effect of the legislation implementing IR35 is likely to be that where the IR35 Test is failed and relevant engagements are held to exist, then a deemed payment is considered to have been made in relation to which, after calculations in accordance with the rules provided, further PAYE and NIC may be payable.

Coping with the effects of such a finding is likely to require speedy action and to be difficult.

Companies with a single contract [CT4.13]

The basic position [CT4.14]

PSC1 Limited has a single shareholder/director, Mr Smith. PSC1 Limited has, during the Year, a single contract with XYZ plc.

During the year, the total income which PSC1 Limited derives from that one contract is £50,000.

During the Year, the expenditure which PSC1 Limited incurs includes:

Salary paid to Mr. Smith	10,000
Telephone	1,000
Travel expenses	500
Motor expenses	1,500
Repairs & Renewals	1,500
Accountancy fees	500
Legal fees	250
Entertainment	250
Rent	2,000
Rates & water	500
Insurance	250

Heat & light	500
Miscellaneous	500
Employer's NIC	953
Pension contributions	4,000
Total	£24,203

The position where the IR 35 Test is passed **[CT4.15]**

During the tax year the Inland Revenue select the affairs of PSC1 Limited for review on a random basis but after considering the employee/self-employed factors the Inland Revenue concluded that PSC1 Limited had passed the IR35 Test.

Accordingly, the IR35 Test having been passed, Mr Smith can freely decide how to extract any funds he wants from the company.

	Remuneration	*Dividends*
Available Profits	25,000	25,000
Less:		
Employer's NIC @ 12.2%	(3,050)	
Corporation Tax @ 20%		(5,000)
	21,950	20,000
Income Tax thereon:	(8,780)	(5,000)
Net cash available	£13,170	£15,000

There will be a saving to Mr Smith of £1,810 in extracting funds by way of dividend rather than by way of remuneration.

The position where the IR35 Test is failed **[CT4.16]**

During the tax year the Inland Revenue select the affairs of PSC1 Limited for review on a random basis but after considering the employee/self-employed factors the Inland Revenue concluded that the single contract is a 'relevant engagement' and that PSC1 Limited had failed the IR35 Test. No appeal is marked against that decision.

Accordingly, the IR35 Test having been failed, it is now necessary for PSC1 Limited to calculate the payment which it has 'deemed' to have made and take that factor into account.

The deemed payment

Total Income		50,000
Total Deductions		
Under the new rules it is not all or some of the £24,203 expenditure incurred by PSC1 Ltd which is taken into account but only certain permissible expenditure is deductible as follows:		
5 % deduction to reflect costs of running the company	2,500	
Schedule E expenses relating to the sole contract (say) (i.e. incurred wholly, exclusively and necessarily)	500	
Pension Contribution (approved scheme)	4000	
Salary paid to Mr Smith during year	10,000	
Employer's NIC paid during the year	953	
Total deductions allowable		17,953
Balance		32,047

Deemed payment $32{,}047 \star \dfrac{100}{100 + 12.2} = £28{,}562$

PSC1 Limited

Income	50,000
Expenditure	
Salary actually paid to Mr Smith	10,000
Salary deemed paid to Mr Smith	28,562
Telephone	1,000
Travel Expenses	500
Motor Expenses	1,500
Repairs & Renewals	1,500
Accountancy fees	500
Legal fees	250
Entertainment	250

Rent	2,000
Rates & Water	500
Insurance	250
Heat & Light	500
Miscellaneous	500
Employer's NIC on actual payment	953
Employer's NIC on deemed payment	3,485
Pension Contributions	4,000
Total Expenditure	56,250
Loss	(£6,250)

Accordingly, the IR35 Test having been failed, Mr Smith has very little freedom to manoeuvre and has in fact made a loss on paper. If Mr Smith did decide to pay himself a dividend then there are provisions to prevent the imposition of what would effectively be double taxation. However, Mr Smith is likely to be more concerned with concentrating upon getting the maximum Corporation Tax relief for PAYE and NIC.

PSC1 Limited will, to avoid penalties, require to pay the Inland Revenue the employer's NIC and the deductions by the due date (19 April). Clearly, however, it would not be in the interests of Mr Smith to pay to himself the whole net amount of the deemed payment since the effect of that would be to drive the company into a loss-making position.

Furthermore, the above example assumes that the whole matter is considered and dealt with in the tax year in question. What is less clear (where clearance in advance has not been sought) is what the position would be where PSC1 Limited is selected for review some years down the line. The sums involved are, cumulatively, by that time likely to be significant. Are the Inland Revenue going to seek interest and penalties? Will the Inland Revenue allow any salary, PAYE and NIC paid then as deductions against Corporation Tax in previous years?

Action to take **[CT4.17]**

In summary, the outlook for the Personal Service Company with a single contract is parlous. Such a company could seek clearance of its contract in advance (see **Chapter CM3** above) and where the view is that the IR35 Test has been failed, tailor its activities accordingly and make actual payments equal to the payments which will be deemed. If not, such a company faces losses as a result of the actual expenditure of the company being cut down to the Schedule E expenses to which an employee would be entitled plus five percent.

The result (whether or not this was the intention of the Government) is to make the advantages of operating a single contract through the commercial vehicle of a Personal Service Company so tenuous and uncertain as to virtually eliminate such advantages as there are to being incorporated at all.

Companies with more than one contract **[CT4.18]**

The basic position **[CT4.19]**

PSC2 Limited has two shareholder/directors, J Jones and A Jones and an employee. PSC2 Limited has, during the year, a number of contracts with a number of clients.

During the year, the total income which PSC2 Limited derives from those contracts is £100,000.

During the Year, the expenditure which PSC1 Limited incurs includes:

Directors' Remuneration	28,000
Wages	10,000
Telephone	2,000
Motor Expenses	3,000
Repairs & Renewals	3,000
Accountancy fees	1,000
Legal fees	500
Entertainment	500
Rent	4,000
Rates & Water	1,000
Insurance	500
Heat & Light	1,000
Miscellaneous	1,000
Employer's NIC	2,857
Pension Contributions	4,000
	£62,357

The position where the IR35 Test is passed **[CT4.20]**

During the tax year the Inland Revenue select the affairs of PSC2 Limited for review on a random basis but after considering the employee/self-employed factors the Inland Revenue concluded that PSC2 Limited had passed the IR35 Test in respect of all its contracts.

Accordingly, the IR 35 test having been passed, J Jones and A Jones can freely decide how to extract any funds they want from the company.

PSC2 Limited

	Remuneration	*Dividends*
Available Profits	35,000	35,000
Less:		
Employer's NIC @ 12.2%	(4,270)	
Corporation Tax @ 20%		(7,000)
	30,730	28,000
Income Tax thereon:		
J Jones	(10,000)	
A Jones	(1,261)	
	(11,261)	(6,250)
Net cash available	£19,469	£21,750

There will be a saving to the Jones of £2,281 in extracting funds by way of dividend rather than by way of remuneration.

The position where the IR35 Test is failed [CT4.21]

During the Tax Year the Inland Revenue select the affairs of PSC2 Limited for review on a random basis but after considering the employee/self-employed factors the Inland Revenue concluded that a number of contracts were 'relevant engagement' and that PSC2 Limited had failed the IR35 Test in respect of those contracts. No appeal is marked against that decision.

Accordingly, the IR35 Test having been failed, it is now necessary for PSC2 Limited to separate its 'relevant engagements' from its 'non-relevant engagements', calculate the payment which it has been 'deemed' to have made in respect of its 'relevant engagements and take that factor into account.

The Deemed Payment

Total Income from 'relevant engagements'		50,000
Total deductions		
Under the new rules it is not all or some of the £62,357 expenditure incurred by PSC2 Ltd which is taken into account but only certain permissible expenditure is deductible as follows:		
5 % deduction to reflect costs of running the Company	2,500	
Schedule E expenses relating to the sole contract (say) (i.e. incurred wholly, exclusively and necessarily)	5000	
Pension Contribution (approved scheme)	4000	
Salary paid to J Jones during year	20,000	
Salary paid to A Jones during year	8,000	
Employer's NIC paid during the year	2,857	
Total deductions allowable		42,357
Balance		7,643

Deemed payment $7{,}643 \star \dfrac{100}{100 + 12.2} =$ £6,812

PSC2 Limited

Income	100,000
Expenditure:	
Directors' Remuneration paid	28,000
Directors' Remuneration deemed	6,812
Wages	10,000
Telephone	2,000
Motor Expenses	3,000
Repairs & Renewals	3,000
Accountancy fees	1,000
Legal fees	500
Entertainment	500

Rent	4,000	
Rates & Water	1,000	
Insurance	500	
Heat & Light	1,000	
Miscellaneous	1,000	
Employer's NIC	3,688	
Pension Contributions	4,000	
Total expenditure		70,000
Profit		£30,000

Accordingly, the IR35 Test having been failed in respect of some contracts only, J Jones and A Jones still have some room to manoeuvre. If the Jones' did decide to pay themselves a dividend then there are provisions to prevent the imposition of what would effectively be double taxation. However, PSC2 Limited is likely to be more concerned with concentrating upon getting the maximum Corporation Tax relief for PAYE and NIC.

PSC2 Limited will, to avoid penalties, require to pay the Inland Revenue the employer's NIC and the deductions by the due date (19 April) and could, if they so wished, pay themselves the whole net amount of the deemed payment and would be best to do so within nine months to ensure that they obtain Corporation Tax relief in that financial year.

The above example assumes, however, that the whole matter is considered and dealt with in the tax year in question. What is less clear (where clearance in advance has not been sought) is what the position would be where PSC2 Limited is selected for review some years down the line. The sums involved are, cumulatively, by that time likely to be significant. Are the Inland Revenue going to seek interest and penalties? Will the Inland Revenue allow any salary, PAYE and NIC paid then as deductions against Corporation Tax in previous years?

Action to take **[CT4.22]**

In summary, the outlook for the Personal Service Company with a more than one contract is better but still a little uncertain. Such a company could seek clearance of its contract in advance and where the view is that the IR35 Test has been failed, tailor its activities accordingly and make actual payments equal to the payments which will be deemed. If not, such a company, to be on the safe side, might be well advised to make actual distributions equal to the payments which would be deemed in the event of any contracts in the 'grey areas' later failing the IR35 Test.

The result (whether or not this was the intention of the Government) is likely to be that even where several contracts are operated through the commercial vehicle of a Personal Service Company, the Government coffers are likely to remain well 'topped up'.

The potential effects of failing the IR35 Test [CT4.23]

The standard deduction [CT4.24]

The first and most obvious effect is that the actual expenditure incurred by the Personal Service Company in achieving its income is disregarded in favour of a standard deduction (currently 5%). It is generally recognised that the present allowance of 5% is less than generous. The substitution is likely to change any profit to a loss in many instances.

Schedule 'E' allowances [CT4.25]

The Personal Service Company is, on the other hand, allowed to deduct those expenses which an employee (taxed under Schedule E) would have been allowed to deduct. The existing tests ('wholly exclusively and necessarily') are likely to be applied in that respect. The interaction with benefit provisions accounted for in the P11D is likely to be a problematic area.

Corporation Tax [CT4.26]

Even where a 'relevant engagement' is established and a 'deemed payment' calculated (resulting in payment of tax and NIC by 19 April) the Personal Service Company must still account for Corporation Tax as a company in the normal manner.

Only where the deemed payment has been anticipated and provided for (and paid within nine months) will the solution be trouble-free. Where no provision has been made and a deemed payment is established later, rolling back the payments later made to that period for Corporation tax purposes is likely to be extremely problematic, if possible at all.

Subsequent payments [CT4.27]

When the IR35 legislation was first proposed, it was somewhat loosely suggested that where a deemed payment was arrived at, then protection would be given against double taxation. In the event, however, the protection actually afforded is considerably more restrictive.

In the first place, having a deemed payment determined and then paying the tax and NIC thereon does *not* mean that the individual behind the Personal Service Company is then free to draw the net salary without further incidence of taxation. To do so would in fact result in a further incidence of tax and NIC.

Only where the taxed money is extracted by way of dividend can further taxation be avoided (*FA 2000, Sch 12, para 13*). Even then, however, there must be both a deemed payment and a dividend resulting in an actual double taxation before the relief will be allowed for which a claim must be made in writing within a stipulated time-period (31 January following the tax year in which the payments are made). Relief may be given by amendment, discharge, repayment or otherwise as appears appropriate to the Inland Revenue.

Summary [CT4.28]

Clearly, the legislation carries the potential to be harsh in application and difficult to administer successfully in practice. Clear forward planning is clearly called for in which respect the uncertainty engendered is unfortunate.

CT5 – Appeals

Introduction [CT5.1]

Most companies are likely to have good relations with the Inland Revenue. From time to time, however, differences of opinion may arise between the taxpayer and the Inland Revenue.

There are a number of ways in which such differences can be resolved but at the end of the day, if all else fails, the taxpayer has – in virtually every field of taxation – a right of appeal to an independent tribunal.

In general, there can be no appeal without a decision to appeal against. In modern practice a lot of correspondence and conversations tend to be exchanged before final positions are taken up and a decision made. These early communications are not decisions and are not appealable. When the Inland Revenue finally adopt a position and reach a decision then that will normally be reflected in some form of formal document such as an assessment, a determination or a formal notice.

Revenue appeals are entirely creatures of statute and therefore unless a right of appeal against a decision can be found in a statute no right of appeal will exist.

Under Inland Revenue best practice, the assessment or formal notice will state the statute and section under which the decision has been made and reference to that statute and section will usually reveal the associated right of appeal.

Professional advice [CT5.2]

Appeals, even though informal, are complex and unusual proceedings the nature of which justify the involvement of professional advisers.

If professional advice is to be taken, however, then it is best if it is taken early. It is of little assistance to a professional adviser coming into a case to find that the client has already adopted a position which they would not have done and has already made a number of damaging admissions which the professional adviser would have counselled the client against making. If a professional adviser is to be used, therefore, it is almost invariably best if the professional adviser is used from the start.

Time limits for appealing [CT5.3]

Virtually every appeal has a generalised time limit of 30 days within which the appeal must be made, failing which the right of appeal may be lost. However, should this time limit of 30 days for making an appeal be exceeded then, provided the matter is raised as soon as possible thereafter and there is a good reason for the delay, it may be possible to persuade the Inland Revenue to accept a late appeal. Failing that, it is possible to apply to the tribunal itself for leave to make a late appeal.

A lot can happen which avoids the need for a formal appeal hearing but where an appeal is being seriously considered, then it is normally prudent to make the appeal in good time since it is normally easier to withdraw a valid appeal than to seek leave to make a late one.

Should the 30 days expire without an appeal being made and no leave for a late appeal being granted, then the decision in the assessment or notice (even if in fact wrong) will in law become final and conclusive.

Reconsideration [CT5.4]

It is the normal practice of the Inland Revenue not to regard any decision as final in the first instance. It will usually be possible for a professional adviser to meet with an Inspector of Taxes and have the issue reconsidered which quite often results in the matter being settled by some middle ground or other agreement being reached. Any such agreement or' settlement' will normally be in writing and will have the same force as if the appeal had been decided by the tribunal. Note that there is no reason why such reconsideration should not take place while the appeal is running.

The form of an appeal [CT5.5]

Under Inland Revenue best practice, the assessment or formal notice will also contain a form which can be used to make an appeal.

Brief grounds of appeal will needed to be provided on the formal appeal form and again, the terms of these should be agreed with the company's professional adviser.

The form may also require other information, types of which are considered below.

Appeal to whom? **[CT5.6]**

There are in fact two tribunals – both independent from the Inland Revenue – to whom an appeal may be marked, one called the General Commissioners and the other called the Special Commissioners.

The General Commissioners **[CT5.7]**

The General Commissioners are lay people although they have usually, through experience, obtained a fair understanding of taxation and they are assisted by a Clerk who is usually a solicitor. They are formally appointed part-time (by the Lord Chancellor in England & Wales and by the Secretary of State in Scotland). They are representative of the area (or 'Division') to which they are appointed and generally represent the views of the reasonable man.

The proceedings of the General Commissioners are confidential, held in private, and they do not have the power to award costs.

The Special Commissioners **[CT5.8]**

The Special Commissioners are professional people who are skilled in all areas of taxation. They, too, are assisted by a Clerk who is usually a Civil Servant. They are formally appointed full-time (by the Lord Chancellor in England & Wales in consultation with the Lord Advocate in Scotland). They are based in London but travel on circuit and generally represent the reasonable application of tax law.

The proceedings of the Special Commissioners are published, normally heard in public (although it is possible to apply for part of the appeal to be heard in private in which case the published decision will be anonymised) and they have the power (not always exercised) to award costs.

Which to choose? [CT5.9]

In the form of appeal you will be asked to which Commissioners your appeal is being marked. There are a very small number of areas where the appeal can only be heard by one of the bodies of Commissioners but in the vast majority of appeals the taxpayer can choose to which Commissioners they wish to appeal. Again, this is a decision best made in consultation with professional advisers.

Considerations include the following.

- How urgent? – an appeal is likely to be heard before the General Commissioners earlier than an appeal before the Special Commissioners.
- How serious? – matters of complex tax law normally go before the Special Commissioners while matters of equity or reasonableness often go before the General Commissioners.
- How long? – it can be difficult to get a longish hearing consistently before the General Commissioners but easier (if later) before the Special Commissioners.
- How sensitive? – General Commissioners will be local but private whereas Special Commissioners will be anonymous but publish.
- How about costs? – these will not be awarded by the General Commissioners but could be by the Special Commissioners.
- How far? – if an appeal to a court of law is a possibility, then the Special Commissioners have more experience of stating a case for the court.

Any such decision is not necessarily irrevocable in any event as in certain circumstances it is open to either body of Commissioners, if they think fit, to transfer an appeal to the other Commissioners where they feel that it is more appropriate that the appeal be dealt with by them.

Payment or postponement [CT5.10]

The treatment of any tax involved, as regards either payment or postponement of that tax while the appeal is proceeding, depends to a large extent upon the nature of the tax involved.

- PAYE – the tax generally may be postponed and need not be paid until the appeal is decided although if the tax is found payable then interest will be charged from the date it was originally due.

- NIC – the tax generally may be postponed and need not be paid until the appeal is decided although if the tax is found payable then interest will be charged from the date it was originally due.
- SSP and SMP – the tax generally may be postponed and need not be paid until the appeal is decided. Interest is not payable.
- Corporation Tax – any postponement of this tax (especially after the introduction of self-assessment) will very much depend upon the circumstances of the case. If allowed, interest is likely to be due.

As a general principle, it is probably the position that any tax is payable pending an appeal unless the Inland Revenue agree to the postponement of the tax.

An application for postponement of the payment of tax should be made at the time of the appeal or within the 30 days from the decision being appealed against. There is provision to ask for a postponement outside the 30 days or to amend any existing postponement but this will normally involve a change of circumstances which is clearly going to result in an overpayment.

The question of postponement can be brought before the tribunal.

An application to withdraw an appeal can be made at any time. Any tax postponed will, together with any interest, normally be due at that time.

The Inland Revenue have the right to refuse to agree to a withdrawal where they feel that the assessment they made was not in fact enough or there is some point of law or principle involved upon which they wish a decision.

The appeal proceedings [CT5.11]

Once an appeal has been formally marked, then the Clerk to the Commissioners concerned will take over.

Notice of the hearing [CT5.12]

The Clerk to the Commissioners will send out a notice simultaneously to the taxpayer and the Inland Revenue specifying – usually on something like 28 days' notice – the date, time and place of the hearing.

Making up the productions [CT5.13]

Where either side intends to rely upon documents to support their case then it is the normal practice for both sides to make up their productions into a numbered 'bundle' and send them both to the other side and the Commissioners in advance of the hearing.

The hearing [CT5.14]

Generally speaking, proceedings before the Commissioners are informal in that no set procedure is laid down. The Commissioners will normally indicate at the outset the procedure which they intend to adopt in relation to the appeal before them. A relevant factor in that decision will be where the onus of proof lies and in most cases the onus of proof will rest on the taxpayer as the appellant.

Only lawyers and professional accountants have a right of audience as representatives and the Commissioners may refuse to let anyone else be a representative.

The appellant usually has to be present and give evidence personally. The appellant will then be cross-examined by the representative of the Inland Revenue and perhaps re-examined by the representative of the appellant. The Commissioners may also ask questions. The same will apply to any witnesses called by the appellant. Unless agreed, any documents produced should be proved.

The Inland Revenue (the respondents) are likely to be represented either by an Inspector of Taxes, a solicitor or counsel. The Inspector of Taxes dealing with the case may or may not give evidence. If so, the Inspector will then be cross-examined by the representative of the appellant and perhaps re-examined by the representative of the Inland Revenue. The Commissioners may also ask questions. The same will apply to any witnesses called by the Respondents.

The decision [CT5.15]

After withdrawing to consider the matter in private, the Commissioners will either issue a decision then or will announce that they will issue a formal decision in writing later.

The decision of the Commissioners may be appealed on a point of law to a court of law but the requirements are complex and beyond the scope of this book.

Part D

Dissolving a Personal Service Company

Introduction

When a person providing personal services through the medium of a Personal Service Company decides to leave that Personal Service Company then there are, in the main, three principal methods of doing so as follows:

- the individual(s) can sell their shares in the Personal Service Company;
- the individual(s) can sell the assets of the Personal Service Company;
- the individual(s) can cease trading and either retain the Personal Service Company or dissolve the Personal Service Company.

In this section, we consider, in outline, some of the legal, management and taxation considerations involved in these decisions.

Law

Making a radical change to the position of a Personal Service Company is no longer a decision which the (majority holding) individual(s) behind a Personal Service Company are entitled to take alone. Different considerations will arise in relation to different circumstances but to a greater or lesser extent the rights of customers, employees and minority shareholders now require to be recognised.

In this section, we consider those rights in relation to the various options.

DL1 – Dealing with the Shares of the Company

Clients' contracts [DL1.1]

The contract which the client has (either directly or through an agency) will be with the Personal Service Company. Unless, therefore, that contract stipulates the involvement of a specified individual (which it often will) a change of shareholder will not affect the Personal Service Company or its contracts.

Employees [DL1.2]

Where effective ownership of a Personal Service Company is changing hands then so far as employees are concerned, the requirements of the *Transfer of Undertakings (Protection of Employment) Regulations 1981* (*SI 1981/1794*) (as amended) will require to be borne in mind.

Shareholders [DL1.3]

So far as shareholders are concerned, in dealing with the shares a number of considerations can come into play which we consider below.

Sale of the shares [DL1.4]

The sale of the shares of the company is a less common and more complicated transaction. It exposes the purchaser to potential unseen liabilities but offers the advantage of instant control over all of the enterprise. From the point of view of the vendor, the prospect of double taxation is avoided in that the price of the shares is received as an individual.

A transaction of this sort usually involves a team of lawyers and accountants performing what is known as 'due diligence' and which effectively amounts to an attempt to exhaustively check every aspect of the business. The vendor is usually asked to sign an extensive range of warranties and indemnities certifying as to the position of the business. They may also be required to stay on for a number of years as a consultant.

A Capital Gain arises, of course, in the hands of the individual selling but this can be mitigated by any retirement relief, a new and improved system of taper relief, and of course the personal allowance. The consideration can be legally structured in a number of ways so as to provide the maximum tax advantages.

Minority protection [DL1.5]

Personal Service Companies are, in general, in exactly the same position as any other private limited company. There will be an established shareholding which has a majority and a minority. That shareholding as a body will have passed the running of the company to a Board of directors.

The Board of directors (notwithstanding that they might be identical in personage to the majority shareholders) ought to conduct the affairs of the company with due regard to the interests of both the majority and the minority of shareholders.

Companies Act 1985 occasionally offers some additional protection in that, for example, extraordinary resolutions (see **CL3.18** above) usually require the approval of a majority of three-quarters of the members but in most situations a simple majority will suffice. Provided that a majority properly exists then the Board are entitled to follow it even where the minority shareholders vehemently disagree.

Against that background, the courts are unwilling to allow a minority of shareholders to interfere with the running of a company in accordance with the wishes of the majority of the shareholders unless the conduct of the majority is oppressive or prejudicial.

This aspect most often comes to the fore when the majority, as a prelude to leaving the company, decide upon some radical action relating to the company such as disposing of the assets of the company or changing the nature of the trade of the company to which the minority takes objection.

Rights of individual members **[DL1.6]**

Each member acquires certain individual rights. In the main, these are to be found in the Memorandum or Articles (which often make individual provision beyond that provided for by the *Companies Acts* and associated Regulations). Beyond that, however, rights may be indirectly acquired by individual shareholders. Thus, should a dividend be declared by the Board then a member would be entitled to enforce their individual right to that dividend.

Similarly, individual members may be able to enforce the right to move resolutions and to speak at meetings in support of them and these are entitlements which the Board (even where reflecting the majority shareholding) should be careful to protect.

A more general complaint (for example, that the company is not being properly run) does not, however, in the eyes of the law arise at the instance of a member as an individual but only by way of what is known as a derivative action.

Derivative action **[DL1.7]**

One of the consequences of a company being a distinct person in law is that it acquires its own bundle of legal rights which are distinct from those of its members.

The law recognises the right of the company to bring an action in its own name to enforce these rights. Should the Board of Directors refuse to initiate such an action, then the law also recognises the right either for the members in general meeting or for an individual member to initiate such proceedings (a 'derivative action').

An individual member cannot enforce every right in this way but only those which clearly point to a breach of the company's rights such as a failure to observe the requirements of the Memorandum or Articles of Association or fraud. These can, however, include the disposal of the assets of the company and, therefore, when deciding to adopt such a course the Board (and/or the majority members behind them) should ensure that they 'go by the book' with due observance of the rights of the minority shareholders.

Statutory protection of the individual member [DL1.8]

Derivative actions are difficult both in theory and in practice. This has been recognised by Parliament which has provided for a new statutory remedy in terms of the *Companies Act 1985, Part XVII – Protection of Company's Members Against Unfair Prejudice.*

This Part (which derives from the insolvency provisions) applies to any body corporate which is liable to be wound up under the *Companies Acts* (which clearly includes Personal Service Companies).

Section 459 provides:

> '(1) A member of a company may apply to the court by petition for an order under this Part on the ground that the company's affairs are being or have been conducted in a manner which is unfairly prejudicial to the interests of its members generally or of some part of its members (including at least himself) or that any actual or proposed act or omission of the company (including an act or omission on its behalf) is or would be prejudicial.
>
> (2) The provisions of this Part apply to a person who is not a member of a company but to whom shares in the company have been transferred or transmitted by operation of law, as those provisions apply to a member of the company; and references to a member or members are to be construed accordingly.'

Accordingly, provided that a minority shareholder could properly make out a case that the affairs of a Personal Service Company are being or have been conducted in a manner which is unfairly prejudicial to the interests of its members generally or some of its members, an application (albeit costly) could be made under this section.

The concept of 'interests' has been interpreted by the Courts as going beyond whatever is contained in the Memorandum or Articles. 'Unfair prejudice' is to receive its ordinary meaning but has been held not to apply to the retention as a director of a family member who was demonstrably incompetent.

Section 461 provides:

> '(1) If the court is satisfied that a petition under this Part is well founded, it may make such order as it thinks fit for

giving relief in respect of the matters complained of.

(2) Without prejudice to the generality of subsection (1), the court's order may–

(a) regulate the conduct of the company's affairs in the future,

(b) require the company to refrain from doing or continuing an act complained of by the petitioner or to do an act which the petitioner has complained it has omitted to do,

(c) authorise civil proceedings to be brought in the name and on behalf of the company by such person or persons and on such terms as the court may direct,

(d) provide for the purchase of the shares of any members of the company by other members or by the company itself and, in the case of a purchase by the company itself, the reduction of the company's capital accordingly.

(3) If an order under this Part requires the company not to make any, or any specified, alteration in the memorandum or articles, the company does not then have power without leave of the court to make any such alteration in breach of that requirement.'

Clearly, therefore, the remedies open to the Court are wide. For example, a majority member who has acted in a dictatorial manner without regard to the requirements of the constitution of the company or the requirements of the *Companies Acts* might well find themselves the subject of a Court Order under which they are removed as director, appointed as a consultant for a fixed period under a fixed salary and made subject to the directions of others who are appointed as directors of the company.

In practice, application to the Courts under the *Companies Acts* have worked best where the individuals behind it have fallen out and are unable to reach an agreement. Where the Court cannot resolve the matter it might order one party to buy the shares of the other at valuation. In an extreme case, the Court might decide that it is just and equitable to wind the company up.

Death and the Personal Service Company [DL1.9]

The death of a member in a Personal Service Company is something which needs to be addressed. Different situations will arise depending upon whether the death is that of a minority shareholder or that of a majority shareholder (who is also providing the essential personal services).

Minority shareholder **[DL1.10]**

The death of a minority shareholder, while doubtless regrettable, generally causes little difficulty for a Personal Service Company. This situation may have been foreseen and provided for in the Articles. Where no such specific provision has been made then the shares in question will usually fall to someone by inheritance and by operation of the *Companies Act 1985, sections 183* and *187* with that person being entitled to have themselves or their nominee entered in the Register of Members.

It sometimes happens, however, that the person inheriting is a complete stranger to others involved in the Personal Service Company or that an existing minority shareholder becomes a majority shareholder. In order to provide for such a situation, the Articles of private limited companies are often amended (in advance) so that no other person can become a shareholder in the company without the consent and approval of those already in the company.

Majority shareholder **[DL1.11]**

The death of the majority shareholder clearly creates a different situation for a Personal Service Company where that person is the main individual providing the personal services. 'Key man' and/or life insurance may be relevant to these circumstances.

Where the Personal Service Company has developed to the stage where it is capable of having a value and existence independent of its majority shareholder hitherto providing the main personal services, then it is possible that a sale of the company might be arranged. This will normally be dealt with by the personal representatives of the deceased who, with the consent of the others involved, will arrange for a sale of the shares.

Sometimes those who have inherited the shares of the deceased majority shareholder simply seek to have themselves entered as shareholders and allow the company to proceed as before. This may be possible where the company is large enough to have an independent Board that is capable of continuing the operation of the company but is less feasible where the majority shareholder was also the director. It is even less feasible where the person succeeding to the shares is incapable of providing the personal services in question.

It will often be the case, therefore, that in an undeveloped Personal Service Company the death of the majority shareholder who is also providing the main personal services will effectively mean the demise of the company. In that situation the personal representatives or the person(s) inheriting the shares should follow through the procedures for the cessation of trading.

Divorce and the Personal Service Company [DL1.12]

Private limited companies are often started up by spouses or partners and Personal Service Companies are no exception in that respect. For so long as these relationships work well, the mutual support provided is often a significant factor in the success of the business as a whole. When these relationships break down, however, then the result can often be a major dislocation of what might be at the time an otherwise successful business.

The greatest danger in these situations is where the business has been started up on the basis that the participants share everything equally. The result is effectively deadlock and where goodwill has been lost, while not impossible it can often be very difficult to resolve matters and doing so often results in the demise of an otherwise sound business. For that reason, provision is often made (in advance) in the Articles to anticipate such a situation and provide for its resolution. Such provision may be required just to keep the business going while these other matters are decided and resolved.

If a deadlock situation does arise the basic law of the land will apply which at present differs depending upon whether a spouse or an unmarried partner is involved.

Spouses [DL1.13]

The shares held by a spouse in a Personal Service Company will essentially be the personal property of that spouse. It may be relevant whether those shares were acquired before the marriage took place or after the marriage took place but after the marriage and separation, in the absence of agreement, a court of law is likely to come to an examination of both the personal assets and the matrimonial assets of the spouses.

Agreement between the parties is almost always preferable if it can be achieved. It is advisable at some stage to consult a specialist practitioner in this area. It is open to the court, under the applicable matrimonial legislation, to make a number of orders which might include the following.

Periodical payments **[DL1.14]**

The respective earning positions of the spouses are likely, in the absence of agreement, to be examined by the court.

It may be that both spouses provide personal services in the company and earn roughly equal amounts, in which case that position may be allowed to continue without any order for a periodical payment being made. It may be that both spouses have entirely separate jobs with roughly comparable earnings in which case again that position may be allowed to continue without any order for a periodical payment being made.

It often happens, however, that one spouse is not working and is looking after any children of the marriage or that one spouse has simply ceased working. In that situation it is usual, in the absence of any agreement, for the court to order the working spouse to make periodical payments of a specified amount for a specified period to the other spouse.

Where there are any children of the marriage then, again, in the absence of any agreement, a court is likely to order the working spouse to make periodical payments for a specified period of a specified amount commensurate with their needs to the children.

A limited amount of tax relief is available for qualifying payments, but in general from 1988/89 such periodical payments are paid gross by the payer but do not form part of the taxable income of the payee.

Lump sum payments **[DL1.15]**

In the absence of any agreement, the courts may adjust the capital assets of the parties by ordering one spouse to make payment of a lump sum to the other.

Guidelines are provided in the matrimonial legislation applicable setting out the factors which the courts should take into account in such circumstances but they are given a considerable discretion with which the Court of Appeal is, in practice, reluctant to interfere.

In the past, one approach by the courts has been to examine the assets which each party has brought to the marriage, examine the matrimonial assets created by the parties together during the marriage and then arrive at the payment by one spouse to the other of a lump sum which in the view of the court would fairly regulate the position. In such circumstances, the fact that only one spouse has ever worked and the other spouse has always kept the house has always been regarded by the court as largely irrelevant on the view that it was the support of the latter which has allowed the former to succeed.

However, in recent years the courts appear to have moved much closer to a position akin to communal property (which would be equally shared) although it would not be accurate to say that that position has been reached anywhere in the UK. This is now supported by a recent House of Lords judgment.

Pension payments **[DL1.16]**

Provision for pension, including the spouse, will often be made and this will also often be made through the company.

Again, this is a situation which has undergone radical change in recent years. Previously, the spouse's pension entitlement was regarded as postponed until the pension became payable but under recent changes in legislation, spouses may now be entitled to a payment reflecting their pension entitlement at the time of divorce.

Providing the funds **[DL1.17]**

At the conclusion of a divorce, the amount to be paid by one spouse to the other will have been decided. Court orders in this area are now more pro-active and imaginative (including orders for the transfer of property) but one of the advantages of reaching an agreement out of court remains the provision of flexibility in relation to the exact manner in which those payments are provided.

This is of particular relevance to Personal Service Companies in that the remaining spouse will normally wish the other spouse to relinquish their shares and directorships in the company (which are still personal assets). The agreement to do so (which will normally involve the valuation of these assets) will often involve the payment of an increased amount of cash by one spouse to the other in return for the relinquishment by the other spouse of all interest of whatever nature in the company. The purchase by a company of its own shares will sometimes be a consideration here but this is an area which requires specialist professional advice in advance.

While retaining the Personal Service Company in such circumstances, raising the money which requires to be paid over and then maintaining that liability out of the company can cause severe difficulties.

It may be that another family member, the remaining spouse shareholder, or an invited stranger would be willing to lend money to the company which it could then use to make payment to the departing spouse. Alternatively, the Personal Service Company may be able to borrow the money to meet the payments required. The taxation consequences of such arrangements is something upon which specialist professional advice should be taken in advance.

In situations like this, any problems posed by IR35 can fade into insignificance. In order to finance the necessary payments the remaining spouse is likely to require to substantially increase the level of remuneration or dividend extracted from the company. This can be detrimental to the Personal Service Companies where the income flow may be uncertain or variable since the payments demanded are fixed and legally enforceable.

In theory, the courts should not make orders that will have the effect of depriving the payer of their livelihood but such orders are often made in the light of a particular set of circumstances prevailing at the time and in practice such orders can be extremely difficult to vary later. This is another reason why negotiated settlements are preferable in that there is a greater scope for variation in the face of a genuine change of circumstances.

Either as part of the process of 'negotiation' or later in relation to non-payment, the departing spouse will often be in a position to force the company into liquidation. To do so, however, or even to impose undue pressure in genuinely difficult situations can have an adverse effect.

Partners **[DL1.18]**

The position has not yet been reached anywhere in the UK where unmarried partners have been recognised as having rights akin to the so-called 'palimony' rights recognised by some States in the USA. Accordingly, the assets of both partners will be regarded as purely personal assets.

Where these are equally shared then, in the event of a loss of goodwill, a deadlock situation can result which can be fatal to the business. If a negotiated settlement cannot be arrived at then resort to the courts may be had, either for a court order (*CA 1985, s459*) or for the liquidation of the company. This will rarely be to the long-term advantage of those involved in a Personal Service Company.

It is, therefore, generally preferable to make provision (in advance) for such a situation in the Articles at the time when the Personal Service Company is being started up.

Dispute deadlock **[DL1.19]**

Advance provision for dealing with deadlock disputes can be achieved either using the Articles or a separate shareholders' agreement. In general, such provisions may be aimed separately at keeping the business going during a dispute deadlock or at resolving the dispute or both.

The Articles might be adjusted to provide, for example, that should a deadlock in the management of the company arise then any member of the company is entitled to convene an EGM. Further provision could then be made for the means by which any deadlock is to be ultimately resolved at that meeting.

Instead, the members may themselves enter into what is known as a shareholder agreement. Such agreements effectively amount to a contract between the members and it is one to which the company will now be recognised as a party. Provided that the agreement does not contradict the *Companies Acts* or the constitution of the company, provision can be made for the procedures to be followed in the event of a deadlock and the means by which any such deadlock is to be ultimately resolved.

While the provisions of the *Companies Acts* and resort to the courts can be utilised, the utilisation of these by Personal Service Companies will rarely be wholly satisfactory (if only on the grounds of cost alone).

Therefore, the Articles or shareholders' agreement may provide for some form of Alternative Dispute Resolution which the parties agree to be bound by. This can range from mediation, conciliation, adjudication to arbitration or indeed a cascading provision containing all of these in order.

The transmission of shares [DL1.20]

Where a member is to leave the company for whatever reason – be it death, divorce, or any other reason then, if the company is to continue in existence there clearly needs to be a procedure for the transmission of the shares in question.

Where *1985 Table A* is adopted without modification then a basic procedure for the transmission of shares is provided for. However, the idea of a stranger entering the company and perhaps disturbing the existing balance of power can be so upsetting that some private limited companies modify their Articles to cater for that eventuality.

Unmodified 1985 Table A [DL1.21]

Where *1985 Table A* is accepted without modification, then the transmission of shares is catered for by *Articles 29–31* as follows:

> '**Article 29**
> If a member dies the survivor or survivors where he was a joint holder, and his personal representatives where he was a sole holder or the only survivor of joint holders, shall be the only person recognised by the company as having any title to his interest; but nothing herein contained shall release the estate of a deceased member from any liability in respect of any share which has been jointly held by him.
>
> **Article 30**
> A person becoming entitled to a share in consequence of the death or bankruptcy of a member may, upon such evidence being produced as the directors may properly require, elect either to become the holder of the share or to have some person nominated by him registered as the transferee. If he elects to become the holder he shall give notice to the company to that effect. If he elects to have another person registered he shall execute an instrument of transfer of that share to that person. All the articles relating to the transfer of shares shall apply to the notice or instrument of transfer as if it were an instrument of transfer executed by the member and the death or bankruptcy of the member had not occurred.

Article 31
A person becoming entitled to a share in consequence of the death or bankruptcy of a member shall have the rights to which he would be entitled if he were the holder of the share, except that he shall not, before being registered as the holder of the share, be entitled in respect of it to attend or vote at any meeting of the company or at any separate meeting of the holders of any class of shares in the company.'

Modified **[DL1.22]**

The Articles of Association might be modified so as to provide that on the death, bankruptcy, divorce, or removal as a director for any reason whatsoever then the directors of the company may, by written notice given within six months of the occurrence of the event, require the sale of the share vested in that shareholder.

That provision might be keyed into the provisions applying where a shareholder wishes to make a voluntary sale of the share vested in that shareholder which might require written notice by the shareholder of an intention to sell the share.

Where written notice is either given or received relating to the sale of a share, then a common set of provisions might apply. These are designed to ensure that the shares are in the first instance offered to the existing shareholders. There would require to be a fairly complicated set of provisions to deal with valuation in the absence of agreement and the effective transmission of the share in the absence of co-operation. In general, however, such provisions are valid at present and are aimed at having the effect of protecting and maintaining the existing balance of power within the private company and they can equally well be applied to Personal Service Companies.

DL2 – Dealing with the Assets of the Company

Client contracts [DL2.1]

Client contracts, together with any associated software, are likely to be the main assets of a Personal Service Company.

Some of these can be sold off and, unless a condition of the sale is a restrictive covenant prohibiting the Personal Service Company or the individuals behind it from trading further within a specified locality for a specified period (as will often be the case), the Personal Service Company would be entitled to trade on with its remaining assets.

If, on a sale of the main assets, the Personal Service Company decides not to trade on then the considerations outlined in the section on ceasing to trade will apply.

Employees [DL2.2]

A sale of major assets will often involve some employees becoming surplus to requirements. Such employees will be entitled to the appropriate termination payments together with any redundancy entitlement.

Shareholders [DL2.3]

In most circumstances, the sale of assets is a decision which the majority shareholder is entitled to make and one with which a minority shareholders must live (always carrying a minority entitlement to the net sale proceeds fed into the company) unless the minority shareholder can point to prejudice in which case the considerations relating to minority protection contained in the section on the sale of shares may apply.

Sale of the assets [DL2.4]

The sale of the assets of the company is the least complicated and most common of the transactions. In principle, this will result in a gain in the hands of the company upon which the company will be required to pay Capital Gains Tax and could result in an element of double taxation in later extracting any funds from the company.

The sale of assets could include the trade and any goodwill of the business. This is more complicated and is likely to involve an assignment of any titles, leases, licenses or contracts of the company. It may also involve the *Transfer of Undertakings (Protection of Employment) Regulations 1981* (*SI 1981/1794*) (as amended) in relation to any employees of the company. This will also usually involve an undertaking by the individuals behind the company entering into a restrictive covenant under which they undertake not to compete with that trade in the future for a defined period and/or geographical locality.

Where the sale of assets does not include the trade then the company can either trade on or cease trading.

DL3 – Ceasing to Trade

Clients' contracts [DL3.1]

When the individual providing the personal services through the commercial vehicle of a Personal Service Company decides to cease trading and leave, it will not be enough to simply announce that fact.

The Personal Service Company will be bound to the clients by a binding and subsisting contract. That contract might have provision for such an eventuality but, if not, the position will require to be negotiated.

It would be open to the Personal Service Company to offer the client a substitute to complete the project but the client would not (unless the contract so provided) be bound to accept any such substitute.

In principle, in the absence of provision in the contract to the contrary, the client will have a right to claim damages from the Personal Service Company (and, in certain circumstances, through that company to the individuals behind it) for the breach of that contract by failing to complete the project.

The amount of any such claim (unless waived by the client) is something which should be taken into account as a factor in ceasing to trade.

Employees [DL3.2]

Any employees become entitled to their pay for the broken period from the last pay day to their date of dismissal with pay in lieu of notice and an entitlement to redundancy. This also is something which should be taken into account as a factor in ceasing to trade.

Shareholders [DL3.3]

Shareholders (especially minority shareholders) have no real claim when a company ceases to trade. Any liabilities incurred along the above lines will be taken into account by the company and balanced against the assets of the company.

Even where the result of that equation results in a deficit it is, of course, in accordance with the principle of limited liability, the position that those shareholders cannot be called upon to pay more than the amount of their shares (unless, being also directors, they have be shown to have assumed some element of personal liability).

Management

DM1 – Dealing with Shares and Assets of the Company

Dealing with the shares of the company [DM1.1]

Any changes in the shareholding of a company is a matter normally dealt with by the company secretary who requires to make the necessary entries in the Register of the company.

Where a sale and purchase of shares is involved this will normally also be overseen by the parties and/or their representatives.

Disposing of the assets of the company [DM1.2]

Where it is decided to cease trading but not to retain the company, then it will be necessary to wind down the company and a director or directors should be appointed to undertake this task.

One aspect of this task will be to dispose of the assets of the company. A company may own its premises and various fittings and fixtures such as desks and chairs within those premises. Companies often also own obscure and long-forgotten assets such as the rights to royalties or licence income.

All of these should be disposed of by the directors for if they are not disposed of then when the company is dissolved ownership of these assets may (if the Crown in the form of the Queen's Remembrancer chooses to accept them) fall to the Crown as *bona vacantia*.

Most assets have a value of some sort or other and can be sold on the market which determines their market value. These proceeds will require to be reflected in the final return of the company.

The assets can be transferred from the business use of the company to the private use of the persons who were behind the company. However, irrespective of the terms of any agreement between the company and these individuals, market value will be used by the Inland Revenue for the purposes of this calculation and these proceeds will require to be reflected in the final return of the company.

The final act of the directors will be to make arrangements for (and presumably have the company pay for – an expense which should also be reflected in the final return of the company) the storage for five or six years of the records relating to VAT, PAYE, NIC, benefits and Corporation Tax for the periods while the company was trading. After that, the directors are in a position to dissolve the company.

DM2 – Ceasing to Trade

Where a Personal Service Company ceases to trade then the management may have a number of tasks to form depending upon the ensuing consequences.

Where the personal Service Company has become insolvent, the management will have a duty to assist any Insolvency Practitioners appointed.

Where the company is to cease to exist after ceasing to trade then the management will require to oversee the death of the company.

Where the company ceases to trade but is to be retained then the responsibilities and duties of the management will be much as before.

DM3 – Insolvency

Introduction [DM3.1]

Personal Service Companies (at least prior to the introduction of IR35) usually had a better chance of avoiding insolvency that most other trading private limited companies.

Rather than having to gamble and risk themselves in the market, a Personal Service Company usually had the advantage of knowing in advance what the income of the company was likely to be and of tailoring its expenditure accordingly. In that way, insolvency could usually be avoided.

It is possible, however, that insolvency could now creep up on even Personal Service Companies. This area has also, for some reason, become increasingly complex and specialised. Once insolvency proceedings have formally commenced they are now the exclusive domain of what are now known as 'insolvency practitioners'. However, again this is an area where, as soon as difficulties threaten, the early advice of a specialist chartered accountant can often avoid a drama becoming more of a disaster than it needs to be.

It is proposed to consider below briefly in outline the various types of insolvency proceedings which, if matters go that far, a Personal Service Company might encounter.

Corporate Voluntary Arrangements [DM3.2]

These, recently developed, offer the most painless proceedings. Essentially, as soon as serious difficulties are recognised a voluntary arrangement is come to with the creditors of the company. From the point of view of the creditors, such arrangements can be attractive in that recovering a little of the cake is usually better than recovering none of the cake at all. This procedure also holds out the prospect of recovery.

Administrations [DM3.3]

This procedure, relatively recently introduced, is intended to act as a moratorium which gives the company a breathing-space in which to attempt to recover. An administrator, if appointed, takes over the running of the company but diligence by creditors is forestalled and the company is given an opportunity to recover.

Receiverships [DM3.4]

This procedure involves, in various ways, a receiver taking control of the company. Recovery is still in theory possible but in practice this will often involve what is known as 'hiving-down' and selling off the best assets of the company.

Liquidation [DM3.5]

This procedure marks the end of the company. It can be achieved in a number of ways:

- members' voluntary winding up;
- creditors' voluntary winding up; and
- compulsory winding up by the court.

DM4 – The Death of a Personal Service Company

Introduction [DM4.1]

Having ceased trading, decided not to retain the company, and disposed of all the company's assets, it remains only to bring the life of the company to an end.

In general, promoters have a specific objective in mind when they create a company. Indeed, in origin, not only were most joint stock companies formed with a specific venture or objective in mind but once that objective had been achieved all of the company's debts were paid off, any surplus was distributed amongst the subscribers, and the life of the company was brought to an end. Today, the lives of companies (at least, those which are successful) tend to continue in perpetuity with fresh objectives overtaking the original objectives and the various shareholders and directors coming and going as the life of the company continued.

For those companies whose purpose has now been served, however, and those companies which have been less than successful, some means are necessary to bring the lives of those companies, either involuntarily or voluntarily, to a tidy end. The Registrar of Companies, whose tasks include maintaining a public Register of extant companies, is particularly keen to have an efficient method of keeping the Register a tidy record of live companies only.

For those companies which have met their end through insolvency, of course, there are the statutory winding-up procedures. Tagged on to the end of these – originally only in relation to compulsory winding-ups but latterly in relation to winding-ups which are both compulsory and voluntary – exists an automatic procedure (a process known as dissolution).

Three months after the liquidator's final return to Companies House, the Registrar will automatically remove the name of that company from the Register and that company will cease to exist. There is also a similar procedure to cater for bringing to an end the life of a company which is insolvent but has insufficient funds for a winding-up.

For those companies whose useful life has come to an end for reasons other than insolvency, however, different procedures are required and here it is proposed to examine the ways in which the life of those companies may be brought to an end.

Striking-off [DM4.2]

One such procedure for bringing the life of a company to an end (indeed, one of the commonest) is striking-off. The requirements leading to this procedure is simply to do nothing. Every now and again (usually triggered by the failure to file an Annual Return) in a tidying-up exercise, the Registrar of Companies, if he has reasonable cause to believe that a company is not carrying on business or in operation, may set in motion the power to have that defunct company struck off the Register.

The power of the Registrar to strike defunct companies off the Register is contained in *Companies Act 1985, section 652* and commences by the Registrar sending the company a letter by post inquiring whether the company is carrying on business or in operation. If no answer is received to that letter within one month the Registrar may then, within 14 days, send the company a letter by registered post referring to these facts and stating that if no reply is received within a further month then a notice will be published in the Gazette with a view to striking the name of the company off the Register. If no answer is received (or an answer to the effect that the company is not in fact carrying on business or in operation) then at the same time as the publication of that notice, the Registrar will send the company (care of the registered office, failing which any officer of the company, failing which to the subscribers at the address in the memorandum) intimation by post that unless cause is shown to the contrary the name of the company will be struck off the Register. At the expiry of that period, in the absence of cause shown, the Registrar will strike the name of that company off the Register and publish notice of that fact in the Gazette publication of which is deemed to mean that the company has been dissolved. Any property in the company will then be deemed to be *bona vacantia* and will (unless disclaimed) vest in the Crown.

Notwithstanding that striking-off, however, a saving contained in *Companies Act 1985, section 652(6)* provides that nothing in the above shall affect the power of the court to wind up a company the name of which has been struck off the Register. Should any reason for doing so arise, therefore, (such as the discovery of hidden assets) a struck-off company may still be wound up although it has been suggested that in practice at the same time as seeking the winding-up order the liquidator should seek an order for the restoration of the company to the Register.

There is also provision that, generally, the liability (if any) of every director, managing officer and member of the company continues and may be enforced as if the company had not been dissolved.

Application for striking-off [DM4.3]

It has been the practice in the past for some to use the above striking-off provisions of *CA 1985, s652* as an informal, cheap and easy method of getting rid of an unwanted company and some have even gone so far as to informally request the Registrar to use his powers in that respect, a request with which the Registrar has sometimes complied in the past.

It is understood, however, that the Registrar will no longer accede to such a request as a result of the introduction of an alternative procedure aimed at being a quick and inexpensive procedure whereby a formal application may be made to the Registrar to strike a private company off the Register. This new procedure was introduced by the *Deregulation and Contracting Out Act 1994* which inserted *sections 652A–F* into *CA 1985*. This procedure is available to a company which has ceased trading and wishes to have its life brought to an end without the expense of a formal winding up.

The guidance notes to this new procedure indicate that it should not be used in circumstances where a formal winding up would be more appropriate but the fact that a company has outstanding assets and liabilities – particularly since there are extensive procedures for notification to creditors (who can object) – should not of itself prevent it from using this new procedure although any assets left in the company will, of course (unless declaimed) vest in the Crown as *bona vacantia*.

The procedure begins with an application from a private company – made on its behalf by a majority of the directors in the prescribed form containing the prescribed information – together with the appropriate fee (currently £10) to the Registrar who is empowered (under *CA 1985, s652A*) to strike the company's name off the Register.

Before doing so, and to ensure that the company is suitably defunct and one which it is appropriate to strike off, it is provided that an application cannot be made (and one made should be withdrawn although it could, presumably, renew the application once the three months have elapsed) if at any time within the previous three months the company has:

- changed its name;
- traded or otherwise carried on business (which does not include the settling of liabilities);
- made a disposal in whole or part for value of property or rights; or
- engaged in any other activity except one which is necessary or expedient for in effect running the company and getting it to this stage. Nor can an application be made at all at a time when there are current proceedings for a company reconstruction; voluntary arrangement; administration; winding-up; or the appointment of a receiver or judicial factor. A failure to observe this is an offence liable to imprisonment or a fine.

Where such an application is appropriate, the person making the application on behalf of the company must, within seven days of the application, provide (delivered, left, or sent by post to the 'proper address' for which extensive provision is made) a copy of the application to every person prescribed by regulation – the current provision relates to anyone who at any time on the day of the application (or at any time while the application is pending) was a:

- member;
- employee;
- creditor (actual, contingent or prospective);
- director;
- manager or trustee of any pension fund of the company.

A failure to observe this is also an offence liable to imprisonment or a fine.

Where such an application is appropriate and the proper steps have been taken, the procedure is for the Registrar to publish in the Gazette a notice stating that on the expiration of three months from the publication of the notice he may exercise his power to strike that company's name off the Register unless any person shows cause why he should not do so.

If any person wishes to show cause, the Guidance Notes suggest that the objection be in writing, be supported by relevant evidence, and specify the cause shown which it is suggested might include:

- breach of the *Companies Acts*;
- the existence of legal proceedings;
- wrongful trading or the like.

The Registrar will consider and deal with any such objection administratively but would presumably be subject in that respect to either an application for judicial review or an application for restoration of the company to the Register.

In the absence of cause shown, the Registrar may, at the expiry of that period, strike the name of that company off the Register and publish notice of that fact in the Gazette. Publication of that notice is deemed to mean that the company has been dissolved and, again, at that point in time, any property remaining in the company will be deemed to be *bona vacantia* and will (unless declaimed) vest in the Crown.

Again, however, by a saving contained in *Companies Act 1985, section 652A(7)*, nothing in the above affects the power of the court to wind up a company the name of which has been struck off the register (and again, in practice, any liquidator should seek an order for restoration to the Register at the same time as seeking a winding-up order) and by *CA 1985, section 652A(6)* it is also provided that the liability (if any) of every director, managing officer and member of the company continues and may be enforced as if the company had not been dissolved.

Restoration to the Register [DM4.4]

There are also procedures for the restoration to the Register of companies which have been struck off.

So far as the Secretary of State is concerned, in the case of either form of striking-off, the Secretary of State may make an application before the expiration of 20 years from publication of the notice in the Gazette in which case the court may order the company's name to be restored to the Register simply if it is satisfied that it is in the public interest to do so.

So far as others are concerned, procedures for the restoration to the Register exist for companies where the company has been struck off by the Registrar:

- using his powers under *CA 1985, s652*; or
- using his powers under *CA 1985, s652A*.

CA 1985, section 652 [DM4.5]

In relation a striking off under *CA 1985, s652*, the procedure for restoration is contained in *CA 1985, s653*. An application made before the expiration of 20 years from publication of the notice in the Gazette (a period which contrasts with the two year time limit placed upon any attempt at a restoration where the company is struck off after a winding-up) may be made by any member or creditor of the company (and, rather oddly given that it theoretically no longer exists, by the company itself) if feeling aggrieved by the company having been struck off.

CA 1985, section 652A [DM4.6]

In relation a striking off under *CA 1985, s652A* the procedure for restoration is contained in CA 1985, s653(2A)–(2D). Only on an application by a notifiable person (a person to whom a copy of the company's application was required to be given) made before the expiration of 20 years from publication of the notice in the Gazette the Court may, if satisfied that the company at the time of striking off was carrying on business or in operation or otherwise that it is just that the company be restored to the Register, order the company's name to be restored. The same principles will presumably apply.

Consequences of restoration [DM4.7]

The consequences of restoration is now statutorily provided for by *CA 1985, s653(3)*. On an office copy of the order for restoration being delivered to the Registrar (who will advertise it in the Gazette) the company to which the order relates is deemed to have continued in existence as if its name had not been struck off and the court is empowered to give such directions and make such provisions as seem just for placing the company and all other persons in the same position (or as nearly as may be) as if the company's name had not been struck off.

One example of the consequences of a restoration is that it would not affect any property actually disposed of by the Crown as *bona vacantia* although the Crown would have to account to the company for the proceeds thereof (*CA 1985, s655*).

The restoration procedures are occasionally used in practice as was recently seen in Scotland in the extraordinary case of *Conti Petitioner 2000 Scots Law Reports*, Petitioner where having personally asked the Registrar of Companies to strike his company off, the petitioner then discovered that the company owned a valuable asset and applied to the court (an application eventually granted by Lord Prosser) as a 'person aggrieved' to have his company restored to the Register of Companies and revived.

In summary **[DM4.8]**

Restoration, therefore, has its place but in many instances when the *raison d'etre* for the existence of a Personal Service Company has come to an end, the most advantageous course (avoiding the difficulties inherent in seeking to maintain and preserve the company) will be to strip out the assets of the company, meet its final liabilities, store its records and arrange for the company to be struck off. The individuals concerned can then relax and, should circumstances permit, it is a relatively easy task to start up another, new, Personal Service Company.

DM5 – Ceasing to Trade but Retaining the Company

Where the company ceases to trade but is to be retained then the responsibilities and duties of the management will be as much as before.

However, in changing from a trading company to an investment company different taxation considerations will apply which management will require to address.

Taxation

DT1 – Taxation on Disposal of Shares

Where another entity is taking over a Personal Service Company – thereby allowing the person hitherto providing the personal services to leave – then the entity taking over may prefer to purchase, rather than the assets of the company, all of the shares of the company and effectively the Personal Service Company itself and everything in it

In this situation, the gain falls not on the shoulders of the company but instead upon the shoulders of the individual(s) holding the shares.

There are a number of ways in which such a potentially significant tax bill can be mitigated but that requires forward planning and specialist professional advice and is beyond the scope of this book.

From a taxation point of view, the exchange of shares will have no effect upon the taxation of the company, the taxation affairs of which will proceed as before.

DT2 – Taxation on Disposal of Assets

Where another entity is taking over a Personal Service Company – thereby allowing the person hitherto providing the personal services to leave – then the entity taking over may prefer to purchase, rather than the company itself, only the assets of the Personal Service Company – most likely, the on-going contracts which the company has with existing clients and/or any software developed specifically for those purposes.

In principle, the value of those contracts and/or software requires to be valued (possibly from a base of zero) and the Personal Service Company itself will be liable for Capital Gains Tax on the gain made thereby (accounted for as part of the Corporation Tax bill reflected by self-assessment in the company Tax Return.

There are a number of ways in which such a potentially significant tax bill can be mitigated but that requires forward planning and specialist professional advice and is beyond the scope of this book.

The individual(s) behind the company will then be left with the shell of the company which (assuming they no longer wish to trade on) they would either retain as an investment company (although that brings its own taxation considerations) or dissolve.

DT3 – Taxation on Cessation of Trading

Introduction [DT3.1]

It may be that neither being sold nor falling into insolvency, a Personal Service Company simply decides for one reason or another to cease trading. In much the same way that the commencement of trading is operated by planned steps, the cessation of trading should, in theory, be operated in the same manner.

VAT [DT3.2]

Once registered for the purposes of VAT, there is a legal obligation (reinforced by penalties) to notify the VAT Office (the Local Business Advice Centre) of any changes in the circumstances of the trader.

Voluntary cancellation [DT3.3]

Where registration for VAT purposes was voluntary in the first place (in the sense that the level of turnover has not been reached which makes registration for VAT purposes compulsory) – or even where registration was originally compulsory but the level of turnover has now fallen below the threshold – then it is possible to voluntarily cancel registration for VAT purposes (while continuing to trade).

The procedure is to apply to HM Customs & Excise for voluntary cancellation of the VAT registration of the business.

Obligatory cancellation [DT3.4]

Where the company ceases to trade or, as Customs & Excise put it, 'the business is closed down' then that is one of the changes which by law the business must intimate to Customs & Excise and where cancellation of the VAT registration is obligatory.

The procedure (and there is a civil penalty for failure) is to apply to Customs & Excise within 30 days of the event quoting the VAT registration number and specifying the date upon which the change took place.

Cancellation procedure **[DT3.5]**

Cancellation will involve the business completing a final VAT Return (on a slightly different Form 193).

It will be appreciated that input VAT might earlier have been reclaimed upon some of the capital assets of the business and some of the stock, if any, which remains unsold within the business. A *de minimus* limit of £250 is currently applied but other than that Customs & Excise will seek to recover that VAT.

From the date of cancellation, the company:

- can no longer charge VAT;
- may no longer reclaim VAT; and
- is no longer required to keep VAT records or make VAT Returns.

However, records generated while trading and registered will require to be kept for a period of six years and arrangements will have to be made by the company to store these.

PAYE, NIC and benefits **[DT3.6]**

It is extremely difficult to ascertain what, if any, are the closing procedures for PAYE, NIC and benefits.

In the course of ceasing to trade, any employees will presumably be gradually paid off leaving only perhaps a single director designated to deal with the formal closing down of the company. For so long as funds remain in the company to do so and that director is in fact paid, then the normal procedures should be followed.

As a matter of logic, common-sense and practice the director should select a point in time at which his or her remuneration and entitlements cease.

That event, that date, and the registration number should be intimated to the Inland Revenue. A final return should be made for the last closing period.

However, records generated while trading will be required to be kept for a period of five years and arrangements will have to be made by the company to store these.

Corporation Tax [DT3.7]

When a company ceases to trade, then it will bring to an end its last accounting period and the last return which the company will have to make will be for that period.

The annual cycle of capital allowances comes to an end in the final period. No writing down allowance is given in the final period. Instead, the disposal proceeds of the assets remaining in the company are compared with the brought-forward capital allowances written-down value and the resulting calculation will produce either a balancing charge or a balancing allowance.

A balancing charge is treated as a taxable receipt but a final balancing allowance will simply be lost to the company.

The final accounting period will produce a calculation of either a profit or a loss. A profit is taxable in the usual manner. A loss, terminal loss, and any losses carried forward are lost to the company.

Included in this calculation will be the disposal of the remaining assets of the company. If disposed of to the members, the transaction may be scrutinised by the Inland Revenue. If disposed of at arm's length then the transaction will either produce a final capital loss (lost to the company) or a final capital gain which the company will require to account for in its final company Tax Return.

Records generated while trading will require to be kept for a period of five years and arrangements will have to be made by the company to store these.

DT4 – The Company after Cessation of Trading

Where the company is then dissolved [DT4.1]

Where a Personal Service Company has ceased trading, completed its last taxation returns, and has then been dissolved then that is an end of taxation matters so far as the Personal Service Company and the individuals behind it are concerned.

As earlier noted, taxation records require to be retained for a stipulated number of years and the Revenue authorities have the right to carry out an investigation in relation to those years (which is why the records must be retained). If they have no reason to do so, however, then they are unlikely to do so and that therefore will be a complete end to the matter.

Where the company ceases trading but is retained [DT4.2]

Where a Personal Service Company has ceased trading but the company is nevertheless retained – perhaps because the company has a number of investments – then the company remains, of course, an entity for taxation purposes.

The company might not be liable to Corporation Tax under Schedule D or other taxes because the company is no longer trading but the company might well be liable to Corporation Tax under one of the other Schedule on the company's investment income.

In fact, the company may no longer be entitled to some of the tax advantages offered to trading companies and again this is an area which requires specialist professional advice.

DT5 – Retaining the Personal Service Company

Introduction [DT5.1]

Having decided to cease trading as a Personal Service Company, there is the option to retain the company not for the purposes of trading but for the purposes of investment.

There are, however, a number of considerations which may apply in these circumstances upon which specialist professional advice should be taken in advance. We consider briefly below a number of the areas of difficulty.

Close companies [DT5.2]

A Personal Service Company is likely to be what is known as a 'close' company but when ceasing to trade is likely to become what is known as a 'close investment' company.

This arises because where a company is controlled by only a few people, the opportunity is there to adjust the position of the company for maximum fiscal advantage. For that reason, such companies are made the subject of a special taxation regime.

A close company is one which is (unless specifically excluded from the definition):

- controlled by five or fewer participators;
- controlled by participators who are directors, or
- a company over half of whose assets could, on a notional winding-up, be distributed among five or fewer participators or director-participators.

A 'participator' is defined as any person who has or is:

- entitled to acquire share capital or voting rights in the company;
- entitled to participate in distributions by the company;

- entitled to have the income or assets of the company applied for his benefit; or
- a loan creditor.

A 'director-participator' is:

- any person who occupies the position of director (whatever their title);
- any person on whose instructions or directions the directors are accustomed to act; or
- the manager of a company if he holds or controls 20 per cent of its ordinary share capital either alone or with associates.

'Control' includes:

- directly or indirectly controlling the company's policies and having the power to appoint or dismiss the directors by ordinary resolution in general meeting; or
- an entitlement to more than half of the nominal or issued share capital or voting power.

Control is determined by aggregating the rights and powers of associates.

An 'Associate' is:

- any relative or partner of a participator;
- a trustee of a settlement created by the participator or a relative; or
- any other company interested in the trust or settlement.

It can safely be said, therefore, that the definition of a close company is widely embracing. All close companies are close investment-holding companies unless they satisfy a list of requirements one of which is that the company is trading. Most Personal Service Companies will be close companies and therefore as soon as they cease trading will revert to being close investment-holding companies.

The immediate effect of that is that such companies are precluded from using the small companies' rate of Corporation Tax. This can make it expensive, on ceasing trading, to retain the Personal Service Company as a close investment-holding company.

Pension [DT5.3]

However, consideration should also be given to the pension position in relation to such companies. There are a number of options open in relation to pensions. Where, however, extensive use of the company and its assets has been used for the purposes of pension provision then it may be difficult to reverse that process.

This is an area upon which expert professional advice should be taken before such pension arrangements are entered into.

APPENDICES

Appendix 1 – Companies House Forms

Form 10

Companies House
— for the record —

10

Please complete in typescript, or in bold black capitals.
CHFP000

First directors and secretary and intended situation of registered office

Notes on completion appear on final page

Company Name in full

Proposed Registered Office
(PO Box numbers only, are not acceptable)

Post town

County / Region

Postcode

If the memorandum is delivered by an agent for the subscriber(s) of the memorandum mark the box opposite and give the agent's name and address.

Agent's Name

Address

Post town

County / Region

Postcode

Number of continuation sheets attached

Please give the name, address, telephone number and, if available, a DX number and Exchange of the person Companies House should contact if there is any query.

Tel

DX number DX exchange

Companies House receipt date barcode

This form has been provided free of charge by Companies House.

Form revised July 1998

When you have completed and signed the form please send it to the Registrar of Companies at:
Companies House, Crown Way, Cardiff, CF14 3UZ DX 33050 Cardiff
for companies registered in England and Wales
or
Companies House, 37 Castle Terrace, Edinburgh, EH1 2EB
for companies registered in Scotland **DX 235 Edinburgh**

Form 10 – continued

Company Secretary (see notes 1-5)

Company name

NAME *Style / Title *Honours etc

* Voluntary details

Forename(s)

Surname

Previous forename(s)

Previous surname(s)

Address

Usual residential address
For a corporation, give the registered or principal office address.

Post town

County / Region Postcode

Country

I consent to act as secretary of the company named on page 1

Consent signature **Date**

Directors (see notes 1-5)

Please list directors in alphabetical order

NAME *Style / Title *Honours etc

Forename(s)

Surname

Previous forename(s)

Previous surname(s)

Address

Usual residential address
For a corporation, give the registered or principal office address.

Post town

County / Region Postcode

Country

Day Month Year

Date of birth **Nationality**

Business occupation

Other directorships

I consent to act as director of the company named on page 1

Consent signature **Date**

Form 10 – continued

Directors (continued) (see notes 1-5)

NAME *Style / Title *Honours etc

* Voluntary details Forename(s)

Surname

Previous forename(s)

Previous surname(s)

Address

Usual residential address
For a corporation, give the registered or principal office address.

Post town

County / Region Postcode

Country

Day Month Year

Date of birth **Nationality**

Business occupation

Other directorships

I consent to act as director of the company named on page 1

Consent signature **Date**

This section must be signed by
Either
an agent on behalf of all subscribers **Signed** **Date**

***Or* the subscribers** **Signed** **Date**

(i.e those who signed as members on the memorandum of association). **Signed** **Date**

Signed **Date**

Signed **Date**

Signed **Date**

Signed **Date**

Form 10 – continued

Notes

1. Show for an individual the full forename(s) NOT INITIALS and surname together with any previous forename(s) or surname(s).

   If the director or secretary is a corporation or Scottish firm - show the corporate or firm name on the surname line.

   Give previous forename(s) or surname(s) except that:

   - for a married woman, the name by which she was known before marriage need not be given,

   - names not used since the age of 18 or for at least 20 years need not be given.

   A peer, or an individual known by a title, may state the title instead of or in addition to the forename(s) and surname and need not give the name by which that person was known before he or she adopted the title or succeeded to it.

   Address:

   Give the usual residential address.

   In the case of a corporation or Scottish firm give the registered or principal office.

   Subscribers:

   The form must be signed personally either by the subscriber(s) or by a person or persons authorised to sign on behalf of the subscriber(s).

2. Directors known by another description:

   - A director includes any person who occupies that position even if called by a different name, for example, governor, member of council.

3. Directors details:

   - Show for each individual director the director's date of birth, business occupation and nationality. **The date of birth must be given for every individual director.**

4. Other directorships:

   - Give the name of every company of which the person concerned is a director or has been a director at any time in the past 5 years. You may exclude a company which either **is** or at **all times during the past 5 years**, when the person was a director, **was**:

   - dormant,

   - a parent company which wholly owned the company making the return,

   - a wholly owned subsidiary of the company making the return, or

   - another wholly owned subsidiary of the same parent company.

   If there is insufficient space on the form for other directorships you may use a separate sheet of paper, which should include the company's number and the full name of the director.

5. Use Form 10 continuation sheets or photocopies of page 2 to provide details of joint secretaries or additional directors.

Form 12

Companies House
— for the record —

12

Declaration on application for registration

Please complete in typescript, or in bold black capitals.

CHFP000

Company Name in full

I,

of

† Please delete as appropriate.

do solemnly and sincerely declare that I am a † [Solicitor engaged in the formation of the company][person named as director or secretary of the company in the statement delivered to the Registrar under section 10 of the Companies Act 1985] and that all the requirements of the Companies Act 1985 in respect of the registration of the above company and of matters precedent and incidental to it have been complied with.

And I make this solemn Declaration conscientiously believing the same to be true and by virtue of the Statutory Declarations Act 1835.

Declarant's signature

Declared at

Day Month Year

On

❶ Please print name.

before me ❶

Signed **Date**

† A Commissioner for Oaths or Notary Public or Justice of the Peace or Solicitor

SPECIMEN

Please give the name, address, telephone number and, if available, a DX number and Exchange of the person Companies House should contact if there is any query.

Tel

DX number DX exchange

Companies House receipt date barcode

This form has been provided free of charge by Companies House.

Form revised June 1998

When you have completed and signed the form please send it to the Registrar of Companies at:

Companies House, Crown Way, Cardiff, CF14 3UZ **DX 33050 Cardiff**
for companies registered in England and Wales

or

Companies House, 37 Castle Terrace, Edinburgh, EH1 2EB
for companies registered in Scotland **DX 235 Edinburgh**

Form 88(2)

Companies House
— for the record —

88(2)
Return of Allotment of Shares

CHFP000

Company Number

Company name in full

Shares allotted (including bonus shares):

	From			To		
	Day	*Month*	*Year*	*Day*	*Month*	*Year*
Date or period during which shares were allotted *(If shares were allotted on one date enter that date in the "from" box).*						

Class of shares *(ordinary or preference etc)*			
Number allotted			
Nominal value of each share			
Amount (if any) paid or due on each share *(including any share premium)*			

List the names and addresses of the allottees and the number of shares allotted to each overleaf

If the allotted shares are fully or partly paid up otherwise than in cash please state:

% that each share is to be treated as paid up			

Consideration for which the shares were allotted
(This information must be supported by the duly stamped contract or by the duly stamped particulars on Form 88(3) if the contract is not in writing)

When you have completed and signed the form send it to the Registrar of Companies at:

Companies House receipt date barcode

This form has been provided free of charge by Companies House.

Companies House, Crown Way, Cardiff CF14 3UZ **DX 33050 Cardiff**
For companies registered in England and Wales

Companies House, 37 Castle Terrace, Edinburgh EH1 2EB **DX 235 Edinburgh**
For companies registered in Scotland

Form 88(2) – continued

Names and addresses of the allottees *(List joint share allotments consecutively)*

Shareholder details	Shares and share class allotted	
Name Address UK Postcode	Class of shares allotted	Number allotted
Name Address UK Postcode	Class of shares allotted	Number allotted
Name Address UK Postcode	Class of shares allotted	Number allotted
Name Address UK Postcode	Class of shares allotted	Number allotted
Name Address UK Postcode	Class of shares allotted	Number allotted

Please enter the number of continuation sheets (if any) attached to this form

Signed ______________________ **Date** ______________________

A director / secretary / administrator / administrative receiver / receiver manager / receiver *Please delete as appropriate*

Please give the name, address, telephone number and, if available, a DX number and Exchange of the person Companies House should contact if there is any query.

Tel	
DX number	DX exchange

Form 287

Companies House

— *for the record* —

287

Change in situation or address of Registered Office

Please complete in typescript, or in bold black capitals.

CHFP000

Company Number

Company Name in full

New situation of registered office

NOTE:

The change in the situation of the registered office does not take effect until the Registrar has registered this notice.

For 14 days beginning with the date that a change of registered office is registered, a person may validly serve any document on the company at its previous registered office.

PO Box numbers only are not acceptable.

Address

Post town

County / Region

Postcode

Signed **Date**

† Please delete as appropriate.

† a director / secretary / administrator / administrative receiver / liquidator / receiver manager / receiver

Please give the name, address, telephone number and, if available, a DX number and Exchange of the person Companies House should contact if there is any query.

Tel

DX number DX exchange

Companies House receipt date barcode

Form revised June 1998

When you have completed and signed the form please send it to the Registrar of Companies at:

Companies House, Crown Way, Cardiff, CF4 3UZ **DX 33050 Cardiff**
for companies registered in England and Wales

or

Companies House, 37 Castle Terrace, Edinburgh, EH1 2EB
for companies registered in Scotland **DX 235 Edinburgh**

Form 288a

Companies House — for the record

288a

APPOINTMENT of director or secretary

(NOT for resignation (use Form 288b) or change of particulars (use Form 288c))

Please complete in typescript, or in bold black capitals.
CHFP000

Company Number

Company Name in full

	Day	Month	Year		Day	Month	Year
Date of appointment				†Date of Birth			

Appointment form

Notes on completion appear on reverse.

Appointment as director | as secretary | *Please mark the appropriate box. If appointment is as a director and secretary mark both boxes.*

NAME *Style / Title | *Honours etc

Forename(s)

Surname

Previous Forename(s) | Previous Surname(s)

Usual residential address

Post town | Postcode

County / Region | Country

†Nationality | †Business occupation

†Other directorships (additional space overleaf)

I consent to act as ** director / secretary of the above named company

Consent signature | **Date**

SPECIMEN

* Voluntary details.
† Directors only.
**Delete as appropriate

A director, secretary etc must sign the form below.

Signed | **Date**

(**a director / secretary / administrator / administrative receiver / receiver manager / receiver)

Please give the name, address, telephone number and, if available, a DX number and Exchange of the person Companies House should contact if there is any query.

Tel

DX number | DX exchange

Companies House receipt date barcode

Form revised July 1998

When you have completed and signed the form please send it to the Registrar of Companies at:

Companies House, Crown Way, Cardiff, CF4 3UZ **DX 33050 Cardiff**
for companies registered in England and Wales **or**
Companies House, 37 Castle Terrace, Edinburgh, EH1 2EB
for companies registered in Scotland **DX 235 Edinburgh**

Form 288a – continued

Company Number

† Directors only. †Other directorships

NOTES
Show the full forenames, NOT INITIALS. If the director or secretary is a corporation or Scottish firm, show the name on surname line and registered or principal office on the usual residential line.

Give previous forenames or surname(s) except:
- for a married woman, the name by which she was known before marriage need not be given.
- for names not used since the age of 18 or for at least 20 years

A peer or individual known by a title may state the title instead of or in addition to the forenames and surname and need not give the name by which that person was known before he or she adopted the title or succeeded to it.

Other directorships.
Give the name of every company incorporated in Great Britain of which the person concerned is a director or has been a director at any time in the past five years.

You may exclude a company which either is, or at all times during the past five years when the person concerned was a director, was
- dormant
- a parent company which wholly owned the company making the return, or
- another wholly owned subsidiary of the same parent company.

Form 288b

Companies House
— for the record —

288b

Please complete in typescript, or in bold black capitals.
CHFP000

Terminating appointment as director or secretary
(NOT for appointment (use Form 288a) or change of particulars (use Form 288c))

Company Number

Company Name in full

	Day	Month	Year
Date of termination of appointment			

as director ☐ as secretary ☐ *Please mark the appropriate box. If terminating appointment as a director and secretary mark both boxes.*

Please insert details as previously notified to Companies House.

NAME *Style / Title *Honours etc

Forename(s)

Surname

	Day	Month	Year
†Date of Birth			

A serving director, secretary etc must sign the form below.

Signed **Date**

(** serving director / secretary / administrator / administrative receiver / receiver manager / receiver)

* Voluntary details.
† Directors only.
** Delete as appropriate

Please give the name, address, telephone number and, if available, a DX number and Exchange of the person Companies House should contact if there is any query.

Tel

DX number DX exchange

Companies House receipt date barcode

This form has been provided free of charge by Companies House.

Form revised 1999

When you have completed and signed the form please send it to the Registrar of Companies at:
Companies House, Crown Way, Cardiff, CF14 3UZ **DX 33050 Cardiff**
for companies registered in England and Wales **or**
Companies House, 37 Castle Terrace, Edinburgh, EH1 2EB
for companies registered in Scotland **DX 235 Edinburgh**

Form 363a

Companies House
— for the record —

Please complete in typescript, or in bold black capitals.

CHFP000

363a

Annual Return

Company Number

Company Name in full

Date of this return
The information in this return is made up to

Day Month Year

Date of next return
If you wish to make your next return to a date earlier than the anniversary of this return please show the date here. Companies House will then send a form at the appropriate time.

Day Month Year

Registered Office
Show here the address **at the date of this return.**

*Any change of registered office **must** be notified on form 287.*

Post town

County / Region

UK Postcode

Principal business activities

Show trade classification code number(s) for the principal activity or activities.

If the code number cannot be determined, give a brief description of principal activity.

Companies House receipt date barcode

Form revised September 1999

When you have completed and signed the form please send it to the Registrar of Companies at:
Companies House, Crown Way, Cardiff, CF14 3UZ **DX 33050 Cardiff**
for companies registered in England and Wales
or
Companies House, 37 Castle Terrace, Edinburgh, EH1 2EB
for companies registered in Scotland **DX 235 Edinburgh**

Page 1

Form 363a – continued

Register of members

If the register of members is not kept at the registered office, state here where it is kept.

Post town

County / Region

UK Postcode

Register of Debenture holders

If there is a register of debenture holders, or a duplicate of any such register or part of it, which is not kept at the registered office, state here where it is kept.

Post town

County / Region

UK Postcode

Company type

Please tick the appropriate box

- Public limited company
- Private company limited by shares
- Private company limited by guarantee without share capital
- Private company limited by shares exempt under section 30
- Private company limited by guarantee exempt under section 30
- Private unlimited company with share capital
- Private unlimited company without share capital

Company Secretary

Details of a new company secretary must be notified on form 288a.

(Please photocopy this area to provide details of joint secretaries).

* Voluntary details.

If a partnership give the names and addresses of the partners or the name of the partnership and office address.

Usual residential address must be given. In the case of a corporation or a Scottish firm, give the registered or principal office address.

Name

* Style / Title

Forename(s)

Surname

Address

Post town

County / Region

UK Postcode

Country

Page 2

Form 363a – continued

Directors

Details of new directors must be notified on form 288a

Please list directors in alphabetical order.

Name * Style / Title

Day Month Year

Directors In the case of a director that is a corporation or a Scottish firm, the name is the corporate or firm name.

Date of birth __ __ / __ __ / __ __ __ __

Forename(s)

Surname

Address

Usual residential address must be given. In the case of a corporation or a Scottish firm, give the registered or principal office address.

Post town

County / Region UK Postcode

Country **Nationality**

Business occupation

* Voluntary details.

Name * Style / Title

Directors In the case of a director that is a corporation or a Scottish firm, the name is the corporate or firm name.

Day Month Year

Date of birth __ __ / __ __ / __ __ __ __

Forename(s)

Surname

Address

Usual residential address must be given. In the case of a corporation or a Scottish firm, give the registered or principal office address.

Post town

County / Region UK Postcode

Country **Nationality**

Business occupation

Form 363a – continued

Directors

Please list directors in alphabetical order.

Details of new directors must be notified on form 288a

Name * Style / Title

Directors In the case of a director that is a corporation or a Scottish firm, the name is the corporate or firm name.

Day Month Year

Date of birth __ __ / __ __ / __ __ __ __

Forename(s)

Surname

Address

Usual residential address must be given. In the case of a corporation or a Scottish firm, give the registered or principal office address.

Post town

County / Region UK Postcode

Country **Nationality**

Business occupation

* Voluntary details.

Name * Style / Title

Directors In the case of a director that is a corporation or a Scottish firm, the name is the corporate or firm name.

Day Month Year

Date of birth __ __ / __ __ / __ __ __ __

Forename(s)

Surname

Address

Usual residential address must be given. In the case of a corporation or a Scottish firm, give the registered or principal office address.

Post town

County / Region UK Postcode

Country **Nationality**

Business occupation

Form 363a – continued

Directors

Details of new directors must be notified on form 288a

Please list directors in alphabetical order.

Name * Style / Title

Directors In the case of a director that is a corporation or a Scottish firm, the name is the corporate or firm name.

Day Month Year

Date of birth __ __ / __ __ / __ __ __ __

Forename(s)

Surname

Address

Usual residential address must be given. In the case of a corporation or a Scottish firm, give the registered or principal office address.

Post town

County / Region UK Postcode

Country **Nationality**

Business occupation

* Voluntary details.

Name * Style / Title

Directors In the case of a director that is a corporation or a Scottish firm, the name is the corporate or firm name.

Day Month Year

Date of birth __ __ / __ __ / __ __ __ __

Forename(s)

Surname

Address

Usual residential address must be given. In the case of a corporation or a Scottish firm, give the registered or principal office address.

Post town

County / Region UK Postcode

Country **Nationality**

Business occupation

Form 363a – continued

Issued share capital
Enter details of all the shares in issue at the date of this return.

Class (e.g. Ordinary/Preference)	Number of shares issued	Aggregate Nominal Value (i.e Number of shares issued multiplied by nominal value per share, or total amount of stock)
Totals		

List of past and present shareholders
(Use attached schedule where appropriate)
A full list is required if one was not included with either of the last two returns.

There were no changes in the period ☐

	on paper	in another format
A list of changes is enclosed	☐	☐
A full list of shareholders is enclosed	☐	☐

Certificate

I certify that the information given in this return is true to the best of my knowledge and belief.

Signed ________ **Date** ________

† Please delete as appropriate.

† a director /secretary

When you have signed the return send it with the fee to the Registrar of Companies. Cheques should be made payable to **Companies House.**

This return includes ________ continuation sheets.
(enter number)

Please give the name, address, telephone number, and if available, a DX number and Exchange, for the person Companies House should contact if there is any query.

____

____

________ Tel ________

DX number ________ DX exchange ________

Page 6

Form 363a – continued

Companies House
— for the record —

List of past and present shareholders
Schedule to form 363a

Company Number

Company Name in full

- Changes to shareholders particulars or details of the amount of stock or shares transferred must be completed each year
- You must provide a "full list" of all the company shareholders on:
  - The company's first annual return following incorporation;
  - Every third annual return after a full list has been provided
- List the company shareholders in alphabetical order or provide an index
- List joint shareholders consecutively

Shareholders' details	Class and number of shares or amount of stock held	Shares or amount of stock transferred (if appropriate)	
		Class and number of shares or amount of stock transferred	Date of registration of transfer
Name Address UK Postcode			
Name Address UK Postcode			
Name Address UK Postcode			

Form 363a – continued

List of past and present shareholders (Continued)

Company Number ____________

Shareholders' details	Class and number of shares or amount of stock held	Shares or amount of stock transferred *(if appropriate)*	
		Class and number of shares or amount of stock transferred	Date of registration of transfer
Name ______ Address ______ ______ ______ UK Postcode ______			
Name ______ Address ______ ______ ______ UK Postcode ______			
Name ______ Address ______ ______ ______ UK Postcode ______			
Name ______ Address ______ ______ ______ UK Postcode ______			
Name ______ Address ______ ______ ______ UK Postcode ______			

Form 363a – continued

Form 363a Continuation Sheet

Company Number

Company Name in full

Company Secretary

Details of a new company secretary must be notified on form 288a.

(Please photocopy this area to provide details of joint secretaries).

* Voluntary details.

Name * Style / Title

Forename(s)

Surname

If a partnership give the names and addresses of the partners or the name of the partnership and office address.

Address

Post town

Usual residential address must be given. In the case of a corporation or a Scottish firm, give the registered or principal office address.

County / Region

UK Postcode

Country

Directors

Please list directors in alphabetical order.

Details of new directors must be notified on form 288a

Name * Style / Title

Day Month Year

Directors In the case of a director that is a corporation or a Scottish firm, the name is the corporate or firm name.

Date of birth __ __ / __ __ / __ __ __ __

Forename(s)

Surname

Address

Usual residential address must be given. In the case of a corporation or a Scottish firm, give the registered or principal office address.

Post town

County / Region

UK Postcode

Country

Nationality

Business occupation

Form 363a – continued

Directors

Please list directors in alphabetical order.

Details of new directors must be notified on form 288a

Directors In the case of a director that is a corporation or a Scottish firm, the name is the corporate or firm name.

Name * Style / Title

Day Month Year

Date of birth __ __ / __ __ / __ __ __ __

Forename(s)

Surname

Address

Usual residential address must be given. In the case of a corporation or a Scottish firm, give the registered or principal office address.

Post town

County / Region UK Postcode

Country **Nationality**

Business occupation

* Voluntary details.

Name * Style / Title

Day Month Year

Directors In the case of a director that is a corporation or a Scottish firm, the name is the corporate or firm name.

Date of birth __ __ / __ __ / __ __ __ __

Forename(s)

Surname

Address

Usual residential address must be given. In the case of a corporation or a Scottish firm, give the registered or principal office address.

Post town

County / Region UK Postcode

Country **Nationality**

Business occupation

Appendix 2 – Contents of the FRSSE

CONTENTS

Appendix 3 – CA 1985, Sch 8

SCHEDULE 8
FORM AND CONTENT OF ACCOUNTS PREPARED BY SMALL COMPANIES

PART I
GENERAL RULES AND FORMATS

SECTION A

1. – (1) Subject to the following provisions of this Schedule–

(a) every balance sheet of a small company shall show the items listed in either of the balance sheet formats set out below in section B of this Part; and

(b) every profit and loss account of a small company shall show the items listed in any one of the profit and loss account formats so set out;

in either case in the order and under the headings and sub-headings given in the format adopted.

(2) Sub-paragraph (1) above is not to be read as requiring the heading or sub-heading for any item to be distinguished by any letter or number assigned to that item in the format adopted.

2. – (1) Where in accordance with paragraph 1 a small company's balance sheet or profit and loss account for any financial year has been prepared by reference to one of the formats set out in section B below, the directors of the company shall adopt the same format in preparing the accounts for subsequent financial years of the company unless in their opinion there are special reasons for a change.

(2) Particulars of any change in the format adopted in preparing a small company's balance sheet or profit and loss account in accordance with paragraph 1 shall be disclosed, and the reasons for the change shall be explained, in a note to the accounts in which the new format is first adopted.

3. – (1) Any item required in accordance with paragraph 1 to be shown in a small company's balance sheet or profit and loss account may be shown in greater detail than required by the format adopted.

(2) A small company's balance sheet or profit and loss account may include an item representing or covering the amount of any asset or liability,

income or expenditure not otherwise covered by any of the items listed in the format adopted, but the following shall not be treated as assets in any small company's balance sheet–

(a) preliminary expenses;

(b) expenses of and commission on any issue of shares or debentures; and

(c) costs of research.

(3) In preparing a small company's balance sheet or profit and loss account the directors of the company shall adapt the arrangement and headings and sub-headings otherwise required by paragraph 1 in respect of items to which an Arabic number is assigned in the format adopted, in any case where the special nature of the company's business requires such adaptation.

(4) Items to which Arabic numbers are assigned in any of the formats set out in section B below may be combined in a small company's accounts for any financial year if either–

(a) their individual amounts are not material to assessing the state of affairs or profit or loss of the company for that year; or

(b) the combination facilitates that assessment;

but in a case within paragraph (b) the individual amounts of any items so combined shall be disclosed in a note to the accounts.

(5) Subject to paragraph 4(3) below, a heading or sub-heading corresponding to an item listed in the format adopted in preparing a small company's balance sheet or profit and loss account shall not be included if there is no amount to be shown for that item in respect of the financial year to which the balance sheet or profit and loss account relates.

(6) Every profit and loss account of a small company shall show the amount of the company's profit or loss on ordinary activities before taxation.

(7) Every profit and loss account of a small company shall show separately as additional items–

(a) any amount set aside or proposed to be set aside to, or withdrawn or proposed to be withdrawn from, reserves;

(b) the aggregate amount of any dividends paid and proposed.

4. – (1) In respect of every item shown in a small company's balance sheet or profit and loss account the corresponding amount for the financial year immediately preceding that to which the balance sheet or profit and loss account relates shall also be shown.

(2) Where that corresponding amount is not comparable with the amount to be shown for the item in question in respect of the financial year to which the balance sheet or profit and loss account relates, the former amount shall be adjusted and particulars of the adjustment and the reasons for it shall be disclosed in a note to the accounts.

(3) Paragraph 3(5) does not apply in any case where an amount can be shown for the item in question in respect of the financial year immediately

preceding that to which the balance sheet or profit and loss account relates, and that amount shall be shown under the heading or sub-heading required by paragraph 1 for that item.

5. Amounts in respect of items representing assets or income may not be set off against amounts in respect of items representing liabilities or expenditure (as the case may be), or vice versa.

SECTION B
THE REQUIRED FORMATS FOR ACCOUNTS

Preliminary

6. References in this Part of this Schedule to the items listed in any of the formats set out below are to those items read together with any of the notes following the formats which apply to any of those items, and the requirement imposed by paragraph 1 to show the items listed in any such format in the order adopted in the format is subject to any provision in those notes for alternative positions for any particular items.

7. A number in brackets following any item in any of the formats set out below is a reference to the note of that number in the notes following the formats.

8. In the notes following the formats–

(a) the heading of each note gives the required heading or sub-heading for the item to which it applies and a reference to any letters and numbers assigned to that item in the formats set out below (taking a reference in the case of Format 2 of the balance sheet formats to the item listed under "Assets" or under "Liabilities" as the case may require); and

(b) references to a numbered format are to the balance sheet format or (as the case may require) to the profit and loss account format of that number set out below.

Balance Sheet Formats
Format 1

A. Called up share capital not paid (1)
B. Fixed assets
  I Intangible assets
    1 Goodwill (2)
    2 Other intangible assets (3)
  II Tangible assets
    1 Land and buildings

2 Plant and machinery etc
III Investments
1 Shares in group undertakings and participating interests
2 Loans to group undertakings and undertakings in which the company has a participating interest
3 Other investments other than loans
4 Other investments (4)
C. Current assets
I Stocks
1 Stocks
2 Payments on account
II Debtors (5)
1 Trade debtors
2 Amounts owed by group undertakings and undertakings in which the company has a participating interest
3 Other debtors
III Investments
1 Shares in group undertakings
2 Other investments
IV Cash at bank and in hand
D. Prepayments and accrued income (6)
E. Creditors: amounts falling due within one year
1 Bank loans and overdrafts
2 Trade creditors
3 Amounts owed to group undertakings and undertakings in which the company has a participating interest
4 Other creditors (7)
F. Net current assets (liabilities) (8)
G. Total assets less current liabilities
H. Creditors: amounts falling due after more than one year
1 Bank loans and overdrafts
2 Trade creditors
3 Amounts owed to group undertakings and undertakings in which the company has a participating interest
4 Other creditors (7)
I. Provisions for liabilities and charges
J. Accruals and deferred income (7)
K. Capital and reserves
I Called up share capital (9)
II Share premium account
III Revaluation reserve
IV Other reserves
V Profit and loss account

Balance Sheet Formats
Format 2

ASSETS

A. Called up share capital not paid (1)

B. Fixed assets

- I Intangible assets
  - 1 Goodwill (2)
  - 2 Other intangible assets (3)
- II Tangible assets
  - 1 Land and buildings
  - 2 Plant and machinery etc
- III Investments
  - 1 Shares in group undertakings and participating interests
  - 2 Loans to group undertakings and undertakings in which the company has a participating interest
  - 3 Other investments other than loans
  - 4 Other investments (4)

C. Current assets

- I Stocks
  - 1 Stocks
  - 2 Payments on account
- II Debtors (5)
  - 1 Trade debtors
  - 2 Amounts owed by group undertakings and undertakings in which the company has a participating interest
  - 3 Other debtors
- III Investments
  - 1 Shares in group undertakings
  - 2 Other investments
- IV Cash at bank and in hand

D. Prepayments and accrued income (6)

LIABILITIES

A. Capital and reserves

- I Called up share capital (9)
- II Share premium account
- III Revaluation reserve
- IV Other reserves
- V Profit and loss account

B. Provisions for liabilities and charges

C. Creditors (10)

- 1 Bank loans and overdrafts
- 2 Trade creditors
- 3 Amounts owed to group undertakings and undertakings in

which the company has a participating interest
4 Other creditors (7)

D. Accruals and deferred income (7)

Notes on the balance sheet formats

(1) *Called up share capital not paid*
(Formats 1 and 2, items A and C.II.3.)
This item may either be shown at item A or included under item C II 3 in Format 1 or 2.

(2) *Goodwill*
(Formats 1 and 2, item B.I.1.)
Amounts representing goodwill shall only be included to the extent that the goodwill was acquired for valuable consideration.

(3) *Other intangible assets*
(Formats 1 and 2, item B.I.2.)
Amounts in respect of concessions, patents, licences, trade marks and similar rights and assets shall only be included in a company's balance sheet under this item if either–

(a) the assets were acquired for valuable consideration and are not required to be shown under goodwill; or
(b) the assets in question were created by the company itself.

(4) *Others: Other investments*
(Formats 1 and 2, items B.III.4 and C.III.2.)
Where amounts in respect of own shares held are included under either of these items, the nominal value of such shares shall be shown separately.

(5) *Debtors*
(Formats 1 and 2, items C.II.1 to 3.)
The amount falling due after more than one year shall be shown separately for each item included under debtors unless the aggregate amount of debtors falling due after more than one year is disclosed in the notes to the accounts.

(6) *Prepayments and accrued income*
(Formats 1 and 2, item D.)
This item may alternatively be included under item C II 3 in Format 1 or 2.

(7) *Other creditors*
(Format 1, items E 4, H 4 and J and Format 2, items C 4 and D.)
There shall be shown separately–

(a) the amount of any convertible loans, and

(b) the amount for creditors in respect of taxation and social security. Payments received on account of orders shall be included in so far as they are not shown as deductions from stocks.
In Format 1, accruals and deferred income may be shown under item J or included under item E 4 or H 4, or both (as the case may require). In Format 2, accruals and deferred income may be shown under item D or within item C 4 under Liabilities.

(8) *Net current assets (liabilities)*
(Format 1, item F.)
In determining the amount to be shown under this item any prepayments and accrued income shall be taken into account wherever shown.

(9) *Called up share capital*
(Format 1, item K I and Format 2, item A.I.)
The amount of allotted share capital and the amount of called up share capital which has been paid up shall be shown separately.

(10) *Creditors*
(Format 2, items C.I to 4.)
Amounts falling due within one year and after one year shall be shown separately for each of these items and for the aggregate of all of these items unless the aggregate amount of creditors falling due within one year and the aggregate amount of creditors falling due after more than one year is disclosed in the notes to the accounts.

Profit and loss account formats
Format 1
(see note (14) below)

1. Turnover
2. Cost of sales (11)
3. Gross profit or loss
4. Distribution costs (11)
5. Administrative expenses (11)
6. Other operating income
7. Income from shares in group undertakings
8. Income from participating interests
9. Income from other fixed asset investments (12)
10. Other interest receivable and similar income (12)
11. Amounts written off investments
12. Interest payable and similar charges (13)
13. Tax on profit or loss on ordinary activities
14. Profit or loss on ordinary activities after taxation
15. Extraordinary income
16. Extraordinary charges

17. Extraordinary profit or loss
18. Tax on extraordinary profit or loss
19. Other taxes not shown under the above items
20. Profit or loss for the financial year

Profit and loss account formats
Format 2

1. Turnover
2. Change in stocks of finished goods and in work in progress
3. Own work capitalised
4. Other operating income
5. (a) Raw materials and consumables
   (b) Other external charges
6. Staff costs:
   (a) wages and salaries
   (b) social security costs
   (c) other pension costs
7. (a) Depreciation and other amounts written off tangible and intangible fixed assets
   (b) Exceptional amounts written off current assets
8. Other operating charges
9. Income from shares in group undertakings
10. Income from participating interests
11. Income from other fixed asset investments (12)
12. Other interest receivable and similar income (12)
13. Amounts written off investments
14. Interest payable and similar charges (13)
15. Tax on profit or loss on ordinary activities
16. Profit or loss on ordinary activities after taxation
17. Extraordinary income
18. Extraordinary charges
19. Extraordinary profit or loss
20. Tax on extraordinary profit or loss
21. Other taxes not shown under the above items
22. Profit or loss for the financial year

Profit and loss account formats
Format 3
(see note (14) below)

A. Charges
1. Cost of sales (11)
2. Distribution costs (11)
3. Administrative expenses (11)
4. Amounts written off investments
5. Interest payable and similar charges (13)

6. Tax on profit or loss on ordinary activities
7. Profit or loss on ordinary activities after taxation
8. Extraordinary charges
9. Tax on extraordinary profit or loss
10. Other taxes not shown under the above items
11. Profit or loss for the financial year

B. Income
1. Turnover
2. Other operating income
3. Income from shares in group undertakings
4. Income from participating interests
5. Income from other fixed asset investments (12)
6. Other interest receivable and similar income (12)
7. Profit or loss on ordinary activities after taxation
8. Extraordinary income
9. Profit or loss for the financial year

Profit and loss account formats
Format 4

A. Charges
1. Reduction in stocks of finished goods and in work in progress
2. (a) Raw materials and consumables
   (b) Other external charges
3. Staff costs:
   (a) wages and salaries
   (b) social security costs
   (c) other pension costs
4. (a) Depreciation and other amounts written off tangible and intangible fixed assets
   (b) Exceptional amounts written off current assets
5. Other operating charges
6. Amounts written off investments
7. Interest payable and similar charges (13)
8. Tax on profit or loss on ordinary activities
9. Profit or loss on ordinary activities after taxation
10. Extraordinary charges
11. Tax on extraordinary profit or loss
12. Other taxes not shown under the above items
13. Profit or loss for the financial year

B. Income
1. Turnover
2. Increase in stocks of finished goods and in work in progress
3. Own work capitalised

4. Other operating income
5. Income from shares in group undertakings
6. Income from participating interests
7. Income from other fixed asset investments (12)
8. Other interest receivable and similar income (12)
9. Profit or loss on ordinary activities after taxation
10. Extraordinary income
11. Profit or loss for the financial year

Notes on the profit and loss account formats

(11) *Cost of sales: distribution costs: administrative expenses*
(Format 1, items 2, 4 and 5 and Format 3, items A.1, 2 and 3.)
These items shall be stated after taking into account any necessary provisions for depreciation or diminution in value of assets.

(12) *Income from other fixed asset investments: other interest receivable and similar income*
(Format 1, items 9 and 10: Format 2, items 11 and 12: Format 3, items B.5 and 6: Format 4, items B.7 and 8.)
Income and interest derived from group undertakings shall be shown separately from income and interest derived from other sources.

(13) *Interest payable and similar charges*
(Format 1, item 12: Format 2, item 14: Format 3, item A.5: Format 4, item A.7.)
The amount payable to group undertakings shall be shown separately.

(14) *Formats 1 and 3*
The amount of any provisions for depreciation and diminution in value of tangible and intangible fixed assets falling to be shown under items 7(a) and A.4(a) respectively in Formats 2 and 4 shall be disclosed in a note to the accounts in any case where the profit and loss account is prepared by reference to Format 1 or Format 3.

PART II
ACCOUNTING PRINCIPLES AND RULES
SECTION A
ACCOUNTING PRINCIPLES

Preliminary

9. Subject to paragraph 15 below, the amounts to be included in respect of all items shown in a small company's accounts shall be determined in accordance with the principles set out in paragraphs 10 to 14.

Accounting principles

10. The company shall be presumed to be carrying on business as a going concern.

11. Accounting policies shall be applied consistently within the same accounts and from one financial year to the next.

12. The amount of any item shall be determined on a prudent basis, and in particular–

(a) only profits realised at the balance sheet date shall be included in the profit and loss account; and

(b) all liabilities and losses which have arisen or are likely to arise in respect of the financial year to which the accounts relate or a previous financial year shall be taken into account, including those which only become apparent between the balance sheet date and the date on which it is signed on behalf of the board of directors in pursuance of section 233 of this Act.

13. All income and charges relating to the financial year to which the accounts relate shall be taken into account, without regard to the date of receipt or payment.

14. In determining the aggregate amount of any item the amount of each individual asset or liability that falls to be taken into account shall be determined separately.

Departure from the accounting principles

15. If it appears to the directors of a small company that there are special reasons for departing from any of the principles stated above in preparing the company's accounts in respect of any financial year they may do so, but particulars of the departure, the reasons for it and its effect shall be given in a note to the accounts.

SECTION B
HISTORICAL COST ACCOUNTING RULES

Preliminary

16. Subject to section C of this Part of this Schedule, the amounts to be included in respect of all items shown in a small company's accounts shall be determined in accordance with the rules set out in paragraphs 17 to 28.

Fixed assets

General rules

17. Subject to any provision for depreciation or diminution in value made in accordance with paragraph 18 or 19 the amount to be included in respect of any fixed asset shall be its purchase price or production cost.

18. In the case of any fixed asset which has a limited useful economic life, the amount of–

(a) its purchase price or production cost; or

(b) where it is estimated that any such asset will have a residual value at the end of the period of its useful economic life, its purchase price or production cost less that estimated residual value;

shall be reduced by provisions for depreciation calculated to write off that amount systematically over the period of the asset's useful economic life.

19. – (1) Where a fixed asset investment of a description falling to be included under item B III of either of the balance sheet formats set out in Part I of this Schedule has diminished in value provisions for diminution in value may be made in respect of it and the amount to be included in respect of it may be reduced accordingly; and any such provisions which are not shown in the profit and loss account shall be disclosed (either separately or in aggregate) in a note to the accounts.

(2) Provisions for diminution in value shall be made in respect of any fixed asset which has diminished in value if the reduction in its value is expected to be permanent (whether its useful economic life is limited or not), and the amount to be included in respect of it shall be reduced accordingly; and any such provisions which are not shown in the profit and loss account shall be disclosed (either separately or in aggregate) in a note to the accounts.

(3) Where the reasons for which any provision was made in accordance with sub-paragraph (1) or (2) have ceased to apply to any extent, that provision shall be written back to the extent that it is no longer necessary; and any amounts written back in accordance with this sub-paragraph which are not shown in the profit and loss account shall be disclosed (either separately or in aggregate) in a note to the accounts.

Rules for determining particular fixed asset items

20. – (1) Notwithstanding that an item in respect of "development costs" is included under "fixed assets" in the balance sheet formats set out in Part I of this Schedule, an amount may only be included in a small company's balance sheet in respect of development costs in special circumstances.

(2) If any amount is included in a small company's balance sheet in respect of development costs the following information shall be given in a note to the accounts–

(a) the period over which the amount of those costs originally capitalised is being or is to be written off; and

(b) the reasons for capitalising the development costs in question.

21. – (1) The application of paragraphs 17 to 19 in relation to goodwill (in any case where goodwill is treated as an asset) is subject to the following provisions of this paragraph.

(2) Subject to sub-paragraph (3) below, the amount of the consideration for any goodwill acquired by a small company shall be reduced by provisions for depreciation calculated to write off that amount systematically over a period chosen by the directors of the company.

(3) The period chosen shall not exceed the useful economic life of the goodwill in question.

(4) In any case where any goodwill acquired by a small company is shown or included as an asset in the company's balance sheet the period chosen for writing off the consideration for that goodwill and the reasons for choosing that period shall be disclosed in a note to the accounts.

Current assets

22. Subject to paragraph 23, the amount to be included in respect of any current asset shall be its purchase price or production cost.

23. – (1) If the net realisable value of any current asset is lower than its purchase price or production cost the amount to be included in respect of that asset shall be the net realisable value.

(2) Where the reasons for which any provision for diminution in value was made in accordance with sub-paragraph (1) have ceased to apply to any extent, that provision shall be written back to the extent that it is no longer necessary.

Miscellaneous and supplementary provisions

Excess of money owed over value received as an asset item

24. – (1) Where the amount repayable on any debt owed by a small company is greater than the value of the consideration received in the transaction giving rise to the debt, the amount of the difference may be treated as an asset.

(2) Where any such amount is so treated–

(a) it shall be written off by reasonable amounts each year and must be completely written off before repayment of the debt; and

(b) if the current amount is not shown as a separate item in the company's balance sheet it must be disclosed in a note to the accounts.

Assets included at a fixed amount

25. – (1) Subject to the following sub-paragraph, assets which fall to be included–

(a) amongst the fixed assets of a small company under the item "tangible assets"; or

(b) amongst the current assets of a small company under the item "raw materials and consumables";

may be included at a fixed quantity and value.

(2) Sub-paragraph (1) applies to assets of a kind which are constantly being replaced, where–

(a) their overall value is not material to assessing the company's state of affairs; and

(b) their quantity, value and composition are not subject to material variation.

Determination of purchase price or production cost

26. – (1) The purchase price of an asset shall be determined by adding to the actual price paid any expenses incidental to its acquisition.

(2) The production cost of an asset shall be determined by adding to the purchase price of the raw materials and consumables used the amount of the costs incurred by the company which are directly attributable to the production of that asset.

(3) In addition, there may be included in the production cost of an asset–

(a) a reasonable proportion of the costs incurred by the company which are only indirectly attributable to the production of that asset, but only to the extent that they relate to the period of production; and

(b) interest on capital borrowed to finance the production of that asset, to the extent that it accrues in respect of the period of production;

provided, however, in a case within paragraph (b) above, that the inclusion of the interest in determining the cost of that asset and the amount of the interest so included is disclosed in a note to the accounts.

(4) In the case of current assets distribution costs may not be included in production costs.

27. – (1) Subject to the qualification mentioned below, the purchase price or production cost of–

(a) any assets which fall to be included under any item shown in a small company's balance sheet under the general item "stocks"; and

(b) any assets which are fungible assets (including investments);

may be determined by the application of any of the methods mentioned in sub-paragraph (2) below in relation to any such assets of the same class. The method chosen must be one which appears to the directors to be appropriate in the circumstances of the company.

(2) Those methods are–

(a) the method known as "first in, first out" (FIFO);

(b) the method known as "last in, first out" (LIFO);

(c) a weighted average price; and

(d) any other method similar to any of the methods mentioned above.

(3) For the purposes of this paragraph, assets of any description shall be regarded as fungible if assets of that description are substantially indistinguishable one from another.

Substitution of original stated amount where price or cost unknown

28. Where there is no record of the purchase price or production cost of any asset of a small company or of any price, expenses or costs relevant for determining its purchase price or production cost in accordance with paragraph 26, or any such record cannot be obtained without unreasonable expense or delay, its purchase price or production cost shall be taken for the purposes of paragraphs 17 to 23 to be the value ascribed to it in the earliest available record of its value made on or after its acquisition or production by the company.

SECTION C
ALTERNATIVE ACCOUNTING RULES
Preliminary

29. – (1) The rules set out in section B are referred to below in this Schedule as the historical cost accounting rules.

(2) Those rules, with the omission of paragraphs 16, 21 and 25 to 28, are referred to below in this Part of this Schedule as the depreciation rules; and references below in this Schedule to the historical cost accounting rules do not include the depreciation rules as they apply by virtue of paragraph 32.

30. Subject to paragraphs 32 to 34, the amounts to be included in respect of assets of any description mentioned in paragraph 31 may be determined on any basis so mentioned.

Alternative accounting rules

31. – (1) Intangible fixed assets, other than goodwill, may be included at their current cost.

(2) Tangible fixed assets may be included at a market value determined as at the date of their last valuation or at their current cost.

(3) Investments of any description falling to be included under item B III of either of the balance sheet formats set out in Part I of this Schedule may be included either–

(a) at a market value determined as at the date of their last valuation; or

(b) at a value determined on any basis which appears to the directors to be appropriate in the circumstances of the company;

but in the latter case particulars of the method of valuation adopted and of the reasons for adopting it shall be disclosed in a note to the accounts.

(4) Investments of any description falling to be included under item C III of either of the balance sheet formats set out in Part I of this Schedule may be included at their current cost.

(5) Stocks may be included at their current cost.

Application of the depreciation rules

32. – (1) Where the value of any asset of a small company is determined on any basis mentioned in paragraph 31, that value shall be, or (as the case may require) be the starting point for determining, the amount to be included in respect of that asset in the company's accounts, instead of its purchase price or production cost or any value previously so determined for that asset; and the depreciation rules shall apply accordingly in relation to any such asset with the substitution for any reference to its purchase price or production cost of a reference to the value most recently determined for that asset on any basis mentioned in paragraph 31.

(2) The amount of any provision for depreciation required in the case of any fixed asset by paragraph 18 or 19 as it applies by virtue of sub-paragraph (1) is referred to below in this paragraph as the adjusted amount, and the amount of any provision which would be required by that paragraph in the case of that asset according to the historical cost accounting rules is referred to as the historical cost amount.

(3) Where sub-paragraph (1) applies in the case of any fixed asset the amount of any provision for depreciation in respect of that asset–

- (a) included in any item shown in the profit and loss account in respect of amounts written off assets of the description in question; or
- (b) taken into account in stating any item so shown which is required by note (11) of the notes on the profit and loss account formats set out in Part I of this Schedule to be stated after taking into

account any necessary provision for depreciation or diminution in value of assets included under it;

may be the historical cost amount instead of the adjusted amount, provided that the amount of any difference between the two is shown separately in the profit and loss account or in a note to the accounts.

Additional information to be provided in case of departure from historical cost accounting rules

33. – (1) This paragraph applies where the amounts to be included in respect of assets covered by any items shown in a small company's accounts have been determined on any basis mentioned in paragraph 31.

(2) The items affected and the basis of valuation adopted in determining the amounts of the assets in question in the case of each such item shall be disclosed in a note to the accounts.

(3) In the case of each balance sheet item affected (except stocks) either–

(a) the comparable amounts determined according to the historical cost accounting rules; or

(b) the differences between those amounts and the corresponding amounts actually shown in the balance sheet in respect of that item;

shall be shown separately in the balance sheet or in a note to the accounts.

(4) In sub-paragraph (3) above, references in relation to any item to the comparable amounts determined as there mentioned are references to–

(a) the aggregate amount which would be required to be shown in respect of that item if the amounts to be included in respect of all the assets covered by that item were determined according to the historical cost accounting rules; and

(b) the aggregate amount of the cumulative provisions for depreciation or diminution in value which would be permitted or required in determining those amounts according to those rules.

Revaluation reserve

34. – (1) With respect to any determination of the value of an asset of a small company on any basis mentioned in paragraph 31, the amount of any profit or loss arising from that determination (after allowing, where appropriate, for any provisions for depreciation or diminution in value made otherwise than by reference to the value so determined and any adjustments of any such provisions made in the light of that determination) shall be credited or (as the case may be) debited to a separate reserve ("the revaluation reserve").

(2) The amount of the revaluation reserve shall be shown in the company's balance sheet under a separate sub-heading in the position

given for the item "revaluation reserve" in Format 1 or 2 of the balance sheet formats set out in Part I of this Schedule, but need not be shown under that name.

(3) An amount may be transferred–

(a) from the revaluation reserve–

(i) to the profit and loss account, if the amount was previously charged to that account or represents realised profit, or

(ii) on capitalisation,

(b) to or from the revaluation reserve in respect of the taxation relating to any profit or loss credited or debited to the reserve;

and the revaluation reserve shall be reduced to the extent that the amounts transferred to it are no longer necessary for the purposes of the valuation method used.

(4) In sub-paragraph (3)(a)(ii) "capitalisation", in relation to an amount standing to the credit of the revaluation reserve, means applying it in wholly or partly paying up unissued shares in the company to be allotted to members of the company as fully or partly paid shares.

(5) The revaluation reserve shall not be reduced except as mentioned in this paragraph.

(6) The treatment for taxation purposes of amounts credited or debited to the revaluation reserve shall be disclosed in a note to the accounts.

PART III
NOTES TO THE ACCOUNTS

Preliminary

35. Any information required in the case of any small company by the following provisions of this Part of this Schedule shall (if not given in the company's accounts) be given by way of a note to those accounts.
Disclosure of accounting policies

36. The accounting policies adopted by the company in determining the amounts to be included in respect of items shown in the balance sheet and in determining the profit or loss of the company shall be stated (including such policies with respect to the depreciation and diminution in value of assets).

Information supplementing the balance sheet

37. Paragraphs 38 to 47 require information which either supplements the information given with respect to any particular items shown in the balance sheet or is otherwise relevant to assessing the company's state of affairs in the light of the information so given.

Share capital and debentures

38. – (1) The following information shall be given with respect to the company's share capital–

- (a) the authorised share capital; and
- (b) where shares of more than one class have been allotted, the number and aggregate nominal value of shares of each class allotted.

(2) In the case of any part of the allotted share capital that consists of redeemable shares, the following information shall be given–

- (a) the earliest and latest dates on which the company has power to redeem those shares;
- (b) whether those shares must be redeemed in any event or are liable to be redeemed at the option of the company or of the shareholder; and
- (c) whether any (and, if so, what) premium is payable on redemption.

39. If the company has allotted any shares during the financial year, the following information shall be given–

- (a) the classes of shares allotted; and
- (b) as respects each class of shares, the number allotted, their aggregate nominal value, and the consideration received by the company for the allotment.

Fixed assets

40. – (1) In respect of each item which is or would but for paragraph 3(4)(b) be shown under the general item "fixed assets" in the company's balance sheet the following information shall be given–

- (a) the appropriate amounts in respect of that item as at the date of the beginning of the financial year and as at the balance sheet date respectively;
- (b) the effect on any amount shown in the balance sheet in respect of that item of–
    - (i) any revision of the amount in respect of any assets included under that item made during that year on any basis mentioned in paragraph 31;
    - (ii) acquisitions during that year of any assets;
    - (iii) disposals during that year of any assets; and
    - (iv) any transfers of assets of the company to and from that item during that year.

(2) The reference in sub-paragraph (1)(a) to the appropriate amounts in respect of any item as at any date there mentioned is a reference to amounts representing the aggregate amounts determined, as at that date, in respect of assets falling to be included under that item on either of the

following bases, that is to say–

(a) on the basis of purchase price or production cost (determined in accordance with paragraphs 26 and 27); or

(b) on any basis mentioned in paragraph 31,

(leaving out of account in either case any provisions for depreciation or diminution in value).

(3) In respect of each item within sub-paragraph (1)–

(a) the cumulative amount of provisions for depreciation or diminution in value of assets included under that item as at each date mentioned in sub-paragraph (1)(a);

(b) the amount of any such provisions made in respect of the financial year;

(c) the amount of any adjustments made in respect of any such provisions during that year in consequence of the disposal of any assets; and

(d) the amount of any other adjustments made in respect of any such provisions during that year;

shall also be stated.

41. Where any fixed assets of the company (other than listed investments) are included under any item shown in the company's balance sheet at an amount determined on any basis mentioned in paragraph 31, the following information shall be given–

(a) the years (so far as they are known to the directors) in which the assets were severally valued and the several values; and

(b) in the case of assets that have been valued during the financial year, the names of the persons who valued them or particulars of their qualifications for doing so and (whichever is stated) the bases of valuation used by them.

Investments

42.– (1) In respect of the amount of each item which is or would but for paragraph 3(4)(b) be shown in the company's balance sheet under the general item "investments" (whether as fixed assets or as current assets) there shall be stated how much of that amount is ascribable to listed investments.

(2) Where the amount of any listed investments is stated for any item in accordance with sub-paragraph (1), the following amounts shall also be stated–

(a) the aggregate market value of those investments where it differs from the amount so stated; and

(b) both the market value and the stock exchange value of any investments of which the former value is, for the purposes of the accounts, taken as being higher than the latter.

Reserves and provisions

43. – (1) Where any amount is transferred–

(a) to or from any reserves; or

(b) to any provisions for liabilities and charges; or

(c) from any provision for liabilities and charges otherwise than for the purpose for which the provision was established;

and the reserves or provisions are or would but for paragraph 3(4)(b) be shown as separate items in the company's balance sheet, the information mentioned in the following sub-paragraph shall be given in respect of the aggregate of reserves or provisions included in the same item.

(2) That information is–

(a) the amount of the reserves or provisions as at the date of the beginning of the financial year and as at the balance sheet date respectively;

(b) any amounts transferred to or from the reserves or provisions during that year; and

(c) the source and application respectively of any amounts so transferred.

(3) Particulars shall be given of each provision included in the item "other provisions" in the company's balance sheet in any case where the amount of that provision is material.

Details of indebtedness

44. – (1) For the aggregate of all items shown under "creditors" in the company's balance sheet there shall be stated the aggregate of the following amounts, that is to say–

(a) the amount of any debts included under "creditors" which are payable or repayable otherwise than by instalments and fall due for payment or repayment after the end of the period of five years beginning with the day next following the end of the financial year; and

(b) in the case of any debts so included which are payable or repayable by instalments, the amount of any instalments which fall due for payment after the end of that period.

(2) In respect of each item shown under "creditors" in the company's balance sheet there shall be stated the aggregate amount of any debts included under that item in respect of which any security has been given by the company.

(3) References above in this paragraph to an item shown under "creditors" in the company's balance sheet include references, where amounts falling due to creditors within one year and after more than one year are distinguished in the balance sheet–

(a) in a case within sub-paragraph (1), to an item shown under the latter of those categories; and

(b) in a case within sub-paragraph (2), to an item shown under either of those categories;

and references to items shown under "creditors" include references to items which would but for paragraph 3(4)(b) be shown under that heading.

45. If any fixed cumulative dividends on the company's shares are in arrear, there shall be stated–

(a) the amount of the arrears; and

(b) the period for which the dividends or, if there is more than one class, each class of them are in arrear.

Guarantees and other financial commitments

46. – (1) Particulars shall be given of any charge on the assets of the company to secure the liabilities of any other person, including, where practicable, the amount secured.

(2) The following information shall be given with respect to any other contingent liability not provided for–

(a) the amount or estimated amount of that liability;

(b) its legal nature; and

(c) whether any valuable security has been provided by the company in connection with that liability and if so, what.

(3) There shall be stated, where practicable, the aggregate amount or estimated amount of contracts for capital expenditure, so far as not provided for.

(4) Particulars shall be given of–

(a) any pension commitments included under any provision shown in the company's balance sheet; and

(b) any such commitments for which no provision has been made;

and where any such commitment relates wholly or partly to pensions payable to past directors of the company separate particulars shall be given of that commitment so far as it relates to such pensions.

(5) Particulars shall also be given of any other financial commitments which–

(a) have not been provided for; and

(b) are relevant to assessing the company's state of affairs.

(6) Commitments within any of sub-paragraphs (1) to (5) which are undertaken on behalf of or for the benefit of–

(a) any parent undertaking or fellow subsidiary undertaking, or

(b) any subsidiary undertaking of the company,

shall be stated separately from the other commitments within that sub-paragraph, and commitments within paragraph (a) shall also be stated separately from those within paragraph (b).

Miscellaneous matters

47. Particulars shall be given of any case where the purchase price or production cost of any asset is for the first time determined under paragraph 28.

Information supplementing the profit and loss account

48. Paragraphs 49 and 50 require information which either supplements the information given with respect to any particular items shown in the profit and loss account or otherwise provides particulars of income or expenditure of the company or of circumstances affecting the items shown in the profit and loss account.

Particulars of turnover

49. – (1) If the company has supplied geographical markets outside the United Kingdom during the financial year in question, there shall be stated the percentage of its turnover that, in the opinion of the directors, is attributable to those markets.
(2) In analysing for the purposes of this paragraph the source of turnover, the directors of the company shall have regard to the manner in which the company's activities are organised.

Miscellaneous matters

50. – (1) Where any amount relating to any preceding financial year is included in any item in the profit and loss account, the effect shall be stated.
(2) Particulars shall be given of any extraordinary income or charges arising in the financial year.
(3) The effect shall be stated of any transactions that are exceptional by virtue of size or incidence though they fall within the ordinary activities of the company.

General

51. – (1) Where sums originally denominated in foreign currencies have been brought into account under any items shown in the balance sheet or profit and loss account, the basis on which those sums have been translated into sterling shall be stated.
(2) Subject to the following sub-paragraph, in respect of every item stated in a note to the accounts the corresponding amount for the financial year immediately preceding that to which the accounts relate shall also be stated and where the corresponding amount is not comparable, it shall be adjusted and particulars of the adjustment and the reasons for it shall be given.
(3) Sub-paragraph (2) does not apply in relation to any amounts stated by virtue of any of the following provisions of this Act–

(a) paragraph 13 of Schedule 4A (details of accounting treatment of acquisitions),
(b) paragraphs 2, 8(3), 16, 21(1)(d), 22(4) and (5), 24(3) and (4) and 27(3) and (4) of Schedule 5 (shareholdings in other undertakings),
(c) Parts II and III of Schedule 6 (loans and other dealings in favour of directors and others), and
(d) paragraphs 40 and 43 above (fixed assets and reserves and provisions).

Dormant Companies Acting as Agents

51A. Where the directors of a company take advantage of the exemption conferred by section 249AA, and the company has during the financial year in question acted as an agent for any person, the fact that it has so acted must be stated.

PART IV
INTERPRETATION OF SCHEDULE

52. The following paragraphs apply for the purposes of this Schedule and its interpretation.

Historical cost accounting rules

53. References to the historical cost accounting rules shall be read in accordance with paragraph 29.

Listed investments

54. "Listed investment" means an investment as respects which there has been granted a listing on a recognised investment exchange other than an overseas investment exchange within the meaning of the Financial Services Act 1986 or on any stock exchange of repute outside Great Britain.

Loans

55. A loan is treated as falling due for repayment, and an instalment of a loan is treated as falling due for payment, on the earliest date on which the lender could require repayment or (as the case may be) payment, if he exercised all options and rights available to him.

Materiality

56. Amounts which in the particular context of any provision of this Schedule are not material may be disregarded for the purposes of that provision.

Provisions

57. – (1) References to provisions for depreciation or diminution in value of assets are to any amount written off by way of providing for depreciation or diminution in value of assets.

(2) Any reference in the profit and loss account formats set out in Part I of this Schedule to the depreciation of, or amounts written off, assets of any description is to any provision for depreciation or diminution in value of assets of that description.

58. References to provisions for liabilities or charges are to any amount retained as reasonably necessary for the purpose of providing for any liability or loss which is either likely to be incurred, or certain to be incurred but uncertain as to amount or as to the date on which it will arise.

Staff costs

59. – (1) "Social security costs" means any contributions by the company to any state social security or pension scheme, fund or arrangement.

(2) "Pension costs" includes any costs incurred by the company in respect of any pension scheme established for the purpose of providing pensions for persons currently or formerly employed by the company, any sums set aside for the future payment of pensions directly by the company to current or former employees and any pensions paid directly to such persons without having first been set aside.

(3) Any amount stated in respect of the item "social security costs" or in respect of the item "wages and salaries" in the company's profit and loss account shall be determined by reference to payments made or costs incurred in respect of all persons employed by the company during the financial year under contracts of service.

Appendix 4 – CA 1985, Sch 8A

SCHEDULE 8A
FORM AND CONTENT OF ABBREVIATED ACCOUNTS OF SMALL COMPANIES DELIVERED TO REGISTRAR

PART I
BALANCE SHEET FORMATS

1. A small company may deliver to the registrar a copy of the balance sheet showing the items listed in either of the balance sheet formats set out in paragraph 2 below in the order and under the headings and sub-headings given in the format adopted, but in other respects corresponding to the full balance sheet.

2. The formats referred to in paragraph 1 are as follows–

Balance Sheet Formats
Format 1

A. Called up share capital not paid
B. Fixed assets
    I Intangible assets
    II Tangible assets
    III Investments
C. Current assets
    I Stocks
    II Debtors (1)
    III Investments
    IV Cash at bank and in hand
D. Prepayments and accrued income
E. Creditors: amounts falling due within one year
F. Net current assets (liabilities)
G. Total assets less current liabilities
H. Creditors: amounts falling due after more than one year
I. Provisions for liabilities and charges
J. Accruals and deferred income
K. Capital and reserves
    I Called up share capital
    II Share premium account

III Revaluation reserve
IV Other reserves
V Profit and loss account

Balance Sheet Formats
Format 2

ASSETS
A. Called up share capital not paid
B. Fixed assets
I Intangible assets
II Tangible assets
III Investments
C. Current assets
I Stocks
II Debtors (1)
III Investments
IV Cash at bank and in hand
D. Prepayments and accrued income

LIABILITIES
A. Capital and reserves
I Called up share capital
II Share premium account
III Revaluation reserve
IV Other reserves
V Profit and loss account
B. Provisions for liabilities and charges
C. Creditors (2)
D. Accruals and deferred income

Notes on the balance sheet formats

(1) *Debtors*
(Formats 1 and 2, item C.II.)
The aggregate amount of debtors falling due after more than one year shall be shown separately, unless it is disclosed in the notes to the accounts.

(2) *Creditors*
(Format 2, Liabilities item C.)
The aggregate amount of creditors falling due within one year and of creditors falling due after more than one year shall be shown separately, unless it is disclosed in the notes to the accounts.

PART II
NOTES TO THE ACCOUNTS

Preliminary

3. Any information required in the case of any small company by the following provisions of this Part of this Schedule shall (if not given in the company's accounts) be given by way of a note to those accounts.

Disclosure of accounting policies

4. The accounting policies adopted by the company in determining the amounts to be included in respect of items shown in the balance sheet and in determining the profit or loss of the company shall be stated (including such policies with respect to the depreciation and diminution in value of assets).

Information supplementing the balance sheet

Share capital and debentures

5. – (1) The following information shall be given with respect to the company's share capital–

(a) the authorised share capital; and

(b) where shares of more than one class have been allotted, the number and aggregate nominal value of shares of each class allotted.

(2) In the case of any part of the allotted share capital that consists of redeemable shares, the following information shall be given—

(a) the earliest and latest dates on which the company has power to redeem those shares;

(b) whether those shares must be redeemed in any event or are liable to be redeemed at the option of the company or of the shareholder; and

(c) whether any (and, if so, what) premium is payable on redemption.

6. If the company has allotted any shares during the financial year, the following information shall be given–

(a) the classes of shares allotted; and

(b) as respects each class of shares, the number allotted, their aggregate nominal value, and the consideration received by the company for the allotment.

Fixed assets

7. – (1) In respect of each item to which a letter or Roman number is assigned under the general item "fixed assets" in the company's balance sheet the following information shall be given–

(a) the appropriate amounts in respect of that item as at the date of the beginning of the financial year and as at the balance sheet date respectively;

(b) the effect on any amount shown in the balance sheet in respect of that item of–

(i) any revision of the amount in respect of any assets included under that item made during that year on any basis mentioned in paragraph 31 of Schedule 8;

(ii) acquisitions during that year of any assets;

(iii) disposals during that year of any assets; and

(iv) any transfers of assets of the company to and from that item during that year.

(2) The reference in sub-paragraph (1)(a) to the appropriate amounts in respect of any item as at any date there mentioned is a reference to amounts representing the aggregate amounts determined, as at that date, in respect of assets falling to be included under that item on either of the following bases, that is to say–

(a) on the basis of purchase price or production cost (determined in accordance with paragraphs 26 and 27 of Schedule 8); or

(b) on any basis mentioned in paragraph 31 of that Schedule,

(leaving out of account in either case any provisions for depreciation or diminution in value).

(3) In respect of each item within sub-paragraph (1)–

(a) the cumulative amount of provisions for depreciation or diminution in value of assets included under that item as at each date mentioned in sub-paragraph (1)(a);

(b) the amount of any such provisions made in respect of the financial year;

(c) the amount of any adjustments made in respect of any such provisions during that year in consequence of the disposal of any assets; and

(d) the amount of any other adjustments made in respect of any such provisions during that year;

shall also be stated.

Details of indebtedness

8. – (1) For the aggregate of all items shown under "creditors" in the company's balance sheet there shall be stated the aggregate of the following amounts, that is to say–

(a) the amount of any debts included under "creditors" which are payable or repayable otherwise than by instalments and fall due for payment or repayment after the end of the period of five years beginning with the day next following the end of the financial year; and

(b) in the case of any debts so included which are payable or repayable by instalments, the amount of any instalments which fall due for payment after the end of that period.

(2) In respect of each item shown under "creditors" in the company's balance sheet there shall be stated the aggregate amount of any debts included under that item, in respect of which any security has been given by the company.

General

9. – (1) Where sums originally denominated in foreign currencies have been brought into account under any items shown in the balance sheet or profit and loss account, the basis on which those sums have been translated into sterling shall be stated.

(2) Subject to the following sub-paragraph, in respect of every item required to be stated in a note to the accounts by or under any provision of this Act, the corresponding amount for the financial year immediately preceding that to which the accounts relate shall also be stated and where the corresponding amount is not comparable, it shall be adjusted and particulars of the adjustment and the reasons for it shall be given.

(3) Sub-paragraph (2) does not apply in relation to any amounts stated by virtue of any of the following provisions of this Act–

(a) paragraph 13 of Schedule 4A (details of accounting treatment of acquisitions),

(b) paragraphs 2, 8(3), 16, 21(1)(d), 22(4) and (5), 24(3) and (4) and 27(3) and (4) of Schedule 5 (shareholdings in other undertakings),

(c) Parts II and III of Schedule 6 (loans and other dealings in favour of directors and others), and

(d) paragraph 7 above (fixed assets).

Dormant Companies Acting as Agents

9A. Where the directors of a company take advantage of the exemption conferred by section 249AA, and the company has during the financial year in question acted as an agent for any person, the fact that it has so acted must be stated.

Appendix 5 – Example Financial Statements

PERSONAL SERVICE COMPANY LIMITED

FINANCIAL STATEMENTS

FOR THE YEAR ENDED 31 JULY 2000

ANDERSONS
Chartered Accountants

PERSONAL SERVICE COMPANY LIMITED

CONTENTS OF THE FINANCIAL STATEMENTS FOR THE YEAR ENDED 31 JULY 2000

PERSONAL SERVICE COMPANY LIMITED

COMPANY INFORMATION FOR THE YEAR ENDED 31 JULY 2000

Directors:	J Jones A Jones
Secretary:	A Jones
Registered Office:	23 Oxford Street London EC1 2XY
Registered Number:	1234567
Accountants:	Andersons Chartered Accountants London
Bankers:	Royal Bank of Scotland London

PERSONAL SERVICE COMPANY LIMITED

REPORT OF THE DIRECTORS FOR THE YEAR ENDED 31 JULY 2000

The directors present their report with the financial statements of the company for the year ended 31 July 2000.

INCORPORATION
The company was incorporated on 1 August 1999 and commenced trading on the same date.

PRINCIPAL ACTIVITY
The principal activity of the company in the year under review was that of providing computing consultancy services.

DIRECTORS
The directors during the year under review were:

J Jones	appointed 01.08.99
A Jones	appointed 01.08.99

The beneficial interests of the directors holding office on 31 July 2000 in the issued share capital of the company were as follows:

	31.07.00	at date of appointment
Ordinary £1 shares		
J Jones	750	750
A Jones	250	250

Both the directors, being eligible, offer themselves for election at the forthcoming first Annual General Meeting.

This report has been prepared in accordance with the special provisions of Part VII of the Companies Act 1985 relating to small companies.

ON BEHALF OF THE BOARD:

J Jones – Director

Dated 15 August 2000

PERSONAL SERVICE COMPANY LIMITED

PROFIT AND LOSS ACCOUNT FOR THE YEAR ENDED 31 JULY 2000

	Notes	£
TURNOVER		100,000
Administrative expenses		76,733
OPERATING PROFIT	2	23,267
Interest receiable and similar income		500
		23,767
Interest payable and similar charges	3	100
PROFIT ON ORDINARY ACTIVITIES BEFORE TAXATION		23,667
Tax on profit on ordinary activities	4	2,176
PROFIT FOR THE FINANCIAL YEAR AFTER TAXATION		21,491
RETAINED PROFIT CARRIED FORWARD		21,491

PERSONAL SERVICE COMPANY LIMITED
BALANCE SHEET
31 July 2000

	Notes	£	£
Fixed Assets:			
Tangible assets	5		44,767
Current Assets:			
Debtors	6	8,000	
Cash at bank		8,000	
		16,000	
Creditors:			
Amounts falling due within one year	7	38,276	
Net Current Liabilities:			(22,276)
Total Assets less Current Liabilities:			£22,491
Capital and reserves:			
Called up share capital	8		1,000
Profit and loss account			21,491
Shareholders' Funds:			£22,491

The company is entitled to exemption from audit under section 249A(1) of the Companies Act 1985 for the year ending 31 July 2000.

No notice has been deposited under section 249B(2) of the Companies Act 1985 in relation to its financial statements for the financial year.

The directors acknowledge their responsibilities for:
(a) ensuring that the company keeps accounting records which comply with section 221 of the Companies Act 1985; and
(b) preparing financial statements which give a true and fair view of the state of affairs of the company as at the end of each financial year and of its profit or loss for each financial year in accordance with the requirements of section 226 and which otherwise comply with the requirements of the Companies Act 1985 relating to financial statements, so far as applicable to the company.

These financial statements have been prepared in accordance with the special provisions of Part VII of the Companies Act 1985 relating to small companies and with the Financial Reporting Standard for Smaller Entities (effective March 2000).

ON BEHALF OF THE BOARD:
J Jones – Director

Approved by the Board on 15 August 2000
The notes form part of these financial statements

PERSONAL SERVICE COMPANY LIMITED

NOTES TO THE FINANCIAL STATEMENTS FOR THE YEAR ENDED 31 JULY 2000

1. Accounting Policies

Accounting convention
The financial statements have been prepared under the historical cost convention and in accordance with the Financial Reporting Standard for Smaller Entities (effective March 2000).

Turnover
Turnover represents net invoiced sales of services, excluding VAT.

Tangible fixed assets
Depreciation is provided at the following annual rates in order to write off each asset over its estimated useful life.

Motor vehicles – 25% on reducing balance
Computer equipment – straight line over 3 years

Deferred taxation
Provision is made at current rates for taxation deferred in respect of all material timing differences except to the extent that, in the opinion of the directors, there is reasonable probability that the liability will not arise in the foreseeable future.

2. Operating Profit

The operating profit is stated after charging/(crediting):

	£
Depreciation – owned assets	22,500
Profit on disposal of fixed assets	(1,267)
Directors' emoluments	28,000

3. Interest Payable and similar Charges

Interest payable and similar charges includes the following:

	£
Bank interest	100

4. Taxation

The tax charge on the profit on ordinary activities for the year was as follows:

	£
UK Corporation Tax	2,176

UK Corporation Tax has been charged at 20%.

5. Tangible Fixed Assets

	Motor Vehicles £	Computer Equipment £	Totals £
Cost:			
Additions	24,000	50,000	74,000
Disposals	(6,000)	(3,350)	(9,350)
At 31 July 2000	18,000	46,650	64,650
Depreciation:			
Charge for year	6,000	16,500	22,500
Eliminated on disposals	(1,500)	(1,117)	(2,617)
At 31 July 2000	4,500	15,383	19,883
Net Book Value:			
At 31 July 2000	13,500	31,267	44,767

6. Debtors: amounts falling due within one year

	£
Trade debtors	8,000

7. Creditors: amounts falling due within one year

	£
Trade creditors	1,000
Directors' current accounts	35,100
Taxation	2,176
	38,276

8. Called up Share Capital

Authorised, allotted, issued and fully paid:

Number	Class	Nominal Value	£
1,000	Ordinary	£1	100,000

PERSONAL SERVICE COMPANY LIMITED

PROFIT AND LOSS ACCOUNT
FOR THE YEAR ENDED 31 JULY 2000

	£	£
Sales		100,000
Other income:		
Deposit account interest		500
		100,500
Expenditure:		
Directors' remuneration	28,000	
Wages	10,000	
Telephone	2,000	
Motor expenses	3,000	
Repairs & renewals	3,000	
Accountancy1,000		
Legal fees	500	
Entertainment	500	
Rent	4,000	
Rates & water	1,000	
Insurance	500	
Light & heat	1,000	
Miscellaneous	1,000	
		55,500
		45,000
Finance costs:		
Bank interest		100
		44,900
Depreciation:		
Motor vehicles	6,000	
Computer equipment	16,500	
		22,500
		22,400
Profit on disposal of fixed assets:		
Computer equipment		1,267
NET PROFIT		23,667

This page does not form part of the statutory financial statements

Appendix 6 – Abbreviated Financial Statements

ABBREVIATED FINANCIAL STATEMENTS

FOR THE YEAR ENDED 31 JULY 2000

FOR

PERSONAL SERVICE COMPANY LIMITED

PERSONAL SERVICE COMPANY LIMITED

CONTENTS OF THE ABBREVIATED FINANCIAL STATEMENTS FOR THE YEAR ENDED 31 JULY 2000

PERSONAL SERVICE COMPANY LIMITED

COMPANY INFORMATION
FOR THE YEAR ENDED 31 JULY 2000

Directors:	J Jones A Jones
Secretary:	A Jones
Registered Office:	23 Oxford Street London EC1 2XY
Registered Number:	1234567
Accountants:	Andersons Chartered Accountants London
Bankers:	Royal Bank of Scotland London

PERSONAL SERVICE COMPANY LIMITED

ABBREVIATED BALANCE SHEET
31 JULY 2000

	Notes	£	£
Fixed Assets:			
Tangible assets	2		44,767
Current Assets:			
Debtors		8,000	
Cash at bank		8,000	
		16,000	
Creditors:			
Amounts falling due within one year		38,276	
Net Current Liabilities:			(22,276)
Total Assets less Current Liabilities:			£22,491
Capital and reserves:			
Called up share capital	3		1,000
Profit and loss account			21,491
Shareholders' Funds:			£22,491

The company is entitled to exemption from audit under section 249A(1) of the Companies Act 1985 for the year ending 31 July 2000.

No notice has been deposited under section 249B(2) of the Companies Act 1985 in relation to its financial statements for the financial year.

The directors acknowledge their responsibilities for:

(a) ensuring that the company keeps accounting records which comply with section 221 of the Companies Act 1985; and

(b) preparing financial statements which give a true and fair view of the state of affairs of the company as at the end of each financial year and of its profit or loss for each financial year in accordance with the requirements of section 226 and which otherwise comply with the requirements of the Companies Act 1985 relating to financial statements, so far as applicable to the company.

These financial statements have been prepared in accordance with the special provisions of Part VII of the Companies Act 1985 relating to small companies.

ON BEHALF OF THE BOARD:
J Jones – Director

Approved by the Board on 15 August 2000
The notes form part of these financial statements

PERSONAL SERVICE COMPANY LIMITED

NOTES TO THE FINANCIAL STATEMENTS FOR THE YEAR ENDED 31 JULY 2000

1. Accounting Policies

Accounting convention

The financial statements have been prepared under the historical cost convention and in accordance with the Financial Reporting Standard for Smaller Entities (effective March 2000).

Turnover

Turnover represents net invoiced sales of services, excluding VAT.

Tangible fixed assets

Depreciation is provided at the following annual rates in order to write off each asset over its estimated useful life.

Motor vehicles – 25% on reducing balance
Computer equipment – straight line over 3 years

Deferred taxation

Provision is made at current rates for taxation deferred in respect of all material timing differences except to the extent that, in the opinion of the directors, there is reasonable probability that the liability will not arise in the foreseeable future.

2. Tangible Fixed Assets

	Total
	£
Cost:	
Additions	74,000
Disposals	(9,350)
At 31 July 2000	64,650
Depreciation:	
Charge for year	22,500
Eliminated on disposals	(2,617)
At 31 July 2000	19,883
Net Book Value:	
At 31 July 2000	44,767

3. Called up Share Capital

Authorised, allotted, issued and fully paid:

Number	Class	Nominal Value	£
1,000	Ordinary	£1	1,000

Appendix 7 – Form CT600

PE001

1

Inland Revenue

Company Tax Return

Form CT600 (1999) Version 1

For accounting periods ending on or after 1 July 1999

This form (or an Inland Revenue approved substitute version of it), together with any relevant *Supplementary Pages*, must be used whenever a company is required by form *CT603 Notice to deliver a company tax return* (the *Notice*) for any period ended on or after 1 July 1999. This form sets out the information we need and provides a standard format for calculations. Please complete the 'Company information' immediately and then read the notes on page 2 before completing any other sections.

Company Information

Company name

Personal Service Company Limited

Company registration number *(if registered)*

1234567

Reference - *as shown on the Notice*

818/12345/67890

Address - *if different from that shown on the Notice*

Period covered by this return *(cannot exceed 12 months)*

From *dd/mm/yyyy*

01/08/1999

To

31/07/2000

Before you begin completing the form, read the notes on page 2 and then go to section 1 on page 3 as this will help you decide whether you need to obtain and complete any of the Supplementary Pages which form part of the return. Fill in the 'Summary' and 'Declaration' below once you have completed the relevant sections, and before you send back the return to the issuing Tax Office

Summary of return information

Put an 'X' in box if Yes

Are you making a repayment claim

- for this period? ☐
- for an earlier period? ☐

I attach

- accounts for the period to which this return relates ☒
- accounts for a different period ☐

Put an 'X' in box if Yes

Are you filing more than one return for this company now? ☐

Are you seeking approved investment trust company status under S842(1) ICTA 1998? *Attach a schedule showing company has met all the conditions* ☐

- if no accounts, say why not

I am sending you the following completed *Supplementary Pages* as part of the return form

Put an 'X' in appropriate box(es)

Loans to participators by close companies (CT600A) ☐

Controlled foreign companies (CT600B) ☐

Group and consortium (CT600C) ☐

Insurance (CT600D) ☐

Charities (CT600E) ☐

Declaration

Warning

Giving false information in the return, or concealing any part of the company's profits or tax payable, can lead to the company and you being prosecuted.

Declaration

The information I have given on this form and in the accompanying Supplementary Pages is correct and complete to the best of my knowledge and belief.

Signature

Date *dd/mm/yyyy*

15/12/2000

Status

Director

Name *(in capital letters)*

J Jones

Except where a liquidator has been appointed, any person who is authorised to do so may sign on behalf of the company. A photo copy of a signature is not acceptable.

CT600 (1999) Version 1(Substitute)(IRIS)

Form CT600 – continued

PE001

2

Important points

- **As soon as you receive the *Notice to deliver a company tax return (the Notice)*** make sure you obtain all the *Supplementary Pages* you need. The information on page 3 in Section 1 should help you decide which you will need and how to get them. Please contact the Tax Office shown on the *Notice* if you need more help.
- **Members' clubs, societies and voluntary associations** may only need to complete the *Company information, Summary and Declaration* sections on page 1, and the short calculation on pages 4 and 5. Note 1 in the *Company Tax Return Guide (Guide)* gives more detail about what to complete but our leaflet *'Clubs societies and voluntary associations' (IR46)* gives more information and includes an example of a completed form *CT600*. The leaflet is available from any Inland Revenue Enquiry Centre or Tax Office (see 'Inland Revenue' in your local Phone Book).
- **'Company' includes** every kind of body, club, society, association or organisation that is chargeable to corporation tax, whether or not it is incorporated.
- **Please no not** make an entry where the company did not have the item specified in the return form. Complete the boxes with whole figures only, except where pence or decimals are indicated.
- **The Guide** and the further notes on this form will help you complete this return.

Which sections you need to complete

After reading the notes on this page, start at Section 1.

All trading companies must complete Section 2. All companies must then complete either the Short Calculation (Section 3) or the Detailed Calculation (Section 4). The notes at the beginning of each Calculation will help you decide which one is appropriate

Complete Section 5 if you want to claim capital allowances.

Complete Section 6 if, in this period, the company has any of the losses or excess amounts listed there. Group companies must also show the maximum amounts available for surrender by way of group or consortium relief.

Complete Section 7 if there is a repayment claim attached to this return.

If the company charges directors' remuneration in the accounts please complete Section 8.

What to do when you have completed the return

When you have completed the appropriate sections make sure you give us all the information requested on page 1. Once you have done this, sign and date the *Declaration* and send the **whole** form to us. Attach any supporting calculations, claims or surrender documentation. Send them along with the relevant completed *Supplementary Pages*, company accounts and, where prepared, directors' and auditors' reports. Note 3 in the *Guide* advises you of the date by which you must do this (the filing date).

It is a good idea to keep a copy of the completed return for your own records.

You must pay any tax outstanding that you calculate is due. A payslip is attached to the *Notice*. Note 20 in the *Guide* tells you about payment dates.

Do not send back the *Guide* but please keep it for reference purposes.

When we receive the return - *see note on page 12 of the Guide*

When we receive your completed return we will process it, based on your figures, and record the amount you have shown in the return as the tax due for this period. At this stage we will acknowledge receipt of the return.

The *Guide* tells you the time limits by which you can amend the return, and the time limits applying to us for correcting or enquiring into it.

Remember

- **Interest is charged on tax paid late.**
- **The company may be liable to penalties if its return is late or incorrect.**

CT600 (1999) Version 1(Substitute)(IRIS)

Form CT600 – continued

PE001

3

Section 1: Which *Supplementary Pages* must be completed?

This page will help you decide if you need any *Supplementary Pages*. The notes in the *Guide* will also help you. Most company agents have supplies but if you do not have an agent, or you agent does not hold stocks, please call the CTSA Orderline on 0845 300 6555, or fax on 0845 300 6777. Make a note of the name and form number of the *Supplementary Page(s)* you want before calling. The CTSA Orderline is open 7 days a week between 8am and 10pm.

If you need further help please contact the Tax Office shown on the *Notice*.

Members' clubs, societies and voluntary associations are unlikely to need any *Supplementary Pages*

Close companies

If the company is close and made a loan, or loans to an individual participator, or associate of a participator, in the return period which has not been repaid within the return period, **you must complete** the detailed calculation on pages 6 to 8 and the *Loans to participators by close companies Supplementary Pages (form CT600A)*.
See Note 2 in the Guide for the meaning of 'close company', 'loan', 'participator' and 'associate'

Controlled foreign companies (CFCs)

If, in this period, the company had an interest of 25% or more in a foreign company which was controlled from the UK, **you must complete** the *Controlled foreign companies Supplementary Pages (form CT600B)*, and, if there is a charge under S747 ICTA 1988, the detailed calculation on pages 6 to 8
Further Guidance on CFCs is available - see *'Other publications of interest'* on page 12 of the *Guide*.

Group and / or consortium companies

If the company is claiming or surrendering any amounts under the group or consortium relief provisions for this period **you must complete**

- Section 4, the detailed calculation on pages 6 to 8, if you are claiming group or consortium relief
- Section 6 on page 9 if you are surrendering relief and
- the *Group and consortium Supplementary Pages (form CT600C)*.

Insurance companies and friendly societies

If in this period, the company or society

- made claims under Sch 19AB ICTA 1988 to provisional payments (including notional repayments in respect of tax on gilt interest) or
- has entered into business in the accounting period which it treats as overseas life assurance business (OLAB)

you must complete the detailed calculation on pages 6 to 8 and the *Insurance Supplementary Pages (form CT600D)*

Charities

If, in this period, the charity is claiming exemption or partial exemption from tax **you must complete** any relevant section of the *CT600* for taxable income and the *Charity Supplementary Pages (form CT600E)*.

Section 2: Turnover of the company

You must complete this Section if the company has trading or professional income.

Members' clubs, societies and voluntary associations that do not trade outside their membership need not complete this Section.

Investment companies and Unit Trusts need not complete this Section.

Turnover

1	**Total turnover from trade or profession** *Enter the total for this return period. See note 4*	1	£ 100000
2	**Banks, building societies, insurance companies and other financial concerns** *Put an 'X' in this box*	2	

This is the end of Section 2. Please now complete either Section 3 on pages 4 and 5, or Section 4 on pages 6 to 8.

CT600 (1999) Version 1(Substitute)(IRIS)

Form CT600 – continued

PE001

Section 3: Short calculation

You may complete this section if it covers all the entries you need to make and any entry is less than £10 million.

In all other cases, or if you prefer, complete Section 4 instead. You should enclose explanations and calculations of any figures you have estimated or which are not immediately recognisable from the company's accounts. If you include a valuation you should state from where you obtained it. The figures to be entered are those adjusted for tax purposes, after deducting capital allowances and adding balancing charges, where appropriate. **References to *notes* are those in the *Guide***

If the company is close and has made loans to an individual participator, or associate of a participator, in this period that were not been repaid within the period, you need to complete Section 4 instead.

Please note that certain box numbers are missing from the short calculation.

Income

3 **Trading and professional profits**
See note 5. Complete Section 6 if there is a loss
3 £ 11945

4 **Trading losses brought forward claimed against profits**
*Only include losses made in the same trade. Include charges treated as losses. **Do not enter any amount larger than is needed to cover the profits in box 3.** See notes 5 and 6*
4 £

5 **Net trading and professional profits**
If box 4 equals box 3, enter '0'. Leave this box blank if there are no trading profits in box 3
box 3 minus box 4
5 £ 11945

7 **Profits and gains from non-trading loan relationships**
Include bank, building society or other interest, and any other profits and gains even if tax has been deducted. You will need to complete the 'Detailed calculation' at Section 4, and Section 6, if you have deficits on non-trading loan relationships from this, earlier or later accounting periods to include. See note 8
7 £ 500

8 **Annuities, annual payments and discounts not arising from loan relationships and from which income tax has not been deducted**
Exclude any amount included in box 7
8 £

10 **Income from which income tax has been deducted**
Enter the gross amount before tax and exclude any amount included in box 7. See note 9
10 £

12 **Income from UK land and buildings**
Enter the amount net of allowable expenses. Complete Section 6 if there is a loss. See note 10
12 £

13 **Annual profits and gains not falling under any other heading**
Enter amount net of losses. Complete Section 6 if there is a loss. See note 7
13 £

Chargeable gains

14 **Gross gains** *See note 11. Complete Section 6 if there is a loss*
14 £

15 **Allowable losses including losses brought forward**
Do not enter an amount larger than the amount of gross gains shown in box 14. See note 11
15 £

16 **Net chargeable gains**
If box 15 equals box 14, enter '0'
box 14 minus box 15
16 £ 0

19 **Profits before other deductions and reliefs**
total of boxes 5,7,8,10 12,13 and 16
19 £ 12445

Deductions and reliefs

26 & 27 **Trading losses of this or a later accounting period under S393A ICTA 1988.**
Put an 'X' in box 26 if amounts carried back from later accounting periods are included in box 27. See note 12
26 [ ] 27 £

30 **Profits before charges**
box 19 minus box 27
30 £ 12445

31 **Charges paid**
This figure must not exceed profits shown in box 30. See note 13
31 £

Corporation tax profits

33 **Profits chargeable to corporation tax**
box 30 minus box 31
33 £ 12445

Carry forward the figure in box 33 to the box on top of page 5

CT600 (1999) Version 1(Substitute)(IRIS)

Form CT600 – continued

PE001

5

Section 3: Short calculation continued

Profits chargeable to corporation tax *Enter the figure from box 33 on page 4* £ 12445

Tax Calculation If you claim tax is chargeable at the small companies' rate, or if you are claiming marginal small companies' relief, complete boxes 34-38. If there are no associated companies, franked investment income or foreign income dividends, please enter the financial year(s) in boxes 35 and 37, and '0' in boxes 34, 36 and, if necessary, 38. *See note 15*

34 Franked investment income and foreign income dividends arising in the period covered by the return. *See note 15* — 34 £

35 - 38 Number of companies associated with this company in the / each financial year(s) covered by this return
Exclude this company. See note 15

Financial year *(yyyy)*		Number of associated companies	
35	1999	36	0
37		38	

39 - 59 Corporation tax chargeable *See note 16*

Financial years beginning 1 April (yyyy)	Amounts of profit	Rates of tax *See note 31*	Tax
39 1999	40 £ 8297	41 20.00%	42 £ 1659 40
49 2000	50 £ 4148	51 20.00%	52 £ 829 60

59 Corporation tax chargeable — box 42 plus box 52 — 59 £ 2489 00

Reliefs and deductions in terms of tax

60 Marginal small companies' relief
Attach your computation. See notes 15 and 16 — 60 £ 312 97

62 Advance corporation tax (restricted if necessary under S239(2) ICTA 1988) *See note 17* — 62 £

63 Total reliefs and deductions in terms of tax
Cannot exceed box 59 amount — total of boxes 60 and 62 — 63 £ 312 97

68 Tax chargeable — box 59 minus box 63 — 68 £ 2176 03

69 Income tax deducted from gross income included in profits
Do not include deductions used to cover income tax for which the company was liable to account to the Inland Revenue on payments it has made. See note 18 — 69 £

70 Income tax repayable to the company
Complete if box 69 is greater than box 68. Also complete Section 7 — 70 £

72 Tax Payable
Enter '0.00' of you have completed box 70. See note 20
This figure is the amount of your self-assessment — box 68 minus box 69 — 72 £ 2176 03

Tax reconciliation

73 Deductions under the Construction Industry Scheme
Enclose forms SC60/CIS25. See note 19 — 73 £

74 Construction industry deductions repayable
Complete Section 7 — box 73 minus box 72 — 74 £

75 Tax already paid (and not repaid)
Exclude amounts entered in boxes 69 and 73. See note 21 — 75 £

76 Tax outstanding
This amount is payable to the Accounts Office. See note 23 — box 72 minus boxes 73 and 75 — 76 £ 2176 03

77 Tax overpaid
Complete Section 7 — box 75 plus box 73 minus box 72 — 77 £

Indicators

79 Put an 'X' in this box if the company should have made quarterly instalment payments under the Corporation Tax (Instalment Payments) Regulations 1998
See note 20 — 79

80 Put an 'X' in this box if the company is within a group payment arrangement for this period — 80

This is the end of the Short calculation

CT600 (1999) Version 1(Substitute)(IRIS)

Form CT600 – continued

PE001 6

Section 4: Detailed calculation

Complete this section if you have not completed Section 3. You should enclose explanations and calculations of any figures you have estimated or which are not immediately recognisable from the company's accounts. If you have included a valuation you should state from where you obtained it. The figures to be entered are those adjusted for tax purposes, after deducting capital allowances and adding balancing charges where appropriate. References to *notes* are those in the *Guide*.

Income

3 **Trading and professional profits**
See note 5. Complete Section 6 if there is a loss — 3 £

4 **Trading losses brought forward claimed against profits**
Only include losses made in the same trade. Include charges treated as losses. ***Do not enter an amount larger than is needed to cover the profits in box 3.*** *See notes 5 and 6* — 4 £

5 **Net trading and professional profits**
If box 4 equals box 3, enter '0'. Leave this box blank if there are no trading profits in box 3 — box 3 minus box 4 — 5 £

6 & 7 **Profits and gains from non-trading loan relationships, exchange fluctuations and certain financial instruments**
Include bank, building society or other interest, and any other profits and gains even if tax has been deducted. Also include intra-group income under S247(4) ICTA 1988 which represents interest in loan relationships. Put an 'X' in box 6 if income is stated net after carrying back deficits on non-trading loan relationships. Complete Section 6 if there are net deficits. See note 8 — 6 — 7 £

8 **Annuities, annual payments and discounts not arising from loan relationships and from which income tax has not been deducted**
Exclude any amount included in box 7 — 8 £

7 **Overseas income within Sch D case V**
Complete Section 6 if there is a loss — 9 £

10 **Income from which income tax has been deducted**
Enter the gross amount before tax and exclude any amount included in box 7. See note 9 — 10 £

11 **Intra-group income under S274(4) ICTA 1988 election where tax has not been deducted** *Exclude any amount included in box 7* — 11 £

12 **Income from UK land and buildings**
Enter the amount net of allowable expenses. Complete Section 6 if there is a loss. See note 10 — 12 £

13 **Annual profits and gains not falling under any other heading**
Enter amount net of losses. Complete Section 6 if there is a loss. See note 7 — 13 £

Chargeable gains

14 **Gross gains**
See note 11. Complete Section 6 if there is a loss — 14 £

15 **Allowable losses including losses brought forward**
Do not enter any amount larger than the amount of gross gains shown in box 14. *See note 11* — 15 £

16 **Net chargeable gains**
If box 15 equals box 14 enter '0' — box 14 minus box 15 — 16 £

Deductions specifically from non-trade profits

17 **Losses brought forward against certain investment income** — 17 £

18 **Non-trade deficits on loan relationships (including interest), exchange fluctuations and certain financial instruments brought forward**
See note 8. Amount cannot exceed total of boxes 7, 8, 9, 10, 11, 12, 13 and 16 — 18 £

19 **Profits before other deductions and reliefs** — total of box 5, and the net sum of boxes 7 to 13 and 16 minus boxes 17 and 18 — 19 £

Carry forward the figure in box 19 to the box at the top of page 7

CT600 (1999) Version 1(Substitute)(IRIS)

Form CT600 – continued

PE001

7

Section 4: Detailed calculation continued

Profits chargeable to corporation tax *Enter the figure from box 19 on page 6* £

Deductions and reliefs

	Box	
20 Losses on unquoted shares	20	£
21 Management expenses under S75 ICTA 1988	21	£
22 Interest distributions under S468L ICTA 1988 *See note 29*	22	£
23 Schedule A losses for this or previous accounting period under S392A ICTA 1988 *See note 10*	23	£
24 Capital allowances for the purpose of management of the business *S28 CAA 1990. Investment companies only. Complete Section 5*	24	£
25 Non-trade deficits for this accounting period from loan relationships, exchange fluctuations or certain financial instruments *See note 8*	25	£
26 & 27 Trading losses of this or a later accounting period under *S393A ICTA 1988* *Put an 'X' in box 26 if amounts carried back from later accounting periods are included in box 27. See note 12* [26]	27	£
28 Non-trade capital allowances *S145(3) CAA 1990. Complete Section 5*	28	£

29 Total of deductions and reliefs *This figure must not exceed profits shown in box 19* — total of boxes 20-25, 27 and 28 — 29 £

30 Profits before charges and group relief — box 19 minus box 29 — 30 £

	Box	
31 Charges paid *This figure must not exceed profits shown in box 30. See note 13*	31	£
32 Group relief *This figure must not exceed box 30 minus box 31. Complete and attach the 'Group and consortium Supplementary Pages'. See note 14*	32	£

33 Profits chargeable to corporation tax — box 30 minus boxes 31 & 32 — 33 £

Tax calculation If you claim tax is chargeable at the small companies' rate, or if you are claiming marginal small companies' relief, complete boxes 34 - 38. If there are no associated companies, franked investment income or foreign income dividends, please enter the financial year(s) in boxes 35 and 37, and '0' in boxes 34, 36 and, if necessary, 38. *See note 15*

34 Franked investment income and foreign income dividends arising in the period covered by the return. *See note 15* — 34 £

35 - 38 Number of companies associated with this company in the/each financial year(s) covered by this return *Exclude this company. See note 15*

Financial year *(yyyy)*	Number of associated companies
35	36
37	38

39 - 59 Corporation tax chargeable *See note 16*

Financial years beginning 1 April (yyyy)	Amounts of profit	Rates of tax *See note 31*	Tax
39	40 £	41	42 £
	43 £	44	45 £
	46 £	47	48 £
49	50 £	51	52 £
	53 £	54	55 £
	56 £	57	58 £

Carry forward the figure in box 59 to the box at the top of page 8 — Total of boxes 42,45,48,52,55 and 58 — 59 £

CT600 (1999) Version 1(Substitute)(IRIS)

Form CT600 – continued

PE001

8

Section 4: Detailed calculation continued

Corporation tax chargeable *Enter the figure from box 59 on page 7* £

60 - 63 Reliefs and deductions in terms of tax

60 Marginal small companies' relief
Attach you computation. See notes 15 and 16 — 60 £

61 Double taxation relief
Exclude any amount included in box 67 — 61 £

61A Put an 'X' in this box if box 61 includes an Underlying Rate relief claim — 61A

62 Advance corporation tax (restricted if necessary under S239(2) ICTA 1988)
See note 17 — 62 £

63 Total reliefs and deductions in terms of tax
Cannot exceed corporation tax chargeable amount in box 59 — 63 £ (total of boxes 60, 61 and 62)

64 - 78 Calculation of tax outstanding or overpaid

64 Net corporation tax liability — 64 £ (box 59 minus box 63)

65 & 66 Tax payable under S419 ICTA 1988
Complete and attach the 'Loans to participators by close companies Supplementary Pages'. Put and 'X' in box 65 if you completed box A11 in the Supplementary Pages. Copy the figure from box A13 to box 66 — 65 — 66 £

67 Tax payable under S747 ICTA 1988
Enter the total figure of tax from the 'Controlled foreign companies Supplementary Pages' — 67 £

68 Tax chargeable — 68 £ (total of boxes 64, 66 and 67)

69 Income tax deducted from gross income included in profits
Do not include deductions used to cover income tax for which the company was liable to account to the Inland Revenue on payments it has made. See note 18 — 69 £

70 Income tax repayable to the company
Complete if box 69 is greater than box 68. Also complete Section 7 — 70 £

71 Advance corporation tax on foreign income dividends and set off to the extent that corporation tax is otherwise unpaid
See note 22 — 71 £

72 Tax payable
Enter '0.00' if you have completed box 70. See note 20
This figure is the amount of your self-assessment — 72 £ (box 68 minus boxes 69 and 7[illegible])

Tax reconciliation

73 Deductions under the Construction Industry Scheme
Enclose forms SC60/CIS25. See note 19 — 73 £

74 Construction industry deductions repayable
Complete Section 7 — 74 £ (box 73 minus box 72)

75 Tax already paid (and not repaid)
Exclude amounts entered in boxes 69, 71 and 73. See note 21 — 75 £

76 Tax outstanding
This amount is payable to the Accounts Office. See note 23 — 76 £ (box 72 minus boxes 73 and 7[illegible])

77 Tax overpaid
Complete Section 7 — 77 £ (box 75 plus box 73 minus box 7[illegible])

78 Tax refunds surrendered to the company under S102 FA 1989
Enclose a copy of the joint Notice. See note 24 — 78 £

Indicators

79 Put an 'X' in this box if the company should have made quarterly instalment payments under the Corporation Tax (Instalment Payments) Regulations 1998
See note 20 — 79

80 Put an 'X' in this box if the company is within a group payment arrangement for this period — 80

This is the end of the Detailed calculation

CT600 (1999) Version 1(Substitute)(IRIS)

Form CT600 – continued

PE001

9

Section 5: Claims for capital allowances and details of balancing charges arising

You must complete this section if you want to claim capital allowances. You should also show balancing charges taken into account in Section3 or 4 calculations. Show details of qualifying expenditure on which writing-down allowances may be claimed, even if you do not want to claim any allowances for this period. *See note 25*

Notice of expenditure on machinery and plant *See note 25*

81	Expenditure on which first year allowance is claimed	81 £	50000
82	Qualifying expenditure on long-life assets	82 £	
83	Qualifying expenditure on other assets	83 £	24000

Charges and allowances included in calculation of trading profit or losses

		Balancing charges	Capital allowances
84 - 85	Cars *Including leased out and 'expensive' cars*	84 £	85 £ 4500
86 - 87	Machinery and plant - long life assets	86 £	87 £
88 - 89	Machinery and plant - other assets	88 £	89 £ 28455
90 - 91	Industrial buildings and structures *Including qualifying hotels and commercial buildings and hotels in enterprise zones*	90 £	91 £
92 - 93	Other charges and allowances *For example agricultural buildings, mineral extraction, scientific research, patents*	92 £	93 £

Charges and allowances not included in calculation of trading profits or losses

	Balancing charges	Capital allowances
94 - 95	94 £	95 £

Section 6: Losses, deficits and excess amounts

Complete this section if the company has incurred, in this period, any of the losses or deficits shown below, or if it has, for this period, any of the excess amounts shown below. Companies that are proposing to surrender any amount as group or consortium relief should also complete the second column. *See note 27.*

		Arising	Maximum available for surrender as group relief
96 - 97	Trading losses *Case I* *See note 5*	calculated under S393 ICTA 1988 96 £	calculated under S393A ICTA 1988 97 £
98	Trading losses Case V	calculated under S393 ICTA 1988 98 £	
99 - 100	Non-trade deficits on loan relationships *See note 8*	calculated under S82 FA 1996 99 £	calculated under S83 FA 1996 100 £
101 - 102	Schedule A losses *UK land and buildings. See note 10*	calculated under S392A ICTA 1988 101 £	calculated under S403 ICTA 1988 102 £
103	Overseas property business losses Case V	calculated under S392A ICTA 1988 103 £	
104	Losses Case VI	calculated under S396 ICTA 1988 104 £	
105	Capital losses	calculated under S16 TCGA 1992 105 £	
		Excess	
106	Excess non-trade capital allowances *Excess over income in period*		calculated under S403 ICTA 1988 106 £
107	Excess charges *See note 13*		calculated under S403 ICTA 1988 107 £
108 - 109	Excess management expenses	calculated under S75(3) ICTA 1988 108 £	calculated under S403 ICTA 1988 109 £
110	Excess interest distributions	calculated under S468L(7) ICTA 198[illegible] 110 £	

CT600 (1999) Version 1(Substitute)(IRIS)

Form CT600 – continued

PE001

10

Section 7: Overpayments and repayments claims

Complete this section if you are claiming a repayment. If you have completed boxes 70, 74 and 77 in Section 3 or 4, attach your calculations. Do not forget to put an 'X' box in the appropriate box of the *Summary of return information* section on page 1. *See note 28*

Please note there is no box 113 in this section

111 Repayment of corporation tax
Include construction industry deductions repayable and enclose forms SC60 / CIS25 — 111 £

112 Repayment of income tax — 112 £

114 Repayment of advance corporation tax
See note 22 — 114 £

Bank details (for person to whom the repayment is to be made)

Repayments of corporation tax (but not income tax, advance corporation tax or construction industry deductions) can be made quickly and safely by direct credit (BACS) to a bank or building society account. You should provide details of the account which is to be credited. If the details are those of the nominee you want to receive the repayment, remember to complete the authority overleaf.

Name of bank or building society

115

Branch sort code — 116

Account Number — 117

Name of account

118

Building society reference

119

Signature

120

Except where a liquidator has been appointed, any person who is authorised to do so may sign the BACS details on behalf of the company. A photocopy of a signature is not acceptable

Name in capitals

120A

CT600 (1999) Version 1(Substitute)(IRIS)

Form CT600 – continued

PE001

11

Section 7: Overpayments and repayment claims continued

Repayment claim

121 The following amount is to be repaid — 121 £

either

122 • to the company — 122

or

123 • to the nominee in the authority given below — 123

(put and 'X' in either box 122 or 123 but not both)

124 The following amount is to be surrendered under S102 Finance Act 1989, and — 124 £

either

125 • the joint Notice is attached — 125

or

126 • will follow — 126

Repayments of advance corporation tax cannot be surrendered

(put an 'X' in appropriate box)

127 Please stop repayment of the following amount until I send you the Notice — 127 £

Payments to a person other than the company

Complete the authority below if you want the repayment to be made to a person **other than the company**. The Inland Revenue reserves the right not to make a repayment to a nominee and will not normally make a repayment to an overseas nominee.

I, as *(enter status - company secretary, treasurer, liquidator or authorised agent etc.)*

128

of *(enter name of company)*

129

authorise *(enter name)*

130

(enter address)

131

Nominee reference

132

to receive on the company's behalf the amount due

Signature

133

Except where a liquidator has been appointed, any person who is authorised to do so may sign the BACS details or an authority on behalf of the company. A photocopy of a signature is not acceptable

Name in capital letters

133A

This is the end of section 7

CT600 (1999) Version 1(Substitute)(IRIS)

Form CT600 – continued

PE001

12

Section 8: Directors' remuneration - optional section

Please complete this section if directors' remuneration is charged in the accounts supporting this form *CT600*
Attach a continuation sheet if you need more space.

Company name

134 Personal Service Company Limited

PAYE District

135 Glasgow 3

PAYE reference

136 818/P1234

Accounts for the period
From *(dd/mm/yyyy)* To

137 1 / 8 / 1999 138 31 / 7 / 2000

Remuneration claimed as a deduction in the accounts
Show total figure for all directors

139 £ 28000

Date when accounts laid before the company in general meeting or, if resolved not to lay accounts, the date on which the accounts were approved by the directors.

140 / /

Analysis

Net remuneration voted after adjustments

Enter the net figure of remuneration after deducting employers' National Insurance contributions, employers' and employees' superannuation contributions and any benefits which have been included in the accounts' figure.

141 Name of director	National Insurance number	Salary £	Bonus, fees or commission £
Jones Mr J	WA 32 58 30 E	20000	0
Jones Mrs A	PS 29 76 25 D	8000	0

Put an 'X' in here if a continuation sheet is used 142

143 Adjustments to reconcile the analysis above with total accounts' deductions claimed - please give details

	£
	£
	£
	£
	£

Date of commencement or cessation of directorship during period of account

144 Name of director	National Insurance number	Date commenced	Date ceased
Jones Mr J	WA 32 58 30 E	01/08/1999	
Jones Mrs A	PS 29 76 25 D	01/08/1999	

CT600 (1999) Version 1(Substitute)(IRIS)

Appendix 8 – Benefits

From relatively obscure beginnings, the concept of a 'benefit' provided for the employee by the employer has expanded to become almost an industry in itself. The provisions are now extremely complex and require not only the existence of a benefit to be identified but also for different benefits to be dealt with in different ways. The requirements are reinforced by penalties which may seem a little severe given the complexity of the requirements.

It is proposed in this appendix to consider in outline the main categories of benefit which a company is likely to encounter cross-referenced to the requirements within the book as regards taxation and reporting. The position in relation to benefits is now so (unnecessarily) complex that it is a matter on which professional advice should now be taken.

The position can also vary in relation to these items which are given as guidance only.

Assets

Assets which are readily convertible such as stocks, shares, bullion, commodities and the like are regarded as non-cash remuneration and are given special treatment

To be included in gross pay?	Yes
Class 1A NIC due?	No
To be entered in P11D?	No

Car fuel

Where an employer pays for or provides fuel for private motoring by a director or higher-paid employee then a benefit may arise which is chargeable to taxation.

The charge applicable varies according to the circumstances as follows.

Company vehicle
Where a lower-paid employee is provided with a company car no charge to taxation arises in respect of fuel for private motoring.

Where a higher-paid employee or director is provided with a company car then – irrespective of the method by which the fuel is paid for – a charge to taxation will arise which will normally be based on the appropriate fuel scale charge and requires to be included in the P11D.

To be included in gross pay?	No
Class 1A NIC due?	Yes
To be entered in P11D?	Yes (Section F)

Private Vehicle
Where a director or employee uses a private car and the employer pays for or provides fuel for private motoring then a charge to taxation will arise depending upon the method used to pay for the fuel:

Credit/agency card or garage account satisfying the following conditions. Employees use the employer's card/account to purchase goods or services bought on the employer's behalf where prior authorisation was given by the employer to make the purchase and the employee explained in advance of the contract being made and the supplier accepted that the purchase was made on behalf of the employer.

To be included in gross pay?	No
Class 1A NIC due?	Yes
To be entered in P11D?	Yes (Section N)

Credit/ Agency Card or Garage Account not satisfying above conditions.

To be included in gross pay?	Yes
Class 1A NIC due?	No
To be entered in P11D?	Yes (Section E or N)

Car parking facilities

The provision by the employer or car parking facilities may give rise to a benefit chargeable to taxation depending upon the circumstances.

Where the car parking facilities are at or near the place of work an exemption applies

To be included in gross pay?	No
Class 1A NIC due?	No
To be entered in P11D?	No

Parking provided elsewhere
If the parking is part of a journey which is qualifying business travel then a charge to taxation may be avoided, otherwise:

To be included in gross pay?	No
Class 1A NIC due?	Yes
To be entered in P11D?	Yes (Section K,L or N)

Car parking fees

Where the employer pays or reimburses car parking fees then that may give rise to a benefit chargeable to taxation depending upon the circumstances.

Where the car parking fees at or near the normal place of employment
Here, the benefit depends upon the circumstances of the contract.

Contract is between the employer and provider of the benefit:

To be included in gross pay?	No
Class 1A NIC due?	No
To be entered in P11D?	No

All other circumstances:

To be included in gross pay?	Yes
Class 1A NIC due?	No
To be entered in P11D?	Yes (Section B)

Where car parking fees for business related journeys

To be included in gross pay?	No
Class 1A NIC due?	No
To be entered in P11D?	Yes (Section O)

Childcare

The provision by the employer of childcare help for the children of employees may constitute a benefit which is subject to a charge to taxation in certain circumstances.

Qualifying nurseries and playschemes
Places in nurseries or playschemes on premises made available by the employer or, if the employer runs the nursery or playscheme jointly with others, on premises made available by one or more of those others provided that the employer has some responsibility for managing and financing the provision of care.

To be included in gross pay?	No
Class 1A NIC due?	No
To be entered in P11D?	No

Childcare help by other means

Contract is between the employer and provider of the benefit.

To be included in gross pay?	No
Class 1A NIC due?	Yes
To be entered in P11D?	Yes (Section N)

Contract is employee/provider and employer reimburses.

To be included in gross pay?	Yes
Class 1A NIC due?	No
To be entered in P11D?	Yes (Section N)

Christmas boxes

The provision by the employer of a christmas box for employees will amount to a benefit chargeable to tax which will be dealt with according to the form the christmas box takes.

Christmas box in cash

To be included in gross pay?	Yes
Class 1A NIC due?	No
To be entered in P11D?	Yes (Section N)

Christmas box in goods

To be included in gross pay?	No
Class 1A NIC due?	Yes
To be entered in P11D?	Yes (Section A or N)

Clothing

The provision by the employer of clothing or uniforms for employees may, depending upon the circumstances, amount to a benefit which is subject to a charge to taxation.

Where provided by the employer

Clothing or uniform provided by employer

To be included in gross pay?	No
Class 1A NIC due?	Yes
To be entered in P11D?	Yes (Section A or N)

Payments to employees for non-durables (e.g. tights)

To be included in gross pay?	Yes
Class 1A NIC due?	Yes
To be entered in P11D?	Yes (Section A or N)

Payments to employees for clothes wearable any time

To be included in gross pay?	Yes
Class 1A NIC due?	Yes
To be entered in P11D?	Yes (Section A or N)

Payments to employees for clothes wearable at work only

To be included in gross pay?	Yes
Class 1A NIC due?	Yes
To be entered in P11D?	Yes (Section A or N)

Contract is employee/provider and employer reimburses

To be included in gross pay? Yes
Class 1A NIC due? No
To be entered in P11D? Yes (Section B or N)

Company vehicles

To be included in gross pay?	No
Class 1A NIC due?	Yes
To be entered in P11D?	Yes

Computers

To be included in gross pay?	No
Class 1A NIC due?	N/A
To be entered in P11D?	No if exemption; yes otherwise

Council Tax

With one exception, the payment by the employer of an employee's Council Tax will amount to a benefit subject to a charge to taxation.

Exceptions

- where it is necessary for the employee to live in the accommodation to do his or her job properly, or

- the accommodation is provided so that the employee can do his or her job better and it is customary for employers to provide living accommodation for this type of job, or
- there is a special threat to security and the employee lives there as part of the special security arrangements.

To be included in gross pay?	No
Class 1A NIC due?	No
To be entered in P11D?	No

All other circumstances

To be included in gross pay?	Yes
Class 1A NIC due?	No
To be entered in P11D?	Yes (Section B)

Credit or charge cards

Where the employer provides the employee with a credit card, charge card or the like, then a benefit may arise which may become the subject of a charge to taxation depending upon the circumstances as follows.

Credit/charge card satisfying the conditions
Employees use the employer's card/account to purchase goods or services bought on the employer's behalf where prior authorisation was given by the employer to make the purchase and the employee explained in advance of the contract being made and the supplier accepted that the purchase was made on behalf of the Employer.

To be included in gross pay?	No
Class 1A NIC due?	No
To be entered in P11D?	No

Credit/Charge Card where:
Employees use the employer's card/account to purchase goods or services for the personal use of the employee.

To be included in gross pay?	Yes
Class 1A NIC due?	No
To be entered in P11D?	Yes (Section C)

Credit/Charge Card where:
Employees use the employer's card/account to purchase goods or services for items relating to specific and distinct expenses actually incurred by the employee.

To be included in gross pay?	No
Class 1A NIC due?	No
To be entered in P11D?	Yes (Section C)

Employee liability insurance

To be included in gross pay?	No
Class 1A NIC due?	N/A if exempt
To be entered in P11D?	Yes

Entertaining clients

To be included in gross pay?	No
Class 1A NIC due?	N/A
To be entered in P11D?	Yes

Entertaining staff

Where an employer provides expenses/allowances for entertaining staff then a benefit may arise which will be subject to a charge to taxation.

Contract is between the employer and provider of the benefit

To be included in gross pay?	No
Class 1A NIC due?	Yes
To be entered in P11D?	Yes (Section K,L or N)

Contract is Employee/Provider and employer reimburses

To be included in gross pay?	Yes
Class 1A NIC due?	No
To be entered in P11D?	Yes (Section O)

Expenses covered by a dispensation

A dispensation (see section on dispensations) removes items covered by the dispensation from the charge to taxation here.

To be included in gross pay?	No
Class 1A NIC due?	No
To be entered in P11D?	No

Expenses not covered by a dispensation

Expenses not covered by a dispensation (see section on dispensations) are naturally not excluded but so far as their being treated as a benefit subject to a charge to taxation is concerned, this is determined by the nature of the payment.

Specific and distinct business expenses

To be included in gross pay?	No
Class 1A NIC due?	No
To be entered in P11D?	Yes (appropriate Section)

Any profit element in the payment

To be included in gross pay?	Yes
Class 1A NIC due?	No
To be entered in P11D?	Yes (appropriate Section)

Food

To be included in gross pay?	No
Class 1A NIC due?	No
To be entered in P11D?	Yes

Goods

Where the employer makes goods (e.g. furniture or TVs) and transfers these to the employee then a benefit may arise which is subject to taxation.

Contract is between the employer and provider of the benefit

To be included in gross pay?	No
Class 1A NIC due?	Yes
To be entered in P11D?	Yes (Section A)

Contract is employee/provider and employer reimburses

To be included in gross pay?	Yes
Class 1A NIC due?	No
To be entered in P11D?	Yes (Section B)

Holidays

Where the employer provides the employee with a holiday then a benefit may arise which is subject to taxation.

Contract is between the employer and provider of the benefit

Not using vouchers

To be included in gross pay?	No
Class 1A NIC due?	Yes
To be entered in P11D?	Yes (Section A, K,L or N)

Using vouchers

To be included in gross pay?	Yes
Class 1A NIC due?	No
To be entered in P11D?	Yes (Section C)

Contract is employee/provider and employer reimburses

To be included in gross pay?	Yes
Class 1A NIC due?	No
To be entered in P11D?	Yes (Section B)

Income tax paid but not deducted from directors

Where the company pays a director's income tax to the Collector of Taxes but fails to deduct that from the remuneration of the director then that may be treated as a benefit subject to taxation.

To be included in gross pay?	Yes
Class 1A NIC due?	No
To be entered in P11D?	Yes (Section N)

Income tax paid on employees' notional payments

Where income tax is borne on notional payments not borne by the employee within 30 days of receipt of each notional payment then that may be treated as a benefit subject to taxation.

To be included in gross pay?	Yes
Class 1A NIC due?	No
To be entered in P11D?	Yes (Section B)

Insurance premiums

Where the contract is between the employee and the insurance provider but reimbursed by the employer then (subject to some exceptions) insurance premiums on pensions, annuities, health and the like may be a benefit subject to a charge to taxation.

To be included in gross pay?	Yes
Class 1A NIC due?	No
To be entered in P11D?	Yes (Section B)

Living accommodation

To be included in gross pay?	Yes
Class 1A NIC due?	No
To be entered in P11D?	Not always

Loans

Where, by reason of employment, an employee or director obtains from the employer and interest-free or cheap loan then that will be treated as a benefit subject to a charge to taxation.The method by which the loan is treated is as follows.

Qualifying loans

To be included in gross pay?	No
Class 1A NIC due?	No
To be entered in P11D?	No

Non-qualifying loans

To be included in gross pay?	No
Class 1A NIC due?	Yes
To be entered in P11D?	Yes (Section H)

Loans written off

To be included in gross pay?	Yes
Class 1A NIC due?	No
To be entered in P11D?	Yes (Section N)

Meal vouchers

Meal vouchers which cannot be transferred to another person, used only for meals and not worth more than 15p per day are non-taxable. Meal vouchers not meeting those conditions, however, will be regarded as a benefit subject to a charge to taxation.

To be included in gross pay?	Yes
Class 1A NIC due?	No
To be entered in P11D?	Yes (Section C)

Meals provided

To be included in gross pay?	Yes
Class 1A NIC due?	No
To be entered in P11D?	Yes

Medical or dental treatment or allowance

The provision of medical or dental treatment for employees can amount to a benefit chargeable to taxation depending upon the circumstances.

Where the contract is between the employer and provider/insurer

To be included in gross pay?	No
Class 1A NIC due?	Yes
To be entered in P11D?	Yes (Section I)

Where the contract is between the employee and provider/insurer

To be included in gross pay?	Yes
Class 1A NIC due?	No
To be entered in P11D?	Yes (Section B)

Mobile phones

Where an employer provides an employee with a mobile telephone for business purposes then provided that ownership is not transferred no benefit will arise.

As regards private calls on that mobile telephone, however, a benefit may arise which is subject to a charge to taxation depending on the circumstances.

Where the contract is between the employer and the provider

To be included in gross pay?	No
Class 1A NIC due?	No
To be entered in P11D?	No

Where the contract is between the employee and the provider

To be included in gross pay?	Yes
Class 1A NIC due?	No
To be entered in P11D?	Yes (Section B,N or O)

Office accommodation

To be included in gross pay?	No
Class 1A NIC due?	N/A
To be entered in P11D?	Yes

Personal bills

Where the personal bills of an employee are paid by the employer then a benefit will arise which is subject to a charge to taxation.

To be included in gross pay?	Yes
Class 1A NIC due?	No
To be entered in P11D?	Yes (Section B)

Personal expenses

To be included in gross pay?	No if exemption
Class 1A NIC due?	No if exemption
To be entered in P11D?	No if exemption

Relocation expenses

Where an employee relocates as a result of employment then certain qualifying expenses up to a certain limit payments or reimburements by the employer but beyond that they will be regasrded as a benefit subject to a charge to taxation the treatment of which will depend on its classification.

Non-qualifying expenses

To be included in gross pay?	Yes
Class 1A NIC due?	No
To be entered in P11D?	Yes (Section O)

Qualifying expenses

To be included in gross pay?	No
Class 1A NIC due?	Yes
To be entered in P11D?	Yes (Section N)

Qualifying expenses below the limit (currently £8,000)

To be included in gross pay?	No
Class 1A NIC due?	No
To be entered in P11D?	No

Qualifying expenses above the limit (currently £8,000)

To be included in gross pay?	No
Class 1A NIC due?	Yes
To be entered in P11D?	Yes (Section J)

Unapproved retirement benefit scheme

Where the employer contributes towards an unapproved retirement benefit scheme for employees then that will be a benefit subject to a charge to taxation.

To be included in gross pay?	Yes
Class 1A NIC due?	No
To be entered in P11D?	Yes (Section N)

Round sum allowances

The way in which an employer makes allowances to employees for expenditure incurred varies and depending upon circumstances can give rise to a benefit which is subject to a charge to taxation.

Specific and distinct business expense identified

To be included in gross pay?	No
Class 1A NIC due?	No
To be entered in P11D?	No

'Round sum' allowance (for which employee not expected to account)

To be included in gross pay?	Yes
Class 1A NIC due?	No
To be entered in P11D?	Yes (appropriate Section)

Scholarships

Scholarships awarded to students by an employer by reason of their parents' employment may be treated as a benefit and made the subject of a charge to taxation depending on the circumstances.

Contract between employer/provider

To be included in gross pay?	No
Class 1A NIC due?	Yes
To be entered in P11D?	Yes (Section N)

Contract between employee/provider

To be included in gross pay?	Yes
Class 1A NIC due?	No
To be entered in P11D?	Yes (Section N)

School fees

School fees paid by an employer by reason of their parents' employment may be treated as a benefit and made the subject of a charge to taxation depending on the circumstances.

Contract between employer/provider

To be included in gross pay?	No
Class 1A NIC due?	Yes
To be entered in P11D?	Yes (Section N)

Contract between employee/provider

To be included in gross pay?	Yes
Class 1A NIC due?	No
To be entered in P11D?	Yes (Section N)

Social functions

To be included in gross pay?	No if written exemption
Class 1A NIC due?	No if written exemption
To be entered in P11D?	No if written exemption

Sport or recreational facilities

To be included in gross pay?	No
Class 1A NIC due?	No (unless reimburses)
To be entered in P11D?	Yes unless exempt

Shares

To be included in gross pay?	No
Class 1A NIC due?	No
To be entered in P11D?	Yes (section N)

Subscriptions and professional fees

Where an employer pays or reimburses subscriptions or professional fees paid in respect of a body membership of which is voluntary then a benefit may arise which is subject to a charge to taxation depending on the circumstances.

Contract between employer and provider

To be included in gross pay?	No
Class 1A NIC due?	Yes
To be entered in P11D?	Yes (Section N)

Contract between Employee and Provider

To be included in gross pay?	Yes
Class 1A NIC due?	No
To be entered in P11D?	Yes (Section N)

Suggestion schemes

Some employers reward employees for suggestions made by them. Under certain conditions, these may be exempt but where the conditions are not met then a benefit may arise which is subject to a charge to taxation.

The suggestion award is wholly discretionary with no contractual entitlement/expectation (and not part of Employees normal duties to make suggestions).

To be included in gross pay?	No
Class 1A NIC due?	No
To be entered in P11D?	No

Where the above conditions are not satisfied

To be included in gross pay?	Yes
Class 1A NIC due?	No
To be entered in P11D?	Yes (Section N)

Training

Generally speaking, no benefit arises where the employer provides the employee with work-related training. In other circumstances, however, a benefit may arise which is subject to a charge to taxation depending upon the circumstances.

Training connected to the employment

To be included in gross pay?	No
Class 1A NIC due?	No
To be entered in P11D?	No

All other circumstances where contract is between employer/provider

To be included in gross pay?	No
Class 1A NIC due?	Yes
To be entered in P11D?	Yes (Section N)

All other circumstances where contract is between employee/provider

To be included in gross pay?	Yes
Class 1A NIC due?	No
To be entered in P11D?	Yes (Section N)

Vouchers

Vouchers provided by employers to employees have long been regarded as benefit subject to a charge to taxation which applies according to circumstances.

Vouchers redeemable for cash or goods

To be included in gross pay?	Yes
Class 1A NIC due?	No
To be entered in P11D?	Yes (Section C)

Vouchers redeemable for goods alone (but not readily convertible)

To be included in gross pay?	Yes
Class 1A NIC due?	No
To be entered in P11D?	Yes (Section C)

Appendix 9 – P9D

Inland Revenue

P9D EXPENSES PAYMENTS AND INCOME FROM WHICH TAX CANNOT BE DEDUCTED 1998-99

Note to employer
Complete this return if you made expenses payments or provided benefits to an employee but you have not completed a form P11D because he or she earned at a rate of less than £8,500 during the year 6 April 1998 to 5 April 1999.

Brief notes are included on this form. Inland Revenue booklet 480 "Expenses and Benefits – A Tax Guide" gives more detailed information.

Send the completed P9D to the Tax Office by 6 July 1999. You must give a copy of this information to the employee by the same date.

Note to employee
Your employer has filled in this form. Keep it in a safe place as you may not be able to get a duplicate. You will need it for your tax records and to complete your 1998-99 Tax Return if you get one.

The box numbers on this P9D have the same numbering as the Employment Pages of the Tax Return, for example, 1.12. Include the total figures in the corresponding box on the Tax Return, unless you think some other figure is more appropriate.

Your tax code may need to be adjusted to take account of the information given on this P9D

Employer's details
Employer's name

PAYE tax reference

Employee's details
Employee's name

Works number or department

National Insurance number

A(1) • **Expenses payments**

If the employee paid expenses solely and necessarily in the performance of his or her duties and/or qualifying travelling expenses and you repaid the amount of those expenses, you do not need to include them here. Total all other expenses payments including

- payments that included Value Added Tax (VAT), even if the VAT was later recovered from HM Customs and Excise
- round sum allowances
- all relocation expenses payments and benefits (see note below).

Some relocation expenses qualify for relief (see booklet 480 Chapter 5 and Appendix 7). The maximum amount that can be paid for any one move is £8,000. You should total all the qualifying payments made for each move including

- any payments made in 1997-98

  and
- any benefits provided under the relocation package in 1998-99 or 1997-98.

The excess over £8,000 of any qualifying expenses payments and benefits for each move should be included in the total expenses payments figure entered below.

If the above amounts total £25 or less they do not need to be returned.

If more than £25 enter the total amount **1.23** £

A(2) • **Any other payments or benefits**

Include here

- payments made to the employee and not included on the End of Year Return for 1998-99
- payments made on the employee's behalf
- gifts in kind – enter the second hand value of any goods provided. That is, the price at which the employee could sell the items as soon as he or she got them.
- any other payments or benefits which could be turned into money not included elsewhere.

Employee's own National Insurance paid by you **1.12** £

Employee's personal telephone bills paid by you **1.12** £

Gifts in kind, for example, Christmas hampers or presents **1.12** £

Anything bought for or paid to the employee other than at market value **1.12** £

Any payment or benefit not included elsewhere enter the value here and give details in the box overleaf. **1.12** £

P9D(1999)

33157 12.98 Niceday Stationery & Print Limited BMSD11/98 R0H1107

Form P9D – continued

B • **Vouchers and credit cards**

Enter the expense of providing the vouchers and the goods and services for which they can be exchanged.
Exclude the value of any vouchers, such as cash vouchers, which have suffered tax under PAYE.

Travel and transport vouchers, including season tickets	1.13 £
Gift vouchers, including National Savings Certificates and Premium Bonds	1.13 £
Meal vouchers – *as requested by page 72 of booklet CWG2 "Employer's Further Guide to PAYE and NICs"*	1.13 £
Any other vouchers exchangeable for goods and services	1.13 £
Credit cards provided for the employee and his or her family – *enter the total amount of expenses met by credit card provided by you for the employee to use unless you have already entered these expenses under one of the above headings*	1.13 £

C • **Accommodation**

Give the cash equivalent of accommodation provided for the employee and/or his or her family/household. Deduct any amounts paid by the employee towards the cost of providing the accommodation – for example, rent.

If the employee is provided with living accommodation give details of the rateable value. This is the gross value that applied before Community Charge was introduced. If the property does not have a gross value, enter "No rateable value established" and give your estimate of what the gross value would have been if rates had continued. If the property costs more than £75,000 special rules apply, see booklet 480, paragraphs 21.16 to 21.22.

If as well as providing the accommodation you paid some of the employee's bills (such as heat and light) show these in the appropriate box or boxes overleaf, whether or not the value of the accommodation itself is exempt from tax.

Enter property address

Enter rateable value of property	£
Enter rent and insurance borne by you	£
The cash value of accomodation provided is the greater of the above figures. Enter that figure here.	1.14

Where necessary use this box to describe the benefits mentioned above and overleaf

Appendix 10 – P11D

Inland Revenue **P11D EXPENSES AND BENEFITS 2000-2001**

Note to employer
Complete this return for a director, or an employee who earned at a rate of £8,500 a year or more during the year 6 April 2000 to 5 April 2001. Do not include expenses and benefits covered by a dispensation or PAYE settlement agreement. Read the P11D Guide and booklet 480, Chapter 24, before you complete the form. Send the completed P11D and form P11D(b) to the Tax Office by 6 July 2001. You must give a copy of this information to the director or employee by the same date. The term employee is used to cover both directors and employees throughout the rest of this form.

Note to employee
Your employer has filled in this form. Keep it in a safe place as you may not be able to get a duplicate. You will need it for your tax records and to complete your 2000-2001 Tax Return if you get one. Your tax code may need to be adjusted to take account of the information given on this P11D. The box numbers on this P11D have the same numbering as the Employment Pages of the Tax Return, for example, 1.12. Include the total figures in the corresponding box on the Tax Return, unless you think some other figure is more appropriate.

Employer's details
Employer's name
PAYE tax reference

Employee's details
Employee's name
If a director tick here
Works number /department
National Insurance number

From 6 April 2000 employers pay Class 1A National Insurance contributions on more benefits. These are shown in boxes which are brown and have a 1A indicator

A Assets transferred (cars, property, goods or other assets)

	Cost/ Market value		Amount made good or from which tax deducted		Cash equivalent	
Description of asset	£	–	£	=	1.12 £	1A

B Payments made on behalf of employee

Description of payment	1.12 £
Tax on notional payments not borne by employee within 30 days of receipt of each notional payment	1.12 £

C Vouchers or credit cards

	Gross amount		Amount made good or from which tax deducted		Cash equivalent
Value of vouchers and payments made using credit cards or tokens	£	–	£	=	1.13 £

D Living accommmodation

	Cash equivalent	
Cash equivalent of accommodation provided for employee, or his/ her family or household	1.14 £	1A

E Mileage allowance

	Gross amount		Amount made good or from which tax deducted		Taxable payment
Car and mileage allowances paid for employee's car	£	–	£	=	1.15 £

F Cars and car fuel *If more than two cars were made available, either at the same time or in succession, please give details on a separate sheet*

	Car 1	Car 2
Make and Model		
Date first registered	/ /	/ /
Dates car was available	From / / to / /	From / / to / /
Business mileage used in calculation *Tick only one box for each car. If the car was not available for part of the year, the business mileage limits are reduced proportionately.*	2,499 or less / 2,500 to 17,999 / 18.000 or more	2,499 or less / 2,500 to 17,999 / 18,000 or more
Enter engine size and tick type of fuel *only if there is a car fuel scale charge*	Engine size in cc: cc; Petrol / Diesel	Engine size in cc: cc; Petrol / Diesel
List price of car *If there is no list price, or if it is a classic car, employers see booklet 480; employees see leaflet IR133*	£	£
Price of optional accessories fitted when car was first made available to the employee	£	£
Price of accessories added after the car was first made available to the employee	£	£
Capital contributions (maximum £5,000) the employee made towards the cost of car or accessories	£	£
Amount paid by employee for private use of the car	£	£
Cash equivalent of each car	£	£
Total cash equivalent of all cars available in 2000-2001		1.16 £ 1A
Cash equivalent of fuel for each car	£	£
Total cash equivalent of fuel for all cars available in 2000-2001		1.17 £ 1A

P11D(2001) BMSD 9/99

Form P11D – continued

G Vans

Cash equivalent of all vans made available for private use — **1.18** £ — 1A

H Interest-free and low interest loans

If the total amount outstanding on all loans does not exceed £5,000 at any time in the year, there is no need for details in this section.

	Loan 1	Loan 2
Number of joint borrowers *(if applicable)*		
Amount outstanding at 5 April 2000 or at date loan was made if later	£	£
Amount outstanding at 5 April 2001 or at date loan was discharged if earlier	£	£
Maximum amount outstanding at any time in the year	£	£
Total amount of interest paid by the borrower in 2000-2001 – *enter "NIL" if none was paid*	£	£
Date loan was made in 2000-2001 if applicable	/ /	/ /
Date loan was discharged in 2000-2001 if applicable	/ /	/ /
Cash equivalent of loans after deducting any interest paid by the borrower	**1.19** £ 1A	**1.19** £ 1A

I Private medical treatment or insurance

	Cost to you		Amount made good or from which tax deducted		Cash equivalent
Private medical treatment or insurance	£	–	£	=	**1.21** £ 1A

J Qualifying relocation expenses payments and benefits

Non-qualifying benefits and expenses go in N and O below

Excess over £8,000 of all qualifying relocation expenses payments and benefits for each move — **1.22** £ — 1A

K Services supplied

	Cost to you		Amount made good or from which tax deducted		Cash equivalent
Services supplied to the employee	£	–	£	=	**1.22** £ 1A

L Assets placed at the employee's disposal

	Annual value plus expenses incurred		Amount made good or from which tax deducted		Cash equivalent
Description of asset	£	–	£	=	**1.22** £ 1A

M Shares

Tick the box if during the year there have been share-related benefits for the employee ☐

N Other items (including subscriptions and professional fees)

	Cost to you		Amount made good or from which tax deducted		Cash equivalent
Description of other items	£	–	£	=	**1.22** 1A
Description of other items	£	–	£	=	**1.22** £
Income tax paid but not deducted from director's remuneration					Tax paid **1.22**

O Expenses payments made to, or on behalf of, the employee

	Cost to you		Amount made good or from which tax deducted		Taxable payment
Travelling and subsistence payments	£	–	£	=	**1.23** £
Entertainment *(trading organisations read P11D Guide and then enter a tick or a cross as appropriate here)* ☐	£	–	£	=	**1.23** £
General expenses allowance for business travel	£	–	£	=	**1.23** £
Payments for use of home telephone	£	–	£	=	**1.23** £
Non-qualifying relocation expenses *(those not shown in section J)*	£	–	£	=	**1.23** £
Description of other expenses	£	–	£	=	**1.23** £

Appendix 11 – Form P46(Car)

Inland Revenue

Notification of a car provided for the private use of an employee or a director

PAYE reference

Employer's name

National Insurance number

Employee's/Director's name

Part 1

You are required to make a return on this form for an employee earning at the rate of £8,500 a year or more or a director for whom a car is made available for private use. The completed form is required within 28 days of the end of the quarter to 5 July, 5 October, 5 January or 5 April in which any of the following takes place.

'√' whichever applies

1 The employee/director is first provided with a car which is available for private use ☐

2 A car provided to the employee/director is replaced by another car which is available for private use ☐

3 The employee/director is provided with a second or further car which is available for private use ☐

4 The employee starts to earn at the rate of £8,500 a year or more or becomes a director ☐

5 A car provided to the employee/director is withdrawn without replacement ☐

Part 2 Details of car provided

Make ☐ Model ☐ Date first registered __ / __ / __

- Price of car (normally the list price at date of first registration) ... £
- Price of accessories not included in price of car ... £
- Date car first made available to employee ... __ / __ / __
- Capital contribution (if any) made by employee to cost of the car and for accessories ... £
- Sum payable (if any) by employee for private use of the car £ *per week* ☐ *per month* ☐ *per quarter* ☐ *per year* ☐
- Is fuel for private use provided with this car ? ... *yes* ☐ *no* ☐

  If so, is the employee required to make good the cost of all fuel used for private motoring **and** do you expect him or her to continue to do so? ... *yes* ☐ *no* ☐
- If the answer to the previous question is 'no' please indicate the type of fuel ... *petrol* ☐ *diesel* ☐

  and the cylinder capacity ... *up to 1400cc* ☐ *1401- 2000cc* ☐ *2001cc or more* ☐
- If you have ticked box 1, 2, 3 or 4 in Part 1 please show the expected level of annual business mileage for this car ... *less than 2500* ☐ *2500 - 17999* ☐ *18000 or more* ☐
- If you have ticked box 2 in Part 1 but the employee has more than one car available for private use please provide details of the car replaced
- If you have ticked box 5 in Part 1 please provide details of the car withdrawn

Make

Model

Date withdrawn *(where appropriate)* __ / __ / __

Declaration

I declare that all particulars required are fully and truly stated according to the best of my knowledge and belief.

Signature

Capacity in which signed

Date __ / __ / __

P46(Car)

41925 12.99 Guilbert UK BMSD11/99 R0J4128

Appendix 12 – The Litmus Test

In their Booklet *Supplying Services through a limited company or a partnership* (*Business Series IR175*), the Inland Revenue propose a form of what we might call a 'litmus test' for the employment/self-employment test. This is not (and nor is it intended to be) a full analysis of the judicial employment/ self-employment test but it does, as suggested, give a litmus-type indication.

Under the heading 'Would I have been an employee of my client' the Inland Revenue suggest the following.

If you can answer 'yes' to the following questions, you will probably be regarded as an employee.

- Do you work set hours, or a given number of hours a week or a month?
- Do you have to do the work yourself rather than hire Somme else to do the work for you?
- Can someone tell you at any time what to do or when and how to do it?
- Are you paid by the hour, week or month?
  Can you get overtime pay?
- Do you work at the premises of the person you work for, or at a place or places he or she decides?
- Do you generally work for one client at a time, rather than having a number of contracts?

If you can answer 'yes' to the following questions, you will probably not be regarded as an employee

- Do you have the final say in how you do the work for the client?
- Can you make a loss on the contract?
- Do you provide the main items of equipment you need to do the job for the client, not just the small tools many employees provide for themselves?
- Are you free to hire other people on your own terms to do the work you have taken on?
- Do you pay them out of your own pocket?
- Do you have to correct unsatisfactory work in your own time and at your own expense?
- Do you have a number of customers at the same time?

Table of Cases

Table of Statutes

1992 Social Security Contributions and Benefits Act	BT2.5
1993 Criminal Justice Act	CL2.70
1994 Deregulation and Contracting Out Act	DM4.3
1994 Trade Marks Act	
s 1	BI1.26
1994 Value Added Tax Act	BM3.13, BT1.15
s 3	CT1.43
s 4	CT1.3
s 5(2)(a)	CT1.4
s 7	CT1.20
s 10	CT1.52
s 12(1)	CT1.54
s 24	CT1.42
s 94	CT1.44
Sch 5	CT1.51
1998 Data Protection Act	CM2.13
1998 Finance Act	BT3.5
Sch 18	BM3.31
para 2(1)	CM8.2
(3)	CM8.2
para 3(1)	CM8.3, CM8.7
para 14(1)(d)	CM8.6
1998 Social Security Act	
s 53	BT2.24
1999 Contracts (Rights of Third Parties) Act	CM2.10
2000 Child Support, Pensions and Security Act	BT2.7, CT3.2
2000 Finance Act	
Sch 12	CT4.2
para 2	CT4.3
(2)(3)	CT4.4
para 7	CT4.5
para 12	CT4.4
para 19	CT4.3

Table of Statutory Instruments

Index